MW01124894

A History of Money and Banking in the United States: The Colonial Era to World War II

The Ludwig von Mises Institute dedicates this volume to all of its generous donors and wishes to thank these Patrons, in particular:

George W. Connell

❧

James L. Bailey, *James Bailey Foundation*;
Robert Blumen; Christopher P. Condon;
John William Galbraith; Hugh E. Ledbetter;
Frederick L. Maier; Mr. and Mrs. R. Nelson Nash;
Dr. Gary G. Schlarbaum

❧

Robert B. Beale; Richard Bleiberg; John Hamilton Bolstad;
Mr. and Mrs. J.R. Bost; Mr. and Mrs. Willard Fischer;
Douglas E. French; Albert L. Hillman, Jr.; L. Charles Hilton, Jr.;
Mr. and Mrs. Truman Johnson; Neil Kaethler;
Robert Kealiher; Dr. Preston W. Keith; David Kramer;
Mr. and Mrs. William W. Massey, Jr.; Hall McAdams;
Dr. Dorothy Donnelley Moller; Francis Powers, M.D.;
Donald Mosby Rembert; James M. Rodney;
Joseph P. Schirrick; Lawrence Van Someren, Sr.; James Whitaker, M.D.

❧

J. Terry Anderson, *Anderson Chemical Company*;
Mr. and Mrs. Ross K. Anderson; Toby O. Baxendale; Robert Bero;
Dr. V.S. Boddicker; Dr. John Brätland; John Cooke;
Carl Creager; Capt. and Mrs. Maino des Granges;
Clyde Evans, *Evans Cabinet Corporation*;
Elton B. Fox, *The Fox Foundation*; James W. Frevert; Larry R. Gies;
Frank W. Heemstra; Donald L. Ifland; Dr. and Mrs. John W. Johnson;
Richard J. Kossmann, M.D.; Alfonso Landa; John Leger;
Arthur L. Loeb; Ronald Mandle;
Ellice McDonald, Jr., CBE, and Rosa Hayward McDonald, CBE;
Norbert McLuckie; In honor of Mikaelah S. Medrano;
Joseph Edward Paul Melville;
Dr. and Mrs. Donald Miller; Reed W. Mower;
Terence Murphree, *United Steel Structures*; James O'Neill;
Victor Pankey; Michael Robb; Catherine Dixon Roland;
John Salvador; Conrad Schneiker; Mark M. Scott;
Robert W. Smiley, Jr., *Benefit Capital Companies*;
Jack DeBar Smith; Val L. Tennent; David W. Tice;
Dr. Jim Walker; Mr. and Mrs. Quinten E. Ward;
Dr. Thomas L. Wenck; Keith S. Wood;
Steven Lee Yamshon; Jeannette Zummo

A History of Money and Banking in the United States: The Colonial Era to World War II

Murray N. Rothbard

Cover art: *Wall Street, 1886*. Permission for use of this print is granted to the Ludwig von Mises Institute by Old World Prints, Ltd.

 For information, write the Ludwig von Mises Institute, 518 West Magnolia Avenue, Auburn, Alabama 36849-5301; www.mises.org.

ISBN: 0-945466-33-1

Contents

INTRODUCTION

In this volume, Murray Rothbard has given us a comprehensive history of money and banking in the United States, from colonial times to World War II, the first to explicitly use the interpretive framework of Austrian monetary theory. But even aside from the explicitly Austrian theoretical framework undergirding the historical narrative, this book does not "look" or "feel" like standard economic histories as they have been written during the past quarter of a century, under the influence of the positivistic "new economic history" or "cliometrics." The focus of this latter approach to economic history, which today completely dominates this field of inquiry, is on the application of high-powered statistical methods to the analysis of quantitative economic data. What profoundly distinguishes Rothbard's approach from the prevailing approach is his insistence upon treating economic quantities and processes as unique and complex historical events. Thus, he employs the laws of economic theory in conjunction with other relevant disciplines to trace each event back to the nonquantifiable values and goals of the particular actors involved. In Rothbard's view, economic laws can be relied upon in interpreting these nonrepeatable historical events because the validity of these laws—or, better yet, their truth—can be established with certainty by praxeology, a science based on the universal experience of human action that is logically anterior to the experience of particular historical episodes.[1] It is in this sense that it can be said that economic theory is an *a priori* science.

In sharp contrast, the new economic historians view history as a laboratory in which economic theory is continually being tested. The economic quantities observed at different dates in history are treated like the homogeneous empirical data generated by a controlled and repeatable experiment. As such, they are used as evidence in statistical tests of hypotheses regarding the causes of a class of events, such as inflations or financial crises, that are observed to recur in history. The hypothesis that best fits the evidence is then tentatively accepted as providing a valid causal explanation of the class of events in question, pending future testing against new evidence that is constantly emerging out of the unfolding historical process.

One of the pioneers of the new economic history, Douglass C. North, a Nobel Prize-winner in economics, describes its method in the following terms:

> It is impossible to analyze and explain the issues dealt with in economic history without developing initial hypotheses and testing them in the light of available evidence. The initial hypotheses come from the body of economic theory that has evolved in the past 200 years and is being continually tested and refined by empirical inquiry. The statistics provide the precise measurement and empirical evidence by which to test the theory. *The limits of inquiry are dictated by the existence of appropriate theory and evidence*. . . . The evidence is, ideally, statistical data that precisely define and measure the issues to be tested.[2]

[1]For good discussions of praxeology, see Ludwig von Mises, *Human Action: A Treatise on Economics,* Scholar's Edition (Auburn, Ala.: Mises Institute, 1998), pp. 1–71; Murray N. Rothbard, *The Logic of Action I: Method, Money, and the Austrian School* (Cheltenham, U.K.: Edward Elgar, 1997), pp. 28–77; and Hans-Hermann Hoppe, *Economic Science and the Austrian Method* (Auburn, Ala.: Mises Institute, 1995).

[2]Douglass C. North, *Growth and Welfare in the American Past: A New Economic History* (Englewood Cliffs, N.J.: Prentice-Hall, 1966), pp. 1–2 (emphasis in original).

This endeavor of North and others to deliberately extend the positivist program to economic history immediately confronts two problems. First, as North emphasizes, this approach narrowly limits the kinds of questions that can be investigated in economic history. Those issues which do not readily lend themselves to formulation in quantitative terms or for which statistical data are not available tend to be downplayed or neglected altogether. Thus the new economic historians are more likely to seek answers to questions like: What was the net contribution of the railroad to the growth of real GNP in the United States? Or, what has been the effect of the creation of the Federal Reserve System on the stability of the price level and real output? They are much less likely to address in a meaningful way the questions of what *motivated* the huge government land grants for railroad rights-of-way or the passage of the Federal Reserve Act.

In general, the question of *"Cui bono?"*—or "Who benefits?"—from changes in policies and institutions receives very little attention in the cliometric literature, because the evidence that one needs to answer it, bearing as it does on human motives, is essentially subjective and devoid of a measurable or even quantifiable dimension. This is not to deny that new economic historians have sought to explain the *ex post* aggregate distribution of income that results from a given change in the institutional framework or in the policy regime. What their method precludes them from doing is identifying the *ex ante* purposes as well as ideas about the most efficacious means of accomplishing these purposes that motivated the specific individuals who lobbied for or initiated the change that effected a new income distribution. However, avoiding such questions leaves the quantitative data themselves ultimately unexplained. The reason is that the institutions that contribute to their formation, such as the railroads or the Fed, are always the complex resultants of the purposive actions of particular individuals or groups of individuals aimed at achieving definite goals by the use of specific means. So the new economic history is not history in the traditional sense of an attempt to "understand" the human motives underlying the emergence of economic institutions and processes.

The second and even more profound flaw in the new economic history is the relationship it posits between theory and history. For North, history is the source of the "empirical evidence"—that is, "ideally, statistical data"—against which the economic theory is tested. This means that the claim to validity of a particular theorem is always tentative and defeasible, resting as it does on its nonfalsification in previous empirical tests. However, this also means that economic history must be continually revised, because the very theory which is employed to identify the causal relations between historical events can always be falsified by new evidence coming to light in the ongoing historical process. In other words, what the new economic historians characterize as "the intimate relationship between measurement and theory" is in reality the vicious circle that ensnares all attempts to invoke positivist precepts in the interpretation of history.[3] For if the theory used to interpret past events can always be invalidated by future events, then it is unclear whether theory is the *explanans* or the *explanand* in historical research.

Rothbard's approach to monetary history does not focus on measurement but on motives. Once the goals of the actors and their ideas about the appropriate means for achieving these goals have been established, economic theory, along with other sciences, is brought to bear to trace out the effects of these actions in producing the complex events and processes of history which are only partially and imperfectly captured in statistical data. This is not to say that Rothbard ignores the quantitative aspects of historical monetary processes. Indeed, his book abounds with money, price, and output data; but these data are

[3]Robert William Fogel, "The New Economic History: Its Findings and Methods," in *The Reinterpretation of American History*, Robert William Fogel and Stanley L. Engerman, eds. (New York: Harper and Row, 1971), p. 7.

always interpreted in terms of the motivations of those who have contributed to their formation. For Rothbard, a particular price datum is, no less than the Spanish-American War, a *historical event,* and its causes must be traced back to the subjective aims governing human plans and choices.

In flatly rejecting the positivist approach to economic history, Rothbard adopts the method of historical research first formulated by Ludwig von Mises. In developing this method, Mises correctly delineated, for the first time, the relationship between theory and history. It is Rothbard's great contribution in this volume—and his earlier *America's Great Depression*—to be the first to consistently apply it to economic history.[4] It is worth summarizing this method here for several reasons. First, Mises's writings on the proper method of historical research have inexplicably been almost completely ignored up to the present, even by those who have adopted Mises's praxeological approach in economics.[5] Second, familiarity with Mises's method of historical research illuminates the source and character of the remarkable distinctiveness of Rothbard's historical writings. In particular, it serves to correct the common but mistaken impression that Rothbard's historical writings, especially on the origin and development of the U.S. monetary system, are grounded in nothing more substantial than an idiosyncratic "conspiracy theory of history." Third, it gives us an opportunity to elucidate the important elaboration of Mises's method that Rothbard contributed and which he deploys to great effect in explicating the topic of this volume. And finally, we find in Mises's method a

[4]Murray N. Rothbard, *America's Great Depression*, 5th ed. (Auburn, Ala.: Mises Institute, 2000).

[5]As Rothbard has written of *Theory and History*, the book in which Mises gives this method its most detailed exposition, this work "has made remarkably little impact, and has rarely been cited even by the young economists of the recent Austrian revival. It remains by far the most neglected masterwork of Mises." Murray N. Rothbard, Preface to Ludwig von Mises's *Theory and History: An Interpretation of Social and Economic Evolution*, 2nd ed. (Auburn, Ala.: Mises Institute, 1985), p. xi.

definitive refutation of the positivist's claim that it is impossible to acquire real knowledge of subjective phenomena like human motives and that, therefore, economic history must deal exclusively with observable and measurable phenomena.

To begin with, Mises grounds his discussion of historical method on the insight that ideas are the primordial stuff of history. In his words:

> History is the record of human action. Human action is the conscious effort of man to substitute more satisfactory conditions for less satisfactory ones. Ideas determine what are to be considered more and less satisfactory conditions and what means are to be resorted to to alter them. Thus ideas are the main theme of the study of history.[6]

This is not to say that all history should be intellectual history, but that ideas are the ultimate cause of all social phenomena, including and especially economic phenomena. As Mises puts it,

> The genuine history of mankind is the history of ideas. It is ideas that distinguish man from all other beings. Ideas engender social institutions, political changes, technological methods of production, and all that is called economic conditions.[7]

Thus, for Mises, history

> establishes the fact that men, inspired by definite ideas, made definite judgments of value, chose definite ends, and resorted to definite means in order to attain the ends chosen, and it deals furthermore with the outcome of their actions, the state of affairs the action brought about.[8]

Ideas—specifically those embodying the purposes and values that direct action—are not only the point of contact

[6]Ibid., pp. 224–25.

[7]Ibid., p. 187.

[8]Ludwig von Mises, *The Ultimate Foundation of Economic Science: An Essay on Method*, 2nd ed. (Kansas City, Mo.: Sheed Andrews and McMeel, 1978), p. 45.

between history and economics, but differing attitudes toward them are precisely what distinguish the methods of the two disciplines. Both economics and history deal with individual choices of ends and the judgments of value underlying them. On the one hand, economic theory as a branch of praxeology takes these value judgments and choices as given data and restricts itself to logically inferring from them the laws governing the valuing and pricing of the means or "goods." As such, economics does not inquire into the individual's motivations in valuing and choosing specific ends. Hence, contrary to the positivist method, the truth of economic theorems is substantiated apart from and without reference to specific and concrete historical experience. They are the conclusions of logically valid deduction from universal experience of the fact that humans adopt means that they believe to be appropriate in attaining ends that they judge to be valuable.[9]

The subject of history, on the other hand, "is action and the judgments of value directing action toward definite ends."[10] This means that for history, in contrast to economics, actions and value judgments are not ultimate "givens" but, in Mises's words, "are the starting point of a specific mode of reflection, of the specific understanding of the historical sciences of human action." Equipped with the method of "specific understanding," the historian, "when faced with a value judgment and the resulting action . . . may try to understand how they originated in the mind of the actor."[11]

[9]It is true that in deriving theorems that apply to the specific conditions characterizing human action in our world, a few additional facts of a lesser degree of generality are inserted into the deductive chain of reasoning. These include the facts that there exists a variety of natural resources, that human labor is differentiated, and that leisure is valued as a consumer's good. See Mises, *Human Action*; Rothbard, *The Logic of Action I*; and Hoppe, *Economic Science and the Austrian Method.*

[10]Mises, *Theory and History*, p. 298.

[11]Ibid., p. 310.

The difference between the methods of economics and history may be illustrated with the following example. The economist qua economist "explains" the Vietnam War-era inflation that began in the mid-1960s and culminated in the inflationary recession of 1973–1975 by identifying those actions of the Fed with respect to the money supply that initiated and sustained it.[12] The historian, including the economic historian, however, must identify and then assign weights to all those factors that *motivated* the various members of the Fed's Board of Governors (or of the Federal Open Market Committee) to adopt this course of action. These factors include: ideology; partisan politics; pressure exerted by the incumbent administration; the grasp of economic theory; the expressed and perceived desires of the Fed's constituencies, including commercial bankers and bond dealers; the informal power and influence of the Fed chairman within the structure of governance; and so on.

In short, the economic historian must supply the motives underlying the actions that are relevant to explaining the historical event. And for this task, his only suitable tool is understanding. Thus, as Mises puts it,

> The scope of understanding is the mental grasp of phenomena which cannot be totally elucidated by logic, mathematics, praxeology, and the natural sciences to the extent that they cannot be cleared up by all these sciences.[13]

To say that a full explanation of any historical event, including an economic one, requires that the method of specific understanding be applied is not to diminish the importance of pure economic theory in the study of history. Indeed, as Mises points out, economics

[12]Some economists would date this inflation from 1965 to 1979, but the precise dates do not matter for our present purposes. See, for example, Thomas Mayer, *Monetary Policy and the Great Inflation in the United States: The Federal Reserve and the Failure of Macroeconomic Policy* (Northampton, Mass.: Edward Elgar, 1999).

[13]Mises, *Human Action*, p. 50.

> provides in its field a consummate interpretation of past events recorded and a consummate anticipation of the effects to be expected from future actions of a definite kind. Neither this interpretation nor this anticipation tells anything about the actual content and quality of the actual individuals' judgments of value. Both presuppose that the individuals are valuing and acting, but their theorems are independent of and unaffected by the particular characteristics of this valuing and acting.[14]

For Mises, then, if the historian is to present a complete explanation of a particular event, he must bring to bear not only his "specific understanding" of the motives of action but the theorems of economic science as well as those of the other "aprioristic," or nonexperimental, sciences, such as logic and mathematics. He must also utilize knowledge yielded by the natural sciences, including the applied sciences of technology and therapeutics.[15] Familiarity with the teachings of all these disciplines is required in order to correctly identify the causal relevance of a particular action to a historical event, to trace out its specific consequences, and to evaluate its success from the point of view of the actor's goals.

For example, without knowledge of the economic theorem that, ceteris paribus, changes in the supply of money cause inverse changes in its purchasing power, a historian of the price inflation of the Vietnam War-era probably would ignore the Fed and its motives altogether. Perhaps, he is under the influence of the erroneous Galbraithian doctrine of administered prices with its implication of cost-push inflation.[16] In this case, he might concentrate exclusively and irrelevantly on the motives of union leaders in demanding large wage increases and on the objectives of the "technostructure" of large business firms in

[14]Mises, *Theory and History*, p. 309.

[15]Ibid., p. 301.

[16]John Kenneth Galbraith, *The New Industrial State* (New York: New American Library, 1967), pp. 189–207, 256–70.

acceding to these demands and deciding what part of the cost increase to pass on to consumers. Thus, according to Mises,

> If what these disciplines [i.e., the aprioristic and the natural sciences] teach is insufficient or if the historian chooses an erroneous theory out of several conflicting theories held by the specialists, his effort is misled and his performance is abortive.[17]

But what exactly is the historical method of specific understanding, and how can it provide true knowledge of a wholly subjective and unobservable phenomenon like human motivation? First of all, as Mises emphasizes, the specific understanding of past events is

> not a mental process exclusively resorted to by historians. It is applied by everybody in daily intercourse with all his fellows. It is a technique employed in all interhuman relations. It is practiced by children in the nursery and kindergarten, by businessmen in trade, by politicians and statesmen in affairs of state. All are eager to get information about other people's valuations and plans and to appraise them correctly.[18]

The reason this technique is so ubiquitously employed by people in their daily affairs is because all action aims at rearranging future conditions so that they are more satisfactory from the actor's point of view. However, the future situation that actually emerges always depends partly on the purposes and choices of others besides the actor. In order to achieve his ends, then, the actor must anticipate not only changes affecting the future state of affairs caused by natural phenomena, but also the changes that result from the conduct of others who, like him, are contemporaneously planning and acting.[19]

[17]Mises, *Theory and History*, p. 301.

[18]Ibid., p. 265.

[19]As Mises puts it, "Understanding aims at anticipating future conditions as far as they depend on human ideas, valuations, and actions." Mises, *Ultimate Foundation*, p. 49.

Understanding the values and goals of others is thus an inescapable prerequisite for successful action.

Now, the method that provides the individual planning action with information about the values and goals of other actors is essentially the same method employed by the historian who seeks knowledge of the values and goals of actors in bygone epochs. Mises emphasizes the universal application of this method by referring to the actor and the historian as "the historian of the future" and "the historian of the past," respectively.[20] Regardless of the purpose for which it is used, therefore, understanding

> aims at establishing the facts that men attach a definite meaning to the state of their environment, that they value this state and, motivated by these judgments of value, resort to definite means in order to preserve or to attain a definite state of affairs different from that which would prevail if they abstained from any purposeful reaction. Understanding deals with judgments of value, with the choice of ends and of the means resorted to for the attainment of these ends, and with the valuation of the outcome of actions performed.[21]

Furthermore, whether directed toward planning action or interpreting history, the exercise of specific understanding is not an arbitrary or haphazard enterprise peculiar to each individual historian or actor; it is the product of a discipline that Mises calls "thymology," which encompasses "knowledge of human valuations and volitions."[22] Mises characterizes this discipline as follows:

> Thymology is on the one hand an offshoot of introspection and on the other a precipitate of historical experience. It is what everybody learns from intercourse with his fellows. It

[20]Mises, *Theory and History*, p. 320.

[21]Mises, *Ultimate Foundation*, p. 48.

[22]Mises, *Theory and History*, p. 265.

> is what a man knows about the way in which people value different conditions, about their wishes and desires and their plans to realize these wishes and desires. It is the knowledge of the social environment in which a man lives and acts or, with historians, of a foreign milieu about which he has learned by studying special sources.[23]

Thus, Mises tells us, thymology can be classified as "a branch of history" since "[i]t derives its knowledge from historical experience."[24] Consequently, the epistemic product of thymological experience is categorically different from the knowledge derived from experiments in the natural sciences. Experimental knowledge consists of "scientific facts" whose truth is independent of time. Thymological knowledge is confined to "historical facts," which are unique and nonrepeatable events. Accordingly, Mises concludes,

> All that thymology can tell us is that in the past definite men or groups of men were valuing and acting in a definite way. Whether they will in the future value and act in the same way remains uncertain. All that can be asserted about their future conduct is speculative anticipation of the future based on specific understanding of the historical branches of the sciences of human action. . . . What thymology achieves is the elaboration of a catalogue of human traits. It can moreover establish the fact that certain traits appeared in the past as a rule in connection with certain other traits.[25]

More concretely, all our anticipations about how family members, friends, acquaintances, and strangers will react in particular situations are based on our accumulated thymological experience. That a spouse will appreciate a specific type of jewelry for her birthday, that a friend will enthusiastically endorse our plan to see a Clint Eastwood movie, that a particular student will complain about his grade—all these expectations are

[23]Ibid., p. 266.

[24]Ibid., p. 272.

[25]Ibid., pp. 272, 274.

based on our direct experience of their past modes of valuing and acting. Even our expectations of how strangers will react in definite situations or what course political, social, and economic events will take are based on thymology. For example, our reservoir of thymological experience provides us with the knowledge that men are jealous of their wives. Thus, it allows us to "understand" and forecast that if a man makes overt advances to a married woman in the presence of her husband, he will almost certainly be rebuffed and runs a considerable risk of being punched in the nose. Moreover, we may forecast with a high degree of certitude that both the Republican and the Democratic nominees will outpoll the Libertarian Party candidate in a forthcoming presidential election; that the price for commercial time during the televising of the Major League Soccer championship will not exceed the price for commercials during the broadcast of the Super Bowl next year; that the average price of a personal computer will be neither $1 million nor $10 in three months; and that the author of this paper will never be crowned king of England. All of these forecasts, and literally millions of others of a similar degree of certainty, are based on the specific understanding of the values and goals motivating millions of nameless actors.

As noted, the source of thymological experience is our interactions with and observations of other people. It is

> acquired either directly from observing our fellow men and transacting business with them or indirectly from reading and from hearsay, as well as out of our special experience acquired in previous contacts with the individuals or groups concerned.[26]

Such mundane experience is accessible to all who have reached the age of reason and forms the bedrock foundation for forecasting the future conduct of others whose actions will affect their plans. Furthermore, as Mises points out, the use of thymological knowledge in everyday affairs is straightforward:

[26]Ibid., p. 313.

> Thymology tells no more than that man is driven by various innate instincts, various passions, and various ideas. The anticipating individual tries to set aside those factors that manifestly do not play any concrete role in the concrete case under consideration. Then he chooses among the remaining ones.[27]

To aid in this task of narrowing down the goals and desires that are likely to motivate the behavior of particular individuals, we resort to the "thymological concept" of "human character."[28] The concrete content of the "character" we attribute to a specific individual is based on our direct or indirect knowledge of his past behavior. In formulating our plans, "We assume that this character will not change if no special reasons interfere, and, going a step farther, we even try to foretell how definite changes in conditions will affect his reactions."[29] It is confidence in our spouse's "character," for example, that permits us to leave for work each morning secure in the knowledge that he or she will not suddenly disappear with the children and the family bank account. And our saving and investment plans involve an image of Alan Greenspan's character that is based on our direct or indirect knowledge of his past actions and utterances. In formulating our intertemporal consumption plans, we are thus led to completely discount or assign a very low likelihood to the possibility that he will either deliberately orchestrate a 10-percent deflation of the money supply or attempt to peg the short-run interest rate at zero percent in the foreseeable future.

Despite reliance on the tool of thymological experience, however, all human understanding of future events remains uncertain, to some degree, for these events are generally a complex resultant of various causal factors operating concurrently. All forecasts of the future, therefore, must involve not only an

[27]Ibid.

[28]Mises, *Ultimate Foundation*, p. 50.

[29]Ibid.

enumeration of the factors that operate in bringing about the anticipated result but also the weighting of the relative influence of each factor on the outcome. Of the two, the more difficult problem is that of apportioning the proper weights among the various operative factors. Even if the actor accurately and completely identifies all the causal factors involved, the likelihood of the forecast event being realized depends on the actor having solved the weighting problem. The uncertainty inherent in forecasting, therefore, stems mainly from the intricacy of assigning the correct weights to different actions and the intensity of their effects.[30]

While thymology powerfully, but implicitly, shapes everyone's understanding of and planning for the future in every facet of life, the thymological method is used deliberately and rigorously by the historian who seeks a specific understanding of the motives underlying the value judgments and choices of the actors whom he judges to have been central to the specific event or epoch he is interested in explaining. Like future events and situations envisioned in the plans of actors, all historical events and the epochs they define are unique and complex outcomes codetermined by numerous human actions and reactions. This is the meaning of Mises's statement,

> History is a sequence of changes. Every historical situation has its individuality, its own characteristics that distinguish it from any other situation. The stream of history never returns to a previously occupied point. History is not repetitious.[31]

It is precisely because history does not repeat itself that thymological experience does not yield certain knowledge of the cause of historical events in the same way as experimentation in the natural sciences. Thus the historian, like the actor, must resort to specific understanding when enumerating the various

[30]Mises, *Theory and History*, pp. 306–08, 313–14.

[31]Ibid., p. 219.

motives and actions that bear a causal relation to the event in question and when assigning each action's contribution to the outcome a relative weight. In this task, "Understanding is in the realm of history the equivalent, as it were, of quantitative analysis and measurement."[32] The historian uses specific understanding to try to gauge the causal "relevance" of each factor to the outcome. But such assessments of relevance do not take the form of objective measurements calculable by statistical techniques; they are expressed in the form of subjective "judgments of relevance" based on thymology.[33] Successful entrepreneurs tend to be those who consistently formulate a superior understanding of the likelihood of future events based on thymology.

The weighting problem that confronts actors and historians may be illustrated with the following example. The Fed increases the money supply by 5 percent in response to a 20-percent plunge in the Dow Jones Industrial Average—or, perhaps now, the Nasdaq—that ignites fears of a recession and a concomitant increase in the demand for liquidity on the part of households and firms. At the same time, OPEC announces a 10-percent increase in its members' quotas and the U.S. Congress increases the minimum wage by 10 percent. In order to answer the question of what the overall impact of these events will be on the purchasing power of money six months hence, specific understanding of individuals' preferences and expectations is required in order to *weight* and *time* the influence of each of these events on the relationship between the supply of and the demand for money. The ceteris-paribus laws of economic theory are strictly qualitative and only indicate the direction of the effect each of these events has on the purchasing power of money and that the change occurs during a sequential adjustment process so that some time must elapse before the full effect emerges. Thus the entrepreneur or economist must always supplement economic theory with an act of historical judgment or understanding when

[32]Mises, *Human Action*, p. 56.

[33]Ibid.

attempting to forecast any economic quantity. The economic historian, too, exercises understanding when making judgments of relevance about the factors responsible for the observed movements of the value of money during historical episodes of inflation or deflation.

Rothbard's contribution to Mises's method of historical research involves the creation of a guide that mitigates some of the uncertainty associated with formulating judgments of relevance about human motives. According to Rothbard, "It is part of the inescapable condition of the historian that he must make estimates and judgments about human motivation even though he cannot ground his judgments in absolute and apodictic certainty."[34] But the task of assigning motives and weighting their relevance is rendered more difficult by the fact that, in many cases, historical actors, especially those seeking economic gain through the political process, are inclined to deliberately obscure the reasons for their conduct. Generally in these situations, Rothbard points out, "the actor himself tries his best to hide his economic motive and to trumpet his more abstract and ideological concerns."[35]

Rothbard contends, however, that such attempts to obfuscate or conceal the pecuniary motive for an action by appeals to

[34]Murray N. Rothbard, "Economic Determinism, Ideology, and The American Revolution," *The Libertarian Forum* 6 (November 1974): 4.

[35]Mises makes a similar point:

> The endeavors to mislead posterity about what really happened and to substitute a fabrication for a faithful recording are often inaugurated by the men who themselves played an active role in the events, and begin with the instant of their happening, or sometimes even precede their occurrence. To lie about historical facts and to destroy evidence has been in the opinion of hosts of statesmen, diplomats, politicians and writers a legitimate part of the conduct of public affairs and of writing history.

Mises concludes that one of the primary tasks of the historian, therefore, "is to unmask such falsehoods." Mises, *Theory and History*, pp. 291–92.

higher goals are easily discerned and exposed by the historian in those cases "where the causal chain of economic interest to action is simple and direct."[36] Thus, for example, when the steel industry lobbies for higher tariffs or reduced quotas, no sane adult, and certainly no competent historian, believes that it is doing so out of its stated concern for the "public interest" or "national security." Despite its avowed motives, everyone clearly perceives that the primary motivation of the industry is economic, that is, to restrict foreign competition in order to increase profits. But a problem arises in those cases "when actions involve longer and more complex causal chains."[37] Rothbard points to the Marshall Plan as an example of the latter. In this instance, the widely proclaimed motives of the architects of the plan were to prevent starvation in Western European nations and to strengthen their resistance to the allures of Communism. Not a word was spoken about the goal that was also at the root of the Marshall Plan: promoting and subsidizing U.S. export industries. It was only through painstaking research that historians were later able to uncover and assess the relevance of the economic motive at work.[38]

Given the propensity of those seeking and dispensing privileges and subsidies in the political arena to lie about their true motives, Rothbard formulates what he describes as "a theoretical guide which will indicate in advance whether or not a historical action will be predominantly for economic, or for ideological, motives."[39] Now, it is true that Rothbard derives this guide from his overall worldview. The historian's worldview, however, should not be interpreted as a purely ideological construction or an unconscious reflection of his normative biases. In fact, every

[36]Rothbard, "Economic Determinism," p. 4.

[37]Ibid.

[38]See, for example, David Eakins, "Business Planners and America's Postwar Expansion," in *Corporations and the Cold War,* David Horowitz, ed. (New York: Modern Reader, 1969), pp. 143–71.

[39]Rothbard, "Economic Determinism," p. 4.

historian must be equipped with a worldview—an interrelated set of ideas about the causal relationships governing how the world works—in order to ascertain which facts are relevant in the explanation of a particular historical event. According to Rothbard, "Facts, of course, must be selected and ordered in accordance with judgments of importance, and such judgments are necessarily tied into the historian's basic world outlook."[40]

Specifically, in Mises's approach to history, the worldview comprises the necessary preconceptions regarding causation with which the historian approaches the data and which are derived from his knowledge of both the aprioristic and natural sciences. According to Mises:

> History is not an intellectual reproduction, but a condensed representation of the past in conceptual terms. The historian does not simply let the events speak for themselves. He arranges them from the aspect of the ideas underlying the formation of the general notions he uses in their presentation. He does not report facts as they happened, but only *relevant* facts. He does not approach the documents without presuppositions, but equipped with the whole apparatus of his age's scientific knowledge, that is, with all the teachings of contemporary logic, mathematics, praxeology, and natural science.[41]

So, for example, the fact that heavy speculation against the German mark accompanied its sharp plunge on foreign-exchange markets is not significant for an Austrian-oriented economic historian seeking to explain the stratospheric rise in commodity prices that characterized the German hyperinflation of the early 1920s. This is because he approaches this event armed with the supply-and-demand theory of money and the purchasing-power–parity theory of the exchange rate.

[40]Murray N. Rothbard, *Conceived in Liberty*, vol. 1, *A New Land, A New People: The American Colonies in the Seventeenth Century*, 2nd ed. (Auburn, Ala.: Mises Institute, 1999), p. 9.

[41]Mises, *Human Action*, pp. 47–48.

These "presuppositions" derived from praxeology lead him to avoid any attribution of causal significance to the actions of foreign exchange speculators in accounting for the precipitous decline of the domestic purchasing power of the mark. Instead they direct his attention to the motives of the German Reichsbank in expanding the money supply. In the same manner, a modern historian investigating the cause and dissemination of bubonic plague in fourteenth-century Europe would presuppose that the blossoming of religious heresy during that period would have no significance for his investigation. Instead he would allow himself to be guided by the conclusions of modern medical science regarding the epidemiology of the disease.

The importance of Rothbard's theoretical guide is that it adds something completely new to the historian's arsenal of scientific preconceptions that aids him in making judgments of relevance when investigating the motives of those who promote or oppose specific political actions. The novelty and brilliance of this guide lies in the fact that it is neither a purely aprioristic law like an economic theorem nor an experimentally established "fact" of the natural sciences. Rather it is a sociological generalization grounded on a creative blend of thymological experience and economic theory. At the core of this generalization is the insight that the State throughout history has been essentially an organization of a segment of the population that forsakes peaceful economic activity to constitute itself as a ruling class. This class makes its living parasitically by establishing a permanent hegemonic or "political" relationship between itself and the productive members of the population. This political relationship permits the rulers to subsist on the tribute or taxes routinely and "legally" expropriated from the income and wealth of the producing class. The latter class is composed of the "subjects" or, in the case of democratic states, the "taxpayers," who earn their living through the peaceful "economic means" of production and voluntary exchange. In contrast, constituents of the ruling class may be thought of as "tax-consumers" who earn their living through the coercive "political means" of taxation and the sale of monopoly privileges.[42]

Rothbard argues that economic logic dictates that the king and his courtiers, or the democratic government and its special interest groups, can never constitute more than a small minority of the country's population—that all States, regardless of their formal organization, must effectively involve oligarchic rule.[43] The reasons for this are twofold. First, the fundamentally parasitic nature of the relationship between the rulers and the ruled by itself necessitates that the majority of the population engages in productive activity in order to be able to pay the tribute or taxes extracted by the ruling class while still sustaining its own existence. If the ruling class comprised the majority of the population, economic collapse and systemic breakdown would swiftly ensue as the productive class died out. The majoritarian ruling class itself then would either be forced into productive activity or dissolve into internecine warfare aimed at establishing a new and more stable—that is, oligarchic—relationship between rulers and producers.

The second reason why the ruling class tends to be an oligarchy is related to the law of comparative advantage. In a world where human abilities and skills vary widely, the division of labor and specialization pervades all sectors of the economy as well as society as a whole. Thus, not only is it the case that a relatively small segment of the populace possesses a comparative advantage in developing new software, selling

[42]For expositions of the view of the origin and nature of the state as a coercive organization of the political means for acquiring income, see Franz Oppenheimer, *The State* (New York: Free Life Editions, [1914] 1975); Albert J. Nock, *Our Enemy, The State* (New York: Free Life Editions, [1935] 1973); and Murray N. Rothbard, *For a New Liberty: The Libertarian Manifesto,* 2nd ed. (San Francisco: Fox and Wilkes, 1996), pp. 45–69.

[43]Rothbard, *For a New Liberty*, pp. 49–50; and idem, "Economic Determinism," pp. 4–5.

mutual funds, or playing professional football, it is also the case that only a fraction of the population tends to excel at wielding coercive power. Moreover, the law of comparative advantage governs the structure of relationships within as well as between organizations, accounting for the hierarchical structure that we almost invariably observe within individual organizations. Whether we are considering a business enterprise, a chess club, or a criminal gang, an energetic and visionary elite invariably comes to the fore, either formally or informally, to lead and direct the relatively inert majority. This "Iron Law of Oligarchy," as this internal manifestation of the law of comparative advantage has been dubbed, operates to transform an initially majoritarian democratic government, or even a decentralized republican government, into a tightly centralized State controlled by a ruling elite.[44]

The foregoing analysis leads Rothbard to conclude that the exercise of political power is inherently an oligarchic enterprise. The small minority that excels in wielding political power will tend to coalesce and devote an extraordinary amount of mental energy and other resources to establishing and maintaining a permanent and lucrative hegemonic bond over the productive majority. Accordingly, since politics is the main source of their income, the policies and actions of the members of this oligarchic ruling class will be driven primarily by economic motives. The exploited producing class, in contrast, will not expend nearly as many resources on politics, and their actions in the political arena will not be motivated by economic gain to the same degree, precisely because they are absorbed in earning their livelihoods in their own chosen areas of specialization on the market. As Rothbard explains:

[44]One of the first expositions of the operation of this law, within the context of social democratic political parties can be found in Robert Michels, *Political Parties: A Sociological Study of the Oligarchical Tendencies of Modern Democracy* (New York: Dover Publications, [1915] 1959).

> the ruling class, being small and largely specialized, is motivated to think about its economic interests twenty-four hours a day. The steel manufacturers seeking a tariff, the bankers seeking taxes to repay their government bonds, the rulers seeking a strong state from which to obtain subsidies, the bureaucrats wishing to expand their empire, are all professionals in statism. They are constantly at work trying to preserve and expand their privileges.[45]

The ruling class, however, confronts one serious and ongoing problem: how to persuade the productive majority, whose tribute or taxes it consumes, that its laws, regulations, and policies are beneficial; that is, that they coincide with "the public interest" or are designed to promote "the common good" or to optimize "social welfare." Given its minority status, failure to solve this problem exposes the political class to serious consequences. Even passive resistance by a substantial part of the producers, in the form of mass tax resistance, renders the income of the political class and, therefore, its continued existence extremely precarious. More ominously, attempts to suppress such resistance may cause it to spread and intensify and eventually boil over into an active revolution whose likely result is the forcible ousting of the minority exploiting class from its position of political power. Here is where the intellectuals come in. It is their task to convince the public to actively submit to State rule because it is beneficial to do so, or at least to passively endure the State's depredations because the alternative is anarchy and chaos. In return for fabricating an ideological cover for its exploitation of the masses of subjects or taxpayers, these "court intellectuals" are rewarded with the power, wealth, and prestige of a junior partnership in the ruling elite. Whereas in pre-industrial times these apologists for State rule were associated with the clergy, in modern times—at

[45]Rothbard, "Economic Determinism," p. 5.

least since the Progressive Era in the U.S.—they have been drawn increasingly from the academy.[46]

Politicians, bureaucrats, and those whom they subsidize and privilege within the economy thus routinely trumpet lofty ideological motives for their actions in order to conceal from the exploited and plundered citizenry their true motive of economic gain. In today's world, these motives are expressed in the rhetoric of "social democracy" in Europe and that of modern—or welfare-state—liberalism in the United States.[47] In the past, ruling oligarchies have appealed to the ideologies of royal absolutism, Marxism, Progressivism, Fascism, National Socialism, New Deal liberalism, and so on to camouflage their economic goals in advocating a continual aggrandizement of State power. In devising his theoretical guide, then, Rothbard seeks to provide historians with a means of piercing the shroud of ideological rhetoric and illuminating the true motives underlying the policies and actions of ruling elites throughout history. As Rothbard describes this guide, whenever the would-be or actual proprietors and beneficiaries of the State act,

> when they form a State, or a centralizing Constitution, when they go to war or create a Marshall Plan or use and

[46]On the alliance between intellectuals and the State, see Rothbard, *For a New Liberty*, pp. 54–69. A particularly graphic example of this alliance can be found in late-nineteenth-century Germany, where the economists of the German Historical School were referred to as "Socialists of the Chair," because they completely dominated the teaching of economics at German universities. They also explicitly viewed their role as providing an ideological shield for the royal line that ruled Germany and proudly proclaimed themselves to be "the Intellectual Bodyguard of the House of Hohenzollern." Ibid., p. 60.

[47]So-called "neoconservatism," which dominates the conservative movement and the Republican Party in the United States, is merely a variant of modern liberalism. Its leading theoreticians envision a slightly smaller and more efficient welfare state, combined with a larger and more actively interventionist global-warfare state.

> increase State power in any way, their *primary* motivation is economic: to increase their plunder at the expense of the subject and taxpayer. The ideology that they profess and that is formulated and spread through society by the Court Intellectuals is merely an elaborate rationalization for their venal economic interests. The ideology is the smoke screen for their loot, the fictitious clothes spun by the intellectuals to hide the naked plunder of the Emperor. The task of the historian, then, is to penetrate to the essence of the transaction, to strip the ideological garb from the Emperor State and to reveal the economic motive at the heart of the issue.[48]

In characterizing the modern democratic State as essentially a means for coercively redistributing income from producers to politicians, bureaucrats, and special interest groups, Rothbard opens himself up to the charge of espousing a conspiracy theory of economic history. But it is his emphasis on the almost universal propensity of those who employ the political means for economic gain to conceal their true motives with ideological cant that makes him especially susceptible to this charge. Indeed, the Chicago School's theory of economic regulation and the public choice theory of the Virginia School also portray politicians, bureaucrats, and industries regulated by the State as interested almost exclusively in maximizing their utility in the narrow sense, which in many, if not most, cases involves a maximization of pecuniary gain.[49] However, economists of both schools are inured against the charge of conspiracy theory because in their applied work they generally eschew a systematic, thymological

[48]Rothbard, "Economic Determinism," p. 5.

[49]For examples, see, respectively, George J. Stigler, "The Theory of Economic Regulation," in *The Citizen and the State: Essays on Regulation* (Chicago: University of Chicago Press, 1975), pp. 114–41; and James M. Buchanan, "Politics without Romance: A Sketch of Positive Public Choice Theory and Its Normative Implications," in *The Theory of Public Choice—II,* James M. Buchanan and Robert D. Tollison, eds. (Ann Arbor: University of Michigan Press, 1984), pp. 11–22.

investigation of the actual motives of those individuals or groups whose actions they are analyzing. Instead, their positivist methodology inclines them to mechanically impute to real actors in concrete historical circumstances a narrowly conceived utility maximization.

James Buchanan, one of the founders of public choice theory, writes, for instance, that economists pursuing this paradigm tend

> to bring with them models of man that have been found useful within economic theory, models that have been used to develop empirically testable and empirically corroborated hypotheses. These models embody the presumption that persons seek to maximize their own utilities, and their own narrowly defined economic well-being is an important component of these utilities.[50]

George Stigler, who pioneered the theory of economic regulation, argues, "There is, in fact, only one theory of human behavior, and that is the utility-maximizing theory." But for Stigler, unlike Rothbard or Mises, the exact arguments of the utility function of flesh-and-blood actors are not ascertained by the historical method of specific understanding but by the empirical method. Thus, Stigler argues:

> The first purpose of the empirical studies [of regulatory policy] is to identify the purpose of the legislation! The announced goals of a policy are sometimes unrelated or perversely related to its actual effects and the *truly intended effects should be deduced from the actual effects*. This is not a tautology designed to gloss over a hard problem, but instead a hypothesis on the nature of political life. . . . If an economic policy has been adopted by many communities, or if it is persistently pursued by a society over a long span of time, it is fruitful to assume that the real effects were known and desired.[51]

[50]Buchanan, "Politics without Romance," p. 13.

[51]Stigler, "Theory of Economic Regulation," p. 140.

By thus discounting the effect of erroneous ideas about the appropriate means for achieving preferred goals on the choices made by historical actors, Stigler the positivist seeks to free himself from the task of delving into the murky and unmeasurable phenomenon of motives. Without doubt, if the historical outcome of a policy or action is always what was aimed at by an individual or organization—because, according to Stigler, "errors are not what men live by or on"—then there is no need to ever address the question of motive. For Stigler, then, there is no reason for the historian to try to subjectively understand the motive for an action because the actor's goal is objectively revealed by the observed result. Now, Stigler would probably agree that it is absurd to assume that Hitler was aiming at defeat in World War II by doggedly pursuing his disastrous policy on the Eastern front over an extended period of time. But this assumption only appears absurd to us in light of the thymological insight into Hitler's mind achieved by examining the records of his actions, policies, utterances, and writings, and those of his associates. This insight leads us to an *understanding,* which cannot be reasonably doubted by anyone of normal intelligence, that Hitler was fervently seeking victory in the war.

Rothbard insists that the same method of specific understanding that allows the historian to grasp Hitler's objectives in directing the German military campaign against the Soviet Union also is appropriate when attempting to discern the motives of those who lobby for a tariff or for the creation of a central bank. Accordingly, the guide that Rothbard originates to direct the economic historian first to a search for evidence of an unspoken economic motive in such instances is only a guide. As such, it can never rule out in advance the possibility that an ideological or altruistic goal may serve as the dominant motivation in a specific case. If his research turns up no evidence of a hidden economic motive, then the historian must explore further for ideological or other noneconomic motives that may be operating. Thus, as Rothbard points out, his approach to economic history, whether it is labeled a "conspiracy theory of history" or not, "is really only praxeology applied to human history, in assuming that men have motives on which they act."[52] This approach also respects what Mises has called "historical individuality" by assuming that "[t]he characteristics of individual men, their ideas and judgments of value as well as the actions guided by those ideas and judgments, cannot be traced back to something of which they would be the derivatives."[53] In sharp contrast, the positivist methods of Stigler and Buchanan attempt to force participants in historical events into the Procrustean bed of *homo economicus*, who ever and unerringly seeks for his own economic gain.

We can more fully appreciate the significance of Rothbard's methodological innovation by briefly contrasting his explanation of the origins of the Federal Reserve System with the explanation given by Milton Friedman and Anna J. Schwartz in their influential work, *A Monetary History of the United States, 1867–1960*.[54] Since its publication in 1963, this book has served as the standard reference work for all subsequent research in U.S. monetary history. While Friedman and Schwartz cannot exactly be classified as new economic historians, their book is written from a strongly positivist viewpoint and its methods are congenial to those pursuing research in this paradigm.[55] For example, in the preface to the book, Friedman and Schwartz write that their aim is "to provide a prologue and a background for a statistical analysis of the secular and cyclical behavior of money in the United States, and to exclude any material not relevant to that purpose." In particular it is not their ambition to write "a full-scale economic and political history that would be

[52]Murray N. Rothbard, "Only One Heartbeat Away," *The Libertarian Forum* 6 (September 1974): 5.

[53]Mises, *Theory and History*, p. 183.

[54]Milton Friedman and Anna Jacobson Schwartz, *A Monetary History of the United States, 1867–1960* (Princeton, N.J.: Princeton University Press, 1963).

[55]See, for example, North, *Growth and Welfare in the American Past*, p. 11, n. 6.

required to record at all comprehensively the role of money in the United States in the past century."[56] Thus, in effect, the behavior of the unmotivated money supply takes center stage in this tome of 808 pages including appendices. Indeed, the opening sentence of the book reads, "This book is about the stock of money in the United States."[57]

Now Friedman and Schwartz certainly do not, and would not, deny that movements in the money supply are caused by the purposeful actions of motivated human beings. Rather, the positivist methodology they espouse constrains them to narrowly focus their historical narrative on the observable outcomes of these actions and never to formally address their motivation. For, according to the positivist philosophy of science, it is only observable and quantifiable phenomena that can be assigned the status of "cause" in a scientific investigation, while human motives are intensive qualities lacking a quantifiable dimension. So, if one is to write a monetary history that is scientific in the strictly positivist sense, the title must be construed quite literally as the chronicling of quantitative variations in a selected monetary aggregate and the measurable effects of these variations on other quantifiable economic variables, such as the price level and real output.

However, even Friedman and Schwartz's *Monetary History* must occasionally emerge from the bog of statistical analysis and address human motivation in order to explain the economic

[56]Friedman and Schwartz, *A Monetary History,* p. xxii.

[57]Ibid., p. 3. As doctrinaire positivists, Friedman and Schwartz consistently refer to the "stock" or "quantity" of money rather than to the "supply" of money, presumably because the former is the observable market outcome of the interaction of the unobservable money supply and money demand curves. However, it is likely that Friedman and Schwartz conceive the money stock as a good empirical proxy for the money supply, because they view the latter as perfectly inelastic with respect to the price level. On this point, compare Peter Temin's interpretation. Peter Temin, *Did Monetary Forces Cause the Great Depression?* (New York: W.W. Norton, 1976), p. 18.

events, intellectual controversies, social conflicts, and political maneuverings that had an undeniable and fundamental impact on the institutional framework of the money supply. Due to the awkward fit of motives into the positivist framework, however, Friedman and Schwartz's forays into human history tend to be cursory and unilluminating, when not downright misleading. For example, their two chapters dealing with the crucial period from 1879 to 1914 in U.S. monetary history comprise one hundred pages, only 11 of which are devoted to discussing the political and social factors that culminated in the establishment of the Federal Reserve System.[58] In these pages, Friedman and Schwartz suggest that the "money 'issue'" that consumed American politics in the last three decades of the nineteenth century was precipitated by "the crime of 1873" and was almost exclusively driven by the silver interests in league with the inflationist and agrarian Populist Party. This movement, moreover, was partly expressive of the 1890s, a decade which, according to C. Vann Woodward as quoted by the authors, "had rather more than its share of zaniness and crankiness, and that these qualities were manifested in the higher and middling as well as lower orders of American society."[59] In thus trivializing the "money issue," the authors completely ignore the calculated and covert drive by the Wall Street banks led by the Morgans and Rockefellers for a cartelization of the entire banking industry, with themselves and their political allies at the helm. This movement, which began in earnest in the 1890s, was also in part a reaction to the proposals of the silverite and agrarian inflationists and was aimed at reserving to the banks the gains forthcoming from monetary inflation.

Friedman and Schwartz thus portray the drive toward a central bank as completely unconnected with the money issue and as only getting under way in reaction to the panic of 1907 and the problem with the "inelasticity of the currency" that was

[58]Friedman and Schwartz, *A Monetary History*, pp. 89–188.

[59]Ibid., p. 115, n. 40.

then commonly construed as its cause. The result is that they characterize the Federal Reserve System as the product of a straightforward, disinterested, bipartisan effort to provide a practical solution to a purely technical problem afflicting the monetary system.[60] Nowhere in their discussion of the genesis of the Federal Reserve System do Friedman and Schwartz raise the all-important question of precisely which groups benefitted from this "solution." Nor do they probe deeply into the motives of the proponents of the Federal Reserve Act. After a brief and superficial account of the events leading up to the enactment of the law, they hasten to return to the main task of their "monetary history" which, as Friedman expresses it in another work, is "to add to our tested knowledge."[61]

For Friedman and Schwartz, then, the central aim of economic history is the testing of hypotheses suggested by empirical regularities observed in the historical data. Accordingly, Friedman and Schwartz describe their approach to economic history as "conjectural history—the tale of 'what might have been.' "[62] In their view, the primary task of the economic historian is to identify the observable set of circumstances that accounts for the emergence of the historical events under investigation by formulating and testing theoretical conjectures about the course of events that would have developed in the absence of these circumstances. This "counterfactual method," as the new economic historians refer to it, explains the historical events in question and, at the same time, adds to the "tested knowledge" of theoretical relationships to be utilized in future investigations in economic history.[63]

[60]Ibid., p. 171.

[61]Milton Friedman, "The Quantity Theory of Money—A Restatement," in *Studies in the Quantity Theory of Money* (Chicago: University of Chicago Press, [1956] 1973), p. 18.

[62]Ibid., p. 168.

[63]For more on the nature and use of the counterfactual method, see Robert William Fogel, "The New Economic History: Its Findings and Methods," in *The Reinterpretation of American History,* Robert William

Friedman and Schwartz exemplify this method in their treatment of the panic of 1907.[64] During this episode, banks swiftly restricted cash payments to their depositors within weeks after the financial crisis struck, and there ensued no large-scale failure or even temporary closing of banks. Friedman and Schwartz formulate from this experience the theoretical conjecture that, when a financial crisis strikes, early restrictions on currency payments work to prevent a large-scale disruption of the banking system. They then test this conjecture by reference to the events of 1929–1933. In this case, although the financial crisis began with the crash of the stock market in October 1929, cash payments to bank depositors were not restricted until March 1933. From 1930 to 1933, there occurred a massive wave of bank failures. The theoretical conjecture, or "counterfactual statement," that a timely restriction of cash payments would have checked the spread of a financial crisis, is therefore empirically validated by this episode because, in the absence of a timely bank restriction, a wave of bank failures did, in fact, occur after 1929.

Granted, Friedman and Schwartz do recognize that these theoretical conjectures cannot be truly tested because "[t]here is no way to repeat the experiment precisely and so to test these conjectures in detail." Nonetheless, they maintain that "all analytical history, history that seeks to interpret and not simply record the past, is of this character, which is why history must be continuously rewritten in the light of new evidence as it unfolds."[65] In other words, history must be revised repeatedly because the very theory that is employed to interpret it is itself subject to constant revision on the basis of "new evidence" that

---

Fogel and Stanley L. Engerman, eds. (New York: Harper and Row, 1971), pp. 8–10; and Donald N. McCloskey, "Counterfactuals," in *The New Palgrave: The New World of Economics*, John Eatwell, Murray Milgate, and Peter Newman, eds. (New York: W.W. Norton, 1991), pp. 149–54.

[64]Friedman and Schwartz, *A Monetary History*, pp. 156–68.

[65]Ibid., p. 168.

is continually coming to light in the ongoing historical process. As pointed out above, this is the vicious circle that characterizes all attempts to apply the positive method to the interpretation of history.

As if to preempt recognition of this vicious circle, Friedman and Schwartz take as the motto of their volume a famous quote from Alfred Marshall, which reads in part:

> Experience . . . brings out the impossibility of learning anything from facts till they are examined and interpreted by reason; and teaches that the most reckless and treacherous of all theorists is he who professes to let facts and figures speak for themselves.[66]

But clearly, reason teaches us that the observable—and, in some cases, countable, but never measurable—events of economic history ultimately are caused by the purposive actions of human beings whose goals and motives can never be directly observed. In rejecting the historical method of specific understanding, Friedman and Schwartz are led not by reason, but by a narrow positivist prepossession with using history as a laboratory, albeit imperfect, for formulating and testing theories that will allow prediction and control of future phenomena. Of the underlying intent of such a positivist approach to history, Mises wrote, "This discipline will abstract from historical experience laws which could render to social 'engineering' the same services the laws of physics render to technological engineering."[67]

Needless to say, for Rothbard, history can never serve even as an imperfect laboratory for testing theory, because of his agreement with Mises that "the subject matter of history . . . is value judgments and their projection into the reality of change."[68] In seeking to explain the origins of the Federal Reserve System, therefore, Rothbard focuses on the question of

[66]Ibid., p. xix.

[67]Mises, *Theory and History,* p. 285.

[68]Mises, *Human Action*, p. 48.

who would reasonably have expected to benefit from and valued such a radical change in the monetary system. Here is where Rothbard's scientific worldview comes into play. As an Austrian monetary theorist, he recognizes that the limits on bank credit inflation confronted by a fractional reserve banking system based on gold are likely to be much less confining under a central bank than under the quasi-decentralized National Banking System put in place immediately prior to the passage of the Federal Reserve Act in 1913. The praxeological reasoning of Austrian monetary theory also leads to the conclusion that those who stand to reap the lion's share of the economic benefits from a bank credit inflation tend to be the lenders and first recipients of the newly created notes and deposits, namely, commercial and investment bankers and their clients. Guided by the implications of this praxeological knowledge and of his thymological rule about the motives of those who lobby for State laws and regulations, Rothbard is led to scrutinize the goals and actions of the large Wall Street commercial and investment bankers, their industrial clientele, and their relatives and allies in the political arena.

Rothbard's analysis of the concrete evidence demonstrates that, beginning in the late 1890s, a full decade before the panic of 1907, this Wall Street banking axis and allied special interests began to surreptitiously orchestrate and finance an intellectual and political movement agitating for the imposition of a central bank. This movement included academic economists who covered up its narrow and venal economic interests by appealing to the allegedly universal economic benefits that would be forthcoming from a central bank operating as a benevolent and disinterested provider of an "elastic" currency and "lender of last resort." In fact, what the banking and business elites dearly desired was a central bank that would provide an elastic supply of paper reserves to supplement existing gold reserves. Banks' access to additional reserves would facilitate a larger and more lucrative bank credit inflation and, more important, would provide the means to ward off or mitigate the recurrent financial crises that had brought past inflationary booms to an abrupt and disastrous end in bank failures and industrial depression.

Rothbard employs the approach to economic history exemplified in this treatment of the origins of the Fed consistently and dazzlingly throughout this volume to unravel the causes and consequences of events and institutions ranging over the course of U.S. monetary history, from colonial times through the New Deal era. One of the important benefits of Rothbard's unique approach is that it naturally leads to an account of the development of the U.S. monetary system in terms of a compelling narrative linking human motives and plans that oftentimes are hidden and devious to outcomes that sometimes are tragic. And one will learn much more about monetary history from reading this exciting story than from poring over reams of statistical analysis.

Although its five parts were written separately, this volume presents a relatively integrated narrative, with very little overlap, that sweeps across three hundred years of U.S. monetary history. Part 1, "The History of Money and Banking Before the Twentieth Century," consists of Rothbard's contribution to the minority report of the U.S. Gold Commission and treats the evolution of the U.S. monetary system from its colonial beginnings to the end of the nineteenth century.[69] In this part, Rothbard gives a detailed account of two early and abortive attempts by the financial elites to shackle the young republic with a quasi-central bank. He demonstrates the inflationary consequences of these privileged banks, the First and Second Banks of the United States, during their years of operation, from 1791 to 1811 and from 1816 to 1833, respectively. Rothbard then discusses the libertarian Jeffersonian and Jacksonian ideological movements that succeeded in destroying these statist and inflationist institutions. This is followed by discussions of the era of

[69]Rep. Ron Paul and Lewis Lehrman, *The Case for Gold: A Minority Report of the U.S. Gold Commission* (Washington, D.C.: Cato Institute, 1982), pp. 17–118.

comparatively free and decentralized banking that extended from the 1830s up to the Civil War, and the pernicious impact of the war on the U.S. monetary system. Part 1 concludes with an analysis and critique of the post–Civil War National Banking System. Rothbard describes how this regime—which was aggressively promoted by the investment banking firm that had acquired the monopoly of underwriting government bonds—centralized banking and destabilized the economy, resulting in a series of financial crises that prepared the way for the imposition of the Federal Reserve System.

Part 2, on the "Origins of the Federal Reserve," is a paper that lay unpublished for a long time and just appeared in a recent issue of *The Quarterly Journal of Austrian Economics*.[70] Its main argument is summarized in the text above.

Part 3 contains a formerly unpublished paper, "From Hoover to Roosevelt: The Federal Reserve and the Financial Elites." Here, Rothbard identifies the financial interests and ideology that drove the Fed to engineer an almost uninterrupted expansion of the money supply from the moment of its inception in 1914 through 1928. This part also includes an analysis of how concordance and conflict between the Morgan and Rockefeller financial interests shaped the politics and behavior of the Fed during the Hoover administration and the first Roosevelt administration as well as international monetary and domestic banking and financial policies under the latter administration.

Part 4, "The Gold-Exchange Standard in the Interwar Years," previously was published as a chapter in a collection of papers on money and the State.[71] The paper appears here for the first

[70]Murray N. Rothbard, "The Origins of the Federal Reserve System," *Quarterly Journal of Economics* 2, no. 3 (Fall 1999): 3–51.

[71]A version of this piece appeared as Murray N. Rothbard, "The Gold-Exchange Standard in the Interwar Years," in *Money and the Nation State: The Financial Revolution, Government and the World Monetary System*, Kevin Dowd and Richard H. Timberlake, Jr., eds. (New Brunswick, N.J.: Transactions Publishers, 1998), pp. 105–63.

time in its original and unexpurgated version. Rothbard elucidates the reasons why the British and U.S. governments in the 1920s so eagerly sought to reconstruct the international monetary system on the basis of this profoundly flawed and inflationary caricature of the classical gold standard. Rothbard also analyzes the "inner contradictions" of the gold-exchange-standard system that led inexorably to its demise in the early 1930s.

Part 5, "The New Deal and the International Monetary System" is the topic of the fifth and concluding part of the book and was previously published in an edited book of essays on New Deal foreign policy.[72] Rothbard argues that an abrupt shift occurred in the international monetary policy of the New Deal just prior to U.S. entry into World War II. He analyzes the economic interests that promoted and benefited from the radical transformation of New Deal policy, from "dollar nationalism" during the 1930s to the aggressive "dollar imperialism" that prevailed during the war and culminated in the Bretton Woods Agreement of 1944.

—Joseph T. Salerno
Pace University

[72]Murray N. Rothbard, "The New Deal and the International Monetary System," in *Watershed of Empire: Essays on New Deal Foreign Policy,* Leonard P. Liggio and James J. Martin, eds. (Colorado Springs, Colo.: Ralph Myles, 1976), p. 19.

Part 1

A History of Money and Banking in the United States Before the Twentieth Century

A HISTORY OF MONEY AND BANKING IN THE UNITED STATES BEFORE THE TWENTIETH CENTURY

As an outpost of Great Britain, colonial America of course used British pounds, pence, and shillings as its money. Great Britain was officially on a silver standard, with the shilling defined as equal to 86 pure Troy grains of silver, and with silver as so-defined legal tender for all debts (that is, creditors were compelled to accept silver at that rate). However, Britain also coined gold and maintained a bimetallic standard by fixing the gold guinea, weighing 129.4 grains of gold, as equal in value to a certain weight of silver. In that way, gold became, in effect, legal tender as well. Unfortunately, by establishing bimetallism, Britain became perpetually subject to the evil known as Gresham's Law, which states that when government compulsorily overvalues one money and undervalues another, the undervalued money will leave the country or disappear into hoards, while the overvalued money will flood into circulation. Hence, the popular catchphrase of Gresham's Law: "Bad money drives out good." But the important point to note is that the triumph of "bad" money is the result, *not* of perverse free-market competition, but of government using the

[*Previously published in a volume edited by U.S. Representative Ron Paul (R-Texas) and Lewis Lehrman,* The Case for Gold: A Minority Report of the U.S. Gold Commission *(Washington, D.C.: Cato Institute, 1983), pp. 17–118.*—Ed.]

compulsory legal tender power to privilege one money above another.

In seventeenth- and eighteenth-century Britain, the government maintained a mint ratio between gold and silver that consistently overvalued gold and undervalued silver in relation to world market prices, with the resultant disappearance and outflow of full-bodied silver coins, and an influx of gold, and the maintenance in circulation of only eroded and "lightweight" silver coins. Attempts to rectify the fixed bimetallic ratios were always too little and too late.[1]

In the sparsely settled American colonies, money, as it always does, arose in the market as a useful and scarce commodity and began to serve as a general medium of exchange. Thus, beaver fur and wampum were used as money in the north for exchanges with the Indians, and fish and corn also served as money. Rice was used as money in South Carolina, and the most widespread use of commodity money was tobacco, which served as money in Virginia. The pound-of-tobacco was the currency unit in Virginia, with warehouse receipts in tobacco circulating as money backed 100 percent by the tobacco in the warehouse.

While commodity money continued to serve satisfactorily in rural areas, as the colonial economy grew, Americans imported gold and silver coins to serve as monetary media in urban centers and in foreign trade. English coins were imported, but so too were gold and silver coins from other European countries. Among the gold coins circulating in America were the French

[1]In the late seventeenth and early eighteenth centuries, the British maintained fixed mint ratios of from 15.1-to-1 of silver grains in relation to gold grains, to about 15.5-to-1. Yet the world market ratio of weight, set by forces of supply and demand, was about 14.9-to-1. Thus, silver was consistently undervalued and gold overvalued. In the eighteenth century, the problem got even worse, for increasing gold production in Brazil and declining silver production in Peru brought the market ratio down to 14.1-to-1 while the mint ratios fixed by the British government continued to be the same.

guinea, the Portuguese "joe," the Spanish doubloon, and Brazilian coins, while silver coins included French crowns and livres.

It is important to realize that gold and silver are international commodities, and that therefore, when not prohibited by government decree, foreign coins are perfectly capable of serving as standard moneys. There is no need to have a national government monopolize the coinage, and indeed foreign gold and silver coins constituted much of the coinage in the United States until Congress outlawed the use of foreign coins in 1857. Thus, if a free market is allowed to prevail in a country, foreign coins will circulate naturally. Silver and gold coins will tend to be valued in proportion to their respective weights, and the ratio *between* silver and gold will be set by the market in accordance with their relative supply and demand.

Shilling and Dollar Manipulations

By far the leading specie coin circulating in America was the Spanish silver dollar, defined as consisting of 387 grains of pure silver. The dollar was divided into "pieces of eight," or "bits," each consisting of one-eighth of a dollar. Spanish dollars came into the North American colonies through lucrative trade with the West Indies. The Spanish silver dollar had been the world's outstanding coin since the early sixteenth century, and was spread partially by dint of the vast silver output of the Spanish colonies in Latin America. More important, however, was that the Spanish dollar, from the sixteenth to the nineteenth century, was relatively the most stable and least debased coin in the Western world.[2]

[2]The name "dollar" came from "thaler," the name given to the coin of similar weight, the "Joachimsthaler" or "schlicken thaler," issued since the early sixteenth century by the Count of Schlick in Joachimsthal in Bohemia. The Joachimsthalers weighed 451 Troy grains of silver. So successful were these coins that similar thalers were minted in Burgundy, Holland, and France; most successful of these was the Maria Theresa thaler, which began being minted in 1751 and formed a considerable portion of American currency after that date. The Spanish "pieces of eight" adopted the name "dollar" after 1690.

Since the Spanish silver dollar consisted of 387 grains, and the English shilling consisted of 86 grains of silver, this meant the natural, free-market ratio between the two coins would be 4 shillings 6 pence per dollar.[3]

Constant complaints, both by contemporaries and by some later historians, arose about an alleged "scarcity of money," especially of specie, in the colonies, allegedly justifying numerous colonial paper money schemes to remedy that "shortage." In reality, there was no such shortage. It is true that England, in a mercantilist attempt to hoard specie, kept minting for its own prerogative and outlawed minting in the colonies; it also prohibited the export of English coin to America. But this did not keep specie from America, for, as we have seen, Americans were able to import Spanish and other foreign coin, including English, from other countries. Indeed, as we shall see, it was precisely paper money issues that led, by Gresham's Law, to outflows and disappearance of specie from the colonies.

In their own mercantilism, the colonial governments early tried to hoard their own specie by debasing their shilling standards in terms of Spanish dollars. Whereas their natural weights dictated a ratio of 4 shillings 6 pence to the dollar, Massachusetts, in 1642, began a general colonial process of competitive debasement of shillings. Massachusetts arbitrarily decreed that the Spanish dollar be valued at 5 shillings; the idea was to attract an inflow of Spanish silver dollars into that colony, and to subsidize Massachusetts exports by making their prices cheaper in terms of dollars. Soon, Connecticut and other colonies followed suit, each persistently upping the ante of debasement. The result was to increase the supply of nominal units of account by debasing the shilling, inflating domestic prices and thereby bringing the temporary export stimulus to a rapid end. Finally, the English government brought a halt to this futile and inflationary practice in 1707.

[3]Since 20 shillings make £1, this meant that the natural ratio between the two currencies was £l = $4.44.

But the colonial governments had already found another, and far more inflationary, arrow for their bow: the invention of government fiat paper money.

Government Paper Money

Apart from medieval China, which invented both paper and printing centuries before the West, the world had never seen government paper money until the colonial government of Massachusetts emitted a fiat paper issue in 1690.[4,5] Massachusetts was accustomed to launching plunder expeditions against the prosperous French colony in Quebec. Generally, the expeditions were successful, and would return to Boston, sell their booty, and pay off the soldiers with the proceeds. This time, however, the expedition was beaten back decisively, and the soldiers returned to Boston in ill humor, grumbling for their pay. Discontented soldiers are ripe for mutiny, so the Massachusetts government looked around in concern for a way to pay the soldiers. It tried to borrow £3,000–£4,000 from Boston merchants, but evidently the Massachusetts credit rating was not the best. Finally, Massachusetts decided in December 1690 to print £7,000 in paper notes and to use them to pay the soldiers. Suspecting that the public would not accept irredeemable paper, the government made a twofold pledge when it issued the notes: that it would redeem them in gold or silver out of tax

[4]Government paper redeemable in gold began in the early ninth century, and after three centuries the government escalated to irredeemable fiat paper, with the usual consequences of boom-bust cycles, and runaway inflation. See Gordon Tullock, "Paper Money—A Cycle in Cathay," *Economic History Review* 9, no. 3 (1957): 393–96.

[5]The only exception was a curious form of paper money issued five years earlier in Quebec, to become known as "card money." The governing *intendant* of Quebec, Monsieur Mueles, divided some playing cards into quarters, marked them with various monetary denominations, and then issued them to pay for wages and materials sold to the government. He ordered the public to accept the cards as legal tender, and this particular issue was later redeemed in specie sent from France.

revenue in a few years and that absolutely no further paper notes would be issued. Characteristically, however, both parts of the pledge went quickly by the board: The issue limit disappeared in a few months, and all the bills continued unredeemed for nearly 40 years. As early as February 1691, the Massachusetts government proclaimed that its issue had fallen "far short" and so it proceeded to emit £40,000 of new money to repay all of its outstanding debt, again pledging falsely that this would be the absolute final note issue.

But Massachusetts found that the increase in the supply of money, coupled with a fall in the demand for paper because of growing lack of confidence in future redemption in specie, led to a rapid depreciation of new money in relation to specie. Indeed, within a year after the initial issue, the new paper pound had depreciated on the market by 40 percent against specie.

By 1692, the government moved against this market evaluation by use of force, making the paper money compulsory legal tender for all debts at par with specie, and by granting a premium of 5 percent on all payment of debts to the government made in paper notes. This legal tender law had the unwanted effect of Gresham's Law: the disappearance of specie circulation in the colony. In addition, the expanding paper issues drove up prices and hampered exports from the colony. In this way, the specie "shortage" became the creature rather than the cause of the fiat paper issues. Thus, in 1690, before the orgy of paper issues began, £200,000 of silver money was available in New England; by 1711, however, with Connecticut and Rhode Island having followed suit in paper money issue, £240,000 of paper money had been issued in New England but the silver had almost disappeared from circulation.

Ironically, then, Massachusetts's and her sister colonies' issue of paper money created rather than solved any "scarcity of money." The new paper drove out the old specie. The consequent driving up of prices and depreciation of paper scarcely relieved any alleged money scarcity among the public. But since the paper was issued to finance government expenditures and pay public debts, the *government,* not the public, benefited from the fiat issue.

After Massachusetts had emitted another huge issue of £500,000 in 1711 to pay for another failed expedition against Quebec, not only was the remainder of the silver driven from circulation, but, despite the legal tender law, the paper pound depreciated 30 percent against silver. Massachusetts pounds, officially 7 shillings to the silver ounce, had now fallen on the market to 9 shillings per ounce. Depreciation proceeded in this and other colonies despite fierce governmental attempts to outlaw it, backed by fines, imprisonment, and total confiscation of property for the high crime of not accepting the paper at par.

Faced with a further "shortage of money" due to the money issues, Massachusetts decided to press on; in 1716, it formed a government "land bank" and issued £100,000 in notes to be loaned on real estate in the various counties of the province.

Prices rose so dramatically that the tide of opinion in Massachusetts began to turn against paper, as writers pointed out that the result of issues was a doubling of prices in the past 20 years, depreciation of paper, and the disappearance of Spanish silver through the operation of Gresham's Law. From then on, Massachusetts, pressured by the British Crown, tried intermittently to reduce the bills in circulation and return to a specie currency, but was hampered by its assumed obligations to honor the paper notes at par of its sister New England colonies.

In 1744, another losing expedition against the French led Massachusetts to issue an enormous amount of paper money over the next several years. From 1744 to 1748, paper money in circulation expanded from £300,000 to £2.5 million, and the depreciation in Massachusetts was such that silver had risen on the market to 60 shillings an ounce, ten times the price at the beginning of an era of paper money in 1690.

By 1740, every colony but Virginia had followed suit in fiat paper money issues, and Virginia succumbed in the late 1750s in trying to finance part of the French and Indian War against the French. Similar consequences—dramatic inflation, shortage of specie, massive depreciation despite compulsory par laws—ensued in each colony. Thus, along with Massachusetts' depreciation of 11-to-1 of its notes against specie compared to the original par, Connecticut's notes had sunk to 9-to-1 and the Carolinas' at 10-to-1 in 1740, and the paper of virulently inflationist Rhode Island to 23-to-1 against specie. Even the least-inflated paper, that of Pennsylvania, had suffered an appreciation of specie to 80 percent over par.

A detailed study of the effects of paper money in New Jersey shows how it created a boom-bust economy over the colonial period. When new paper money was injected into the economy, an inflationary boom would result, to be followed by a deflationary depression when the paper money supply contracted.[6]

At the end of King George's War with France in 1748, Parliament began to pressure the colonies to retire the mass of paper money and return to a specie currency. In 1751, Great Britain prohibited all further issues of legal tender paper in New England and ordered a move toward redemption of existing issues in specie. Finally, in 1764, Parliament extended the prohibition of new issues to the remainder of the colonies and required the gradual retirement of outstanding notes.

Following the lead of Parliament, the New England colonies, apart from Rhode Island, decided to resume specie payment and retire their paper notes rapidly at the current depreciated market rate. The panicky opponents of specie resumption and monetary contraction made the usual predictions in such a situation: that the result would be a virtual absence of money in New England and the consequent ruination of all trade. Instead, however, after a brief adjustment, the resumption and retirement led to a far more prosperous trade and production—the harder money and lower prices attracting an inflow of specie. In fact, with

[6]Donald L. Kemmerer, "Paper Money in New Jersey, 1668–1775," New Jersey Historical Society, *Proceedings* 74 (April 1956): 107–44.

Massachusetts on specie and Rhode Island still on depreciated paper, the result was that Newport, which had been a flourishing center for West Indian imports for western Massachusetts, lost its trade to Boston and languished in the doldrums.[7, 8]

In fact, as one student of colonial Massachusetts has pointed out, the return to specie occasioned remarkably little dislocation, recession, or price deflation. Indeed, wheat prices fell by less in Boston than in Philadelphia, which saw no such return to specie in the early 1750s. Foreign exchange rates, after the resumption of specie, were highly stable, and "the restored specie system operated after 1750 with remarkable stability during the Seven Years War and during the dislocation of international payments in the last years before the Revolution."[9]

Not being outlawed by government decree, specie remained in circulation throughout the colonial period, even during the

[7]Before Massachusetts went back to specie, it was committed to accept the notes of the other New England colonies at par. This provided an incentive for Rhode Island to inflate its currency wildly, for this small colony, with considerable purchases to make in Massachusetts, could make these purchases in inflated money at par. Thereby Rhode Island could export its inflation to the larger colony, but make its purchases with the new money before Massachusetts prices could rise in response. In short, Rhode Island could expropriate wealth from Massachusetts and impose the main cost of its inflation on the latter colony.

[8]If Rhode Island was the most inflationary of the colonies, Maryland's monetary expansion was the most bizarre. In 1733, Maryland's public land bank issued £70,000 of paper notes, of which £30,000 was *given away* in a fixed amount to each inhabitant of the province. This was done to universalize the circulation of the new notes, and is probably the closest approximation in history of Milton Friedman's "helicopter" model, in which a magical helicopter lavishes new paper money in fixed amounts of proportions to each inhabitant. The result of the measure, of course, was rapid depreciation of new notes. However, the inflationary impact of the notes was greatly lessened by tobacco still being the major money of the new colony. Tobacco was legal tender in Maryland and the paper was not receivable for all taxes.

[9]Roger W. Weiss, "The Colonial Monetary Standard of Massachusetts," *Economic History Review* 27 (November 1974): 589.

operation of paper money. Despite the inflation, booms and busts, and shortages of specie caused by paper issues, the specie system worked well overall:

> Here was a silver standard . . . in the absence of institutions of the central government intervening in the silver market, and in the absence of either a public or private central bank adjusting domestic credit or managing a reserve of specie or foreign exchange with which to stabilize exchange rates. The market . . . kept exchange rates remarkably close to the legislated par. . . . What is most remarkable in this context is the continuity of the specie system through the seventeenth and eighteenth centuries.[10]

Private Bank Notes

In contrast to government paper, private bank notes and deposits, redeemable in specie, had begun in western Europe in Venice in the fourteenth century. Firms granting credit to consumers and businesses had existed in the ancient world and in medieval Europe, but these were "money lenders" who loaned out their own savings. "Banking" in the sense of lending out the savings of others only began in England with the "scriveners" of the early seventeenth century. The scriveners were clerks who wrote contracts and bonds and were therefore in a position to learn of mercantile transactions and engage in money lending and borrowing.[11]

There were, however, no banks of deposit in England until the civil war in the mid-seventeenth century. Merchants had been in the habit of storing their surplus gold in the king's mint for safekeeping. That habit proved to be unfortunate, for when

[10]Ibid., p. 591.

[11]During the sixteenth century, before the rise of the scriveners, most English money-lending was not even conducted by specialized firms, but by wealthy merchants in the clothing and woolen industries, as outlets for their surplus capital. See J. Milnes Holden, *The History of Negotiable Instruments in English Law* (London: Athlone Press, 1955), pp. 205–06.

Charles I needed money in 1638, shortly before the outbreak of the civil war, he confiscated the huge sum of £200,000 of gold, calling it a "loan" from the owners. Although the merchants finally got their gold back, they were understandably shaken by the experience, and forsook the mint, depositing their gold instead in the coffers of private goldsmiths, who, like the mint, were accustomed to storing the valuable metal. The warehouse receipts of the goldsmiths soon came to be used as a surrogate for the gold itself. By the end of the civil war, in the 1660s, the goldsmiths fell prey to the temptation to print pseudo-warehouse receipts not covered by gold and lend them out; in this way fractional reserve banking came to England.[12]

Very few private banks existed in colonial America, and they were short-lived. Most prominent was the Massachusetts Land Bank of 1740, issuing notes and lending them out on real estate. The land bank was launched as an inflationary alternative to government paper, which the royal governor was attempting to restrict. The land bank issued irredeemable notes, and fear of its unsound issue generated a competing private silver bank, which emitted notes redeemable in silver. The land bank promptly issued over £49,000 in irredeemable notes, which depreciated very rapidly. In six months' time the public was almost universally refusing to accept the bank's notes and land bank sympathizers vainly accepting the notes. The final blow came in 1741, when Parliament, acting at the request of several Massachusetts merchants and the royal governor, outlawed both the land and the silver banks.

[12]Once again, ancient China pioneered in deposit banking, as well as in fractional reserve banking. Deposit banking per se began in the eighth century A.D., when shops would accept valuables, in return for warehouse receipts, and receive a fee for keeping them safe. After a while, the deposit receipts of these shops began to circulate as money. Finally, after two centuries, the shops began to issue and lend out more receipts than they had on deposit; they had caught on to fractional reserve banking. Tullock, "Paper Money," p. 396.

One intriguing aspect of both the Massachusetts Land Bank and other inflationary colonial schemes is that they were advocated and lobbied for by some of the wealthiest merchants and land speculators in the respective colonies. Debtors benefit from inflation and creditors lose; realizing this fact, older historians assumed that debtors were largely poor agrarians and creditors were wealthy merchants and that therefore the former were the main sponsors of inflationary nostrums. But, of course, there are no rigid "classes" of debtors and creditors; indeed, wealthy merchants and land speculators are often the heaviest debtors. Later historians have demonstrated that members of the latter group were the major sponsors of inflationary paper money in the colonies.[13, 14]

[13]On the Massachusetts Land Bank, see the illuminating study by George Athan Billias, "The Massachusetts Land Bankers of 1740," *University of Maine Bulletin* 61 (April 1959). On merchant enthusiasm for inflationary banking in Massachusetts, see Herman J. Belz, "Paper Money in Colonial Massachusetts," Essex Institute, *Historical Collections* 101 (April 1965): 146–63; and Herman J. Belz, "Currency Reform in Colonial Massachusetts, 1749–1750," Essex Institute, *Historical Collections* 103 (January 1967): 66–84. On the forces favoring colonial inflation in general, see Bray Hammond, *Banks and Politics in America* (Princeton, N.J.: Princeton University Press, 1957), chap. 1; and Joseph Dorfman, *The Economic Mind in American Civilization, 1606–1865* (New York: Viking Press, 1946), p. 142.

[14]For an excellent biographical essay on colonial money and banking, see Jeffrey Rogers Hummel, "The Monetary History of America to 1789: A Historiographical Essay," *Journal of Libertarian Studies* 2 (Winter 1978): 373–89. For a summary of colonial monetary experience, see Murray N. Rothbard, *Conceived in Liberty,* vol. 2, *Salutary Neglect, The American Colonies in the First Half of the Eighteenth Century* (New Rochelle, N.Y.: Arlington House, 1975), pp. 123–40. A particularly illuminating analysis is in the classic work done by Charles Jesse Bullock, *Essays on the Monetary History of the United States* (New York: Greenwood Press, [1900] 1969), pp. 1–59. Up-to-date data on the period is in Roger W. Weiss, "The Issue of Paper Money in the American Colonies, 1720–1774," *Journal of Economic History* 30 (December 1970): 770–84.

Revolutionary War Finance

To finance the Revolutionary War, which broke out in 1775, the Continental Congress early hit on the device of issuing fiat paper money. The leader in the drive for paper money was Gouverneur Morris, the highly conservative young scion of the New York landed aristocracy. There was no pledge to redeem the paper, even in the future, but it was supposed to be retired in seven years by taxes levied pro rata by the separate states. Thus, a heavy future tax burden was supposed to be added to the inflation brought about by the new paper money. The retirement pledge, however, was soon forgotten, as Congress, enchanted by this new, seemingly costless form of revenue, escalated its emissions of fiat paper. As a historian has phrased it, "such was the beginning of the 'federal trough,' one of America's most imperishable institutions."[15]

The total money supply of the United States at the beginning of the Revolution has been estimated at $12 million. Congress launched its first paper issue of $2 million in late June 1775, and before the notes were printed it had already concluded that another $1 million was needed. Before the end of the year, a full $6 million in paper issues was issued or authorized, a dramatic increase of 50 percent in the money supply in one year.

The issue of this fiat "Continental" paper rapidly escalated over the next few years. Congress issued $6 million in 1775, $19 million in 1776, $13 million in 1777, $64 million in 1778, and $125 million in 1779. This was a total issue of over $225 million in five years superimposed upon a pre-existing money supply of $12 million. The result was, as could be expected, a rapid price inflation in terms of the paper notes, and a corollary accelerating depreciation of the paper in terms of specie. Thus, at the end of 1776, the Continentals were worth $1 to $1.25 in specie; by the fall of the following year, its value had fallen to 3-to-1; by December 1778 the value was 6.8-to-1; and by December 1779,

[15]Edmund Cody Burnett, *The Continental Congress* (New York: W.W. Norton, 1964), p. 83.

to the negligible 42-to-1. By the spring of 1781, the Continentals were virtually worthless, exchanging on the market at 168 paper dollars to one dollar in specie. This collapse of the Continental currency gave rise to the phrase, "not worth a Continental."

To top this calamity, several states issued their own paper money, and each depreciated at varying rates. Virginia and the Carolinas led the inflationary move, and by the end of the war, state issues added a total of 210 million depreciated dollars to the nation's currency.

In an attempt to stem the inflation and depreciation, various states levied maximum price controls and compulsory par laws. The result was only to create shortages and impose hardships on large sections of the public. Thus, soldiers were paid in Continentals, but farmers understandably refused to accept payment in paper money despite legal coercion. The Continental Army then moved to "impress" food and other supplies, seizing the supplies and forcing the farmers and shopkeepers to accept depreciated paper in return. By 1779, with Continental paper virtually worthless, the Continental Army stepped up its impressments, "paying" for them in newly issued paper tickets or "certificates" issued by the army quartermaster and commissary departments. The states followed suit with their own massive certificate issues. It understandably took little time for these certificates, federal and state, to depreciate in value to nothing; by the end of the war, federal certificate issues alone totaled $200 million.

The one redeeming feature of this monetary calamity was that the federal and state governments at least allowed these paper issues to sink into worthlessness without insisting that taxpayers shoulder another grave burden by being forced to redeem these issues specie at par, or even to redeem them at all.[16] Continentals

[16]As one historian explained, "Currency and certificates were the 'common debt' of the Revolution, most of which at war's end had been sunk at its depreciated value. Public opinion . . . tended to grade claims against the government according to their real validity. Paper money had

were not redeemed at all, and state paper was only redeemed at depreciating rates, some at the greatly depreciated market value.[17] By the end of the war, all the wartime state paper had been withdrawn from circulation.

Unfortunately, the same policy was not applied to another important device that Congress turned to after its Continental paper had become almost worthless in 1779: loan certificates. Technically, loan certificates were public debt, but they were scarcely genuine loans. They were simply notes issued by the government to pay for supplies and accepted by the merchants because the government would not pay anything else. Hence, the loan certificates became a form of currency, and rapidly depreciated. As early as the end of 1779, they had depreciated to 24-to-1 in specie. By the end of the war, $600 million of loan certificates had been issued. Some of the later loan certificate issues were liquidated at a depreciated rate, but the bulk remained after the war to become the substantial core of the permanent, peacetime federal debt.

The mass of federal and state debt could have depreciated and passed out of existence by the end of the war, but the process was stopped and reversed by Robert Morris, wealthy Philadelphia merchant and virtual economic and financial czar of the Continental Congress in the last years of the war. Morris, leader of the nationalist forces in American politics, moved to make the depreciated federal debt ultimately redeemable in par and also agitated for federal assumption of the various state debts. The reason for this was twofold: (a) to confer a vast subsidy on speculators who had purchased the public debt at highly depreciated values, by paying interest and principal at

---

the least status." E. James Ferguson, *The Power of the Purse: A History of American Public Finance, 1776–1790* (Chapel Hill: University of North Carolina Press, 1961), p. 68.

[17]In Virginia and Georgia, the state paper was redeemed at the highly depreciated market rate of 1,000-to-1 in specie.

par in specie;[18] and (b) to build up agitation for taxing power in the Congress, which the Articles of Confederation refused to allow to the federal government. The decentralist policy of the states' raising taxes or issuing new paper money to pay off the pro rata federal debt as well as their own was thwarted by the adoption of the Constitution, which brought about the victory of the nationalist program, led by Morris's youthful disciple and former aide, Alexander Hamilton.

The Bank of North America

Robert Morris's nationalist vision was not confined to a strong central government, the power of the federal government to tax, and a massive public debt fastened permanently upon the taxpayers. Shortly after he assumed total economic power in Congress in the spring of 1781, Morris introduced a bill to create the first commercial bank, as well as the first central bank, in the history of the new Republic. This bank, headed by Morris himself, the Bank of North America, was not only the first fractional reserve commercial bank in the U.S.; it was to be a privately owned central bank, modeled after the Bank of England. The money system was to be grounded upon specie, but with a controlled monetary inflation pyramiding an expansion of money and credit upon a reserve of specie.

The Bank of North America, which quickly received a federal charter and opened its doors at the beginning of 1782, received the privilege from the government of its notes being receivable in all duties and taxes to all governments, at par with specie. In addition, no other banks were to be permitted to operate in the country. In return for its monopoly license to issue paper

[18]As Morris candidly put it, this windfall to the public debt speculators at the expense of the taxpayers would cause wealth to flow "into those hands which could render it most productive." Ferguson, *Power of the Purse*, p. 124.

money, the bank would graciously lend most of its newly created money to the federal government to purchase public debt and be reimbursed by the hapless taxpayer. The Bank of North America was made the depository for all congressional funds. The first central bank in America rapidly loaned $1.2 million to the Congress, headed also by Robert Morris.[19]

Despite Robert Morris's power and influence, and the monopoly privileges conferred upon his bank, it was perceived in the market that the bank's notes were being inflated compared with specie. Despite the nominal redeemability of the Bank of North America's notes in specie, the market's lack of confidence in the inflated notes led to their depreciation outside its home base in Philadelphia. The bank even tried to shore up the value of the notes by hiring people to urge redeemers of its notes not to ruin everything by insisting upon specie—a move scarcely calculated to improve ultimate confidence in the bank.

After a year of operation, however, Morris, his political power slipping after the end of the war, moved quickly to end his bank's role as a central bank and to shift it to the status of a private commercial bank chartered by the state of Pennsylvania. By the end of 1783, all of the federal government's stock in the Bank of North America, which had the previous year amounted to five-eighths of its capital, had been sold by Morris into private hands, and all U.S. government debt to the bank

[19]When Morris failed to raise the legally required specie capital to launch the Bank of North America, Morris, in an act tantamount to embezzlement, simply appropriated specie loaned to the U.S. by France and invested it for the government in his own bank. In this way, the bulk of specie capital for his bank was appropriated by Morris out of government funds. A multiple of these funds was then borrowed back from Morris's bank by Morris as government financier for the pecuniary benefit of Morris as banker; and finally, Morris channeled most of the money into war contracts for his friends and business associates. Murray N. Rothbard, *Conceived in Liberty*, vol. 4, *The Revolutionary War, 1775–1784* (New Rochelle, N.Y.: Arlington House, 1979), p. 392.

had been repaid. The first experiment with a central bank in the United States had ended.[20]

At the end of the Revolutionary War, the contraction of the swollen mass of paper money, combined with the resumption of imports from Great Britain, combined to cut prices by more than half in a few years. Vain attempts by seven state governments, in the mid-1780s, to cure the "shortage of money" and reinflate prices were a complete failure. Part of the reason for the state paper issues was a frantic attempt to pay the wartime public debt, state and pro rata federal, without resorting to crippling burdens of taxation. The increased paper issues merely added to the "shortage" by stimulating the export of specie and the import of commodities from abroad. Once again, Gresham's Law was at work. State paper issues—despite compulsory par laws—merely depreciated rapidly, and aggravated the shortage of specie. A historian discusses what happened to the paper issues of North Carolina:

> In 1787–1788 the specie value of the paper had shrunk by more than fifty percent. Coin vanished, and since the paper had practically no value outside the state, merchants could not use it to pay debts they owed abroad; hence they suffered severe losses when they had to accept it at inflated values in the settlement of local debts. North Carolina's performance warned merchants anew of the menace of depreciating paper money which they were forced to receive at par from their debtors but which they could not pass on to their creditors.[21]

Neither was the situation helped by the expansion of banking following the launching of the Bank of North America in 1782. The Bank of New York and the Massachusetts Bank

[20]See ibid., pp. 409–10. On the Bank of North America and on Revolutionary War finance generally, see Curtis P. Nettels, *The Emergence of a National Economy, 1775–1815* (New York: Holt, Rinehart, and Winston, 1962), pp. 23–34.

[21]Nettels, *National Economy*, p. 82.

(Boston) followed two years later, with each institution enjoying a monopoly of banking in its region.[22] Their expansion of bank notes and deposits helped to drive out specie, and in the following year the expansion was succeeded by a contraction of credit, which aggravated the problems of recession.[23]

THE UNITED STATES: BIMETALLIC COINAGE

Since the Spanish silver dollar was the major coin circulating in North America during the colonial and Confederation periods, it was generally agreed that the "dollar" would be the basic currency unit of the new United States of America.[24] Article I, section 8 of the new Constitution gave to Congress the power "to coin money, regulate the value thereof, and of foreign coin"; the power was exclusive because the state governments were prohibited, in Article I, section 10, from coining money, emitting paper money, or making anything but gold and silver coin legal tender in payment of debts. (Evidently the Founding Fathers were mindful of the bleak record of colonial and Revolutionary paper issues and provincial juggling of the weights and denominations of coin.) In accordance with this power, Congress passed the Coinage Act of 1792 on the recommendation of Secretary of Treasury Alexander Hamilton's "Report on the Establishment of a Mint" of the year before.[25]

[22]See Hammond, *Banks and Politics*, pp. 67, 87–88.

[23]Nettels, *National Economy*, pp. 61–62. See also Hammond, *Banks and Politics*, pp. 77–80, 85.

[24]As Jefferson put it at the time: "The unit or dollar is a known coin, and the most familiar of all to the mind of the public. It is already adopted from South to North, has identified our currency, and therefore happily offers itself a unit already introduced." Cited in J. Laurence Laughlin, *The History of Bimetallism in the United States*, 4th ed. (New York: D. Appleton, 1901), p. 11, n. 3.

[25]The text of the Coinage Act of 1792 may be found in ibid., pp. 300–01. See also pp. 21–23; and A. Barton Hepburn, *A History of Currency in the United States with a Brief Description of the Currency Systems of all Commercial Nations* (New York: MacMillan, 1915), pp. 43–45.

The Coinage Act established a bimetallic dollar standard for the United States. The dollar was defined as *both* a weight of 371.25 grains of pure silver *and/or* a weight of 24.75 grains of pure gold—a fixed ratio of 15 grains of silver to 1 grain of gold.[26] Anyone could bring gold and silver bullion to the mint to be coined, and silver and gold coins were both to be legal tender at this fixed ratio of 15-to-1. The basic silver coin was to be the silver dollar, and the basic gold coin the $10 eagle, containing 247.5 grains of pure gold.[27]

The 15-to-1 fixed bimetallic ratio almost precisely corresponded to the market gold/silver ratio of the early 1790s,[28] but of course the tragedy of any bimetallic standard is that the fixed mint ratio must always come a cropper against inevitably changing market ratios, and that Gresham's Law will then come inexorably into effect. Thus, Hamilton's express desire to keep both metals in circulation in order to increase the supply of money was doomed to failure.[29]

Unfortunately for the bimetallic goal, the 1780s saw the beginning of a steady decline in the ratio of the market values of silver to gold, largely due to the massive increases over the next three decades of silver production from the mines of Mexico. The result was that the market ratio fell to 15.5-to-1 by the 1790s, and after 1805 fell to approximately 15.75-to-1. The latter figure was enough of a gap between the market and mint ratios to set Gresham's Law into operation so that by 1810 gold

[26]The current Spanish silver dollars in use were lighter than the earlier dollars, weighing 387 grains. See Laughlin, *History of Bimetallism*, pp. 16–18.

[27]Golden half-eagles (worth $5) and quarter-eagles (worth $2.50) were also to be coined, of corresponding proportional weights, and, for silver coins, half-dollars, quarter-dollars, dimes, and half-dimes of corresponding weights.

[28]Silver had declined in market value from the 14.1-to-1 ratio of 1760, largely due to the declining production of gold from Russian mines in this period and therefore the rising relative value of gold.

[29]See Laughlin, *History of Bimetallism*, p. 14.

coins began to disappear from the United States and silver coins began to flood in. The fixed government ratio now significantly overvalued silver and undervalued gold, so it paid people to bring in silver to exchange for gold, melt the gold coins into bullion and ship it abroad. From 1810 until 1834, only silver coin, domestic and foreign, circulated in the United States.[30]

Originally, Congress provided in 1793 that all foreign coins circulating in the United States be legal tender. Indeed, foreign coins have been estimated to form 80 percent of American domestic specie circulation in 1800. Most of the foreign coins were Spanish silver, and while the legal tender privilege was progressively canceled for various foreign coins by 1827, Spanish silver coins continued as legal tender and to predominate in circulation.[31] Spanish dollars, however, soon began to be heavier in weight by 1 to 5 percent over their American equivalents, even though they circulated at face value here, and so the American mint ratio overvalued American more than Spanish dollars. As a result, the Spanish silver dollars were re-exported, leaving American silver dollars in circulation. On the other hand, fractional Spanish silver coins—half-dollars, quarter-dollars, dimes, and half-dimes—were considerably overvalued in the U.S., since they circulated at face value and yet were far lighter weight. Gresham's Law again came into play, and the result was that American silver fractional coins were exported and disappeared, leaving Spanish silver fractional coins as the major currency. To make matters still more complicated, American silver dollars, though lighter weight than the Spanish, circulated equally by name in the West Indies. As a result,

[30]For a lucid explanation of the changing silver-gold ratios and how Gresham's Law operated in this period, see ibid., pp. 10–51. See also J. Laurence Laughlin, *A New Exposition of Money, Credit and Prices* (Chicago: University of Chicago Press, 1931), pp. 93–111.

[31]These "Spanish" coins were almost exclusively minted in the Spanish colonies of Latin America. After the Latin American nations achieved independence in the 1820s, the coins circulated freely in the United States without being legal tender.

American silver dollars were exported to the Caribbean. Thus, by the complex workings of Gresham's Law, the United States was left, especially after 1820, with no gold coins and only Spanish fractional silver coin in circulation.[32]

The First Bank of the United States: 1791–1811

A linchpin of the Hamiltonian financial program was a central bank, the First Bank of the United States, replacing the abortive Bank of North America experiment. Hamilton's "Report on a National Bank" of December 1790 urged such a bank, to be owned privately with the government owning one-fifth of the shares. Hamilton argued that the alleged "scarcity" of specie currency needed to be overcome by infusions of paper and the new bank was to issue such paper, to be invested in the assumed federal debt and in subsidy to manufacturers. The bank notes were to be legally redeemable in specie on demand, and its notes were to be kept at par with specie by the federal government's accepting its notes in taxes—giving it a quasi–legal tender status. Also, the federal government would confer upon the bank the prestige of being the depository for its public funds.

In accordance with Hamilton's wishes, Congress quickly established the First Bank of the United States in February 1791. The charter of the bank was for 20 years, and it was assured a monopoly of the privilege of having a national charter during that period. In a significant gesture of continuity with the Bank of North America, the latter's longtime Bank of North America president and former partner of Robert Morris, Thomas Willing of Philadelphia, was made president of the new Bank of the United States.

The Bank of the United States promptly fulfilled its inflationary potential by issuing millions of dollars in paper money

[32]On the complex workings of fractional coins as against dollar coins in this period, see the excellent article by David A. Martin, "Bimetallism in the United States before 1850," *Journal of Political Economy* 76 (May–June 1968): 428–34.

and demand deposits, pyramiding on top of $2 million in specie. The Bank of the United States invested heavily in loans to the United States government. In addition to $2 million invested in the assumption of pre-existing long-term debt assumed by the new federal government, the Bank of the United States engaged in massive temporary lending to the government, which reached $6.2 million by 1796.[33] The result of the outpouring of credit and paper money by the new Bank of the United States was an inflationary rise in prices. Thus, wholesale prices rose from an index of 85 in 1791 to a peak of 146 in 1796, an increase of 72 percent.[34] In addition, speculation boomed in government securities and real estate values were driven upward.[35] Pyramiding on top of the Bank of the United States's expansion and aggravating the paper money expansion and the inflation was a flood of newly created commercial banks. Whereas there were only three commercial banks before the founding of the United States, and only four by the establishment of the Bank of the United States, eight new banks were founded shortly thereafter, in 1791 and 1792, and 10 more by

[33]Schultz and Caine are severely critical of these operations: "In indebting itself heavily to the Bank of the United States, the Federal Government was obviously misusing its privileges and seriously endangering the Bank's stability." They also charged that

> the Federalists had saddled the government with a military and interest budget that threatened to topple the structure of federal finances. Despite the addition of tax after tax to the revenue system, the Federal Government's receipts through the decade of the '90s were barely able to cling to the skirts of its expenditures. (William J. Schultz and M.R. Caine, "Federalist Finance," in *Hamilton and the National Debt*, G.R. Taylor, ed. [Boston: D.C. Heath, 1950], pp. 6–7)

[34]Similar movements occurred in wholesale prices in Philadelphia, Charleston, and the Ohio River Valley. U.S. Department of Commerce, *Historical Statistics of the United States, Colonial Times to 1957* (Washington, D.C.: Government Printing Office, 1960), pp. 116, 119–21.

[35]Nettels, *National Economy*, pp. 121–22.

1796. Thus, the Bank of the United States and its monetary expansion spurred the creation of 18 new banks in five years.[36]

The establishment of the Bank of the United States precipitated a grave constitutional argument, the Jeffersonians arguing that the Constitution gave the federal government no power to establish a bank. Hamilton, in turn, paved the way for virtually unlimited expansion of federal power by maintaining that the Constitution "implied" a grant of power for carrying out vague national goals. The Hamiltonian interpretation won out officially in the decision of Supreme Court Justice John Marshall in *McCulloch v. Maryland* (1819).[37]

Despite the Jeffersonian hostility to commercial and central banks, the Democratic-Republicans, under the control of quasi-Federalist moderates rather than militant Old Republicans, made no move to repeal the charter of the Bank of the United States before its expiration in 1811 and happily multiplied the number of state banks and bank credit in the next two decades.[38] Thus, in 1800 there were 28 state banks; by 1811, the number had escalated to 117, a fourfold increase. In 1804, there were 64 state banks, of which we have data on 13, or 20 percent of the banks. These reporting banks had $0.98 million in specie, as against notes and demand deposits outstanding of $2.82 million, a

[36]J. Van Fenstermaker, "The Statistics of American Commercial Banking, 1782–1818," *Journal of Economic History* (September 1965): 401; J. Van Fenstermaker, *The Development of American Commercial Banking 1782–1837* (Kent, Ohio: Kent State University, 1965), pp. 111–83; William M. Gouge, *A Short History of Paper Money and Banking in the United States* (New York: Augustus M. Kelley, [1833] 1968), p. 42.

[37]Marshall, a disciple of Hamilton, repeated some of Hamilton's arguments virtually word for word in the decision. See Gerald T. Dunne, *Monetary Decisions of the Supreme Court* (New Brunswick, N.J.: Rutgers University Press, 1960), p. 30.

[38]On the quasi-Federalists as opposed to the Old Republicans, on banking and on other issues, see Richard E. Ellis, *The Jeffersonian Crisis: Courts and Politics in the Young Republic* (New York: Oxford University Press, 1971), pp. 277 ff.

reserve ratio of 0.35 (or, a notes plus deposits pyramiding on top of specie of 2.88-to-1). By 1811, 26 percent of the 117 banks reported a total of $2.57 million; but the two-and-a-half-fold increase in specie was more than matched by an emission of $10.95 million of notes and deposits, a nearly fourfold increase. This constituted a pyramiding of 4.26-to-1 on top of specie, or a reserve ratio of these banks of 0.23.[39]

As for the Bank of the United States, which acted in conjunction with the federal government and with the state banks, in January 1811 it had specie assets of $5.01 million, and notes and deposits outstanding of $12.87 million, a pyramid ratio of 2.57-to-1, or a reserve ratio of 0.39.[40]

Finally, when the time for rechartering the Bank of the United States came in 1811, the recharter bill was defeated by one vote each in the House and Senate. Recharter was fought for by the Madison administration aided by nearly all the Federalists in Congress, but was narrowly defeated by the bulk of the Democratic-Republicans, including the hard-money Old Republican forces. In view of the widely held misconception among historians that central banks serve, and are looked upon, as restraints upon state or private bank inflation, it is

[39]Van Fenstermaker notes that there has been a tendency of historians to believe that virtually all bank emissions were in the form of notes, but that actually a large portion was in the form of demand deposits. Thus, in 1804, bank liabilities were $1.70 million in notes and $1.12 million in deposits; in 1811 they were $5.68 million and $5.27 million respectively. He points out that deposits exceeded notes in the large cities such as Boston and Philadelphia, sometimes by two- or threefold, whereas bank notes were used far more widely in rural areas for hand-to-hand transactions. Van Fenstermaker, "Statistics," pp. 406–11.

[40]Of the Bank of the United States's liabilities, bank notes totaled $5.04 million and demand deposits $7.83 million. John Jay Knox, *A History of Banking in the United States* (New York: Bradford Rhodes, 1900), p. 39. There are no other reports for the Bank of the United States extant except for 1809. The others were destroyed by fire. John Thom Holdsworth, *The First Bank of the United States* (Washington, D.C.: National Monetary Commission, 1910), pp. 111 ff., 138–44.

instructive to note that the major forces in favor of recharter were merchants, chambers of commerce, and most of the state banks. Merchants found that the bank had expended credit at cheap rates and had eased the eternal complaint about a "scarcity of money." Even more suggestive is the support of the state banks, which hailed the bank as "advantageous" and worried about the contraction of credit if the bank were forced to liquidate. The Bank of New York, which had been founded by Alexander Hamilton, in fact lauded the Bank of the United States because it had been able "in case of any sudden pressure upon the merchants to step forward to their aid in a degree which the state institutions were unable to do."[41]

The War of 1812 and Its Aftermath

War has generally had grave and fateful consequences for the American monetary and financial system. We have seen that the Revolutionary War occasioned a mass of depreciated fiat paper, worthless Continentals, a huge public debt, and the beginnings of central banking in the Bank of North America. The Hamiltonian financial system, and even the Constitution itself, was in large part shaped by the Federalist desire to fund the federal and state public debt via federal taxation, and a major reason for the establishment of the First Bank of the United States was to contribute to the funding of the newly assumed federal debt. The Constitutional prohibition against state paper money, and the implicit rebuff to all fiat paper were certainly influenced by the Revolutionary War experience.

[41]Holdsworth, *First Bank*, p. 83. See also ibid., pp. 83–90. Holdsworth, the premier historian of the First Bank of the United States, saw the overwhelming support by the state banks, but still inconsistently clung to the myth that the Bank of the United States functioned as a restraint on their expansion: "The state banks, *though their note issues and discounts had been kept in check by the superior resources and power of the Bank of the United States,* favored the extension of the charter, and memorialized Congress to that effect." Ibid., p. 90 (italics added).

The War of 1812–15 had momentous consequences for the monetary system. An enormous expansion in the number of banks and in bank notes and deposits was spurred by the dictates of war finance. New England banks were more conservative than in other regions, and the region was strongly opposed to the war with England, so little public debt was purchased in New England. Yet imported goods, textile manufactures, and munitions had to be purchased in that region by the federal government. The government therefore encouraged the formation of new and recklessly inflationary banks in the Mid-Atlantic, Southern, and Western states, which printed huge quantities of new notes to purchase government bonds. The federal government thereupon used these notes to purchase manufactured goods in New England.

Thus, from 1811 to 1815 the number of banks in the country increased from 117 to 212; in addition, there had sprung up 35 private unincorporated banks, which were illegal in most states but were allowed to function under war conditions. Specie in the 30 reporting banks, 26 percent of the total number of banks of 1811, amounted to $2.57 million in 1811; this figure had risen to $5.40 million in the 98 reporting banks in 1815, or 40 percent of the total. Notes and deposits, on the other hand, were $10.95 million in 1811 and had increased to $31.6 million in 1815 among the reporting banks.

If we make the heroic assumption that we can estimate the money supply for the country by multiplying by the proportion of unreported banks and we then add in the Bank of the United States's totals for 1811, specie in all banks would total $14.9 million in 1811 and $13.5 million in 1815, or a 9.4 percent decrease. On the other hand, total bank notes and deposits aggregated to $42.2 million in 1811 and $79 million four years later, so that an increase of 87.2 percent, pyramided on top of a 9.4 percent decline in specie. If we factor in the Bank of the United States, then, the bank pyramid ratio was 3.70-to-1 and the reserve ratio 0.27 in 1811; while the pyramid ratio four years later was 5.85-to-1 and the reserve ratio 0.17.

But the aggregates scarcely tell the whole story since, as we have seen, the expansion took place solely outside of New England, while New England banks continued on their relatively sound basis and did not inflate their credit. The record expansion of the number of banks was in Pennsylvania, which incorporated no less than 41 new banks in the month of March 1814, contrasting to only four banks which had existed in that state—all in Philadelphia—until that date. It is instructive to compare the pyramid ratios of banks in various reporting states in 1815: to only 1.96-to-1 in Massachusetts, 2.7-to-1 in New Hampshire, and 2.42-to-1 in Rhode Island, as contrasted to 19.2-to-1 in Pennsylvania, 18.46-to-1 in South Carolina, and 18.73-to-1 in Virginia.[42]

This monetary situation meant that the United States government was paying for New England manufactured goods with a mass of inflated bank paper outside the region. Soon, as the New England banks called upon the other banks to redeem their notes in specie, the mass of inflating banks faced imminent insolvency.

It was at this point that a fateful decision was made by the U.S. government and concurred in by the governments of the states outside New England. As the banks all faced failure, the governments, in August 1814, permitted all of them to suspend specie payments—that is, to stop all redemption of notes and deposits in gold or silver—and yet to continue in operation. In short, in one of the most flagrant violations of property rights in American history, the banks were permitted to waive their contractual obligations to pay in specie while they themselves could expand their loans and operations and force their own debtors to repay their loans as usual.

Indeed, the number of banks, and bank credit, expanded rapidly during 1815 as a result of this governmental carte

[42]Van Fenstermaker, "Statistics," pp. 401–09. For the list of individual incorporated banks, see Van Fenstermaker, *Development*, pp. 112–83, with Pennsylvania on pp. 169–73.

blanche. It was precisely during 1815 when virtually all the private banks sprang up, the number of banks increasing in one year from 208 to 246. Reporting banks increased their pyramid ratios from 3.17-to-1 in 1814 to 5.85-to-1 the following year, a drop of reserve ratios from 0.32 to 0.17. Thus, if we measure bank expansion by pyramiding and reserve ratios, we see that a major inflationary impetus during the War of 1812 came during the year 1815 after specie payments had been suspended throughout the country by government action.

Historians dedicated to the notion that central banks restrain state or private bank inflation have placed the blame for the multiplicity of banks and bank credit inflation during the War of 1812 on the absence of a central bank. But as we have seen, both the number of banks and bank credit grew apace during the period of the First Bank of the United States, pyramiding on top of the latter's expansion, and would continue to do so under the Second Bank, and, for that matter, the Federal Reserve System in later years. And the federal government, not the state banks themselves, is largely to blame for encouraging new, inflated banks to monetize the war debt. Then, in particular, it allowed them to suspend specie payment in August 1814, and to continue that suspension for two years after the war was over, until February 1817. Thus, for two and a half years banks were permitted to operate and expand while issuing what was tantamount to fiat paper and bank deposits.

Another neglected responsibility of the U.S. government for the wartime inflation was its massive issue of Treasury notes to help finance the war effort. While this Treasury paper was interest-bearing and was redeemable in specie in one year, the cumulative amount outstanding functioned as money, as it was used in transactions among the public and was also employed as reserves or "high-powered money" by the expanding banks. The fact that the government received the Treasury notes for all debts and taxes gave the notes a quasi–legal tender status. Most of the Treasury notes were issued in 1814 and 1815, when their outstanding total reached $10.65 million and $15.46 million, respectively. Not only did the Treasury notes fuel the bank inflation, but their quasi–legal tender status brought Gresham's Law into operation and specie flowed out of the banks and public circulation outside of New England, and into New England and out of the country.[43]

The expansion of bank money and Treasury notes during the war drove up prices in the United States. Wholesale price increases from 1811 to 1815 averaged 35 percent, with different cities experiencing a price inflation ranging from 28 percent to 55 percent. Since foreign trade was cut off by the war, prices of imported commodities rose far more, averaging 70 percent.[44] But more important than this inflation, and at least as important as the wreckage of the monetary system during and after the war, was the precedent that the two-and-a-half-year-long suspension of specie payment set for the banking system for the future. From then on, every time there was a banking crisis brought on by inflationary expansion and demands for redemption in specie, state and federal governments looked the other way and permitted general suspension of specie payments while bank operations continued to flourish. It thus became clear to the banks that in a general crisis they would not be required to meet the ordinary obligations of contract law or of respect for property rights, so their inflationary expansion was permanently encouraged by this massive failure of government to fulfill its obligation to enforce contracts and defend the rights of property.

Suspensions of specie payments informally or officially permeated the economy outside of New England during the panic

[43]For a perceptive discussion of the nature and consequences of Treasury note issue in this period, see Richard H. Timberlake, Jr., *The Origins of Central Banking in the United States* (Cambridge, Mass.: Harvard University Press, 1978), pp. 13–18. The Gresham Law effect probably accounts for the startling decline of specie held by the reporting banks, from $9.3 million to $5.4 million, from 1814 to 1815. Van Fenstermaker, "Statistics," p. 405.

[44]*Historical Statistics*, pp. 115–24; Murray N. Rothbard, *The Panic of 1819: Reactions and Policies* (New York: Columbia University Press, 1962), p. 4.

of 1819, occurred everywhere outside of New England in 1837, and in all states south and west of New Jersey in 1839. A general suspension of specie payments occurred throughout the country once again in the panic of 1857.[45]

It is important to realize, then, in evaluating the American banking system before the Civil War, that even in the later years when there was no central bank, the system was not "free" in any proper economic sense. "Free" banking can only refer to a system in which banks are treated as any other business, and that therefore failure to obey contractual obligations—in this case, prompt redemption of notes and deposits in specie—must incur immediate insolvency and liquidation. Burdened by the tradition of allowing general suspensions that arose in the United States in 1814, the pre–Civil War banking system, despite strong elements of competition when not saddled with a central bank, must rather be termed in the phrase of one economist, as "Decentralization without Freedom."[46]

[45]On the suspensions of specie payments, and on their importance before the Civil War, see Vera C. Smith, *The Rationale of Central Banking* (London: P.S. King and Son, 1936), pp. 38–46. See also Dunne, *Monetary Decisions*, p. 26.

[46]Smith, *Rationale*, p. 36. Smith properly defines "free banking" as

> a regime where note-issuing banks are allowed to set up in the same way as any other type of business enterprise, so long as they comply with the general company law. The requirement for their establishment is not special conditional authorization from a government authority, but the ability to raise sufficient capital, and public confidence, to gain acceptance for their notes and ensure the profitability of the undertaking. Under such a system all banks would not only be allowed the same rights, but would also be subjected to the same responsibilities as other business enterprises. If they failed to meet their obligations they would be declared bankrupt and put into liquidation, and their assets used to meet the claims of their creditors, in which case the shareholders would lose the whole or part of their capital, and the penalty for failure would be paid, at least for the most part, by those responsible for the policy of the bank. Notes issued

From the 1814–1817 experience on, the notes of state banks circulated at varying rates of depreciation, depending on public expectations of how long they would be able to keep redeeming their obligations in specie. These expectations, in turn, were heavily influenced by the amount of notes and deposits issued by the bank as compared with the amount of specie held in its vaults.

In that era of poor communications and high transportation costs, the tendency for a bank note was to depreciate in proportion to its distance from the home office. One effective, if time-consuming, method of enforcing redemption on nominally specie-paying banks was the emergence of a class of professional "money brokers." These brokers would buy up a mass of depreciated notes of nominally specie-paying banks, and then travel to the home office of the bank to demand redemption in specie. Merchants, money brokers, bankers, and the general public were aided in evaluating the various state bank notes by the development of monthly journals known as "bank note detectors." These "detectors" were published by money brokers and periodically evaluated the market rate of various bank notes in relation to specie.[47]

"Wildcat" banks were so named because in that age of poor transportation, banks hoping to inflate and not worry about redemption attempted to locate in "wildcat" country where money brokers would find it difficult to travel. It should be noted that if it were not for periodic suspension, there would

---

> under this system would be "promises to pay," and such obligations must be met on demand in the generally accepted medium which we will assume to be gold. No bank would have the right to call on the government or on any other institution for special help in time of need. . . . A general abandonment of the gold standard is inconceivable under these conditions, and with a strict interpretation of the bankruptcy laws any bank suspending payments would at once be put into the hands of a receiver. (Ibid., pp. 148–49)

[47]See Richard H. Timberlake, Jr., *Money, Banking, and Central Banking* (New York: Harper and Row, 1965), p. 94.

have been no room for wildcat banks or for varying degrees of lack of confidence in the genuineness of specie redemption at any given time.

It can be imagined that the advent of the money broker was not precisely welcomed in the town of an errant bank, and it was easy for the townspeople to blame the resulting collapse of bank credit on the sinister stranger rather than on the friendly neighborhood banker. During the panic of 1819, when banks collapsed after an inflationary boom lasting until 1817, obstacles and intimidation were often the lot of those who attempted to press the banks to fulfill their contractual obligation to pay in specie.

Thus, Maryland and Pennsylvania, during the panic of 1819, engaged in almost bizarre inconsistency in this area. Maryland, on February 15, 1819, enacted a law "to compel . . . banks to pay specie for their notes, or forfeit their charters." Yet two days after this seemingly tough action, it passed another law relieving banks of any obligation to redeem notes held by money brokers, "the major force ensuring the people of this state from the evil arising from the demands made on the banks of this state for gold and silver by brokers." Pennsylvania followed suit a month later. In this way, these states could claim to maintain the virtue of enforcing contract and property rights while moving to prevent the most effective method of ensuring such enforcement.

During the 1814–1817 general suspension, noteholders who sued for specie payment seldom gained satisfaction in the courts. Thus, Isaac Bronson, a prominent Connecticut banker in a specie-paying region, sued various New York banks for payment of notes in specie. He failed to get satisfaction, and for his pains received only abuse in the New York press as an agent of "misery and ruin."[48]

[48]Hammond, *Banks and Politics*, pp. 179–80. Even before the suspension, in 1808, a Bostonian named Hireh Durkee who attempted to demand specie for $9,000 in notes of the state-owned Vermont State Bank, was met by an indictment for an attempt by this "evil-disposed person" to "realize

The banks south of Virginia largely went off specie payment during the panic of 1819, and in Georgia at least general suspension continued almost continuously to the 1830s. One customer complained during 1819 that in order to collect in specie from the largely state-owned Bank of Darien, Georgia, he was forced to swear before a justice of the peace in the bank that each and every note he presented to the bank was his own and that he was not a money broker or an agent for anyone else; he was forced to swear to the oath in the presence of at least five bank directors and the bank's cashier; and he was forced to pay a fee of $1.36 on each note in order to acquire specie on demand. Two years later, when a noteholder demanded $30,000 in specie at the Planters' Bank of Georgia, he was told he would be paid in pennies only, while another customer was forced to accept pennies handed out to him at the rate of $60 a day.[49]

During the panic, North Carolina and Maryland in particular moved against the money brokers in a vain attempt to prop up the depreciated notes of their states' banks. In North Carolina, banks were not penalized by the legislature for suspending specie payments to "brokers," while maintaining them to others. Backed by government, the three leading banks of the state met and agreed, in June 1819, not to pay specie to brokers or their agents. Their notes immediately fell to a 15-percent discount outside the state. However, the banks continued to require—ignoring the inconsistency—that their own debtors pay them at par in specie. Maryland, during the same year, moved to require a license of $500 per year for money brokers, in addition to an enormous $20,000 bond to establish the business.

---

a filthy gain" at the expense of the resources of the state of Vermont and the ability of "good citizens thereof to obtain money." Ibid., p. 179. See also Gouge, *Short History*, p. 84.

[49]Gouge, *Short History*, pp. 141–42. Secretary of the Treasury William H. Crawford, a Georgia politician, tried in vain to save the Bank of Darien from failure by depositing Treasury funds there during the panic. Rothbard, *Panic of 1819*, p. 62.

Maryland tried to bolster the defense of banks and the attack on brokers by passing a compulsory par law in 1819, prohibiting the exchange of specie for Maryland bank notes at less than par. The law was readily evaded, however, with the penalty merely adding to the discount as compensation for the added risk. Specie furthermore was driven out of the state by the operation of Gresham's Law.[50]

In Kentucky, Tennessee, and Missouri, stay laws were passed requiring creditors to accept depreciated and inconvertible bank paper in payment of debts, else suffer a stay of execution of the debt. In this way, quasi–legal tender status was conferred on the paper.[51] Many states permitted banks to suspend specie payment, and four western states—Tennessee, Kentucky, Missouri, and Illinois—established state-owned banks to try to overcome the depression by issuing large issues of inconvertible paper money. In all states trying to prop up inconvertible bank paper, a quasi-legal status was also conferred on the paper by agreeing to receive the notes in taxes or debts due to the state. The result of all the inconvertible paper schemes was rapid and massive depreciation, disappearance of specie, succeeded by speedy liquidation of the new state-owned banks.[52]

An amusing footnote on the problem of banks being protected against their contractual obligations to pay in specie

[50]Ibid., pp. 64–68. Other compulsory par laws were passed by Ohio and Delaware.

[51]The most extreme proposal was Tennessee politician Felix Grundy's scheme, never adopted, to compel creditors to accept bank notes of the state bank or forfeit the debt; that would have conferred full legal tender status on the bank. Ibid., p. 91; and Joseph H. Parks, "Felix Grundy and the Depression of 1819 in Tennessee," *Publications of the East Tennessee Historical Society* 10 (1938): 22.

[52]Only New England, New York, New Jersey, Virginia, Mississippi, and Louisiana were comparatively untouched by the inconvertible paper contagion, either in the form of suspended specie banks continuing in operation or new state-owned banks emitting more paper. For an analysis of the events and controversies in each state, see Rothbard, *The Panic of 1819*, pp. 57–111.

occurred in the course of correspondence between one of the earliest economists in America, the young Philadelphia state Senator Condy Raguet, and the eminent English economist David Ricardo. Ricardo had evidently been bewildered by Raguet's statement that banks technically required to pay in specie often were not called upon to do so. On April 18, 1821, Raguet replied, explaining the power of banks in the United States:

> You state in your letter that you find it difficult to comprehend, why persons who had a right to demand coin from the Banks in payment of their notes, so long forebore to exercise it. This no doubt appears paradoxical to one who resides in a country where an act of parliament was necessary to protect a bank, but the difficulty is easily solved. The whole of our population are either stockholders of banks or in debt to them. It is not the *interest* of the first to press the banks and the rest are *afraid*. This is the whole secret. An independent man, who was neither a stockholder or debtor, who would have ventured to compel the banks to do justice, would have been persecuted as an enemy of society.[53]

The Second Bank of the United States, 1816–1833

The United States emerged from the War of 1812 in a chaotic monetary state, with banks multiplying and inflating ad lib, checked only by the varying rates of depreciation of their notes. With banks freed from redeeming their obligations in specie, the number of incorporated banks increased during 1816, from 212 to 232.[54] Clearly, the nation could not continue indefinitely with the issue of fiat money in the hands of discordant sets of

[53]Raguet to Ricardo, April 18, 1821, in David Ricardo, *Minor Papers on the Currency Question*, 1809–23, Jacob H. Hollander, ed. (Baltimore: Johns Hopkins Press, 1932), pp. 199–201; Rothbard, *Panic of 1819*, pp. 10–11. See also Hammond, *Banks and Politics*, p. 242.

[54]New note issue series by banks reached a heavy peak in 1815 and 1816 in New York and Pennsylvania. D.C. Wismar, *Pennsylvania Descriptive List of Obsolete State Bank Notes, 1782–1866* (Frederick, Md.:

individual banks. It was apparent that there were two ways out of the problem: one was the hard-money path, which was advocated by the Old Republicans and, for their own purposes, the Federalists. The federal and state governments would have sternly compelled the rollicking banks to redeem promptly in specie, and, when most of the banks outside of New England could not, to force them to liquidate. In that way, the mass of depreciated and inflated notes and deposits would have been swiftly liquidated, and specie would have poured back out of hoards and into the country to supply a circulating medium. The inflationary experience would have been over.

Instead, the Democratic-Republican establishment in 1816 turned to the old Federalist path: a new central bank, a Second Bank of the United States. Modeled closely after the First Bank, the Second Bank, a private corporation with one-fifth of the shares owned by the federal government, was to create a national paper currency, purchase a large chunk of the public debt, and receive deposits of Treasury funds. The Second Bank of the United States's notes and deposits were to be redeemable in specie, and they were given quasi–legal tender status by the federal government's receiving them in payment of taxes.

That the purpose of establishing the Second Bank of the United States was to support the state banks in their inflationary course rather than crack down on them is seen by the shameful deal that the Second Bank made with the state banks as soon as it opened its doors in January 1817. At the same time that it was establishing the new bank in April 1816, Congress passed a resolution of Daniel Webster, at that time a Federalist champion of hard money, requiring that after February 20, 1817, the United States should accept as payments for debts or taxes only specie, Treasury notes, Bank of the United States notes, or state bank notes redeemable in specie on demand. In short, no irredeemable state bank notes would be accepted after that

---

J.W. Stovell, 1933); and idem, *New York Descriptive List of Obsolete Paper Money* (Frederick, Md.: J.W. Stovell, 1931).

date. Instead of using the opportunity to compel the banks to redeem, however, the Second Bank of the United States, in a meeting with representatives from the leading urban banks, excluding Boston, agreed to issue $6 million worth of credit in New York, Philadelphia, Baltimore, and Virginia before insisting on specie payments from debts due to it from the state banks. In return for that agreed-upon massive inflation, the state banks graciously consented to resume specie payments.[55] Moreover, the Second Bank and the state banks agreed to mutually support each other in any emergency, which of course meant in practice that the far stronger Bank of the United States was committed to the propping up of the weaker state banks.

The Second Bank of the United States was pushed through Congress by the Madison administration and particularly by Secretary of the Treasury Alexander J. Dallas, whose appointment was lobbied for, for that purpose. Dallas, a wealthy Philadelphia lawyer, was a close friend, counsel, and financial associate of Philadelphia merchant and banker Stephen Girard, reputedly one of the two wealthiest men in the country. Toward the end of its term, Girard was the largest stockholder of the First Bank of the United States, and during the War of 1812 Girard became a very heavy investor in the war debt of the federal government. Both as a prospective large stockholder and as a way to unload his public debt, Girard began to agitate for a new Bank of the United States. Dallas's appointment as secretary of Treasury in 1814 was successfully engineered by Dallas and his close friend, wealthy New York merchant and fur trader John Jacob Astor, also a heavy investor in the war debt. When the Second Bank of the United States was established, Stephen Girard purchased the $3 million of the $28 million that

[55]On the establishment of the Bank of the United States and on the deal with the state banks, see Ralph C.H. Catterall, *The Second Bank of the United States* (Chicago: University of Chicago Press, 1902), pp. 9–26, 479–90. See also Hammond, *Banks and Politics*, pp. 230–48; and Davis R. Dewey, *The Second United States Bank* (Washington, D.C.: National Monetary Commission, 1910), pp. 148–76.

remained unsubscribed, and he and Dallas managed to secure for the post of president of the new bank their good friend William Jones, former Philadelphia merchant.[56]

Much of the opposition to the founding of the Bank of the United States seems keenly prophetic. Thus, Senator William H. Wells, Federalist from Delaware, in arguing against the bank bill, said that it was

> ostensibly for the purpose of correcting the diseased state of our paper currency by restraining and curtailing the overissue of bank paper, and yet it came prepared to inflict upon us the same evil, being itself nothing more than simply a paper-making machine.[57]

In fact, the result of the deal with the state banks was that their resumption of specie payments after 1817 was more nominal than real, thereby setting the stage for the widespread suspensions of the 1819–21 depression. As Bray Hammond writes:

> [S]pecie payments were resumed, with substantial shortcomings. Apparently the situation was better than it had been, and a pretense was maintained of its being better than it was. But redemption was not certain and universal; there was still a premium on specie and still a discount on bank notes, with considerable variation in both from place to place. Three years later, February 1820, Secretary [of the Treasury] Crawford reported to Congress that during the greater part of the time that had elapsed since the resumption of specie payments, the convertibility of bank notes into

[56]On the Girard-Dallas connection, see Hammond, *Banks and Politics,* pp. 231–46, 252; Philip H. Burch, Jr., *Elites in American History,* vol. 1, *The Federalist Years to the Civil War* (New York: Holmes and Meier, 1981), pp. 88, 97, 116–17, 119–21; and Kenneth L. Brown, "Stephen Girard, Promoter of the Second Bank of the United States," *Journal of Economic History* (November 1942): 125–32.

[57]*Annals of Congress,* 14th Cong., 1st sess., April 1, 1816, pp. 267–70. See also ibid., pp. 1066, 1091, 1110 ff; cited in Murray N. Rothbard, *The Case for a 100 Percent Gold Dollar* (Washington, D.C.: Libertarian Review Press, 1974), p. 18 n. See also Gouge, *Short History,* pp. 79–83.

specie had been nominal rather than real in the largest portion of the Union.[58]

One problem is that the Bank of the United States lacked the courage to insist on payment of its notes from the state banks. As a result, state banks had large balances piled up against them at the Bank of the United States, totaling over $2.4 million during 1817 and 1818, remaining on the books as virtual interest-free loans. As Catterall points out, "so many influential people were interested in the [state banks] as stockholders that it was not advisable to give offense by demanding payment in specie, and borrowers were anxious to keep the banks in the humor to lend." When the Bank of the United States did try to collect on state bank notes in specie, bank President Jones reported, "the banks, our debtors, plead inability, require unreasonable indulgence, or treat our reiterated claims and expostulations with settled indifference."[59]

From its inception, the Second Bank launched a spectacular inflation of money and credit. Lax about insisting on the required payment of its capital in specie, the bank failed to raise the $7 million legally supposed to have been subscribed in specie; instead, during 1817 and 1818, its specie held never rose above $2.5 million. At the peak of its initial expansion, in July 1818, the Bank of the United States's specie totaled $2.36 million, and its aggregate notes and deposits totaled $21.8 million. Thus, in a scant year and a half of operation, the Second Bank of the United States had added a net of $19.2 million to the nation's money supply, for a pyramid ratio of 9.24, or a reserve ratio of 0.11.

Outright fraud abounded at the Second Bank of the United States, especially at the Philadelphia and Baltimore branches,

[58]Hammond, *Banks and Politics*, p. 248. See also Condy Raguet, *A Treatise on Currency and Banking*, 2nd ed. (New York: Augustus M. Kelley, [1840] 1967), pp. 302–03; Catterall, *Second Bank*, pp. 37–39; and Walter Buckingham Smith, *Economic Aspects of the Second Bank of the United States* (Cambridge, Mass.: Harvard University Press, 1953), p. 104.

[59]Catterall, *Second Bank*, p. 36.

particularly the latter. It is no accident that three-fifths of all of the bank's loans were made at these two branches.[60] Also, the bank's attempt to provide a uniform currency throughout the nation floundered on the fact that the western and southern branches could inflate credit and bank notes and that the inflated notes would wend their way to the more conservative branches in New York and Boston, which would be obligated to redeem the inflated notes at par. In this way, the conservative branches were stripped of specie while the western branches could continue to inflate unchecked.[61]

The expansionary operations of the Second Bank of the United States, coupled with its laxity toward insisting on specie payment by the state banks, impelled a further inflationary expansion of state banks on top of the spectacular enlargement of the central bank. Thus, the number of incorporated state banks rose from 232 in 1816 to 338 in 1818. Kentucky alone chartered 40 new banks in the 1817–18 legislative session. The estimated total money supply in the nation rose from $67.3 million in 1816 to $94.7 million in 1818, a rise of 40.7 percent in two years. Most of this increase was supplied by the Bank of the United States.[62]

[60]On the expansion and fraud at the Second Bank of the United States, see Catterall, *Second Bank*, pp. 28–50, 503. The main culprits were James A. Buchanan, president of the Baltimore mercantile firm of Smith and Buchanan, and the Baltimore Bank of the United States cashier James W. McCulloch, who was simply an impoverished clerk at the mercantile house. Smith, an ex-Federalist, was a senator from Maryland and a powerful member of the National Democratic-Republican establishment.

[61]As a result of the contractionary influence on the Boston branch of the Bank of the United States, the notes of the Massachusetts banks actually declined in this period, from $1 million in June 1815 to $850,000 in June 1818. See Rothbard, *Panic of 1819*, p. 8.

[62]Total notes and deposits of 39 percent of the nation's reporting state banks was $26.3 million in 1816, while 38 percent of the banks had total notes and deposits of $27.7 million two years later. Converting this pro rata to 100 percent of the banks gives an estimated $67.3 million in 1816,

The huge expansion of money and credit impelled a full-scale inflationary boom throughout the country. Import prices had fallen in 1815, with the renewal of foreign trade after the war, but domestic prices were another story. Thus, the index of export staples in Charleston rose from 102 in 1815 to 160 in 1818; the prices of Louisiana staples at New Orleans rose from 178 to 224 in the same period. Other parts of the economy boomed; exports rose from $81 million in 1815 to a peak of $116 million in 1818. Prices rose greatly in real estate, land, farm improvement projects, and slaves, much of it fueled by the use of bank credit for speculation in urban and rural real estate. There was a boom in turnpike construction, furthered by vast federal expenditures on turnpikes. Freight rates rose on steamboats, and shipbuilding shared in the general prosperity. Also, general boom conditions expanded stock trading so rapidly that traders, who had been buying and selling stocks on the curbs on Wall Street for nearly a century, found it necessary to open the first indoor stock exchange in the country, the New York Stock Exchange, in March 1817. Also, investment banking began in the United States during this boom period.[63]

Starting in July 1818, the government and the Second Bank began to see what dire straits they were in; the enormous inflation of money and credit, aggravated by the massive fraud, had put the Bank of the United States in real danger of going under and illegally failing to sustain specie payments. Over the next year, the bank began a series of heroic contractions, forced curtailment of loans, contractions of credit in the south and west, refusal to provide uniform national currency by redeeming its

---

and $72.9 million in 1818. Add to the latter figure $21.8 million for Bank of the United States notes and deposits, and this yields $94.7 million in 1818, or a 40.7-percent increase. Adapted from tables in Van Fenstermaker, "Statistics," pp. 401, 405, 406.

[63]Rothbard, *Panic of 1819*, pp. 6–10; *Historical Statistics*, pp. 120, 122, 563. See also George Rogers Taylor, *The Transportation Revolution, 1815–1860* (New York: Rinehart, 1951), pp. 334–36.

shaky branch notes at par, and seriously enforcing the requirement that its debtor banks redeem in specie. In addition, it purchased millions of dollars of specie from abroad. These heroic actions, along with the ouster of bank President William Jones, managed to save the Bank of the United States, but the massive contraction of money and credit swiftly brought the United States its first widespread economic and financial depression. The first nationwide "boom-bust" cycle had arrived in the United States, impelled by rapid and massive inflation, quickly succeeded by contraction of money and credit. Banks failed, and private banks curtailed their credits and liabilities and suspended specie payments in most parts of the country.

Contraction of money and credit by the Bank of the United States was almost unbelievable, total notes and deposits falling from $21.9 million in June 1818 to $11.5 million only a year later. The money supply contributed by the Bank of the United States was thereby contracted by no less than 47.2 percent in one year. The number of incorporated banks at first remained the same, and then fell rapidly from 1819 to 1822, falling from 341 in mid-1819 to 267 three years later. Total notes and deposits of state banks fell from an estimated $72 million in mid-1818 to $62.7 million a year later, a drop of 14 percent in one year. If we add in the fact that the U.S. Treasury contracted total Treasury notes from $8.81 million to zero during this period, we get the following estimated total money supply: in 1818, $103.5 million; in 1819, $74.2 million, a contraction in one year of 28.3 percent.[64]

The result of the contraction was a massive rash of defaults, bankruptcies of business and manufacturers, and liquidation of unsound investments during the boom. There was a vast drop in real estate values and rents and in the prices of freight rates and slaves. Public land sales dropped greatly as a result of the contraction, declining from $13.6 million in 1818 to $1.7 million

[64]These estimates are adapted from the tables in Van Fenstermaker, "Statistics," pp. 401–06, and *Development*, pp. 66–68. The data for 38 percent of incorporated banks in 1818, and for 54 percent in 1819, are

in 1820.[65] Prices in general plummeted: The index of export staples fell from 158 in November 1818 to 77 in June 1819, an annualized drop of 87.9 percent during those seven months. South Carolina export staples dropped from 160 to 96 from 1818 to 1819, and commodity prices in New Orleans dropped from 200 in 1818 to 119 two years later.

Falling money incomes led to a precipitous drop in imports, which fell from $122 million in 1818 to $87 million the year later. Imports from Great Britain fell from $43 million in 1818 to $14 million in 1820, and cotton and woolen imports from Britain fell from over $14 million each in 1818 to about $5 million each in 1820.

The great fall in prices aggravated the burden of money debts, reinforced by the contraction of credit. Bankruptcies abounded, and one observer estimated that $100 million of mercantile debts to Europe were liquidated by bankruptcy during the crisis. Western areas, shorn of money by the collapse of the previously swollen paper and debt, often returned to barter conditions, and grain and whiskey were used as media of exchange.[66]

In the dramatic summing up of the hard-money economist and historian William Gouge, by its precipitous and dramatic contraction "the Bank was saved, and the people were ruined."[67]

The Jacksonian Movement and the Bank War

Out of the bitter experiences of the panic of 1819 emerged the beginnings of the Jacksonian movement, dedicated to hard money, the eradication of fractional reserve banking in general,

---

converted pro rata to 100-percent figures. Bank of the United States figures are in Catterall, *Second Bank*, p. 502. On the contraction by the Second Bank, see ibid., pp. 51–72.

[65]On Treasury note contraction in this period, see Timberlake, *Origins of Central Banking*, pp. 21–26.

[66]See Rothbard, *Panic of 1819*, pp. 11–16.

[67]Gouge, *Short History*, p. 110.

and of the Bank of the United States in particular. Andrew Jackson himself, Senator Thomas Hart "Old Bullion" Benton of Missouri, future President James K. Polk of Tennessee, and Jacksonian economists Amos Kendall of Kentucky and Condy Raguet of Philadelphia, were all converted to hard money and 100-percent reserve banking by the experience of the panic of 1819.[68] The Jacksonians adopted, or in some cases pioneered in, the Currency School analysis, which pinned the blame for boom-bust cycles on inflationary expansions followed by contractions of bank credit. Far from being the ignorant bumpkins that most historians have depicted, the Jacksonians were steeped in the knowledge of sound economics, particularly of the Ricardian Currency School.

Indeed, no movement in American politics has been as flagrantly misunderstood by historians as the Jacksonians. They were emphatically *not*, as historians until recently have depicted, either "ignorant anti-capitalist agrarians," or "representatives of the rising entrepreneurial class," or "tools of the inflationary state banks," or embodiments of an early proletarian anticapitalist movement or a nonideological power group or "electoral machine." The Jacksonians were libertarians, plain and simple. Their program and ideology were libertarian; they strongly favored free enterprise and free markets, but they just as strongly opposed special subsidies and monopoly privileges conveyed by government to business or to any other group. They favored absolutely minimal government, certainly at the federal level, but also at the state level. They believed that government should be confined to upholding the rights of private property. In the monetary sphere, this meant the separation of government from the banking system and a shift from inflationary paper money and fractional reserve banking to pure specie and banks confined to 100-percent reserves.

In order to put this program into effect, however, the Jacksonians faced the grueling task of creating a new party out of

[68]Rothbard, *Panic of 1819*, p. 188.

what had become a one-party system after the War of 1812, in which the Democrat-Republicans had ended up adopting the Federalist program, including the re-establishing of the Bank of the United States. The new party, the Democratic Party, was largely forged in the mid-1820s by New York political leader, Martin Van Buren, newly converted by the aging Thomas Jefferson to the laissez-faire cause. Van Buren cemented an alliance with Thomas Hart Benton of Missouri and the Old Republicans of Virginia, but he needed a charismatic leader to take the presidency away from Adams and what was becoming known as the National Republican Party. He found that leader in Andrew Jackson, who was elected president under the new Democratic banner in 1828.

The Jacksonians eventually managed to put into effect various parts of their free-market and minimal-government economic program, including a drastic lowering of tariffs, and for the first and probably the last time in American history, paying off the federal debt. But their major concentration was on the issue of money and banking. Here they had a coherent program, which they proceeded to install in rapidly succeeding stages.

The first important step was to abolish central banking, in the Jacksonian view the major inflationary culprit. The object was not to eliminate the Bank of the United States in order to free the state banks for inflationary expansion, but, on the contrary, to eliminate the major source of inflation before proceeding, on the state level, to get rid of fractional reserve banking. The Bank of the United States's charter was up for renewal in 1836, but Jackson denounced the bank in his first annual message, in 1829. The imperious Nicholas Biddle,[69]

[69]Biddle continued the chain of control over both Banks of the United States by the Philadelphia financial elite, from Robert Morris and William Bingham, to Stephen Girard and William Jones. See Burch, *Elites*, p. 147. See also Thomas P. Govan, *Nicholas Biddle: Nationalist and Public Banker, 1786–1844* (Chicago: University of Chicago Press, 1959), pp. 45, 74–75, 79.

head of the Second Bank, decided to precipitate a showdown with Jackson before his re-election effort, so Biddle filed for renewal early, in 1831. The host of National Republicans and non-Jacksonian Democrats proceeded to pass the recharter bill, but Jackson, in a dramatic message, vetoed the bill, and Congress failed to pass it over his veto.

Triumphantly re-elected on the bank issue in 1832, President Jackson lost no time in disestablishing the Bank of the United States as a central bank. The critical action came in 1833, when Jackson removed the public Treasury deposits from the Bank of the United States and placed them in a number of state banks (soon labeled as "pet banks") throughout the country. The original number of pet banks was seven, but the Jacksonians were not interested in creating a privileged bank oligarchy to replace the previous monopoly; so the number of pet banks had increased to 91 by the end of 1836.[70] In that year, Biddle managed to secure a Pennsylvania charter for his bank, and the new United States Bank of Pennsylvania functioned as a much-reduced but still influential state bank for a few years thereafter.

Orthodox historians have long maintained that by his reckless act of destroying the Bank of the United States and shifting government funds to the numerous pet banks, Andrew Jackson freed the state banks from the restraints imposed on them by a central bank. Thus, the banks were supposedly allowed to pyramid notes and deposits rashly on top of existing specie and precipitate a wild inflation that was later succeeded by two bank panics and a disastrous deflation.

Recent historians, however, have totally reversed this conventional picture.[71] In the first place, the record of bank inflation under the regime of the Bank of the United States was

[70]Hammond, *Banks and Politics*, p. 420.

[71]For an excellent biographical essay and critique of historical interpretations of Jacksonism and the Bank War, see Jeffrey Rogers Hummel, "The Jacksonians, Banking, and Economic Theory: A Reinterpretation," *Journal of Libertarian Studies* 2 (Summer 1978): 151–65.

scarcely ideal. From the depths of the post-1819 depression in January 1820 to January 1823, under the regime of the conservative Langdon Cheves, the Bank of the United States increased its notes and deposits at an annual rate of 5.9 percent. The nation's total money supply remained about the same in that period. Under the far more inflationist regime of Nicholas Biddle, however, the Bank of the United States's notes and deposits rose, after January 1823, from $12 million to $42.1 million, an annual increase of 27.9 percent. As a consequence of this base of the banking pyramid inflating so sharply, the total money supply during this period vaulted from $81 million to $155 million, an annual increase of 10.2 percent. It is clear that the driving force for monetary expansion was the Bank of the United States, which acted as an inflationary rather than a restraining force upon the state banks. Looking at the figures another way, the 1823 data represented a pyramid ratio of money liabilities to specie of 3.86-to-1 on the part of the Bank of the United States and 4-to-1 of the banking system as a whole, or respective reserve ratios of 0.26 and 0.25. By 1832, in contrast, the Bank of the United States's reserve ratio had fallen to 0.17 and the country as a whole to 0.15. Both sets of institutions had inflated almost precisely proportionately on top of specie.[72]

The fact that wholesale prices remained about the same over this period is no indication that the monetary inflation was not improper and dangerous. As "Austrian" business cycle theory has pointed out, any bank credit inflation sets up conditions for boom-and-bust; there is no need for prices actually to rise. The reason that prices did not rise was that the increased production of goods and services sufficed to offset the monetary expansion during this period. But similar conditions of the 1920s precipitated the great crash of 1929, an event that

[72]For the Bank of the United States data, see Catterall, *Second Bank*, p. 503; for total money supply, see Peter Temin, *The Jacksonian Economy* (New York: W.W. Norton, 1969), p. 71.

shocked most economists, who had adopted the proto-monetarist position of Irving Fisher and other economists of the day that a stable wholesale price level cannot, by definition, be inflationary. In reality, the unhampered free-market economy will usually increase the supply of goods and services and thereby bring about a gently falling price level, as happened in most of the nineteenth century except during wartime.

What, then, of the consequences of Jackson's removal of the deposits? What of the fact that wholesale prices rose from 84 in April 1834, to 131 in February 1837, a remarkable increase of 52 percent in a little less than three years? Wasn't that boom due to the abolition of central banking?

An excellent reversal of the orthodox explanation of the boom of the 1830s, and indeed of the ensuing panic, has been provided by Professor Temin.[73] First, he points out that the price inflation really began earlier, when wholesale prices reached a trough of 82 in July 1830 and then rose by 20.7 percent in three years to reach 99 in the fall of 1833. The reason for the price rise is simple: The total money supply had risen from $109 million in 1830 to $159 million in 1833, an increase of 45.9 percent, or an annual rise of 15.3 percent. Breaking the figures down further, the total money supply had risen from $109 million in 1830 to $155 million a year and a half later, a spectacular expansion of 35 percent. Unquestionably, this monetary expansion was spurred by the still-flourishing Bank of the United States, which increased its notes and deposits from January 1830 to January 1832 from a total of $29 million to $42.1 million, a rise of 45.2 percent.

Thus, the price and money inflation in the first few years of the 1830s were again sparked by the expansion of the still-dominant central bank. But what of the notable inflation after 1833? There is no doubt that the cause of the price inflation was the

[73]Temin, *Jacksonian Economy*, passim. See also Hugh Rockoff, "Money, Prices, and Banks in the Jacksonian Era," in *The Reinterpretation of American Economic History*, R. Fogel and S. Engerman, eds. (New York: Harper and Row, 1971), pp. 448–58.

remarkable monetary inflation during the same period. For the total money supply rose from $150 million at the beginning of 1833 to $267 million at the beginning of 1837, an astonishing rise of 84 percent, or 21 percent per annum.

But as Temin points out, this monetary inflation was not caused by the liberated state banks expanding to a fare-thee-well. If it were true that the state banks used their freedom and their new federal government deposits to pyramid wildly on the top of specie, then their pyramid ratio would have risen a great deal, or, conversely, their reserve ratio of specie to notes and deposits would have fallen sharply. Yet the banks' reserve ratio was 0.16 at the beginning of 1837. During the intervening years, the reserve ratio was never below this figure. But this means that the state banks did no more pyramiding after the demise of the Bank of the United States as a central bank than they had done before.[74]

Conventional historians, believing that the Bank of the United States *must* have restrained the expansion of state banks, naturally assumed that they were hostile to the central bank. But now Jean Wilburn has discovered that the state banks overwhelmingly supported the Bank of the United States:

> We have found that Nicholas Biddle was correct when he said, "state banks in the main are friendly." Specifically, only in Georgia, Connecticut, and New York was there positive evidence of hostility. A majority of state banks in some states of the South, such as North Carolina and Alabama, gave strong support to the Bank as did both the Southwest states of Louisiana and Mississippi. Since Virginia gave some support, we can claim that state banks in the South and Southwest for the most part supported the Bank. New England, contrary to expectations, showed the banks of Vermont and New Hampshire behind the Bank, but support of Massachusetts was both qualitatively and quantitatively weak.

[74]Temin, *Jacksonian Economy*, pp. 68–74.

> The banks of the Middle states all supported the Second Bank except for those of New York.[75]

What, then, was the cause of the enormous monetary expansion of the 1830s? It was a tremendous and unusual expansion of the stock of specie in the nation's banks. The supply of specie in the country had remained virtually constant at about $32 million, from the beginning of 1823 until the beginning of 1833. But the proportion of specie to bank notes, held by the public as money, dropped during this period from 23 percent to 5 percent, so that more specie flowed from the public into the banks to fuel the relatively moderate monetary expansion of the 1820s. But starting at the beginning of 1833, the total specie in the country rose swiftly from $31 million to $73 million at the beginning of 1837, for a rise of 141.9 percent or 35.5 percent per annum. Hence, even though increasing distrust of banks led the public to withdraw some specie from them, so that the public now held 13 percent of its money in specie instead of 5 percent, the banks were able to increase their notes and deposits at precisely the same rate as the expansion of specie flowing into their coffers.

Thus, the Jackson administration is absolved from blame for the 1833–37 inflation. In a sense, the state banks are as well; certainly, they scarcely acted as if being "freed" by the demise of the Bank of the United States. Instead, they simply increased their money issues proportionately with the huge increase of specie. Of course, the basic fractional reserve banking system is scarcely absolved from responsibility, since otherwise the monetary expansion in absolute terms would not have been as great.[76]

[75]Jean Alexander Wilburn, *Biddle's Bank: The Crucial Years* (New York: Columbia University Press, 1979), pp. 118–19, quoted in Hummel, "Jacksonians," p. 155.

[76]Moreover, if the Jacksonians had been able to move more rapidly in returning the banking system to a 100-percent-specie basis, they could have used the increase in specie to ease the monetary contraction required by a return to a pure specie money.

The enormous increase in specie was the result of two factors: first and foremost, a large influx of silver coin from Mexico, and second, the sharp cut in the usual export of silver to the Orient. The latter was due to the substantial increases in China's purchase of opium instead of silver from abroad. The influx of silver was the result of paper money inflation by the Mexican government, which drove Mexican silver coins into the United States, where they circulated as legal tender. The influx of Mexican coin has been attributed to a possible increase in the productivity of the Mexican mines, but this makes little sense, since the inflow stopped permanently as soon as 1837. The actual cause was an inflation of the Mexican currency by the Santa Anna regime, which financed its deficits during this period by minting highly debased copper coins. Since the debased copper grossly overvalued copper and undervalued gold and silver, both of the latter metals proceeded to flow rapidly out of Mexico until they virtually disappeared. Silver, of course, and not gold, was flowing into the United States during this period. Indeed, the Mexican government was forced to rescind its actions in 1837 by shifting the copper coinage to its proper ratio. The influx of Mexican silver into the U.S. promptly ceased.[77]

A bank credit inflation the magnitude of that of the 1830s is bound to run into shoals that cause the banks to stop the expansion and begin to contract. As the banks expand, and prices rise, specie is bound to flow out of the country and into the hands of the domestic public, and the pressure on the banks to redeem in specie will intensify, forcing cessation of the boom and even monetary contraction. In a sense, the immediate precipitating cause is of minor importance. Even so, the Jackson administration has been unfairly blamed for precipitating the panic of 1837 by issuing the Specie Circular in 1836.

[77]Mexico was pinpointed as the source of the inflow of specie by Temin, *Jacksonian Economy*, p. 80, while the disclosure of the cause in Mexican copper inflation came in Rockoff, "Money, Prices, and Banks," p. 454.

In 1836 the Jackson administration decided to stop the enormous speculation in Western public lands that had been fueled during the past two years by the inflation of bank credit. Hence, Jackson decreed that public land payments would have to be made in specie. This had the healthy effect of stopping public land speculation, but recent studies have shown that the Specie Circular had very little impact in putting pressure on the banks to pay specie.[78] From the point of view of the Jacksonian program, however, it was as important as moving toward putting the U.S. government finances on a purely specie basis.

Another measure advancing the Jacksonian program was also taken in 1836. Jackson, embarrassed at the government having amassed a huge budget surplus during his eight years in office, ordered the Treasury to distribute the surplus proportionately to the states. The distribution was made in notes presumably payable in specie. But again, Temin has shown that the distribution had little impact on movements of specie between banks and therefore in exerting contractionist pressure upon them.[79]

What, then, was the precipitating factor in triggering the panic of 1837? Temin plausibly argues that the Bank of England, worried about inflation in Britain, and the consequent outflow of gold, tightened the money supply and raised interest rates in the latter half of 1836. As a result, credit contraction severely

[78]Public land sales by the federal government, which had been going steadily at approximately $4 million–$6 million per year, suddenly spurted upward in 1835 and 1836, to $16.2 million and $24.9 million respectively. The latter was the largest sale of public lands in American history, and the 1835 figure was the second largest. Temin, *Jacksonian Economy*, p. 124. The first demonstration of the negligible impact of the Specie Circular on the position of the banks was Richard H. Timberlake, Jr., "The Specie Circular and Distribution of the Surplus," *Journal of Political Economy* 68 (April 1960): 109–17, reprinted in Timberlake, *Origins*, pp. 50–62. Timberlake defended his thesis in idem, "The Specie Circular and the Sale of Public Lands: A Comment," *Journal of Economic History* 25 (September 1965): 414–16.

[79]Temin, *Jacksonian Economy*, pp. 128–36.

restricted the American cotton export trade in London, exports declined, cotton prices fell, capital flowed into England, and contractionist pressure was put upon American trade and the American banks. Banks throughout the United States—including the Bank of the United States—promptly suspended specie payments in May 1837, their notes depreciated at varying rates, and interregional trade within the country was crippled.

While banks were able to evade specie payments and continue operations, they were still obliged to contract credit in order to go back on specie eventually, since they could not hope to be creating fiat money indefinitely and be allowed to remain in business. Finally, the New York banks were compelled by law to resume paying their contractual obligations, and the other banks followed in the fall of 1838. During the year 1837, the money supply fell from $276 million to $232 million, a large drop of 15.6 percent in one year. Total specie in the country continued to increase in 1837, up to $88 million, but growing public distrust of the banks (reflected in an increase in the proportion of money held as specie from 13 percent to 23 percent) put enough pressure upon the banks to force the contraction. The banks' reserve ratio rose from 0.16 to 0.20. In response to the monetary contraction, wholesale prices fell precipitately, by over 30 percent in seven months, declining from 131 in February 1837 to 98 in September of that year.

In 1838 the economy revived. Britain resumed easy credit that year, cotton prices rose, and a short-lived boomlet began. Public confidence in the banks unwisely returned as they resumed specie payment, and as a result, the money supply rose slightly during the year, and prices rose by 25 percent, increasing from 98 in September 1837 to 125 in February 1839.

Leading the boom of 1838 were state governments, who, finding themselves with the unexpected windfall of a distributed surplus from the federal government, proceeded to spend the money wildly and borrow even more extravagantly on public works and other uneconomic forms of "investment." But the state governments engaged in rashly optimistic plans that their public works would be financed heavily from Britain and other countries, and the cotton boom on which these hopes depended collapsed again in 1839. The states had to abandon their projects en masse. Cotton prices declined, and severe contractionist pressure was put on trade. Furthermore, the Philadelphia-based Bank of the United States had invested heavily in cotton speculation, and the falling price of cotton forced the Bank of the United States, once again, to suspend payments in October 1839. This touched off a wave of general bank suspensions in the south and west, but this time the banks of New York and New England continued to redeem their obligations in specie. Finally, the Bank of the United States, having for the last time played a leading role in generating a recession and monetary crisis, was forced to close its doors two years later.

With the crisis of 1839 there ensued four years of massive monetary and price deflation. Unsound banks were finally eliminated; unsound investments generated in the boom were liquidated. The number of banks during these four years fell by 23 percent. The money supply fell from $240 million at the beginning of 1839 to $158 million in 1843, a seemingly cataclysmic drop of 34 percent, or 8.5 percent per annum. Prices fell even further, from 125 in February 1839 to 67 in March 1843, a tremendous drop of 42 percent, or 10.5 percent per year.

During the boom, as we have indicated, state governments went heavily into debt, issuing bonds to pay for wasteful public works. In 1820, the total indebtedness of American states was a modest $12.8 million; by 1830, it rose to $26.5 million. But then it started to escalate, reaching $66.5 million in 1835 and skyrocketing to $170 million by 1839. The collapse of money, credit banking, and prices after 1839 brought these state debts into jeopardy. At this point, the Whigs, taking a leaf from their forebears, the Federalists, agitated for the federal government to bail out the states and assume their debts.[80] After the crisis of 1839

[80]See Reginald C. McGrane, *Foreign Bondholders and American State Debts* (New York: Macmillan, 1935), pp. 6–7, 24ff.

arrived, some of the southern and western states were clearly in danger of default, their plight made worse by the fact that the bulk of the debt was held by British and Dutch capitalists and that specie would have to be sent abroad to meet the heavy interest payments. The Whigs pressed further for federal assumption of the debt, with the federal government to issue $200 million worth of bonds in payment. Furthermore, British bankers put severe pressure on the United States to assume the state debts if it expected to float further loans abroad.

The American people, however, spurned federal aid, including even the citizens of the states in difficulty, and the advent of the Polk administration ended any prospects for federal assumption. The British noted in wonder that the average American was far more concerned about his personal debts to other individuals and banks than about the debts of his state. In fact, the people were quite willing to have the states repudiate their debts outright. Demonstrating an astute perception of the reckless course the states had taken, the typical American response to the problem, "Suppose foreign capitalists did not lend any more to the states?" was the sharp retort was, "Well who cares if they don't? We are now as a community heels over head in debt and can scarcely pay the interest."[81] The implication was that the disappearance of foreign credit to the states would have the healthy effect of cutting off their wasteful spending—as well as avoiding the imposition of a crippling tax burden to pay for the interest and principal. There was in this response an awareness by the public that they and their government were separate and sometimes even hostile entities rather than one and the same organism.[82]

[81]McGrane, *Foreign Bondholders*, pp. 39–40.

[82]The Americans also pointed out that the banks, including the Bank of the United States, which were presuming to denounce repudiation of state debt, had already suspended specie payments and were largely responsible for the contraction. "Let the bondholders look to the United States Bank and to the other banks for their payment declared the people." Ibid., p. 48.

By 1847, four western and southern states (Mississippi, Arkansas, Michigan, and Florida) had repudiated all or part of their debts. Six other states (Maryland, Illinois, Indiana, Louisiana, Arkansas, and Pennsylvania) had defaulted from three to six years before resuming payment.

It is evident, then, that the 1839–1843 contraction was healthful for the economy in liquidating unsound investments, debts, and banks, including the pernicious Bank of the United States. But didn't the massive deflation have catastrophic effects—on production, trade, and employment, as we have been led to believe? In a fascinating analysis and comparison with the deflation of 1929–1933 a century later, Professor Temin shows that the percentage of deflation over the comparable four years (1839–1843 and 1929–1933) was almost the same.[83] Yet the effects on real production of the two deflations were very different. Whereas in 1929–1933, real gross investment fell catastrophically by 91 percent, real consumption by 19 percent, and real GNP by 30 percent; in 1839–1843, investment fell by 23 percent, but real consumption *increased* by 21 percent and real GNP by 16 percent. The interesting problem is to account for the enormous fall in production and consumption in the 1930s, as contrasted to the rise in production and consumption in the 1840s. It seems that only the initial months of the contraction worked a hardship on the American public and that most of the earlier deflation was a period of economic growth. Temin properly suggests that the reason can be found in the downward flexibility of prices in the nineteenth century, so that massive monetary contraction would lower prices but not particularly cripple the world of real production or standards of living. In contrast, in the 1930s government placed massive roadblocks on the downward fall of prices and wage rates and hence

[83]In 1839–43, the money supply, as we have seen, fell by 34 percent, wholesale prices by 42 percent, and the number of banks by 23 percent. In 1929–33, the money supply fell by 27 percent, prices by 31 percent, and the number of banks by 42 percent. Temin, *Jacksonian Economy*, pp. 155 ff.

brought about severe and continuing depression of production and living standards.

The Jacksonians had no intention of leaving a permanent system of pet banks, and so after the retirement of Jackson, his successor, Martin Van Buren, fought to establish the Independent Treasury System, in which the federal government conferred no special privilege or inflationary prop on any bank; instead of a central bank or pet banks, the government was to keep its funds purely in specie, in its own Treasury vaults—or its "subtreasury" branches—and simply take in and spend funds from there. Van Buren finally managed to establish the Independent Treasury System, which would last until the Civil War. At long last, the Jacksonians had achieved their dream of severing the federal government totally from the banking system and placing its finances on a purely hard-money, specie basis.

The Jacksonians and the Coinage Legislation of 1834

We have seen that the Coinage Act of 1792 established a bimetallic system in which the dollar was defined as equaling both 371.25 grains of pure silver and 24.75 grains of pure gold—a fixed weight ratio of 15 grains of silver to 1 grain of gold. But bimetallism foundered on Gresham's Law. After 1805, the world market value of silver fell to approximately 15.75-to-1, so that the U.S. fixed mint ratio greatly undervalued gold and overvalued silver. As a result gold flowed out of the country and silver flowed in, so that after 1810 only silver coin, largely overvalued Spanish-American fractional silver coin, circulated within the United States. The rest of the currency was inflated bank paper in various stages of depreciation.

The Jacksonians, as we have seen, were determined to eliminate inflationary paper money and substitute a hard money consisting of specie—or, at the most—of paper 100-percent-backed by gold or silver. On the federal level, this meant abolishing the Bank of the United States and establishing the independent Treasury. The rest of the fight would have to be conducted during the 1840s and later, at the state level where the banks were chartered. But one thing the federal government could do was readjust the specie coinage. In particular, the Jacksonians were anxious to eliminate small-denomination bank notes ($20 and under) and substitute gold and silver coins for them. They reasoned that the average American largely used these coins, and they were the ones bilked by inflated paper money. For a standard to be really gold and silver, it was vital that gold or silver coins circulate and be used as a medium of exchange by the average American.

To accomplish this goal, the Jacksonians set about to establish a comprehensive program. As one vital step, one of the Coinage Acts of 1834 readjusted the old mint ratio of 15-to-1 that had undervalued gold and driven it out of circulation. The Coinage Act devalued the definition of the gold dollar from the original 24.75 grains to 23.2 grains, a debasement of gold by 6.26 percent. The silver dollar was left at the old weight of 371.25 grains, so that the mint ratio between silver and gold was now fixed at a ratio of 16-to-1, replacing the old 15-to-1. It was unfortunate that the Jacksonians did not appreciate silver (to 396 grains) instead of debasing gold, for this set a precedent for debasement that was to plague America in 1933 and after.[84]

The new ratio of 16-to-1, however, now undervalued silver and overvalued gold, since the world market ratio had been approximately 15.79-to-1 in the years before 1834. Until recently, historians have assumed that the Jacksonians deliberately tried to bring in gold and expel silver and establish a monometallic gold standard by the back door. Recent study has shown, however, that the Jacksonians only wanted to give

[84]Probably the Jacksonians did so to preserve the illusion that the original silver dollar, the "dollar of our fathers" and the standard currency of the day, remained fixed in value. Laughlin, *History of Bimetallism*, p. 70.

gold inflow a little push through a slight undervaluation and that they anticipated a full coin circulation of both gold and silver.[85] In 1833, for example, the world market ratio was as high as 15.93-to-1. Indeed, it turns out that for two decades the Jacksonians were right, and that the slight 1-percent premium of silver over gold was not enough to drive the former coins out of circulation.[86] Both silver and gold were imported from then on, and silver and gold coins both circulated successfully side by side until the early 1850s. Lightweight Spanish fractional silver remained overvalued even at the mint ratio, so it flourished in circulation, replacing depreciated small notes. Even American silver dollars were now retained in circulation since they were "shielded" and kept circulating by the presence of new, heavyweight Mexican silver dollars, which were exported instead.[87]

In order to stimulate the circulation of both gold and silver coins instead of paper notes, the Jacksonians also passed two companion coinage acts in 1834. The Jacksonians were not monetary nationalists; specie was specie, and they saw no reason that foreign gold or silver coins should not circulate with the same full privileges as American-minted coins. Hence, the Jacksonians, in two separate measures, legalized the circulation of

[85]For the illuminating discovery that the Jacksonians were interested in purging small bank notes by bringing in gold, see Paul M. O'Leary, "The Coinage Legislation of 1834," *Journal of Political Economy* 45 (February 1937): 80–94. For the development of this insight by Martin, who shows that the Jacksonians anticipated a coinage of both gold and silver, and reveals the comprehensive Jacksonian coinage program, see David A. Martin, "Metallism, Small Notes, and Jackson's War with the B.U.S.," *Explorations in Economic History* 11 (Spring 1974): 227–47.

[86]For the next 16 years, from 1835 through 1850, the market ratio averaged 18.5-to-1, a silver premium of only 1 percent over the 16-to-1 mint ratio. For the data, see Laughlin, *History of Bimetallism*, p. 291.

[87]Martin, "Bimetallism," pp. 436–37. Spanish fractional silver coins were from 5 percent to 15 percent underweight, so their circulation in the U.S. at par by name (or "tale") meant that they were still considerably overvalued.

all foreign silver and gold coins, and they flourished in circulation until the 1850s.[88, 89]

A third plank in the Jacksonian coinage platform was to establish branch U.S. mints so as to coin the gold found in newly discovered mines in Georgia and North Carolina. The Jackson administration finally succeeded in getting Congress to do so in 1835 when it set up branch mints to coin gold in North Carolina and Georgia, and silver and gold at New Orleans.[90]

Finally, on the federal level, the Jacksonians sought to levy a tax on small bank notes and to prevent the federal government from keeping its deposits in state banks, issuing small notes, or accepting small bank notes in taxes. They were not successful, but the independent Treasury eliminated public deposit in state banks and the Specie Circular, as we have seen, stopped the receipt of bank notes for public land sales. From 1840 on, the hard-money battle would be waged at the state level.

In the early 1850s, Gresham's Law finally caught up with the bimetallist idyll that the Jacksonians had forged in the 1830s, replacing the earlier de facto silver monometallism. The sudden

[88]As Jackson's Secretary of the Treasury Levi Woodbury explained the purpose of this broad legalization of foreign coins: "to provide a full supply and variety of coins, instead of bills below five and ten dollars," for this would be "particularly conducive to the security of the poor and middling classes, who, as they own but little in, and profit but little by, banks, should be subjected to as small risk as practicable by their bills." Quoted in Martin, "Metallism," p. 242.

[89]In 1837 another coinage act made a very slight adjustment in the mint ratios. In order to raise the alloy composition of gold coins to have them similar to silver, the definition of the gold dollar was raised slightly from 23.2 grains to 23.22 grains. With the weight of the silver dollar remaining the same, the silver-gold ratio was now very slightly lowered from 16.002-to-1 to 15.998-to-1. Further slight adjustments in valuations of foreign coins in the Coinage Act of 1843 resulted in the undervaluation of many foreign coins and their gradual disappearance. The major ones—Spanish fractional silver—continued, however, to circulate widely. Ibid., p. 436.

[90]Ibid., p. 240.

discovery of extensive gold mines in California, Russia, and Australia greatly increased gold production, reaching a peak in the early 1850s. From the 1720s through the 1830s, annual world gold production averaged $12.8 million, never straying very far from that norm. Then, world gold production increased to an annual average of $38.2 million in the 1840s, and spurted upward to a peak of $155 million in 1853. World gold production then fell steadily from that peak to an annual average of $139.9 million in the 1850s and to $114.7 million from 1876 to 1890. It was not to surpass this peak until the 1890s.[91]

The consequence of the burst in gold production was, of course, a fall in the price of gold relative to silver in the world market. The silver-gold ratio declined from 15.97 in January 1849 to an average of 15.70 in 1850 to 15.46 in 1851 and to an average of 15.32-to-1 in the eight years from 1853 to 1860.[92] As a result, the market premium of American silver dollars over gold quickly rose above the 1-percent margin, which was the estimated cost of shipping silver coins abroad. That premium, which had hovered around 1 percent since the mid-1830s, suddenly rose to 4.5 percent at the beginning of 1851, and after falling back to about 2 percent at the turn of 1852, bounced back up and remained at the 4- to 5-percent level.

The result was a rapid disappearance of silver from the country, the heaviest and therefore most undervalued coins vanishing first. Spanish-milled dollars, which contained 1 percent to 5 percent more silver than American dollars, commanded a premium of 7 percent and went first. Then went the full-weight American silver dollars and after that, American fractional silver coins, which were commanding a 4-percent premium by the fall of 1852. The last coins left were the worn Spanish and Mexican fractions, which were depreciated by 10

[91]On gold production, see Laughlin, *History of Bimetallism*, pp. 283–86; and David A. Martin, "1853: The End of Bimetallism in the United States," *Journal of Economic History* 33 (December 1973): 830.

[92]The silver-gold ratio began to slide sharply in October and November 1850. Laughlin, *History of Bimetallism*, pp. 194, 291.

to 15 percent. By the beginning of 1851, however, even these worn foreign silver fractions had gone to a 1-percent premium and were beginning to go.

It was clear that America was undergoing a severe small-coin crisis. Gold coins were flowing into the country, but they were too valuable to be technically usable for small-denomination coins. The Democratic Pierce administration saw with horror millions of dollars of unauthorized private small notes flood into circulation in early 1853 for the first time since the 1830s. The Jacksonians were in grave danger of losing the fight for hard-money coinage, at least for the smaller and medium denominations. Something had to be done quickly.[93]

The ultimate breakdown of bimetallism had never been clearer. If bimetallism is not in the long run viable, this leaves two free-market, hard-money alternatives: (a) silver monometallism with the dollar defined as a weight of silver only, and gold circulating freely by weight at freely fluctuating market rates; or (b) gold monometallism with the dollar defined only as a weight of gold, with silver circulating by weight. Each of these is an example of what has been called "parallel standards" or "free metallism," in which two or more metal coins are allowed to fluctuate freely within the same area and exchange at free-market prices. As we have seen, colonial America was an example of such parallel standards, since foreign gold and silver coins circulated freely and at fluctuating market prices.[94]

[93]Martin, "Metallism," p. 240.

[94]For an account of how parallel standards worked in Europe from the medieval period through the eighteenth century, see Luigi Einaudi, "The Theory of Imaginary Money from Charlemagne to the French Revolution," in *Enterprise and Secular Change,* F. Lane and J. Riemersma, eds. (Homewood, Ill.: Irwin, 1953), pp. 229–61. Robert Lopez contrasts the ways in which Florence and Genoa each returned to gold coinage in the mid-thirteenth century, after a gap of half a millennium:

> Florence, like most medieval states, made bimetallism and trimetallism a base of its monetary policy . . . it committed

The United States could have taken this opportunity of monetary crisis to go on either version of a parallel standard.[95] Apparently, however, few thought of doing so. Another viable though inferior solution to the problem of bimetallism was to establish a monometallic system, either de facto or de jure, with the other metal circulating in the form of lightweight, and therefore overvalued, or "token" coinage. Silver monometallism was immediately unfeasible since it was rapidly flowing out of the country, and because gold, being far more valuable than silver,

---

> the government to the Sysiphean labor of readjusting the relations between different coins as the ratio between the different metals changes, or as one or another coin was debased. . . . Genoa on the contrary, *in conformity with the principle of restricting state intervention as much as possible* did not try to enforce a fixed relation between coins of different metals. . . . Basically, the gold coinage of Genoa was not meant to integrate the silver and bullion coinages but to form an independent system. (Robert Sabatino Lopez, "Back to Gold, 1252," *Economic History Review* [April 1956]: 224; emphasis added)

See also James Rolph Edwards, "Monopoly and Competition in Money," *Journal of Libertarian Studies* 4 (Winter 1980): 116. For an analysis of parallel standards, see Ludwig von Mises, *The Theory of Money and Credit,* 3rd ed. (Indianapolis: Liberty Classics, 1980), pp. 87, 89–91, 205–07.

[95]Given parallel standards, the ultimate, admittedly remote solution would be to eliminate the term "dollar" altogether, and simply have both gold and silver coins circulate by regular units of weight: "grain," "ounce," or "gram." If that were done, all problems of bimetallism, debasement, Gresham's Law, etc., would at last disappear. While such a pure free-market solution seems remote today, the late nineteenth century saw a series of important international monetary conferences trying to move toward a universal gold or silver gram, with each national currency beginning as a simple multiple of each other, and eventually only units of weight being used. Before the conferences foundered on the gold-silver problem, such a result was not as remote or utopian as we might now believe. See the fascinating account of these conferences in Henry B. Russell, *International Monetary Conferences* (New York: Harper and Bros., 1898).

could not technically function easily as a lightweight subsidiary coin. The only feasible solution, then, within a monometallic framework, was to make gold the basic standard and let highly overvalued, essentially token, silver coins function as subsidiary small coinage. Certainly if a parallel standard was not to be adopted, the latter solution would be far better than allowing depreciated paper notes to function as small currency.

Under pressure of the crisis, Congress decided, in February 1853, to keep the de jure bimetallic standard but to adopt a de facto gold monometallic standard, with fractional silver coins circulating as a deliberately overvalued subsidiary coinage, legal tender up to a maximum of only $5. The fractional silver coins were debased by 6.91 percent. With silver commanding about a 4-percent market premium over gold, this meant that fractional silver was debased 3 percent below gold. At that depreciated rate, fractional silver was not overvalued in relation to gold, and remained in circulation. By April, the new subsidiary quarter-dollars proved to be popular and by early 1854 the problem of the shortage of small coins in America was over.

In rejecting proposals either to go over completely to de jure gold monometallism or to keep the existing bimetallic system, Congress was choosing a gold standard temporarily, but keeping its options open. The fact that it continued the old full-bodied silver dollar, the "dollar of our fathers," demonstrates that an eventual return to de facto bimetallism was by no means being ruled out—albeit Gresham's Law could not then maintain the American silver dollar in circulation.[96]

In 1857, an important part of the Jacksonian coinage program was repealed, as Congress, in an exercise of monetary nationalism, eliminated all legal tender power of foreign coins.[97]

[96]For an excellent portrayal of the congressional choice in 1853, see Martin, "1853," pp. 825–44.

[97]Only Spanish-American fractional silver coins were to remain legal tender, and they were to be received quickly at government offices and

Decentralized Banking from the 1830s to the Civil War

After the central bank was eliminated in the 1830s, the battle for hard money largely shifted to the state governmental arena. During the 1830s, the major thrust was to prohibit the issue of small notes, which was accomplished for notes under five dollars in 10 states by 1832, and subsequently, five others restricted or prohibited such notes.[98]

The Democratic Party became ardently hard-money in the various states after the shock of the financial crisis of 1837 and 1839. The Democratic drive was toward the outlawry of all fractional reserve bank paper. Battles were fought also, in the late 1840s, at constitutional conventions of many states, particularly in the west. In some western states, the Jacksonians won temporary success, but soon the Whigs would return and repeal the bank prohibition. The Whigs, trying to find some way to overcome the general revulsion against banks after the crisis of the late 1830s, adopted the concept of "free" banking, which had been enacted by New York and Michigan in the late 1830s. From New York, the idea spread outward to the rest of the country and triumphed in 15 states by the early 1850s. On the eve of the Civil War, 18 out of the 33 states in the Union had adopted "free" banking laws.[99]

It must be realized that "free" banking, as it came to be known in the United States before the Civil War, was unrelated to the philosophic concept of free banking analyzed by economists. As we have seen earlier, genuine free banking is a system where entry into banking is totally free; the banks are neither subsidized nor regulated, and at the first sign of failure to

---

immediately reminted into American coins. Hepburn, *History of Currency*, pp. 66–67.

[98]See Martin, "Metallism," pp. 242–43.

[99]Hugh Rockoff, *The Free Banking Era: A Re-Examination* (New York: Arno Press, 1975), pp. 3–4.

redeem in specie payments, a bank is forced to declare insolvency and close its doors.

"Free" banking before the Civil War, on the other hand, was very different.[100] As we have pointed out, the government allowed periodic general suspensions of specie payments whenever the banks overexpanded and got into trouble—the latest episode was in the panic of 1857. It is true that bank incorporation was now more liberal since any bank that met the legal regulations could become incorporated automatically without lobbying for special legislative charters, as had been the case before. But the banks were now subject to a myriad of regulations, including edicts by state banking commissioners and high minimum capital requirements that greatly restricted entry into the banking business. But the most pernicious aspect of "free" banking was that the expansion of bank notes and deposits was directly tied to the amount of state government securities that the bank had invested in and posted as bond with the state. In effect, then, state government bonds became the reserve base upon which banks were allowed to pyramid a multiple expansion of bank notes and deposits. Not only did this system provide explicitly or implicitly for fractional reserve banking, but the pyramid was tied rigidly to the amount of government bonds purchased by the banks. This provision deliberately tied banks and bank credit expansion to the public debt; it meant that the more public debt the banks purchased, the more they could create and lend out new money. Banks, in short, were encouraged to monetize the public debt, state governments were thereby encouraged to go into debt, and hence, government and bank inflation were intimately linked.

[100]Rockoff goes so far as to call free banking the "antithesis of *laissez-faire* banking laws." Hugh Rockoff, "Varieties of Banking and Regional Economic Development in the United States, 1840–1860," *Journal of Economic History* 35 (March 1975): 162. Quoted in Hummel, "Jacksonians," p. 157.

In addition to allowing periodic suspension of specie payments, federal and state governments conferred upon the banks the privilege of their notes being accepted in taxes. Moreover, the general prohibition of interstate branch banking—and often of intrastate branches as well—greatly inhibited the speed by which one bank could demand payment from other banks in specie. In addition, state usury laws, pushed by the Whigs and opposed by the Democrats, made credit excessively cheap for the riskiest borrowers and encouraged inflation and speculative expansion of bank lending.

Furthermore, the desire of state governments to finance internal improvements was an important factor in subsidizing and propelling expansion of bank credit. As Hammond admits: "The wild cats lent no money to farmers and served no farmer interest. They arose to meet the credit demands not of farmers [who were too economically astute to accept wildcat money] but of states engaged in public improvements."[101]

Despite the flaws and problems, the decentralized nature of the pre–Civil War banking system meant banks were free to experiment on their own with improving the banking system. The most successful such device was the creation of the Suffolk system.

[101]Hammond, *Banks and Politics*, p. 627. On free banking, see Hummel, "Jacksonians," p. 154–60; Smith, *Rationale*, pp. 44–45; and Rockoff, "American Free Banking," pp. 417–20. On the effect of usury laws, see William Graham Sumner, *A History of American Currency* (New York: Henry Holt, 1876), p. 125. On the Jacksonians versus their opponents on the state level after 1839, see William G. Shade, *Banks or No Banks: The Money Issue in Western Politics, 1832–1865* (Detroit: Wayne State University Press, 1972); Herbert Ershkowitz and William Shade, "Consensus or Conflict? Political Behavior in the State Legislatures During the Jaksonian Era," *Journal of American History* 58 (December 1971): 591–621; and James Roger Sharp, *Jacksonians versus the Banks: Politics in the States After the Panic of 1837* (New York: Columbia University Press, 1970).

A Free-Market "Central Bank"

It is a fact, almost never recalled, that there once existed an American private bank that brought order and convenience to a myriad of privately issued bank notes. Further, this Suffolk Bank restrained the overissuance of these notes. In short, it was a private central bank that kept the other banks honest. As such, it made New England an island of monetary stability in an America contending with currency chaos.

Chaos was, in fact, that condition in which New England found herself just before the Suffolk Bank was established. There was a myriad of bank notes circulating in the area's largest financial center, Boston. Some were issued by Boston banks which all in Boston knew to be solvent. But others were issued by state-chartered banks. These could be quite far away, and in those days such distance impeded both general knowledge about their solvency and easy access in bringing the banks' notes in for redemption into gold or silver. Thus, while at the beginning these country notes were accepted in Boston at par value, this just encouraged some faraway banks to issue far more notes than they had gold to back them. So country bank notes began to be generally traded at discounts to par, of from 1 percent to 5 percent.

City banks finally refused to accept country bank notes altogether. This gave rise to the money brokers mentioned earlier in this chapter. But it also caused hardship for Boston merchants, who had to accept country notes whose real value they could not be certain of. When they exchanged the notes with the brokers, they ended up assuming the full cost of discounting the bills they had accepted at par.

A False Start

Matters began to change in 1814. The New England Bank of Boston announced it too would go into the money broker business, accepting country notes from holders and turning them over to the issuing bank for redemption. The note holders, though, still had to pay the cost. In 1818, a group of prominent merchants formed the Suffolk Bank to do the same thing. This enlarged competition brought the basic rate of country-note discount down from 3 percent in 1814 to 1 percent in 1818 and finally to a bare one-half of 1 percent in 1820. But this did not necessarily mean that country banks were behaving more responsibly in their note creation. By the end of 1820 the business had become clearly unprofitable, and both banks stopped competing with the private money brokers. The Suffolk became just another Boston bank.

Operation Begins

During the next several years city banks found their notes representing an ever smaller part of the total New England money supply. Country banks were simply issuing far more notes in proportion to their capital (that is, gold and silver) than were the Boston banks.

Concerned about this influx of paper money of lesser worth, both Suffolk Bank and New England Bank began again in 1824 to purchase country notes. But this time they did so not to make a profit on redemption, but simply to reduce the number of country notes in circulation in Boston. They had the foolish hope that this would increase the use of their (better) notes, thus increasing their own loans and profits.

But the more they purchased country notes, the more notes of even worse quality (particularly from faraway Maine banks) would replace them. Buying these latter involved more risk, so the Suffolk proposed to six other city banks a joint fund to purchase and send these notes back to the issuing bank for redemption. These seven banks, known as the Associated Banks, raised $300,000 for this purpose. With the Suffolk acting as agent and buying country notes from the other six, operations began March 24, 1824. The volume of country notes bought in this way increased greatly, to $2 million per month by the end of 1825. By then, Suffolk felt strong enough to go it alone. Further, it now had the leverage to pressure country banks into depositing gold and silver with the Suffolk, to make note redemption easier. By 1838, almost all banks in New England did so, and were redeeming their notes through the Suffolk Bank.

The Suffolk ground rules from beginning (1825) to end (1858) were as follows: Each country bank had to maintain a permanent deposit of specie of at least $2,000 for the smallest bank, plus enough to redeem all its notes that Suffolk received. These gold and silver deposits did not have to be at Suffolk, as long as they were at some place convenient to Suffolk, so that the notes would not have to be sent home for redemption. But in practice, nearly all reserves were at Suffolk. (City banks had only to deposit a fixed amount, which decreased to $5,000 by 1835.) No interest was paid on any of these deposits. But, in exchange, the Suffolk began performing an invaluable service: It agreed to accept at par all the notes it received as deposits from other New England banks in the system, and credit the depositor banks' accounts on the following day.

With the Suffolk acting as a "clearing bank," accepting, sorting, and crediting bank notes, it was now possible for any New England bank to accept the notes of any other bank, however far away, and at face value. This drastically cut down on the time and inconvenience of applying to each bank separately for specie redemption. Moreover, the certainty spread that the notes of the Suffolk member banks would be valued at par: It spread at first among other bankers and then to the general public.

The Country Banks Resist

How did the inflationist country banks react to this? Not very well, for as one could see the Suffolk system put limits on the amount of notes they could issue. They resented par redemption and detested systematic specie redemption because that forced them to stay honest. But country banks knew that any bank that did not play by the rules would be shunned by the banks that did (or at least see its notes accepted only at discount, and not in a very wide area, at that). All legal means to stop Suffolk failed: The Massachusetts Supreme Court upheld in 1827 Suffolk's right to demand gold or silver for country bank notes, and the state legislature refused to charter a clearing bank run by country banks, probably rightly assuming that these banks would run much less strict operations. Stung by these setbacks, the country banks played by the rules, bided their time, and awaited their revenge.

Suffolk's Stabilizing Effects

Even though Suffolk's initial objective had been to increase the circulation of city banks, this did not happen. In fact, by having their notes redeemed at par, country banks gained a new respectability. This came, naturally, at the expense of the number of notes issued by the worst former inflationists. But at least in Massachusetts, the percentage of city bank notes in circulation fell from 48.5 percent in 1826 to 35.8 percent in 1833.

Circulation of Notes of Massachusetts Banks (in Thousands)

Date	All Banks	Boston Banks	Boston Percentage
1823	$3,129	$1,354	43.3
1824	3,843	1,797	46.8
1825	4,091	1,918	46.9
1826	4,550	2,206	48.5
1827	4,936	2,103	42.6
1828	4,885	2,067	42.3
1829	4,748	2,078	43.8
1830	5,124	2,171	42.3
1831	7,139	3,464	44.8
1832	7,123	3,060	43.0
1833	7,889	2,824	35.8

Source: Wilfred S. Lake, "The End of the Suffolk System," *Journal of Economic History* 7, no. 4 (1947), p. 188.

The biggest, most powerful weapon Suffolk had to keep stability was the power to grant membership into the system. It accepted only banks whose notes were sound. While Suffolk could not prevent a bad bank from inflating, denying it membership ensured that the notes would not enjoy wide circulation. And the member banks that were mismanaged could be stricken from the list of Suffolk-approved New England banks in good standing. This caused an offending bank's notes to trade at a discount at once, even though the bank itself might be still redeeming its notes in specie.

In another way, Suffolk exercised a stabilizing influence on the New England economy. It controlled the use of overdrafts in the system. When a member bank needed money, it could apply for an overdraft, that is, a portion of the excess reserves in the banking system. If Suffolk decided that a member bank's loan policy was not conservative enough, it could refuse to sanction that bank's application to borrow reserves at Suffolk. The denial of overdrafts to profligate banks thus forced those banks to keep their assets more liquid. (Few government central banks today have succeeded in that.) This is all the more remarkable when one considers that Suffolk—or any central bank—could have earned extra interest income by issuing overdrafts irresponsibly.

But Dr. George Trivoli, whose excellent monograph, *The Suffolk Bank*, we rely on in this study, states that by providing stability to the New England banking system, "it should not be inferred that the Suffolk bank was operating purely as public benefactor." Suffolk, in fact, made handsome profits. At its peak in 1858, the last year of existence, it was redeeming $400 million in notes, with a total annual salary cost of only $40,000. The healthy profits were derived primarily from loaning out those reserve deposits which Suffolk itself, remember, did not pay interest on. These amounted to more than $1 million in 1858. The interest charged on overdrafts augmented that. Not surprisingly, Suffolk stock was the highest priced bank stock in Boston, and by 1850, regular dividends were 10 percent.

The Suffolk Difference

That the Suffolk system was able to provide note redemption much more cheaply than the U.S. government was stated by a U.S. comptroller of the currency. John Jay Knox compared the two systems from a vantage point of half a century:

> [I]n 1857 the redemption of notes by the Suffolk Bank was almost $400,000,000 as against $137,697,696, in 1875, the highest amount ever reported under the National banking system. The redemptions in 1898 were only $66,683,476, at a cost of $1.29 per thousand. The cost of redemption under the Suffolk system was ten cents per $1,000, which does not appear to include transportation. If this item is deducted from the cost of redeeming National bank notes, it would reduce it to about ninety-four cents. This difference is accounted for by the relatively small amount of redemptions by the Treasury, and the increased expense incident to the necessity of official checks by the Government, and by the higher salaries paid. But allowing for these differences, the fact is established that private enterprise could be entrusted with the work of redeeming the circulating notes of the banks, and it could thus be done as safely and much more economically than the same service can be performed by the Government.[102]

The volume of redemptions was much larger under Suffolk than under the national banking system. During Suffolk's existence (1825–57) they averaged $229 million per year. The average of the national system from its start in 1863 to about 1898 is put by Mr. Knox at only $54 million. Further, at its peak in 1858, $400 million was redeemed. But the New England money supply was only $40 million. This meant that, astoundingly, the average note was redeemed ten times per year, or once every five weeks.

[102]John Jay Knox, *A History of Banking in the United States* (New York: Augustus M. Kelley, [1900] 1969), pp. 368–69.

Bank capital, note circulation, and deposits, considered together as "banking power," grew in New England on a per capita basis much faster than in any other region of the country from 1803 to 1850. And there is some evidence that New England banks were not as susceptible to disaster during the several banking panics during that time. In the panic of 1837, not one Connecticut bank failed, nor did any suspend specie payments. All remained in the Suffolk system. And when in 1857 specie payment was suspended in Maine, all but three banks remained in business. As the Bank Commission of Maine stated,

> The Suffolk system, though not recognized in banking law, has proved to be a great safeguard to the public; whatever objections may exist to the system in theory, its practical operation is to keep the circulation of our banks within the bounds of safety.

The Suffolk's Demise

The extraordinary profits—and power—that the Suffolk had by 1858 attained spawned competitors. The only one to become established was the Bank for Mutual Redemption in 1858. This bank was partially a response to the somewhat arrogant behavior of the Suffolk by this time, after 35 years of unprecedented success. But further, and more important, the balance of power in the state legislature had shifted outside of Boston, to the country bank areas. The politicians were more amenable to the desires of the overexpanding country banks. Still, it must be said that Suffolk acted toward the Bank of Mutual Redemption with spite where conciliation would have helped. Trying to force Mutual Redemption out of business, Suffolk, starting October 8, 1858, refused to honor notes of banks having deposits in the newcomer. Further, Suffolk in effect threatened any bank withdrawing deposits from it. But country banks rallied to the newcomer, and on October 16, Suffolk announced that it would stop clearing any country bank notes, thus becoming just another bank.

Only the Bank for Mutual Redemption was left, and though it soon had half the New England banks as members, it was much more lax toward overissuance by country banks. Perhaps the Suffolk would have returned amid dissatisfaction with its successor, but in 1861, just over two years after Suffolk stopped clearing, the Civil War began and all specie payments were stopped. As a final nail in the coffin, the national banking system Act of 1863 forbade the issuance of any state bank notes, giving a monopoly to the government that has continued ever since.

While it lasted, though, the Suffolk banking system showed that it is possible in a free-market system to have private banks competing to establish themselves as efficient, safe, and inexpensive clearinghouses limiting overissue of paper money.

The Civil War

The Civil War exerted an even more fateful impact on the American monetary and banking system than had the War of 1812. It set the United States, for the first time except for 1814–1817, on an irredeemable fiat currency that lasted for two decades and led to reckless inflation of prices. This "greenback" currency set a momentous precedent for the post-1933 United States, and even more particularly for the post-1971 experiment in fiat money.

Perhaps an even more important consequence of the Civil War was the permanent change wrought in the American banking system. The federal government in effect outlawed the issue of state bank notes, and created a new, quasi-centralized, fractional reserve national banking system which paved the way for the return of outright central banking in the Federal Reserve System. The Civil War, in short, ended the separation of the federal government from banking, and brought the two institutions together in an increasingly close and permanent symbiosis. In that way, the Republican Party, which inherited the Whig admiration for paper money and governmental control and sponsorship of inflationary banking, was able to implant the soft-money tradition permanently in the American system.

Greenbacks

The Civil War led to an enormous ballooning of federal expenditures, which skyrocketed from $66 million in 1861 to $1.30 billion four years later. To pay for these swollen expenditures, the Treasury initially attempted, in the fall of 1861, to float a massive $150 million bond issue, to be purchased by the nation's leading banks. However, Secretary of the Treasury Salmon P. Chase, a former Jacksonian, tried to require the banks to pay for the loan in specie that they did not have. This massive pressure on their specie, as well as an increased public demand for specie due to a well-deserved lack of confidence in the banks, brought about a general suspension of specie payments a few months later, at the end of December 1861. This suspension was followed swiftly by the Treasury itself, which suspended specie payments on its Treasury notes.

The U.S. government quickly took advantage of being on an inconvertible fiat standard. In the Legal Tender Act of February 1862, Congress authorized the printing of $150 million in new "United States notes" (soon to be known as "greenbacks") to pay for the growing war deficits. The greenbacks were made legal tender for all debts, public and private, except that the Treasury continued its legal obligation of paying the interest on its outstanding public debt in specie.[103] The

[103]To be able to keep paying interest in specie, Congress provided that customs duties, at least, had to be paid in gold or silver. For a comprehensive account and analysis of the issue of greenbacks in the Civil War, see Wesley Clair Mitchell, *A History of the Greenbacks* (Chicago: University of Chicago Press, 1903). For a summary, see Paul Studenski and Herman E. Kross, *Financial History of the United States* (New York: McGraw-Hill, 1952), pp. 141–49.

greenbacks were also made convertible at par into U.S. bonds, which remained a generally unused option for the public, and was repealed a year later.

In creating greenbacks in February, Congress resolved that this would be the first and last emergency issue. But printing money is a heady wine, and a second $150 million issue was authorized in July, and still a third $150 million in early 1863. Greenbacks outstanding reached a peak in 1864 of $415.1 million.

Greenbacks began to depreciate in terms of specie almost as soon as they were issued. In an attempt to drive up the price of government bonds, Secretary Chase eliminated the convertibility of greenbacks in July 1863, an act that simply drove their value down further. Chase and the Treasury officials, instead of acknowledging their own premier responsibility for the continued depreciation of the greenbacks, conveniently placed the blame on anonymous "gold speculators." In March 1863, Chase began a determined campaign, which would last until he was driven from office, to stop the depreciation by controlling, assaulting, and eventually eliminating the gold market. In early March, he had Congress to levy a stamp tax on gold sales and to forbid loans on a collateral of coin above its par value. This restriction on the gold market had little effect, and when depreciation resumed its march at the end of the year, Chase decided to de facto repeal the requirement that customs duties be paid in gold. In late March 1864, Chase declared that importers would be allowed to deposit greenbacks at the Treasury and receive gold in return at a premium below the market. Importers could then use the gold to pay the customs duties. This was supposed to reduce greatly the necessity for importers to buy gold coin on the market and therefore to reduce the depreciation. The outcome, however, was that the greenback, at 59¢ in gold when Chase began the experiment, had fallen to 57¢ by mid-April. Chase was then forced to repeal his customs-duties scheme.

With the failure of this attempt to regulate the gold market, Chase promptly escalated his intervention. In mid-April, he sold the massive amount of $11 million in gold in order to drive down the gold premium of greenbacks. But the impact was trifling, and the Treasury could not continue this policy indefinitely, because it had to keep enough gold in its vaults to pay interest on its bonds. At the end of the month, the greenback was lower than ever, having sunk to below 56¢ in gold.

Indefatigably, Chase tried yet again. In mid-May 1864, he sold foreign exchange in London at below-market rates in order to drive down pounds in relation to dollars, and, more specifically, to replace some of the U.S. export demand for gold in England. But this, too, was a failure, and Chase ended this experiment before the end of the month.

Finally, Secretary Chase decided to take off the gloves. He had failed to regulate the gold market; he would therefore end the depreciation of greenbacks by destroying the gold market completely. By mid-June, he had driven through Congress a truly despotic measure to prohibit under pain of severe penalties all futures contracts in gold, as well as all sales of gold by a broker outside his own office.

The result was disaster. The gold market was in chaos, with wide ranges of prices due to the absence of an organized market. Businessmen clamored for repeal of the "gold bill," and, worst of all, the object of the law—to lower the depreciation of the paper dollar—had scarcely been achieved. Instead, public confidence in the greenback plummeted, and its depreciation in terms of gold got far worse. At the beginning of June, the greenback dollar was worth over 52¢ in gold. Apprehensions about the emerging gold bill drove the greenback down slightly to 51¢ in mid-June. Then, after the passage of the bill, the greenback plummeted, hitting 40¢ at the end of the month.

The disastrous gold bill was hastily repealed at the end of June, and perhaps not coincidentally, Secretary Chase was ousted from office at the same time. The war against the speculators was over.[104, 105]

As soon as greenbacks depreciated to less than 97¢ in gold, fractional silver coins became undervalued and so were exported to be exchanged for gold. By July 1862, in consequence, no coin higher than the copper-nickel penny remained in circulation. The U.S. government then leaped in to fill the gap with small tickets, first issuing postage stamps for the purpose, then bits of unglued paper, and finally, after the spring of 1863, fractional paper notes.[106] A total of $28 million in postage currency and fractional notes had been issued by the middle of 1864. Even the nickel-copper pennies began to disappear from circulation, as greenbacks depreciated, and the nickel-copper coins began to move toward being undervalued. The expectation and finally the reality of undervaluation drove the coins into hoards and then into exports. Postage and fractional notes

[104]Chase and the administration should have heeded the advice of Republican Senator Jacob Collamer of Vermont: "Gold does not fluctuate in price . . . because they gamble in it; but they gamble in it because it fluctuates. . . . But the fluctuation is not in the gold; the fluctuation is in the currency, and it is a fluctuation utterly beyond the control of individuals." Mitchell, *History of Greenbacks*, pp. 229–30.

[105]On the war against the gold speculators, see ibid., pp. 223–35. The greenbacks fell further to 35¢ in mid-July on news of military defeats for the North. Military victories, and consequently rising prospects of possible future gold redemption of the greenbacks, caused a rise in greenbacks in terms of gold, particularly after the beginning of 1865. At war's end, the greenback dollar was worth 69¢ in gold. Ibid., pp. 232–38, 423–28.

[106]Some of the greenbacks had been decorated with portraits of President Lincoln ($5) and Secretary Chase ($1). However, when Spencer Clark, chief clerk of the Treasury's National Currency Division, put his own portrait on 5¢ fractional notes, the indignant Republican Representative Martin R. Thayer of Pennsylvania put through a law, still in force, making it illegal to put the picture of any living American on any coin or paper money. See Gary North, "Greenback Dollars and Federal Sovereignty, 1861–1865," in *Gold Is Money*, Hans Sennholz, ed. (Westport, Conn.: Greenwood Press, 1975), pp. 124, 150.

did not help matters, because their lowest denominations were 5¢ and 3¢, respectively. The penny shortage was finally alleviated when a debased and lighter-weight penny was issued in the spring of 1864, consisting of bronze instead of nickel and copper.[107]

As soon as the nation's banks and the Treasury itself suspended specie payments at the end of 1861, Gresham's Law went into operation and gold coin virtually disappeared from circulation, except for the government's interest payments and importers' customs duties. The swift issuance of legal tender greenbacks, which the government forced creditors to accept at par, ensured the continued disappearance of gold from then on.

The fascinating exception was California. There were very few banks during this period west of Nebraska, and in California the absence of banks was ensured by the fact that note-issuing banks, at least, were prohibited by the California constitution of 1849.[108] The California gold discoveries of the late 1840s ensured a plentiful supply for coinage.

Used to a currency of gold coin only, with no intrusion of bank notes, California businessmen took steps to maintain gold circulation and avoid coerced payment in greenbacks. At first, the merchants of San Francisco, in November 1862 jointly agreed to refrain from accepting or paying out greenbacks at any but the (depreciated) market value, and to keep gold as the monetary standard. Any firms that refused to abide by the agreement would be blacklisted and required to pay gold in cash for any goods which they might purchase in the future.

Voluntary efforts did not suffice to overthrow the federal power standing behind legal tender, however, and so California merchants obtained the passage in the California legislature of

[107]See Mitchell, *History of Greenbacks*, pp. 156–63.

[108]Banks of deposit existed in California, but of course they could not supply the public's demand for cash. See Knox, *History of Banking*, pp. 843–45.

a "specific contracts act" at the end of April 1863. The specific contracts act provided that contracts for the payment of specific kinds of money would be enforceable in the courts. After passage of that law, California businessmen were able to protect themselves against tenders of greenbacks by inserting gold coin payment clauses in all their contracts. Would that the other states, and even the federal government, had done the same![109] Furthermore, the private banks of deposit in California refused to accept greenbacks on deposit, newspapers used their influence to warn citizens about the dangers of greenbacks, and the state government refused to accept greenbacks in payment of taxes. In that way, all the major institutions in California joined in refusing to accept or give their imprimatur to federal inconvertible paper.

Judicial institutions also helped maintain the gold standard and repel the depreciated U.S. paper. Not only did the California courts uphold the constitutionality of the specific contracts act, but the California Supreme Court ruled in 1862 that greenbacks could not be accepted in state or county taxes, since the state constitution prohibited any acceptance of paper money for taxes.

The state of Oregon was quick to follow California's lead. Oregon's constitution had also outlawed banks of issue, and gold had for years been the exclusive currency. Two weeks after the agreement of the San Francisco merchants, the merchants of Salem, Oregon, unanimously backed gold as the monetary standard and refused to accept greenbacks at par. Two months later, the leading merchants of Portland agreed to accept greenbacks only at rates current in San Francisco; the

[109]This experience illustrates a continuing problem in contract law: It is not sufficient for government to allow contracts to be made in gold or gold coin. It is necessary for government to enforce *specific performance* of the contracts so that debtors must pay in the weight or value of the gold (or anything else) required in the contract, and not in some paper-dollar equivalent decided by law or the courts.

merchants in the rest of the state were quick to follow suit. The Portland merchants issued a circular warning of a blacklist of all customers who insisted on settling their debts in greenbacks, and they would be quickly boycotted, and dealings with them would only be in cash.

Oregon deposit banks also refused to accept greenbacks, and the Oregon legislature followed California a year and a half later in passing a specific performance law. Oregon, too, refused to accept greenbacks in taxes and strengthened the law in 1864 by requiring that "all taxes levied by state, counties, or municipal corporations therein, shall be collected and paid in gold and silver coin of the United States and not otherwise."[110]

In the same year, the Oregon Supreme Court followed California in ruling that greenbacks could not constitutionally be received in payment of taxes.

The banking story during the Civil War is greatly complicated by the advent of the national banking system in the latter part of the war. But it is clear that the state banks, being able to suspend specie and to pyramid money and credit on top of the federal greenbacks, profited greatly by being able to expand during this period. Thus, total state bank notes and deposits were $510 million in 1860, and by 1863 rose to $743 million, an increase in state bank demand liabilities in those three years of 15.2 percent per year.[111]

It is no wonder, then, that contrary to older historical opinion, many state banks were enthusiastic about the greenbacks,

[110]Cited in Richard A. Lester, *Monetary Experiments* (London: David and Charles Reprints, [1939] 1970), p. 166. On the California and Oregon maintenance of the gold standard in this period, see ibid., pp. 161–71. On California, see Bernard Moses, "Legal Tender Notes in California," in *Quarterly Journal of Economics* (October 1892): 1–25; and Mitchell, *History of Greenbacks*, pp. 142–44. On Oregon, see James H. Gilbert, *Trade and Currency in Early Oregon* (New York: Columbia University Press, 1907), pp. 101–22.

[111]*Historical Statistics*, pp. 625, 648–49.

which provided them with legal tender that could function as a reserve base upon which they could expand. As Hammond puts it, "Instead of being curbed (as some people supposed later), the powers of the banks were augmented by the legal tender issues. As the issues increased, the deposits of the banks would increase."[112] Indeed, Senator Sherman (R-Ohio) noted that the state banks favored greenbacks. And the principal author of the greenback legislation, Representative Elbridge G. Spaulding (R-N.Y.), the chairman of the House Ways and Means subcommittee that introduced the bill, was himself a Buffalo banker.

The total money supply of the country (including gold coin, state bank notes, subsidiary silver, and U.S. currency including fractional and greenbacks) amounted to $745.4 million in 1860. By 1863, the money supply had skyrocketed to $1.435 billion, an increase of 92.5 percent in three years, or 30.8 percent per annum. By the end of the war, the money supply, which now included national bank notes and deposits, totaled $1.773 billion, an increase in two years of 23.6 percent or 11.8 percent per year. Over the entire war, the money supply rose from $45.4 million to $1.773 billion, an increase of 137.9 percent, or 27.69 percent per annum.[113]

The response to this severe monetary inflation was a massive inflation of prices. It is no wonder that the greenbacks, depreciating rapidly in terms of gold, depreciated in terms of goods as well. Wholesale prices rose from 100 in 1860 to 210.9

[112]Bray Hammond, *Sovereignty and an Empty Purse: Banks and Politics in the Civil War* (Princeton, N.J.: Princeton University Press, 1970), pp. 246, 249–50. See also North, "Greenback Dollars," pp. 143–48.

[113]*Historical Statistics*, pp. 625, 648–49. In a careful analysis, North estimates the total money supply at approximately $2 billion and also points out that conterfeit notes in the Civil War have been estimated to amount to no less than one-third of the total currency in circulation. North, "Greenback Dollars," p. 134. The counterfeiting estimates are in William P. Donlon, *United States Large Size Paper Money, 1861 to 1923,* 2nd ed. (Iola, Wis.: Krause, 1970), p. 15.

at the end of the war, a rise of 110.9 percent, or 22.2 percent per year.[114]

The Republican administration argued that its issue of greenbacks was required by stern wartime "necessity." The spuriousness of this argument is seen by the fact that greenbacks were virtually not issued after the middle of 1863. There were three alternatives to the issuance of legal tender fiat money. (1) The government could have issued paper money but not made it legal tender; it would have depreciated even more rapidly. At any rate, they would have had quasi–legal tender status by being receivable in federal dues and taxes. (2) It could have increased taxes to pay for the war expenditures. (3) It could have issued bonds and other securities and sold the debt to banks and non-bank institutions. In fact, the government employed both the latter alternatives, and after 1863 stopped issuing greenbacks and relied on them exclusively, especially a rise in the public debt. The accumulated deficit piled up during the war was $2.614 billion, of which the printing of greenbacks only financed $431.7 million. Of the federal deficits during the war, greenbacks financed 22.8 percent in fiscal 1862, 48.5 percent in 1863, 6.3 percent in 1864, and none in 1865.[115] This is particularly striking if we consider that the peak

[114]Ralph Andreano, ed., *The Economic Impact of the American Civil War* (Cambridge, Mass.: Schenckman, 1961), p. 178.

[115]The Confederacy, on the other hand, financed virtually all of its expenditures through mammoth printing of fiat paper, the Southern version of the greenback. Confederate notes, which were first issued in June 1861 at a sum of $1.1 million, skyrocketed until the total supply of Confederate notes in January 1864 was no less than $826.8 million, an increase of 750.6 percent for three and a half years, or 214.5 percent per year. Bank notes and deposits in the Confederacy rose from $119.3 million to $268.1 million in this period, so that the total money supply rose from $120.4 million to $1.095 billion, an increase of 1,060 percent—or 302.9 percent per year. Prices in the eastern Confederacy rose from 100 in early 1861 to over 4,000 in 1864, and to 9,211 at the end of the war in April 1865. Thus, in four years, prices rose by 9,100 percent or an average of

deficit came in 1865, totaling $963.8 million. All the rest was financed by increased debt. Taxes also increased greatly, revenues rising from $52 million in 1862 to $333.7 million in 1865. Tax revenues as a percentage of the budget rose from a miniscule 10.7 percent in fiscal 1862 to over 26 percent in 1864 and 1865.

It is clear, then, that the argument of "necessity" in the printing of greenbacks was specious, and indeed the greenback advocates conceded that it was perfectly possible to issue public debt, provided that the administration was willing to see the prices of its bonds rise and its interest payments rise considerably. At least for most of the war, they were not willing to take their chances in the competitive bond market.[116]

The Public Debt and the National Banking System

The public debt of the Civil War brought into American financial history the important advent of one Jay Cooke. The Ohio-born Cooke had joined the moderately successful Philadelphia investment banking firm of Clark and Dodge as a clerk at the age of 18. In a few years, Cooke worked himself up to the status of junior partner, and, in 1857, he left the firm to branch out on his own in canal and railroad promotion and other business ventures. There he doubtless would have remained, except for the lucky fact that he and his brother Henry, editor of the leading Republican newspaper in Ohio,

---

2,275 percent per annum. See Eugene M. Lerner, "Inflation in the Confederacy, 1861–65," in *Studies in the Quantity Theory of Money*, Milton Friedman, ed. (Chicago: University of Chicago Press, 1956), pp. 163–75; and Eugene M. Lerner, "Money, Prices, and Wages in the Confederacy, 1861–65," in Andreano, *Economic Impact*, pp. 11–40.

[116]Mitchell, *History of the Greenbacks*, pp. 61–74, 119 f., 128–31. See also Don C. Barrett, *The Greenbacks and Resumption of Specie Payments, 1862–1879* (Cambridge, Mass.: Harvard University Press, 1931), pp. 25–57.

the *Ohio State Journal*, were close friends of U.S. Senator Salmon P. Chase. Chase, a veteran leader of the antislavery movement, fought for and lost the Republican presidential nomination in 1860 to Abraham Lincoln. At that point, the Cookes determined to feather their nest by lobbying to make Salmon Chase secretary of the Treasury. After heavy lobbying by the Cookes, the Chase appointment was secured, so Jay Cooke quickly set up his own investment banking house of Jay Cooke and Company.

Everything was in place; it now remained to seize the opportunity. As the Cookes' father wrote of Henry:

> I took up my pen principally to say that H.S.'s [Henry's] plan in getting Chase into the Cabinet and [John] Sherman into the Senate is accomplished, and that now is the time for making money, by honest contracts out of the government.[117]

Now indeed was their time for making money, and Cooke lost no time in doing so. It did not take much persuasion, including wining and dining, for Cooke to induce his friend Chase to take an unprecedented step in the fall of 1862: granting the House of Cooke a monopoly on the underwriting of the public debt. With enormous energy, Cooke hurled himself into the task of persuading the mass of public to buy U.S. government bonds. In doing so, Cooke perhaps invented the art of public relations and of mass propaganda; certainly, he did so in the realm of selling bonds. As Kirkland writes:

> With characteristic optimism, he [Cooke] flung himself into a bond crusade. He recruited a small army of 2,500 subagents among bankers, insurance men, and community leaders and kept them inspired and informed by mail and

[117]In Henrietta Larson, *Jay Cooke, Private Banker* (Cambridge, Mass: Harvard University Press, 1936), p. 103. See also Edward C. Kirkland, *Industry Comes of Age: Business, Labor and Public Policy, 1860–1897* (New York: Holt, Rinehart and Winston, 1961), p. 20.

> telegraph. He taught the American people to buy bonds, using lavish advertising in newspapers, broadsides, and posters. God, destiny, duty, courage, patriotism—all summoned "Farmers, Mechanics, and Capitalists" to invest in loans[118]

—loans which of course they had to purchase from Jay Cooke.

And purchase the loans they did, for Cooke's bond sales soon reached the enormous figure of $1 million to $2 million dollars a day. Perhaps $2 billion in bonds were bought and underwritten by Jay Cooke during the war. Cooke lost his monopoly in 1864, under pressure of rival bankers; but a year later he was reappointed to keep that highly lucrative post until the House of Cooke crashed in the panic of 1873.

In the Civil War, Jay Cooke began as a moderately successful promoter; he emerged at war's end a millionaire, a man who had spawned the popular motto, "as rich as Jay Cooke." Surely he must have counted the $100,000 he had poured into Salmon Chase's political fortunes by 1864 as one of the most lucrative investments he had ever made.

It is not surprising that Jay Cooke acquired enormous political influence in the Republican administration of the Civil War and after. Hugh McCulloch, secretary of the Treasury from 1865 to 1869, was a close friend of Cooke's, and when McCulloch left office he assumed the post as head of Cooke's London office. The Cooke brothers were also good friends of General Ulysses Grant, so they wielded great influence during the Grant administration.

No sooner had Cooke secured the monopoly of government bond underwriting than he teamed up with his associates, Secretary of the Treasury Chase and Ohio's Senator John Sherman, to drive through a measure which was destined to have far more fateful effects than greenbacks on the American monetary system: the national banking system. The National Banking

[118]Kirkland, *Industry*, pp. 20–21.

Acts destroyed the previously decentralized and fairly successful state banking system, and substituted a new, centralized, and far more inflationary banking system under the aegis of Washington and a handful of Wall Street banks. Whereas the effects of the greenbacks were finally eliminated by the resumption of specie payments in 1879, the effects of the national banking system are still with us. Not only was this system in place until 1913, but it paved the way for the Federal Reserve System by instituting a quasi–central banking type of monetary system. The "inner contradictions" of the national banking system were such that the nation was driven either to go onward to a frankly central bank or else to scrap centralized banking altogether and go back to decentralized state banking. Given the inner dynamic of state intervention to keep intensifying, coupled with the almost universal adoption of statist ideology after the turn of the twentieth century, which course the nation would take was unfortunately inevitable.

Chase and Sherman drove the new system through under cover of war necessity, but it was designed to alter the banking system permanently. The wartime ground was to set up national banks, which were so structured as to necessarily purchase large amounts of U.S. government bonds. Patterned after the "free" banking systems, this tied the nation's banks with the federal government and the public debt in a close symbiotic relationship. The Jacksonian embarrassment of the independent Treasury was de facto swept away, and the Treasury would now keep its deposits in a new series of "pets": the national banks, chartered directly by the federal government. In this way, the Republican Party was able to use the wartime emergency to fulfill the Whig-Republican dream of a federally-controlled centralized banking system able to inflate the supply of money and credit in a uniform manner. Meshing with this was a profound political goal: As Sherman expressly pointed out, a vital object of the national banking system was to eradicate the embarrassing doctrine of state's rights and to nationalize American politics.[119]

As established in the bank acts of 1863 and 1864, the national banking system provided for the chartering of national banks by the Office of the Comptroller of the Currency in Washington, D.C. The banks were "free" in that any institution meeting the requirements could obtain a charter, but the requirements were so high (from $50,000 for rural banks to $200,000 in the bigger cities) that small national banks were ruled out, particularly in the large cities.[120]

The national banking system created three sets of national banks: *central reserve city*, which was only New York; *reserve city*, others cities with over 500,000 population; and *country*, which included all other national banks.

Central reserve city banks were required to keep 25 percent of their notes and deposits in reserve of vault cash or "lawful money," which included gold, silver, and greenbacks. This

[119]In his important work on Northern intellectuals and the Civil War, George Frederickson discusses an influential article by one Samuel Fowler written at the end of the war:

> The Civil War which has changed the current of our ideas, and crowded into a few years the emotions of a lifetime," Fowler wrote, "has in measure given to the preceding period of our history the character of a remote state of political existence." Fowler described the way in which the war, a triumph of nationalism and a demonstration of "the universal tendency to combination," had provided the *coup de grace* for the Jefferson philosophy of government with its emphasis on decentralization and the protection of local and individual liberties. (George Frederickson, *The Inner Civil War: Northern Intellectuals and the Crisis of the Union* [New York: Harper and Row, 1965], p. 184)

See also Merrill D. Peterson, *The Jeffersonian Image in the American Mind* (New York: Oxford University Press, 1960), pp. 217–18.

[120]For a particularly lucid exposition of the structure of the national banking system, see John J. Klein, *Money and the Economy*, 2nd ed. (New York: Harcourt, Brace and World, 1970), pp. 140–47.

provision incorporated the "reserve requirement" concept that had been a feature of the "free" banking system. Reserve city banks, on the other hand, were allowed to keep one-half of their required reserves in vault cash, while the other half could be kept as demand deposits (checking deposits) in central reserve city banks. Finally, country banks only had to keep a minimum reserve ratio of 15 percent of their notes and deposits; and only 40 percent of these reserves had to be in the form of vault cash. The other 60 percent could be in the form of demand deposits either at reserve city or central reserve city banks.

The upshot of this system was to replace the individualized structure of the pre–Civil War state banking system by an inverted pyramid of country banks expanding on top of reserve city banks, which in turn expanded on top of New York City banks. Before the Civil War, every bank had to keep its own specie reserves, and any pyramiding of notes and deposits on top of that was severely limited by calls for redemption in specie by other, competing banks as well as by the general public. But now, reserve city banks could keep half of their reserves as deposits in New York City banks, and country banks could keep most of theirs in one or the other, so that as a result, all the national banks in the country could pyramid in two layers on top of the relatively small base of reserves in the New York banks. And furthermore, those reserves could consist of inflated greenbacks as well as specie.

A simplified schematic diagram can portray the essence of this revolution in American banking:

Figure 1

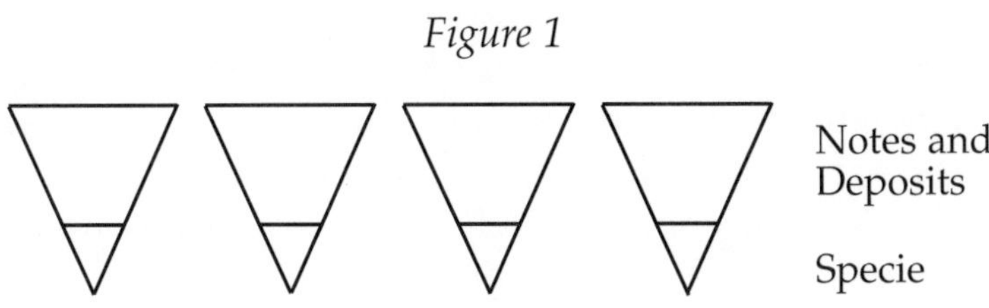

Figure 1 shows state banks in the decentralized system before the Civil War. Every bank must stand or fall on its bottom. It can pyramid notes and deposits on top of specie, but its room for such inflationary expansion is limited, because any bank's expansion will cause increased spending by its clients on the goods or services of other banks. Notes or checks on the expanding bank will go into the coffers of other banks, which will call on the expanding bank for redemption. This will put severe pressure on the expanding bank, which cannot redeem all of its liabilities as it is, and whose reserve ratio has declined, so it will be forced to either contract its loans and liabilities or else go under.

Figure 2

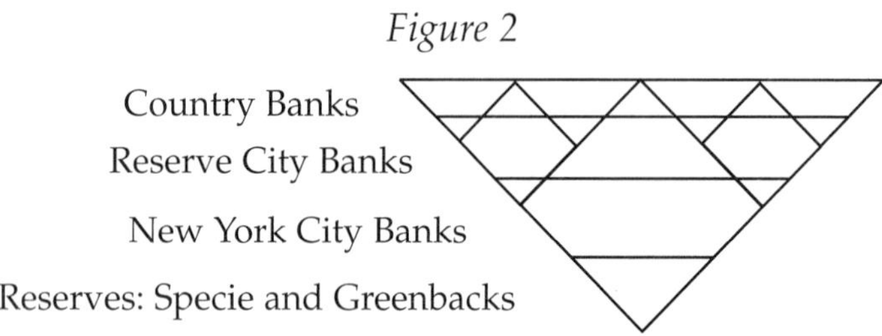

Figure 2 depicts the inverted pyramid of the national banking system. New York City banks pyramid notes and deposits on top of specie and greenbacks; reserve city banks pyramid their notes and deposits on top of specie, greenbacks, *and* deposits at New York City; and country banks pyramid on top of both. This means that, for example, if New York City banks inflate and expand their notes and deposits, they will not be checked by other banks calling upon them for redemption. Instead, reserve city banks will be able to expand their own loans and liabilities by pyramiding on top of their own increased deposits at New York banks. In turn, the country banks will be able to inflate their credit by pyramiding on top of their increased deposits at both reserve city and New York banks. The whole nation is able to inflate uniformly and relatively unchecked by pyramiding on top of a few New York City banks.

The national banks were not compelled to keep part of their reserves as deposits in larger banks, but they tended to do so—in the long run, so that they could expand uniformly on top of the larger banks, and in the short run because of the advantages of having a line of credit with a larger "correspondent" bank as well as earning interest on demand deposits at that bank.[121]

Let us illustrate in another way how the national banking system pyramided by centralizing reserves. Let us consider the hypothetical balance sheets of the various banks.[122] Suppose that the country banks begin with $1 million in vault cash as their reserves. With the national banking system in place, the country banks can now deposit three-fifths, or $600,000, of their cash in reserve city banks, in return for interest-paying demand deposits at those banks.

The balance-sheet changes are now as follows:

COUNTRY BANKS

Assets		Liabilities + Equity	
Reserves			
Vault cash	– $600,000		
Deposits at reserve city banks	+ $600,000		

RESERVE CITY BANKS

Assets		Liabilities + Equity	
Reserves			
Vault cash	+ $600,000	Demand deposits due country banks	+ $600,000

[121]Banks generally paid interest on demand deposits until the practice was outlawed in 1934.

[122]Adapted from Klein, *Money and the Economy*, pp. 144–45.

Total reserves for the two sets of banks have not changed. But now because the country banks can use as their reserves deposits in reserve city banks, the same total reserves can be used by the banks to expand far more of their credit. For now $400,000 in cash supports the same total of notes and deposits that the country banks had previously backed by $1 million, and the reserve city banks can now expand $2.4 million on top of the new $600,000 in cash—or rather, $1.8 million in addition to the $600,000 due to the city banks. In short, country bank reserves have remained the same, but reserve city bank reserves have increased by $600,000, and they can engage in 4-to-1 pyramiding of credit on top of that.

But that is not all. The reserve city banks can deposit half of their reserves at the New York banks. When they do that, then the balance sheets of the respective banks change as follows:

RESERVE CITY BANKS

Assets		Liabilities + Equity	
Reserves			
Vault cash	+ $300,000		
Deposits at central reserve city banks	+ $300,000	Demand deposits due country banks	+ $600,000

CENTRAL RESERVE CITY BANKS

Assets		Liabilities + Equity	
Reserves			
Vault cash	+ $300,000	Demand deposits due reserve city banks	+ $300,000

Note that since the reserve city banks are allowed to keep half of their reserves in the central reserve city banks, the former can still pyramid $2.4 million on top of their new $600,000, and yet deposit $300,000 in cash at the New York banks. The latter, then, can expand another 4-to-1 on top of the new cash of $300,000, or increase their total notes and deposits to $1.2 million.

In short, not only did the national banking system allow pyramiding of the entire banking structure on top of a few large Wall Street banks, but the very initiating of the system allowed a multiple expansion of all bank liabilities by centralizing a large part of the nation's cash reserves from the individual state banks into the hands of the larger, and especially the New York, banks. For the expansion of $1.2 million on top of the new $300,000 at New York banks served to expand the liabilities going to the smaller banks, which in turn could pyramid on top of their increased deposits. But even without that further expansion, $1 million which, we will assume, originally supported $6 million in notes and deposits, will now support, in addition to that $6 million, $2.4 million issued by the reserve city banks, and $1.2 million by the New York banks—to say nothing of further expansion by the latter two sets of banks which will allow country banks to pyramid more liabilities.

In June 1874, the fundamental structure of the national banking system was changed when Congress, as part of an inflationist move after the panic of 1873, eliminated all reserve requirements on notes, keeping them only on deposits. This released over $20 million of lawful money from bank reserves and allowed a further pyramiding of demand liabilities.[123] In the long run, it severed the treatment of notes from deposits, with notes tied rigidly to bank holdings of government debt, and demand deposits pyramiding on top of reserve ratios in specie and greenbacks.

[123]See Hepburn, *History of Currency*, pp. 317–18.

But this centralized inverse pyramiding of bank credit was not all. For, in a way modeled by the "free" banking system, every national bank's expansion of notes was tied intimately to its ownership of U.S. government bonds. Every bank could only issue notes if it deposited an equivalent of U.S. securities as collateral at the U.S. Treasury,[124] so that national banks could only expand their notes to the extent that they purchased U.S. government bonds. This provision tied the national banking system intimately to the federal government, and more particularly, to its expansion of public debt. The federal government had an assured, built-in market for its debt, and the more the banks purchased that debt, the more the banking system could inflate. Monetizing the public debt was not only inflationary per se, it provided the basis—when done by the larger city banks—of other banks pyramiding on top of their own monetary expansion.

The tie-in and the pyramiding process were cemented by several other provisions. Every national bank was obliged to redeem the obligations of every other national bank at par. Thus, the severe market limitation on the circulation of inflated notes and deposits—depreciation as the distance from the bank increases—was abolished. And while the federal government could not exactly make the notes of a private bank legal tender, it conferred quasi–legal tender status on every national bank by agreeing to receive all its notes and deposits at par for dues and taxes.[125] It is interesting and even heartening to discover that despite these enormous advantages conferred by the federal government, national bank notes fell below par with greenbacks in the financial crisis of 1867, and a number of national banks failed the next year.[126]

[124]Originally, national banks could only issue notes to the value 90 percent of their U.S. government bonds. This limitation was changed to 100 percent in 1900.

[125]Except, of course, as we have seen with the greenbacks, for payment of customs duties, which had to be paid in gold, to build up a fund to pay interest on the government debt in gold.

[126]See Smith, *Rationale*, p. 48.

Genuine redeemability, furthermore, was made very difficult under the national banking system. Laxity was ensured by the fact that national banks were required to redeem the notes and deposits of every other national bank at par, and yet it was made difficult for them to actually redeem those liabilities in specie; for one of the problems with the pre–Civil War state banking system was that interstate or even intrastate branches were illegal, thereby hobbling the clearing system for swiftly redeeming another bank's notes and deposits. One might think that a national banking system would at least eliminate this problem, but on the contrary, branch banking continued to be prohibited, and interstate branch banking is illegal to this day.* A bank would only have to redeem its notes at its own counter in its home office. Furthermore, the redemption of notes was crippled by the fact that the federal government imposed a maximum limit of $3 million a month by which national bank notes could be contracted.[127]

Reserve requirements are now considered a sound and precise way to limit bank credit expansion, but the precision can work two ways. Just as government safety codes can *decrease* safety by setting a lower limit for safety measures and inducing private firms to reduce safety *downward* to that common level, so reserve requirements can and ordinarily do serve as lowest common denominators for bank reserve ratios. Free competition can and generally will result in banks voluntarily keeping higher reserve ratios. But a uniform legal requirement will tend to push all the banks down to that minimum ratio. And indeed we can see this now in the universal propensity of all banks to be "fully loaned up," that is, to expand as much as is legally possible up to the limits imposed by the legal reserve ratio. Reserve

[127]Ibid., p. 132.

*[*Congress eliminated federal restrictions on interstate banking and branching in September 1994, with the passage of the Riegle-Neal Interstate Banking and Branching Efficiency Act.*—Ed.]

requirements of less than 100 percent are more an inflationary than a restrictive monetary device.

The national banking system was intended to replace the state banks, but many state banks continued aloof and refused to join, despite the special privileges accorded to the national banks. The reserve and capital requirements were more onerous, and at that period, national banks were prohibited from making loans on real estate. With the state banks refusing to come to heel voluntarily, Congress, in March 1865, completed the Civil War revolution of the banking system by placing a prohibitive 10-percent tax on all bank notes—which had the desired effect of virtually outlawing all note issues by the state banks. From 1865 on, the national banks had a legal monopoly on the issue of bank notes.

At first, the state banks contracted and disappeared under the shock, and it looked as if the United States would only have national banks. The number of state banks fell from 1,466 in 1863 to 297 in 1866, and total notes and deposits in state banks fell from $733 million in 1863 to only $101 million in 1866. After several years, however, the state banks readily took their place as an expanding element in the banking system, albeit subordinated to the national banks. In order to survive, the state banks had to keep deposit accounts at national banks, from whom they could "buy" national bank notes in order to redeem their deposits. In short, the state banks now became the fourth layer of the national pyramid of money and credit, on top of the country and other banks, for the reserves of the state banks became, in addition to vault cash, demand deposits at national banks, which they could redeem in cash. The multi-layered structure of bank inflation under the national banking system was intensified.

In this new structure, the state banks began to flourish. By 1873, the total number of state banks had increased to 1,330, and their total deposits were $789 million.[128]

[128]*Historical Statistics*, pp. 628–29.

The Cooke-Chase connection with the new national banking system was simple. As secretary of the Treasury, Chase wanted an assured market for the government bonds that were being issued so heavily during the Civil War. And as the monopoly underwriter of U.S. government bonds for every year except one from 1862 to 1873, Jay Cooke was even more directly interested in an assured and expanding market for his bonds. What better method of obtaining such a market than creating an entirely new banking system, the expansion of which was directly tied to the banks' purchases of government bonds—from Jay Cooke?

The Cooke brothers played a major role in driving the National Banking Act of 1863 through a reluctant Congress. The Democrats, devoted to hard money, opposed the legislation almost to a man. Only a majority of Republicans could be induced to agree on the bill. After John Sherman's decisive speech in the Senate for the measure, Henry Cooke—now head of the Washington office of the House of Cooke—wrote jubilantly to his brother:

> It will be a great triumph, Jay, and one to which we have contributed more than any other living man. The bank had been repudiated by the House, and was without a sponsor in the Senate, and was thus virtually dead and buried when I induced Sherman to take hold of it, and we went to work with the newspapers.[129]

Going to work with the newspapers meant something more than mere persuasion for the Cooke brothers; as monopoly underwriter of government bonds, Cooke was paying the newspapers large sums for advertising, and so the Cookes thought—as it turned out correctly—that they could induce the newspapers to grant them an enormous amount of free space "in which to set forth the merits of the new national banking

[129]Quoted in Robert P. Sharkey, *Money, Class, and Party: An Economic Study of Civil War and Reconstruction* (Baltimore, Md.: The Johns Hopkins Press, 1959), p. 245.

system." Such space meant not only publicity and articles, but even more important, the fervent editorial support of most of the nation's press. And so the press, implicitly bought for the occasion, kept up a drumfire of propaganda for the new national banking system. As Cooke himself related:

> For six weeks or more nearly all the newspapers in the country were filled with our editorials [written by the Cooke brothers] condemning the state bank system and explaining the great benefits to be derived from the national banking system now proposed.

And every day the indefatigable Cookes put on the desks of every member of Congress the relevant editorials from newspapers in their respective districts.[130]

While many state bankers, especially the conservative old-line New York bankers, opposed the national banking system, Jay Cooke, once the system was in place, plunged in with a will. Not only did he sell the national banks their required bonds, he also set up new national banks which would have to buy his government securities. His agents formed national banks in the smaller towns of the south and west. Furthermore, he set up two large national banks, the First National Bank of Philadelphia and the First National Bank of Washington, D.C.

But the national banking system was in great need of a mighty bank in New York City to serve as the base of the inflationary pyramid for a host of country and reserve city banks. Shortly after the inception of the system, three national banks had been organized in New York, but none of them were large enough or prestigious enough to serve as the key fulcrum of the new banking structure. Jay Cooke, however, was happy to oblige, and he quickly established the Fourth National Bank of New York, capitalized at a huge $5 million. After the war, Jay Cooke favored resumption of specie payments, but only if greenbacks could be replaced one-to-one by new national bank notes. In his unbounded enthusiasm for national bank

[130]See Hammond, *Sovereignty*, pp. 289–90.

notes and their dependence on the federal debt, Cooke urged repeal of the $300 million legal limit on national bank note issue. In 1865, he published a pamphlet proclaiming that in less than 20 years national bank note circulation would total $1 billion.[131]

The title of the pamphlet Cooke published is revealing: *How Our National Debt May Be A National Blessing. The Debt is Public Wealth, Political Union, Protection of Industry, Secure Basis for National Currency*.[132]

By 1866, it was clear that the national banking system had replaced the state as the center of the monetary system of the United States. Only a year earlier, in 1865, state bank notes had totaled $142.9 million; by 1866 they had collapsed to $20 million. On the one hand, national bank notes grew from a mere $31.2 million in 1864, their first year of existence, to $276 million in 1866. And while, as we have seen, the number of state banks in existence was falling drastically from 1,466 to 297, the number of national banks grew in that same period, from 66 in 1863 to 1,634 three years later.

THE POST–CIVIL WAR ERA: 1865–1879

The United States ended the war with a depreciated inconvertible greenback currency, and a heavy burden of public debt. The first question on the monetary agenda was what to do about the greenbacks. A powerful group of industrialists calling for continuation of greenbacks, opposing resumption and, of course, any contraction of money to prepare for specie resumption, was headed by the Pennsylvania iron and steel manufacturers. The Pennsylvania ironmasters, who had been in the forefront of the organized protective tariff movement since its beginnings in

[131]Actually, Cooke erred, and national bank notes never reached that total. Instead, it was demand deposits that expanded, and reached the billion-dollar mark by 1879.

[132]See Sharkey, *Money, Class, and Party*, p. 247.

1820,[133] were led here and instructed by their intellectual mentor—himself a Pennsylvania ironmaster—the elderly economist Henry C. Carey. Carey and his fellow iron manufacturers realized that during an inflation, since the foreign exchange market anticipates further inflation, domestic currency tends to depreciate faster than domestic prices are rising. A falling dollar and a rising price of gold, they realized, make domestic prices cheaper and imported prices higher, and hence function as a surrogate tariff. A cheap-money, inflationist policy, then, could not only provide easy credit for manufacturing, it could also function as an extra tariff because of the depreciation of the dollar and the rise in the gold premium.

Imbibers of the Carey gospel of high tariffs and soft money were a host of attendees at the famous "Carey Vespers"—evenings of discussion of economics and politics. Influential Carey disciples included economist and Pennsylvania ironmaster Stephen Colwell; Eber Ward, president of the Iron and Steel Association; John A. Williams, editor of the association's journal, *Iron Age*; Representative Daniel Morrell, Pennsylvania iron manufacturer; I. Smith Homans, Jr., editor of *The Bankers Magazine*; and powerful U.S. Representative William D. Kelley of Pennsylvania, whose lifelong devotion to the interest of the ironmasters earned him the proud sobriquet "Old Pig Iron." The Carey circle also dominated the American Industrial League, which spread the Carey doctrines of protection and paper money. Influential allies in Congress, if not precisely Carey followers, were the radical leader Representative Thaddeus Stevens, himself a Pennsylvania ironmaster, and Representative John A. Griswold, an ironmaster from New York.

Also sympathetic to greenbacks were many manufacturers who desired cheap credit, gold speculators who were betting on

[133]The leader of the protectionists in Congress in 1820 was Representative Henry Baldwin, a leading iron manufacturer from Pittsburgh. Rothbard, *Panic of 1819*, pp. 164 ff.

higher gold prices, and railroads, which as heavy debtors to their bondholders, realized that inflation benefits debtors by cheapening the dollar whereas it also tends to expropriate creditors by the same token. One of the influential Carey disciples, for example, was the leading railroad promoter, the Pennsylvanian Thomas A. Scott, leading entrepreneur of the Pennsylvania and the Texas and Pacific Railroads.[134]

One of the most flamboyant advocates of greenback inflation in the postwar era was the Wall Street stock speculator Richard Schell. In 1874, Schell became a member of Congress, where he proposed an outrageous pre-Keynesian scheme in the spirit of Keynes's later dictum that so long as money is *spent*, it doesn't matter what the money is spent on, be it pyramid-building or digging holes in the ground.[135] Schell seriously urged the federal government to dig a canal from New York to San Francisco, financed wholly by the issue of greenbacks. Schell's enthusiasm was perhaps matched only by that of the notorious railroad speculator and economic adventurer George Francis Train, who called repeatedly for immense issues of greenbacks. Train thundered in 1867:

[134]On the Carey circle and its influence, see Irwin Unger, *The Greenback Era: A Social and Political History of American Finance, 1865–1879* (Princeton, N.J.: Princeton University Press, 1964), pp. 53–59; and Joseph Dorfman, *The Economic Mind in American Civilization*, vol. 3, *1864–1918* (New York: Viking Press, 1949), pp. 7–8. Dorfman notes that Congressman Kelley dedicated his collected *Speeches, Addresses, and Letters on Industrial and Financial Questions* of 1872 to "The Great Master of Economic Science, The Profound Thinker, and the Careful Observer of Social Phenomena, My Venerable Friend and Teacher, Henry C. Carey." Ibid., p. 8. On the link between high tariffs and greenbacks for the Pennsylvania ironmasters, see Sharkey, *Money, Class, and Party*, chap. 4.

[135]Thus, Keynes wrote: "'To dig holes in the ground,' paid for out of savings will increase, not only employment, but the real national dividend of useful goods and services." John Maynard Keynes, *The General Theory of Employment, Interest and Money* (New York: Harcourt, Brace, 1936), p. 220. On pyramid-building, see ibid., pp. 131, 220.

> Give us greenbacks we say, and build cities, plant corn, open coal mines, control railways, launch ships, grow cotton, establish factories, open gold and silver mines, erect rolling mills. . . . Carry my resolution and there is sunshine in the sky.[136]

The panic of 1873 was a severe blow to many overbuilt railroads, and it was railroad men who led in calling for more greenbacks to stem the tide. Thomas Scott; Collis P. Huntington, leader of the Central Pacific Railroad; Russel Sage; and other railroad men joined in the call for greenbacks. So strong was their influence that the *Louisville Courier-Journal*, in April 1874, declared: "The strongest influence at work in Washington upon the currency proceeded from the railroads. . . . The great inflationists after all, are the great trunk railroads."[137]

The greenback problem after the Civil War was greatly complicated by the massive public debt that lay over the heads of the American people. A federal debt, which had tallied only $64.7 million in 1860, amounted to the huge amount of $2.32 billion in 1866. Many ex-Jacksonian Democrats, led by Senator George H. Pendleton of Ohio, began to agitate for further issue of greenbacks *solely* for the purpose of redeeming the principal of federal debts contracted in greenbacks during the war.[138] In a sense, then, hard-money hostility to both inflation and the public debt were now at odds. In a sense, the Pendletonians were motivated by a sense of poetic justice, of paying inflated debts in inflated paper, but in doing so they lost sight of the broader hard-money goal.[139] This program confused the party struggles

[136]Unger, *Greenback Era*, p. 46.

[137]Ibid., p. 222.

[138]The federal government had contracted to redeem the *interest* on the wartime public debt in gold, but nothing was contracted about the repayment of the principal.

[139]Similar motivations had impelled many hard-money anti-Federalists during the 1780s to advocate the issue of state paper money for the *sole* purpose of redeeming swollen wartime public debts.

of the post–Civil War period, but ultimately it is safe to say that the Democrats had a far greater proportion of congressmen devoted to hard money and to resumption than did the Republicans. Thus, Secretary of the Treasury Hugh McCulloch's "Loan Bill" of March 1866, which provided for contraction of greenbacks in preparation for resumption of specie payments, was passed in the House by a Republican vote of 56–52, and a Democratic vote of 27–1. And in April 1874, the "Inflation Bill," admittedly vetoed later by President Grant, which provided for expansion of greenbacks and of national bank notes, was passed in the House by a Republican vote of 105–64, while the Democrats voted against by the narrow margin of 35–37.[140]

In the meantime, despite repeated resolutions for resumption of specie payments in 1865 and 1869, the dominant Republican Party continued to do nothing for actual resumption. The Pendleton Plan was adopted by the Democrats in their 1868 platform, and the Republican victory in the presidential race that year was generally taken as a conclusive defeat for that idea. Finally, however, the Democratic sweep in the congressional elections of 1874 forced the Republicans into a semblance of unity on monetary matters, and, in the lame-duck congressional session led by Senator John Sherman, they came up with the Resumption Act of January 1875.

Despite the fact that the Resumption Act ultimately resulted in specie resumption, it was not considered a hard-money victory by contemporaries. Sherman had forged a compromise between hard- and soft-money forces. It is true that the U.S. government was supposed to buy gold with government bonds to prepare for resumption on January 1, 1879. But this resumption was four years off, and Congress had expressed intent to resume several times before. And in the meantime, the soft-money men were appeased by the fact that the bill immediately eliminated the

[140]On the McCulloch Loan Bill, see Sharkey, *Money, Class, and Party,* p. 75; on the Inflation Bill, see Unger, *Greenback Era*, p. 410.

$300 million limit on national bank notes, in a provision known as "free banking." The only hard-money compensation was an 80-percent pro rata contraction of greenbacks to partially offset any new national bank notes.[141] The bulk of the opposition to the Resumption Act was by hard-money congressmen, who, in addition to pointing out its biased ambiguities, charged that the contracted greenbacks could be reissued instead of retired. Hard-money forces throughout the country had an equally scornful view of the Resumption Act. In a few years, however, they rallied as resumption drew near.

That the Republicans were generally less than enthusiastic about specie resumption was revealed by the Grant administration's reaction to the Supreme Court's decision in the first legal tender case. After the end of the war, the question of the constitutionality of legal tender came before the courts (we have seen that the California and Oregon courts decided irredeemable paper to be unconstitutional). In the large number of state court decisions on greenbacks before 1870, every Republican judge but one upheld their constitutionality, whereas every Democratic judge but two declared them unconstitutional.[142]

The greenback question reached the U.S. Supreme Court in 1867, and was decided in February 1870, in the case of *Hepburn v. Griswold*. The Court held, by a vote of 5–3, with all the Democratic judges voting with the majority and the Republicans in the minority. Chief Justice Salmon P. Chase, who delivered the decision denouncing his own action as secretary of the Treaury as unnecessary and unconstitutional, had swung back to the Democratic Party and had actually been a candidate for the presidential nomination at the 1868 convention.

[141]This political and compromise interpretation of the Resumption Act successfully revises the previous hard-money view of this measure. See Unger, *Greenback Era*, pp. 249–63.

[142]See Charles Fairman, "Mr. Justice Bradley's Appointment to the Supreme Court and the Legal Tender Cases," *Harvard Law Review* (May 1941): 1131; cited in Unger, *Greenback Era*, p. 174.

The Grant administration was upset by *Hepburn v. Griswold*, as were the railroads, who had accumulated a heavy long-term debt, which would now be payable in more valuable gold. As luck would have it, however, there were two vacancies on the Court, one of which was created by the retirement of one of the majority judges. Grant appointed not only two Republican judges, but two railroad lawyers whose views on the subject were already known.[143] The new 5–4 majority dutifully and quickly reconsidered the question, and, in May 1871, reversed the previous Court in the fateful decision of *Knox v. Lee*. From then on, paper money would be held consonant with the U.S. Constitution.

The national banking system was ensconced after the Civil War. The number of banks, national bank notes, and deposits all pyramided upward, and after 1870 state banks began to boom as deposit-creating institutions. With lower requirements and fewer restrictions than the national banks, they could pyramid on top of national banks. The number of national banks increased from 1,294 in 1865 to 1,968 in 1873, while the number of state banks rose from 349 to 1,330 in the same period. Total state and national bank notes and deposits rose from $835 million in 1865 to $1.964 billion in 1873, an increase of 135.2 percent or an increase of 16.9 percent per year. The following year, the supply of bank money leveled off as the panic of 1873 struck and caused numerous bankruptcies.

[143]The first new justice, William Strong of Pennsylvania, had been a top attorney for the Philadelphia and Reading Railroad, and a director of the Lebanon Valley Railroad. The second jurist, Joseph P. Bradley, was a director of the Camden and Amboy Railroad and of the Morris and Essex Railroad, in New Jersey. On the railroad ties of Strong and Bradley, see Philip H. Burch, Jr., *Elites in American History*, vol. 2, *The Civil War to the New Deal* (New York: Holmes and Meier, 1981), pp. 44–45. On the reaction of the Grant administration, see Unger, *Greenback Era*, pp. 172–78. For a legal analysis of the decisions, see Hepburn, *History of Currency*, pp. 254–64; and *Government's Money Monopoly*, Henry Mark Holzer, ed. (New York: Books in Focus, 1981), pp. 99–168.

As a general overview of the national banking period, we can agree with Klein that

> The financial panics of 1873, 1884, 1893, and 1907 were in large part an outgrowth of . . . reserve pyramiding and excessive deposit creation by reserve city and central reserve city banks. These panics were triggered by the currency drains that took place in periods of relative prosperity when banks were loaned up.[144]

And yet it must be pointed out that the total money supply, even merely the supply of bank money, did not decrease after the panic, but merely leveled off.

Orthodox economic historians have long complained about the "great depression" that is supposed to have struck the United States in the panic of 1873 and lasted for an unprecedented six years, until 1879. Much of this stagnation is supposed to have been caused by a monetary contraction leading to the resumption of specie payments in 1879. Yet what sort of "depression" is it which saw an extraordinarily large expansion of industry, of railroads, of physical output, of net national product, or real per capita income? As Friedman and Schwartz admit, the decade from 1869 to 1879 saw a 3-percent-per-annum increase in money national product, an outstanding real national product growth of 6.8 percent per year in this period, and a phenomenal rise of 4.5 percent per year in real product per capita. Even the alleged "monetary contraction" never took place, the money supply increasing by 2.7 percent per year in this period. From 1873 through 1878, before another spurt of monetary expansion, the total supply of bank money *rose* from $1.964 billion to $2.221 billion—a rise of 13.1 percent or 2.6 percent per year. In short, a modest but definite rise, and scarcely a *contraction*.

It should be clear, then, that the "great depression" of the 1870s is merely a myth—a myth brought about by misinterpretation of

[144]Klein, *Money and the Economy*, pp. 145–46.

the fact that prices in general fell sharply during the entire period. Indeed they fell from the end of the Civil War until 1879. Friedman and Schwartz estimated that prices in general fell from 1869 to 1879 by 3.8 percent per annum. Unfortunately, most historians and economists are conditioned to believe that steadily and sharply falling prices *must* result in depression: hence their amazement at the obvious prosperity and economic growth during this era. For they have overlooked the fact that in the natural course of events, when government and the banking system do not increase the money supply very rapidly, free-market capitalism will result in an increase of production and economic growth so great as to swamp the increase of money supply. Prices will fall, and the consequences will be not depression or stagnation, but prosperity (since costs are falling, too) economic growth, and the spread of the increased living standard to all the consumers.[145]

Indeed, recent research has discovered that the analogous "great depression" in England in this period was also a myth, and due to a confusion between a contraction of prices and its alleged inevitable effect on a depression of prices and its alleged inevitable effect on a depression of business activity.[146]

It might well be that the major effect of the panic of 1873 was, not to initiate a great depression, but to cause bankruptcies in overinflated banks and in railroads riding on the tide of vast government subsidy and bank speculation. In particular, we may note Jay Cooke, one of the creators of the national banking system and paladin of the public debt. In 1866, he favored contraction of the greenbacks and early resumption

[145]For the bemusement of Friedman and Schwartz, see Milton Friedman and Anna Jacobson Schwartz, *A Monetary History of the United States, 1867–1960* (New York: National Bureau of Economic Research, 1963), pp. 33–44. On totals of bank money, see *Historical Statistics,* pp. 624–25.

[146]S.B. Saul, *The Myth of the Great Depression, 1873–1896* (London: Macmillan, 1969).

because he feared that inflation would destroy the value of government bonds. By the late 1860s, however, the House of Cooke was expanding everywhere, and in particular, had gotten control of the new Northern Pacific Railroad. Northern Pacific had been the recipient of the biggest federal largesse to railroads during the 1860s: a land grant of no less than 47 million acres.

Cooke sold Northern Pacific bonds as he had learned to sell government securities: hiring pamphleteers to write propaganda about the alleged Mediterranean climate of the Northwest. Many leading government officials and politicians were on the Cooke–Northern Pacific payroll, including President Grant's private secretary, General Horace Porter.

In 1869, Cooke expressed his monetary philosophy in keeping with his enlarged sphere of activity:

> Why should this Grand and Glorious Country be stunted and dwarfed—its activities chilled and its very life blood curdled by these miserable "hard coin" theories—the musty theories of a by gone age—These men who are urging on premature resumption know nothing of the great growing west which would grow twice as fast if it was not cramped for the means necessary to build RailRoads and improve farms and convey the produce to market.

But in 1873, a remarkable example of poetic justice struck Jay Cooke. The overbuilt Northern Pacific was crumbling, and a Cooke government bond operation provided a failure. So the mighty House of Cooke—"stunted and dwarfed" by the market economy—crashed and went bankrupt, touching off the panic of 1873.[147]

After passing the Resumption Act in 1875, the Republicans finally stumbled their way into resumption in 1879, fully 14 years after the end of the Civil War. The money supply did not contract in the late 1870s because the Republicans did not have

[147]Unger, *Greenback Era*, pp. 47 and 221.

the will to contract in order to pave the way for resumption. Resumption was finally achieved after substantial sales of U.S. bonds for gold in Europe by Secretary of the Treasury Sherman.

Return to the gold standard in 1879 was almost blocked, in the last three years before resumption, by the emergence of a tremendous agitation, heavily in the West but also throughout the country, for the free coinage of silver. The United States mint ratios had been undervaluing silver since 1834, and in 1853 de facto gold monometallism was established because silver was so far undervalued as to drive fractional silver coins out of the country. Since 1853, the United States, while de jure on a bimetallic standard at 16-to-1, with the silver dollar still technically in circulation though nonexistent, was actually on a gold monometallic standard with lightweight subsidiary silver coins for fractional use.

In 1872, it became apparent to a few knowledgeable men at the U.S. Treasury that silver, which had held at about 15.5-to-1 since the early 1860s, was about to suffer a huge decline in value. The major reason was the realization that European nations were shifting from a silver to a gold standard, thereby decreasing their demand for silver. A subsidiary reason was the discovery of silver mines in Nevada and other states in the West. Working rapidly, these Treasury men, along with Senator Sherman, slipped through Congress in February 1873 a seemingly innocuous bill which in effect discontinued the minting of any further silver dollars. This was followed by an act of June 1874, which completed the demonetization of silver by ending the legal tender quality of all silver dollars above the sum of $5. The timing was perfect, since it was in 1874 that the market value of silver fell to greater than 16-to-1 to gold for the first time. From then on, the market price of silver fell steadily, declining to nearly 18-to-1 in 1876, over 18-to-1 in 1879, and reaching the phenomenal level of 32-to-1 in 1894.

In short, after 1874, silver was no longer undervalued but overvalued, and increasingly so, in terms of gold, at 16-to-1.

Except for the acts of 1873 and 1874, labeled by the pro-silver forces as "The Crime of 1873," silver would have flowed into the United States, and the country would have been once again on a de facto monometallic silver standard. The champions of greenbacks, the champions of inflation, saw a "hard-money" way to increase greatly the amount of American currency: the remonetization of a flood of new overvalued silver. The agitation was to remonetize silver by "the free and unlimited coinage of silver at 16-to-1."

It should be recognized that the silverites had a case. The demonetization of silver was a "crime" in the sense that it was done shiftily, deceptively, by men who knew that they wanted to demonetize silver before it was too late and have silver replace gold. The case for gold over silver was a strong one, particularly in an era of rapidly falling value of silver, but it should have been made openly and honestly. The furtive method of demonetizing silver, the "crime against silver," was in part responsible for the vehemence of the silver agitation for the remainder of the century.[148]

Ultimately, the administration was able to secure the resumption of payments in gold, but at the expense of submitting to the Bland-Allison Act of 1878, which mandated that the Treasury purchase $2 million to $4 million of silver per month from then on.

It should be noted that this first silver agitation of the late 1870s, at least, cannot be considered an "agrarian" or a particularly Southern and Western movement. The silver agitation was broadly based throughout the nation, except in New England, and was, moreover, an urban movement. As Weinstein points out:

[148]For the best discussion of the crime against silver, see Allen Weinstein, *Prelude to Populism: Origins of the Silver Issue, 1867–1878* (New Haven, Conn.: Yale University Press, 1970), pp. 8–32. See also Paul M. O'Leary, "The Scene of the Crime of 1873 Revisited: A Note," *Journal of Political Economy* 68 (1960): 388–92.

> Silver began as an urban movement, furthermore, not an agrarian crusade. Its original strongholds were the large towns and cities of the Midwest and middle Atlantic states, not the country's farming communities. The first batch of bimetallist leaders were a loosely knit collection of hard money newspaper editors, businessmen, academic reformers, bankers, and commercial groups.[149]

With the passage of the Silver Purchase Act of 1878, silver agitation died out in America, to spring up again in the 1890s.

THE GOLD STANDARD ERA WITH THE NATIONAL BANKING SYSTEM, 1879–1913

The record of 1879–1896 was very similar to the first stage of the alleged great depression from 1873 to 1879. Once again, we had a phenomenal expansion of American industry, production, and real output per head. Real reproducible, tangible wealth per capita rose at the decadal peak in American history in the 1880s, at 3.8 percent per annum. Real net national product rose at the rate of 3.7 percent per year from 1879 to 1897, while per-capita net national product increased by 1.5 percent per year.

Once again, orthodox economic historians are bewildered, for there should have been a great depression, since prices fell at a rate of over 1 percent per year in this period. Just as in the previous period, the money supply grew, but not fast enough to overcome the great increases in productivity and the supply of products. The major difference in the two periods is that money supply rose more rapidly from 1879 to 1897, by 6 percent per year, compared with the 2.7 percent per year in the earlier era. As a result, prices fell by less, by over 1 percent per annum as contrasted to 3.8 percent. Total bank money, notes, and deposits rose from $2.45 billion to $6.06 billion in this period, a rise of

[149]Weinstein, *Prelude to Populism*, p. 356.

10.45 percent per annum—surely enough to satisfy all but the most ardent inflationists.[150]

For those who persist in associating a gold standard with deflation, it should be pointed out that price deflation in the gold standard 1879–1897 period was considerably less than price deflation from 1873 to 1879, when the United States was still on a fiat greenback standard.

After specie resumption occurred successfully in 1879, the gold premium to greenbacks fell to par and the appreciated greenback promoted confidence in the gold-backed dollar. More foreigners willing to hold dollars meant an inflow of gold into the United States and greater American exports. Some historians have attributed the boom of 1879–1882, culminating in a financial crisis in the latter year, to the inflow of gold coin to the U.S., which rose from $110.5 million in 1879 to $358.3 million in 1882.[151] In a sense this is true, but the boom would never have taken on considerable proportions without the pyramiding of the national banking system, the deposits of which increased from $2.149 billion in 1879 to $2.777 billion in 1882, a rise of 29.2 percent, or 9.7 percent per annum. Wholesale prices were driven up from 90 in 1879 to 108 three years later, a 22.5 percent increase, before resuming their long-run downward path.

A financial panic in 1884, coming during a mild contraction after 1882, lowered the supply of bank money. Total bank notes and deposits dropped slightly, from $3.19 billion in 1883 to $3.15 billion. The panic was triggered by an overflow of gold abroad, as foreigners began to lose confidence in the willingness of the United States to remain on the gold standard. This understandable loss of confidence resulted from the inflationary sop to the pro-silver forces in the Bland-Allison Silver Purchase Act of

[150]Friedman and Schwartz, *Monetary History*, pp. 91–93; and *Historical Statistics*, p. 625.

[151]Friedman and Schwartz, *Monetary History*, pp. 98–99.

1878. The shift in Treasury balances from gold to silver struck a disquieting note in foreign financial circles.[152]

Before examining the critical decade of the 1890s, it is well to point out in some detail the excellent record of the first decade after the return to gold, 1879–1889.

America went off the gold standard in 1861 and remained off after the war's end. Arguments between hard-money advocates who wanted to eliminate unbacked greenbacks and soft-money men who wanted to increase them raged through the 1870s until the Grant administration decided in 1875 to resume redemption of paper dollars into gold at prewar value on the first day of 1879. At the time (1875) greenbacks were trading at a discount of roughly 17 percent against the prewar gold dollar. A combination of outright paper-money deflation and an increase in official gold holdings enabled a return to gold four years later, which set the scene for a decade of tremendous economic growth.

Economic recordkeeping a century ago was not nearly as well developed as today, but a clear picture comes through nonetheless. The *Encyclopedia of American Economic History* calls the period under review "one of the most expansive in American history. Capital investment was high; . . . there was little unemployment; and the real costs of production declined rapidly."

Prices, Wages, and Real Wages

This is shown most graphically with a look at wages and prices during the decade before and after convertibility. While prices fell during the 1870s and 1880s, wages only fell during the greenback period, and rose from 1879 to 1889.

The figures tell a remarkable story. Both consumer prices and nominal wages fell by about 30 percent during the last decade of greenbacks. But from 1879–1889, while prices kept falling, wages rose 23 percent. So real wages, after taking inflation—or the lack of it—into effect, soared.

[152]See Rendigs Fels, *American Business Cycle, 1865–1897* (Chapel Hill: University of North Carolina Press, 1959), pp. 130–31.

WHOLESALE PRICE INDEX

(1910–1914 = 100)

Year	Index	% Change
1869	151	—
1879	90	-40.4%
1889	81	-10.0%

CONSUMER PRICE INDEX

Year	Index	% Change
1869	138	—
1879	97	-28.8%
1889	93	-4.2%

WAGES

(1900–1914 = 100)

	Urban Labor	Farm Labor	Combined
1869	77	96	87
1879	61	61	61
1889	72	78	75

No decade before or since produced such a sustainable rise in real wages. Two possible exceptions are the periods 1909–1919 (when the index rose from 99 to 140) and 1929–1939 (134 to 194). But during the first decade real wages plummeted the next year—to 129 in 1920, and did not reach 1919's level until 1934. And during the 1930s real wages also soared, for those fortunate enough to have jobs.

In any event, the contrast to this past decade is astonishing. And while there are many reasons why real wages increase, three necessary conditions must be present. Foremost, an absence of sustained inflation. This contributes to the second condition, a rise in savings and capital formation.

People will not save if they believe their money will be worth less in the future. Finally, technological advancement is obviously important. But it is not enough. The 1970s saw this third factor present, but the absence of the first two caused real wages to fall.

Interest Rates

Sidney Homer writes in his monumental *History of Interest Rates, 2000 B.C. to the Present* that "during the last two decades of the nineteenth century (1880–1900), long-term bond yields in the United States declined almost steadily. The nation entered its first period of low long-term interest rates," finally experiencing the 3- to 3.5-percent long-term rates which had characterized Holland in the seventeenth century and Britain in the eighteenth and nineteenth: in short, the economic giants of their day.

To gauge long-term rates of the day, it is best not to use the long-term government bonds we would use today as a measure. The National Banking Acts of 1863–1864 stipulated that these bonds had to be used to secure bank notes. This created such a demand for them that, as Homer says, "by the mid 1870s [it] put government bond prices up to levels where their yields were far below acceptable rates of long-term interest." But the Commerce Department tracks the unadjusted index of yields of American railroad bonds. We list the yields for 1878, the year before gold, and for 1879, and 1889.

Railroad Bond Yields

1878	6.45%
1879	5.98%
1889	4.43%

We stress that with consumer prices about 7 percent lower in 1889 than they had been the decade before, the *real* rate of return by decade's end was well into double-digit range, a bonanza for savers and lenders.

Short-term rates during the last century were considerably more skittish than long-term rates. But even here the decennial averages of annual averages of both three- to six-month commercial paper rates and (overnight) call money during the 1880s declined from what it had been the previous decades:

	COMMERCIAL PAPER	CALL MONEY
1870–1879	6.46%	5.73%
1880–1889	5.14%	3.98%

A BURST IN PRODUCTIVITY

By some measures the 1880s was the most productive decade in our history. In their *A Monetary History of the United States, 1867–1960,* Professors Friedman and Schwartz quote R.W. Goldsmith on the subject:

> The highest decadal rate [of growth of real reproducible, tangible wealth per head from 1805 to 1950] for periods of about ten years was apparently reached in the eighties with approximately 3.8 percent.

The statistics give proof to this outpouring of new wealth.

GROSS NATIONAL PRODUCT
(1958 prices)

	Total (billions of dollars)	Per capita (in dollars)
Decade average 1869–78	$23.1	$531
Decade average 1879–88	$42.4	$774
Decade average 1889–98	$49.1	$795

This dollar growth was occurring, remember, in the face of general price declines.

GROSS DOMESTIC PRODUCT
(1929 prices in billions of dollars)

1869–1878	$11.6 (average per year)
1879–1888	$21.2 (average per year)

Gross domestic product almost doubled from the decade before, a far larger percentage jump decade-on-decade than any time since.

Labor Productivity Manufacturing Output Per Man-Hour (1958 = 100)	
1869	14.7
1879	16.2
1889	20.5

The 26.5-percent increase here ranks among the best in our history. Labor productivity reflects increased capital investment.

Capital Formation

From 1869 to 1879 the total number of business establishments barely rose, but the next decade saw a 39.4-percent increase. Nor surprisingly, a decade of falling prices, rising real income, and lucrative interest returns made for tremendous capital investment, ensuring future gains in productivity.

Purchase of Structures and Equipment (total, in 1958 prices, in billions of dollars)	
1870	$0.4
1880	$0.4
1890	$2.0

This massive 500-percent decade-on-decade increase has never since been even closely rivaled. It stands in particular contrast to the virtual stagnation witnessed by the 1970s.

Private and Public Capital Formation (total gross, in billions, 1929 prices)		
Average	1872–1876	$2.6
Average	1877–1881	$3.7
Average	1882–1886	$4.5
Average	1887–1891	$5.9

These five-year averages are not as "clean" as some other figures, but still show a rough doubling of total capital formation from the '70s to the '80s.

It has repeatedly been alleged that the late nineteenth century, the "golden age of the gold standard" in the United States, was a period especially harmful to farmers. The facts, however, tell a different story. While manufacturing in the 1880s grew more rapidly than did agriculture ("The Census of 1890," report Friedman and Schwartz, "was the first in which the net value added by manufacturing exceeded the value of agricultural output"), farmers had an excellent decade.

Number of Farms (in thousands)	
1880	4,009
1890	4,565

Farm Land (in millions of acres)	
1880	536,182
1890	623,219

Farm Productivity (persons supplied by farm worker)	
1880	5.1
1890	5.6

Value of Farm Gross Output and Product (1910-1914 dollars, in millions)	
1880	$4,129
1890	$4,990

So farms, farmland, productivity, and production all increased in the 1880s, even while commodity prices were falling. And as we see below, farm wage rates, even in nominal terms, rose during this time.

Farm Wage Rates (per month, with board and room, in 1879, 1889 dollars)	
1879 or 1880	$11.50
1889 or 1890	$13.50

This phenomenal economic growth during the decade immediately after the return to gold convertibility cannot be attributed solely to the gold standard. Indeed all during this time there was never a completely free-market monetary system. The National Banking Acts of 1863–1864 had semi-cartelized the banking system.

Only certain banks could issue money, but all other banks had to have accounts at these. The financial panics throughout the late nineteenth century were a result of the arbitrary credit-creation powers of the banking system. While not as harmful as today's inflation mechanism, it was still a storm in an otherwise fairly healthy economic climate.

The fateful decade of the 1890s saw the return of the agitation for free silver, which had lain dormant for a decade. The Republican Party intensified its longtime flirtation with inflation by passing the Sherman Silver Purchase Act of 1890, which roughly doubled the Treasury purchase requirement of silver. The Treasury was now mandated to buy 4.5 million ounces of silver per month. Furthermore, payment was to be made in a new issue of redeemable greenback currency, Treasury notes of 1890, which were to be a full legal tender, redeemable in either gold or silver at the discretion of the Treasury. Not only was this an increased commitment to silver, it was a significant step on the road to bimetallism which—at the depreciated market rates—would mean inflationary silver monometallism. In the same year, the Republicans passed the high McKinley Tariff Act of 1890, which reaffirmed their commitment to high tariffs and soft money.

Another unsettling inflationary move made in the same year was that the New York Subtreasury altered its longstanding practice of settling its clearinghouse balances in gold coin. Instead, in August 1890, it began using the old greenbacks and the new Treasury notes of 1890. As a result, these paper currencies largely replaced gold paid in customs receipts in New York.[153]

[153]See Friedman and Schwartz, *Monetary History,* pp. 106, n. 25.

Uneasiness about the shift from gold to silver and the continuing free-silver agitation caused foreigners to lose further confidence in the U.S. gold standard, and to cause a drop in capital imports and severe gold outflows from the country. This loss of confidence exerted contractionist pressure on the American economy and reduced potential economic growth during the early 1890s.

Fears about the American gold standard were intensified in March 1891, when the Treasury suddenly imposed a stiff fee on the export of gold bars taken from its vaults so that most gold exported from then on was American gold coin rather than bars. A shock went through the financial community, in the U.S. and abroad, when the United States Senate passed a free-silver coinage bill in July 1892; the fact that the bill went no further was not enough to restore confidence in the gold standard. Banks began to insert clauses in loans and mortgages requiring payment in gold coin; clearly the dollar was no longer trusted. Gold exports intensified in 1892, the Treasury's gold reserve declined, and a run ensued on the U.S. Treasury. In February 1893, the Treasury persuaded New York banks, which had drawn down $6 million on gold from the Treasury by presenting Treasury notes for redemption, to return the gold and reacquire the paper. This act of desperation was scarcely calculated to restore confidence in the paper dollar. The Treasury was paying the price for specie resumption without bothering to contract the paper notes in circulation. The gold standard was therefore inherently shaky, resting only on public confidence, and that was giving way under the silver agitation and under desperate acts by the Treasury.

Poor Grover Cleveland, a hard-money Democrat, assumed the presidency in the middle of this monetary crisis. Two months later, the stock market collapsed, and a month afterward, in June 1893, distrust of the fractional reserve banks led to massive bank runs and bank failures throughout the country. Once again, however, many banks, national and state, especially in the West and South, were allowed to suspend specie payments. The panic of 1893 was on. In a few months, Eastern bank suspension occurred, beginning with New York City. The total money supply—gold coin, Treasury paper, national bank notes, and national and state bank deposits—fell by 6.3 percent in one year, from June 1892 to June 1893. Suspension of specie payments resulted in deposits—which were no longer immediately redeemable in cash—going to a discount in relation to currency during the month of August. As a result, deposits became less useful, and the public tried its best to intensify its exchange of deposits for currency.

By the end of 1893, the panic was over as foreign confidence rose with the Cleveland administration's successful repeal of the Sherman Silver Purchase Act in November of that year. Further silver agitation of 1895 endangered the Treasury's gold reserve, but heroic acts of the Treasury, including buying gold from a syndicate of bankers headed by J.P. Morgan and August Belmont, restored confidence in the continuance of the gold standard.[154] The victory of the free-silver Bryanite forces at the 1896 Democratic convention caused further problems for gold, but the victory of the pro-gold Republicans put an end to the problem of domestic and foreign confidence in the gold standard.

1896: The Transformation of the American Party System

Orthodox economic historians attribute the triumph of William Jennings Bryan in the Democratic Convention of 1896, and his later renominations for president, to a righteous rising up of the "people" demanding inflation over the "interests" holding out for gold. Friedman and Schwartz attribute the rise of Bryanism to the price contraction of the last three decades of the nineteenth century, and the triumph of gold and disappearance of the "money" issue to the price rise after 1896.[155]

[154]On silver agitation, the gold reserves, and the panic of 1893, see Friedman and Schwartz, *Monetary History*, pp. 104–33, 705.

[155]Ibid., *Monetary History*, pp. 113–19.

This conventional analysis overlooks several problems. First, if Bryan represented the "people" versus the "interests," why did Bryan lose and lose soundly, not once but three times? Why did gold triumph long before any price inflation became obvious, in fact at the depths of price contraction in 1896?

But the main neglect of the conventional analysis is the disregard of the highly illuminating insights provided in the past fifteen years by the "new political history" of nineteenth-century American politics and its political culture. The new political history began by going beyond national political issues (largely economic) and investigating state and local political contests.[156] It also dug into the actual voting records of individual parishes, wards, and counties, and discovered how people voted and why they voted the way they did. The work of the new political history is truly interdisciplinary, for its methods range from sophisticated techniques for voting analysis to illuminating insights into American ethnic religious history.

In the following pages, we shall present a summary of the findings of the new political history on the American party structure of the late nineteenth century and after, and on the transformation of 1896 in particular.

First, the history of American political parties is one of successive "party systems." Each party system lasts several

[156]The locus classicus of the new political history in late nineteenth-century politics is Paul Kleppner, *The Cross of Culture: A Social Analysis of Midwestern Politics, 1859–1900* (New York: Free Press, 1970). See also other writings of the prolific Kleppner, especially his magnum opus, *The Third Electoral System, 1853–1892: Parties, Voters, and Political Cultures* (Chapel Hill: University of North Carolina Press, 1979). On the late nineteenth century, see also Richard J. Jensen, *The Winning of the Midwest: Social and Political Conflict, 1888–1896* (Chicago: University of Chicago Press, 1971). On the Civil War period and earlier, see the works of Ronald Formisano, Joel Sibley, and William Shade. For Eastern confirmation on the Kleppner and Jensen findings on the Middle West, see Samuel T. McSeveney, *The Politics of Depression: Political Behavior in the Northeast, 1893–1896* (Oxford: Oxford University Press, 1972).

decades, with each particular party having a certain central character; in many cases, the name of the party can remain the same but its essential character can drastically change—in the so-called "critical elections." In the nineteenth century the nation's second party system (Whigs v. Democrats), lasting from about 1832 to 1854, was succeeded by the third system (Republicans v. Democrats), lasting from 1854 to 1896.

Characteristic of both party systems was that each party was committed to a distinctive ideology clashing with the other, and these conflicting worldviews made for fierce and close contests. Elections were particularly hard fought. Interest was high since the parties offered a "choice, not an echo," and so the turnout rate was remarkably high, often reaching 80 to 90 percent of eligible voters. More remarkably, candidates did not, as we are used to in the twentieth century, fuzz their ideology during campaigns in order to appeal to a floating, ideologically indifferent, "independent voter." There were very few independent voters. The way to win elections, therefore, was to bring out your vote, and the way to do that was to intensify and strengthen your ideology during campaigns. Any fuzzing over would lead the Republican or Democratic constituents to stay home in disgust, and the election would be lost. Very rarely would there be a crossover to the other, hated party.

One problem that strikes anyone interested in nineteenth-century political history is: How come the average person exhibited such great and intense interest in such arcane economic topics as banking, gold and silver, and tariffs? Thousands of half-literate people wrote embattled tracts on these topics, and voters were intensely interested. Attributing the answer to inflation or depression, to seemingly economic interests, as do Marxists and other economic determinists, simply won't do. The far greater depressions and inflations of the twentieth century have not educed nearly as much mass interest in economics as did the milder economic crises of the past century.

Only the findings of the new political historians have cleared up this puzzle. It turns out that the mass of the public was not necessarily interested in what the elites, or national politicians, were talking about. The most intense and direct interest of the voters was applied to local and state issues, and on these local levels the two parties waged an intense and furious political struggle that lasted from the 1830s to the 1890s.

The beginning of the century-long struggle began with the profound transformation of American Protestantism in the 1830s. This transformation swept like wildfire across the Northern states, particularly Yankee territory, during the 1830s, leaving the South virtually untouched. The transformation found particular root among Yankee culture, with its aggressive and domineering spirit.[157]

This new Protestantism—called "pietism"—was born in the fires of Charles Finney and the great revival movement of the 1830s. Its credo was roughly as follows: Each individual is responsible for his own salvation, and it must come in an emotional moment of being "born again." Each person can achieve salvation; each person must do his best to save everyone else. This compulsion to save others was more than simple missionary work; it meant that one would go to hell unless he did his best to save others. But since each person is alone and facing the temptation to sin, this role can only be done by the use of the State. The role of the State was to stamp out sin and create a new Jerusalem on Earth.[158, 159]

[157]"Yankees" originated in rural New England and then emigrated westward in the early nineteenth century, settling in upstate (particularly western) New York, northern Ohio, northern Indiana, and northern Illinois.

[158]These pietists have been called "evangelical pietists" to contrast them with the new Southern pietists, called "salvational pietists," who did not include the compulsion to save everyone else in their doctrine.

[159]These pietists are distinguished from contemporary "fundamentalists" because the former were "postmillennialists" who believe that the

The pietists defined sin very broadly. In particular, the most important politically was "demon rum," which clouded men's minds and therefore robbed them of their theological free will. In the 1830s, the evangelical pietists launched a determined and indefatigable prohibitionist crusade on the state and local level that lasted a century. Second was any activity on Sunday except going to church, which led to a drive for Sabbatarian blue laws. Drinking on Sunday was of course a double sin, and hence was particularly heinous. Another vital thrust of the new Yankee pietism was to try to extirpate Roman Catholicism, which robs communicants of their theological free will by subjecting them to the dictates of priests who are agents of the Vatican. If Roman Catholics could not be prohibited per se, their immigration could be slowed down or stopped. And since their adults were irrevocably steeped in sin, it became vital for crusading pietists to try to establish public schools as compulsory forces for Protestantizing society or, as the pietists liked to put it, to "Christianize the Catholics." If the adults are hopeless, the children must be saved by the public school and compulsory attendance laws.

Such was the political program of Yankee pietism. Not all immigrants were scorned. British, Norwegian, or other immigrants who belonged to pietist churches (whether nominally Calvinist or Lutheran or not) were welcomed as "true Americans." The Northern pietists found their home, almost to a man, first in the Whig Party, and then in the Republican Party. And they did so, too, among the Greenback and Populist parties, as we shall see further below.

---

world must be shaped up and Christianized for a millennium before Jesus will return. In contrast, contemporary fundamentalists are "premillennials" who believe that the Second Coming of Jesus will usher in the millennium. Obviously, if everyone must be shaped up before Jesus can return, there is a much greater incentive to wield State power to stamp out sin.

There came to this country during the century an increasing number of Catholic and Lutheran immigrants, especially from Ireland and Germany. The Catholics and High Lutherans, who have been called "ritualists" or "liturgicals," had a very different kind of religious culture. Each person is not responsible for his own salvation directly; if he is to be saved, he joins the church and obeys its liturgy and sacraments. In a profound sense, then, the church is responsible for one's salvation, and there was no need for the State to stamp out temptation. These churches, then, especially the Lutheran, had a laissez-faire attitude toward the State and morality. Furthermore, their definitions of "sin" were not nearly as broad as the pietists'. Liquor is fine in moderation; and drinking beer with the family in beer parlors on Sunday after church was a cherished German (Catholic and Lutheran) tradition; and parochial schools were vital in transmitting religious values to their children in a country where they were in a minority.

Virtually to a man, Catholics and High Lutherans[160] found their home during the nineteenth century in the Democratic Party. It is no wonder that the Republicans gloried in calling themselves throughout this period "the party of great moral ideas," while the Democrats declared themselves to be "the party of personal liberty." For nearly a century, the bemused liturgical Democrats fought a defensive struggle against people whom they considered "pietist-fanatics" constantly swooping down trying to outlaw their liquor, their Sunday beer parlors, and their parochial schools.

How did all this relate to the economic issues of the day? Simply that the leaders of each party went to their voting constituents and "raised their consciousness" to get them vitally

[160]Lutherans, then as now, were split into many different synods, some highly liturgical, others highly pietist, and still others in between. Paul Kleppner has shown a 1-to-1 correlation between the degree of liturgicalness and the percentage of Democratic Party votes among the different synods.

interested in national economic questions. Thus, the Republican leaders would go to their rank and file and say: "Just as we need Big Paternalistic Government on the local and state level to stamp out sin and compel morality, so we need Big Government on the national level to increase everyone's purchasing power through inflation, keeping out cheap foreign goods (tariffs), or keeping out cheap foreign labor (immigration restrictions)."

And for their part, the Democratic leaders would go to their constituents and say: "Just as the Republican fanatics are trying to take away your liquor, your beer parlors, and your parochial schools, so the same people are trying to keep out cheap foreign goods (tariffs), and trying to destroy the value of your savings through inflation. Paternalistic government on the federal level is just as evil as it is at home."

So statism and libertarianism were expanded to other issues and other levels. Each side infused its economic issues with a moral fervor and passion stemming from deeply held religious values. The mystery of the passionate interest of Americans in economic issues in the epoch is solved.

Both in the second and third party systems, however, the Whigs and then the Republicans had a grave problem. Partly because of demographics—greater immigration and higher birth rates—the Democratic-liturgicals were slowly but surely becoming the majority party in the country. The Democrats were split asunder by the slavery question in the 1840s and '50s. But now, by 1890, the Republicans saw the handwriting on the wall. The Democratic victory in the congressional races in 1890, followed by the unprecedented landslide victory of Grover Cleveland carrying *both* houses of Congress in 1892, indicated to the Republicans that they were becoming doomed to be a permanent minority.

To remedy the problem, the Republicans, in the early 1890s, led by Ohio Republicans William McKinley and Mark Hanna, launched a shrewd campaign of reconstruction. In particular, in state after state, they ditched the prohibitionists, who were becoming an embarrassment and losing the Republicans large numbers of German Lutheran votes. Also, they modified their hostility to immigration. By the mid-1890s, the Republicans had moved rapidly toward the center, toward fuzzing over their political pietism.

In the meanwhile, an upheaval was beginning to occur in the Democratic Party. The South, by now a one-party Democratic region, was having its own pietism transformed by the 1890s. Quiet pietists were now becoming evangelical, and Southern Protestant organizations began to call for prohibition. Then the new, sparsely settled Mountain states, many of them with silver mines, were also largely pietist. Moreover, a power vacuum, which would ordinarily have been temporary, had been created in the national Democratic Party. Poor Grover Cleveland, a hard-money laissez-faire Democrat, was blamed for the panic of 1893, and many leading Cleveland Democrats lost their gubernatorial and senatorial posts in the 1894 elections. The Cleveland Democrats were temporarily weak, and the Southern-Mountain coalition was ready to hand. Seeing this opportunity, William Jennings Bryan and his pietist coalition seized control of the Democratic Party at the momentous convention of 1896. The Democratic Party was never to be the same again.[161]

The Catholics, Lutherans, and laissez-faire Cleveland Democrats were in mortal shock. The "party of our fathers" was lost. The Republicans, who had been moderating their stance anyway, saw the opportunity of a lifetime. At the Republican convention, Representative Henry Cabot Lodge, representing the Morgans and the pro-gold-standard Boston financial interests, told McKinley and Hanna: Pledge yourself to the gold standard—the basic Cleveland economic issue—and drop your silverite and greenback tendencies, and

[161]Grover Cleveland himself, of course, was neither a Roman Catholic nor a Lutheran. But he was a Calvinist Presbyterian who detested the takeover of the Presbyterian Church by the pietists.

we will all back you. Refuse, and we will support Bryan or a third party. McKinley struck the deal, and from then on, the Republicans, in nineteenth-century terms, were a centrist party. Their principles were now high tariffs and the gold standard, and prohibition was quietly forgotten.

What would the poor liturgicals do? Many of them stayed home in droves, and indeed the election of 1896 marks the beginning of the great slide downward in voter turnout rates that continues to the present day. Some of them, in anguish at the pietist, inflationist, and prohibitionist Bryanites, actually conquered their anguish and voted Republican for the first time in their lives. The Republicans, after all, had dropped the hated prohibitionists and adopted gold.

The election of 1896 inaugurated the fourth party system in America. From a third party system of closely fought, seesawing races between a pietist-statist Republican Party vs. a liturgical-libertarian Democratic Party, the fourth party system consisted of a majority centrist Republican Party as against a minority pietist Democratic Party. After a few years, the Democrats lost their pietist nature, and they too became a centrist, though usually minority party, with a moderately statist ideology scarcely distinguishable from the Republicans. So went the fourth party system until 1932.

A charming anecdote, told us by Richard Jensen, sums up much of the 1896 election. The heavily German city of Milwaukee had been mainly Democratic for years. The German Lutherans and Catholics in America were devoted, in particular, to the gold standard and were bitter enemies of inflation. The Democratic nomination for Congress in Milwaukee had been obtained by a Populist-Democrat, Richard Schilling. Sounding for all the world like modern monetarists or Keynesians, Schilling tried to explain to the assembled Germans of Milwaukee in a campaign speech that it didn't really matter what commodity was chosen as money, that "gold, silver, copper, paper, sauerkraut or sausages" would do equally well as money. At that point, the German masses of Milwaukee laughed Schilling off the stage, and the shrewdly opportunistic Republicans adopted as their campaign slogan, "Schilling and Sauerkraut" and swept Milwaukee. [162]

The Greenbackers and later the pro-silver, inflationist, Bryanite Populist Party were not "agrarian parties"; they were collections of pietists aiming to stamp out personal and political sin. Thus, as Kleppner points out, "The Greenback Party was less an amalgamation of economic pressure groups than an ad hoc coalition of 'True Believers,' 'ideologues,' who launched their party as a 'quasi-religious' movement that bore the indelible hallmark of 'a transfiguring faith.'" The Greenbackers perceived their movement as the "religion of the Master in motion among men." And the Populists described their 1890 free-silver contest in Kansas not as a "political campaign," but as "a religious revival, a crusade, a pentecost of politics in which a tongue of flame sat upon every man, and each spake as the spirit gave him utterance." The people had "heard the word and could preach the gospel of Populism." It was no accident, we see now, that the Greenbackers almost invariably endorsed prohibition, compulsory public schooling, and crushing of parochial schools. Or that Populists in many states "declared unequivocally for prohibition" or entered various forms of fusion with the Prohibition Party.[163]

The Transformation of 1896 and the death of the third party system meant the end of America's great laissez-faire, hard-money libertarian party. The Democratic Party was no longer the party of Jefferson, Jackson, and Cleveland. With no further political embodiment for laissez-faire in existence, and with both parties offering "an echo not a choice," public interest in

[162]So intense was the German-American devotion to gold and hard money that even German communist-anarchist Johann Most, leader of a movement that sought the abolition of money itself, actually came out for the gold standard during the 1896 campaign! See Jensen, *Winning of the Midwest*, pp. 293–95.

[163]Kleppner, *Third Electoral System*, pp. 291–96.

politics steadily declined. A power vacuum was left in American politics for the new corporate statist ideology of progressivism, which swept both parties (and created a short-lived Progressive Party) in America after 1900. The Progressive Era of 1900–1918 fastened a welfare-warfare state on America which has set the mold for the rest of the twentieth century. Statism arrived after 1900 not because of inflation or deflation, but because a unique set of conditions had destroyed the Democrats as a laissez-faire party and left a power vacuum for the triumph of the new ideology of compulsory cartelization through a partnership of big government, business, unions, technocrats, and intellectuals.

Part 2

THE ORIGINS OF THE FEDERAL RESERVE

THE ORIGINS OF THE FEDERAL RESERVE

THE PROGRESSIVE MOVEMENT

The Federal Reserve Act of December 23, 1913, was part and parcel of the wave of Progressive legislation, on local, state, and federal levels of government, that began about 1900. Progressivism was a bipartisan movement which, in the course of the first two decades of the twentieth century, transformed the American economy and society from one of roughly laissez-faire to one of centralized statism.

Until the 1960s, historians had established the myth that Progressivism was a virtual uprising of workers and farmers who, guided by a new generation of altruistic experts and intellectuals, surmounted fierce big business opposition in order to curb, regulate, and control what had been a system of accelerating monopoly in the late nineteenth century. A generation of research and scholarship, however, has now exploded that myth for all parts of the American polity, and it has become all too clear that the truth is the reverse of this well-worn fable. In contrast, what actually happened was that business became increasingly competitive during the late nineteenth century, and that various big-business interests, led by the powerful financial house of J.P. Morgan and Company, had tried desperately to

[*Originally published as "The Origins of the Federal Reserve,"* Quarterly Journal of Austrian Economics *2, no. 3 (Fall): 3–51.*—Ed.]

establish successful cartels on the free market. The first wave of such cartels was in the first large-scale business, railroads, and in every case, the attempt to increase profits, by cutting sales with a quota system and thereby to raise prices or rates, collapsed quickly from internal competition within the cartel and from external competition by new competitors eager to undercut the cartel. During the 1890s, in the new field of large-scale industrial corporations, big-business interests tried to establish high prices and reduced production via mergers, and again, in every case, the mergers collapsed from the winds of new competition. In both sets of cartel attempts, J.P. Morgan and Company had taken the lead, and in both sets of cases, the market, hampered though it was by high protective tariff walls, managed to nullify these attempts at voluntary cartelization.

It then became clear to these big-business interests that the only way to establish a cartelized economy, an economy that would ensure their continued economic dominance and high profits, would be to use the powers of government to establish and maintain cartels by coercion. In other words, to transform the economy from roughly laissez-faire to centralized and coordinated statism. But how could the American people, steeped in a long tradition of fierce opposition to government-imposed monopoly, go along with this program? How could the public's consent to the New Order be engineered?

Fortunately for the cartelists, a solution to this vexing problem lay at hand. Monopoly could be put over *in the name of* opposition to monopoly! In that way, using the rhetoric beloved by Americans, the *form* of the political economy could be maintained, while the *content* could be totally reversed. Monopoly had always been defined, in the popular parlance and among economists, as "grants of exclusive privilege" by the government. It was now simply redefined as "big business" or business competitive practices, such as price-cutting, so that regulatory commissions, from the Interstate Commerce Commission to the Federal Trade Commission to state insurance commissions, were lobbied for and staffed by big-business men from the regulated industry, all done in the name of curbing "big business monopoly" on the free market. In that way, the regulatory commissions could subsidize, restrict, and cartelize in the name of "opposing monopoly," as well as promoting the general welfare and national security. Once again, it was railroad monopoly that paved the way.

For this intellectual shell game, the cartelists needed the support of the nation's intellectuals, the class of professional opinion-molders in society. The Morgans needed a smoke screen of ideology, setting forth the rationale and the apologetics for the New Order. Again, fortunately for them, the intellectuals were ready and eager for the new alliance. The enormous growth of intellectuals, academics, social scientists, technocrats, engineers, social workers, physicians, and occupational "guilds" of all types in the late nineteenth century led most of these groups to organize for a far greater share of the pie than they could possibly achieve on the free market. These intellectuals needed the State to license, restrict, and cartelize their occupations, so as to raise the incomes for the fortunate people already in these fields. In return for their serving as apologists for the new statism, the State was prepared to offer not only cartelized occupations, but also ever increasing and cushier jobs in the bureaucracy to plan and propagandize for the newly statized society. And the intellectuals were ready for it, having learned in graduate schools in Germany the glories of statism and organicist socialism, of a harmonious "middle way" between dog-eat-dog laissez-faire on the one hand and proletarian Marxism on the other. Instead, big government, staffed by intellectuals and technocrats, steered by big business and aided by unions organizing a subservient labor force, would impose a cooperative commonwealth for the alleged benefit of all.

Unhappiness With the National Banking System

The previous big push for statism in America had occurred during the Civil War, when the virtual one-party Congress after secession of the South emboldened the Republicans to enact their cherished statist program under cover of the war. The alliance of big business and big government with the Republican Party drove through an income tax, heavy excise taxes on such sinful products as tobacco and alcohol, high protective tariffs, and huge land grants and other subsidies to transcontinental railroads. The overbuilding of railroads led directly to Morgan's failed attempts at railroad pools, and finally to the creation, promoted by Morgan and Morgan-controlled railroads, of the Interstate Commerce Commission in 1887. The result of *that* was the long secular decline of the railroads beginning before 1900. The income tax was annulled by Supreme Court action, but was reinstated during the Progressive period.

The most interventionary of the Civil War actions was in the vital field of money and banking. The approach toward hard money and free banking that had been achieved during the 1840s and 1850s was swept away by two pernicious inflationist measures of the wartime Republican administration. One was fiat money greenbacks, which depreciated by half by the middle of the Civil War, and were finally replaced by the gold standard after urgent pressure by hard-money Democrats, but not until 1879, some 14 full years after the end of the war. A second, and more lasting, intervention was the National Banking Acts of 1863, 1864, and 1865, which destroyed the issue of bank notes by state-chartered (or "state") banks by a prohibitory tax, and then monopolized the issue of bank notes in the hands of a few large, federally chartered "national banks," mainly centered on Wall Street. In a typical cartelization, national banks were compelled by law to accept each other's notes and demand deposits at par, negating the process by which the free market had previously been discounting the notes and deposits of shaky and inflationary banks.

In this way, the Wall Street–federal government establishment was able to control the banking system, and inflate the supply of notes and deposits in a coordinated manner.

But there were still problems. The national banking system provided only a halfway house between free banking and government central banking, and by the end of the nineteenth century, the Wall Street banks were becoming increasingly unhappy with the status quo. The centralization was only limited, and, above all, there was no governmental central bank to coordinate inflation, and to act as a lender of last resort, bailing out banks in trouble. No sooner had bank credit generated booms when they got into trouble and bank-created booms turned into recessions, with banks forced to contract their loans and assets and to deflate in order to save themselves. Not only that, but after the initial shock of the National Banking Acts, state banks had grown rapidly by pyramiding their loans and demand deposits on top of national bank notes. These state banks, free of the high legal capital requirements that kept entry restricted in national banking, flourished during the 1880s and 1890s and provided stiff competition for the national banks themselves. Furthermore, St. Louis and Chicago, after the 1880s, provided increasingly severe competition to Wall Street. Thus, St. Louis and Chicago bank deposits, which had been only 16 percent of the St. Louis, Chicago, and New York City total in 1880, rose to 33 percent of that total by 1912. All in all, bank clearings outside of New York City, which were 24 percent of the national total in 1882, had risen to 43 percent by 1913.

The complaints of the big banks were summed up in one word: "inelasticity." The national banking system, they charged, did not provide for the proper "elasticity" of the money supply; that is, the banks were not able to expand money and credit as much as they wished, particularly in times of recession. In short, the national banking system did not provide sufficient room for inflationary expansions of credit by the nation's banks.[1]

[1]On the national banking system background and on the increasing unhappiness of the big banks, see Murray N. Rothbard, "The Federal Reserve as a Cartelization Device: The Early Years, 1913–1920," in *Money in Crisis,* Barry Siegel, ed. (San Francisco: Pacific Institute, 1984), pp. 89–94; Ron Paul and Lewis Lehrman, *The Case for Gold: A Minority Report on the U.S. Gold Commission* (Washington, D.C.: Cato Institute, 1982); and Gabriel Kolko, *The Triumph of Conservatism: A Reinterpretation of American History* (Glencoe, Ill.: Free Press, 1983), pp. 139–46.

By the turn of the century the political economy of the United States was dominated by two generally clashing financial aggregations: the previously dominant Morgan group, which had begun in investment banking and expanded into commercial banking, railroads, and mergers of manufacturing firms; and the Rockefeller forces, which began in oil refining and then moved into commercial banking, finally forming an alliance with the Kuhn, Loeb Company in investment banking and the Harriman interests in railroads.[2]

Although these two financial blocs usually clashed with each other, they were as one on the need for a central bank. Even though the eventual major role in forming and dominating the Federal Reserve System was taken by the Morgans, the Rockefeller and Kuhn, Loeb forces were equally enthusiastic in pushing, and collaborating on, what they all considered to be an essential monetary reform.

The Beginnings of the "Reform" Movement: The Indianapolis Monetary Convention

The presidential election of 1896 was a great national referendum on the gold standard. The Democratic Party had been captured, at its 1896 convention, by the Populist, ultra-inflationist, anti-gold forces, headed by William Jennings Bryan. The older Democrats, who had been fiercely devoted to hard money and the gold standard, either stayed home on election day or voted, for the first time in their lives, for the hated Republicans. The Republicans had long been the party of prohibition and of greenback inflation and opposition to gold. But since the early 1890s,

[2]Indeed, much of the political history of the United States from the late nineteenth century until World War II may be interpreted by the closeness of each administration to one of these sometimes cooperating, more often conflicting, financial groupings: Cleveland (Morgan), McKinley (Rockefeller), Theodore Roosevelt (Morgan), Taft (Rockefeller), Wilson (Morgan), Harding (Rockefeller), Coolidge (Morgan), Hoover (Morgan), and Franklin Roosevelt (Harriman–Kuhn, Loeb–Rockefeller).

the Rockefeller forces, dominant in their home state of Ohio and nationally in the Republican Party, had decided to quietly ditch prohibition as a political embarrassment and as a grave deterrent to obtaining votes from the increasingly powerful bloc of German-American voters. In the summer of 1896, anticipating the defeat of the gold forces at the Democratic convention, the Morgans, previously dominant in the Democratic Party, approached the McKinley–Mark Hanna–Rockefeller forces through their rising young satrap, Congressman Henry Cabot Lodge of Massachusetts. Lodge offered the Rockefeller forces a deal: The Morgans would support McKinley for president and neither sit home nor back a third, Gold Democrat party, provided that McKinley pledged himself to a gold standard. The deal was struck, and many previously hard-money Democrats shifted to the Republicans. The nature of the American political party system was now drastically changed: previously a tightly fought struggle between hard-money, free-trade, laissez-faire Democrats on the one hand, and protectionist, inflationist, and statist Republicans on the other, with the Democrats slowly but surely gaining ascendancy by the early 1890s, was now a party system that would be dominated by the Republicans until the depression election of 1932.

The Morgans were strongly opposed to Bryanism, which was not only Populist and inflationist, but also anti–Wall Street bank; the Bryanites, much like Populists of the present day, preferred congressional, greenback inflationism to the more subtle, and more privileged, big-bank-controlled variety. The Morgans, in contrast, favored a gold standard. But, once gold was secured by the McKinley victory of 1896, they wanted to press on to use the gold standard as a hard-money camouflage behind which they could change the system into one less nakedly inflationist than populism but far more effectively controlled by the big-banker elites. In the long run, a controlled Morgan-Rockefeller gold standard was far more pernicious to the cause of genuine hard money than a candid free-silver or greenback Bryanism.

As soon as McKinley was safely elected, the Morgan-Rockefeller forces began to organize a "reform" movement to cure the "inelasticity" of money in the existing gold standard and to move slowly toward the establishment of a central bank. To do so, they decided to use the techniques they had successfully employed in establishing a pro–gold standard movement during 1895 and 1896. The crucial point was to avoid the public suspicion of Wall Street and banker control by acquiring the patina of a broad-based grassroots movement. To do so, the movement was deliberately focused in the Middle West, the heartland of America, and organizations developed that included not only bankers, but also businessmen, economists, and other academics, who supplied respectability, persuasiveness, and technical expertise to the reform cause.

Accordingly, the reform drive began just after the 1896 elections in authentic Midwest country. Hugh Henry Hanna, president of the Atlas Engine Works of Indianapolis, who had learned organizing tactics during the year with the pro–gold standard Union for Sound Money, sent a memorandum, in November, to the Indianapolis Board of Trade, urging a grassroots Midwestern state like Indiana to take the lead in currency reform.[3]

In response, the reformers moved fast. Answering the call of the Indianapolis Board of Trade, delegates from boards of trade from 12 Midwestern cities met in Indianapolis on December 1, 1896. The conference called for a large monetary convention of businessmen, which accordingly met in Indianapolis on January 12, 1897. Representatives from 26 states and the District of Columbia were present. The monetary reform movement was now officially under way. The influential *Yale Review* commended the convention for averting the danger of arousing popular hostility to bankers. It reported that "the conference was a gathering of businessmen in general rather than bankers in particular."[4]

[3]For the memorandum, see James Livingston, *Origins of the Federal Reserve System: Money, Class, and Corporate Capitalism, 1890–1913* (Ithaca, N.Y.: Cornell University Press, 1986), pp. 104–05.

[4]*Yale Review* 5 (1897): 343–45, quoted in ibid., p. 105.

The conventioneers may have been businessmen, but they were certainly not very grassrootsy. Presiding at the Indianapolis Monetary Convention of 1897 was C. Stuart Patterson, dean of the University of Pennsylvania Law School and a member of the finance committee of the powerful, Morgan-oriented Pennsylvania Railroad. The day after the convention opened, Hugh Hanna was named chairman of an executive committee which he would appoint. The committee was empowered to act for the convention after it adjourned. The executive committee consisted of the following influential corporate and financial leaders:

John J. Mitchell of Chicago, president of the Illinois Trust and Savings Bank, and a director of the Chicago and Alton Railroad; the Pittsburgh, Fort Wayne and Chicago Railroad; and the Pullman Company. Mitchell was named treasurer of the executive committee.

H.H. Kohlsaat, editor and publisher of the *Chicago Times-Herald* and the Chicago *Ocean Herald*, trustee of the Chicago Art Institute, and a friend and adviser of Rockefeller's main man in politics, President William McKinley.

Charles Custis Harrison, provost of the University of Pennsylvania, who had made a fortune as a sugar refiner in partnership with the powerful Havemeyer ("Sugar Trust") interests.

Alexander E. Orr, New York City banker in the Morgan ambit, who was a director of the Morgan-run Erie and Chicago, Rock Island, and Pacific Railroads; of the National Bank of Commerce; and of the influential publishing house, Harper Brothers. Orr was also a partner in the country's largest grain merchandising firm and a director of several life insurance companies.

Edwin O. Stanard, St. Louis grain merchant, former governor of Missouri, and former vice president of the National Board of Trade and Transportation.

E.B. Stahlman, owner of the *Nashville Banner*, commissioner of the cartelist Southern Railway and Steamship Association, and former vice president of the Louisville, New Albany, and Chicago Railroad.

A.E. Willson, influential attorney from Louisville and a future governor of Kentucky.

But the two most interesting and powerful executive committee members of the Indianapolis Monetary Convention were Henry C. Payne and George Foster Peabody. Henry Payne was a Republican Party leader from Milwaukee and president of the Morgan-dominated Wisconsin Telephone Company, long associated with the railroad-oriented Spooner-Sawyer Republican machine in Wisconsin politics. Payne was also heavily involved in Milwaukee utility and banking interests, in particular as a longtime director of the North American Company, a large public utility holding company headed by New York City financier Charles W. Wetmore. So close was North American to the Morgan interests that its board included two top Morgan financiers. One was Edmund C. Converse, president of Morgan-run Liberty National Bank of New York City, and soon-to-be founding president of Morgan's Bankers Trust Company. The other was Robert Bacon, a partner in J.P. Morgan and Company, and one of Theodore Roosevelt's closest friends, whom Roosevelt would make assistant secretary of state. Furthermore, when Theodore Roosevelt became president as the result of the assassination of William McKinley, he replaced Rockefeller's top political operative, Mark Hanna of Ohio, with Henry C. Payne as postmaster general of the United States. Payne, a leading Morgan lieutenant, was reportedly appointed to what was then the major political post in the Cabinet, specifically to break Hanna's hold over the national Republican Party. It seems clear that replacing Hanna with Payne was part of the savage assault that Theodore Roosevelt would soon launch against Standard Oil as part of the open warfare about to break out between the Rockefeller–Harriman–Kuhn, Loeb camp and the Morgan camp.[5]

Even more powerful in the Morgan ambit was the secretary of the Indianapolis Monetary Convention's executive committee,

[5]See Philip H. Burch, Jr., *Elites in American History,* vol. 2, *The Civil War to the New Deal* (New York: Holmes and Meier, 1981), p. 189, n. 55.

George Foster Peabody. The entire Peabody family of Boston Brahmins had long been personally and financially closely associated with the Morgans. A member of the Peabody clan had even served as best man at J.P. Morgan's wedding in 1865. George Peabody had long ago established an international banking firm of which J.P. Morgan's father, Junius, had been one of the senior partners. George Foster Peabody was an eminent New York investment banker with extensive holdings in Mexico, who was to help reorganize General Electric for the Morgans, and was later offered the job of secretary of the Treasury during the Wilson administration. He would function throughout that administration as a "statesman without portfolio."[6]

Let the masses be hoodwinked into regarding the Indianapolis Monetary Convention as a spontaneous grassroots outpouring of small Midwestern businessmen. To the *cognoscenti*, any organization featuring Henry Payne, Alexander Orr, and especially George Foster Peabody meant but one thing: J.P. Morgan.

The Indianapolis Monetary Convention quickly resolved to urge President McKinley to (1) continue the gold standard, and (2) create a new system of "elastic" bank credit. To that end, the convention urged the president to appoint a new monetary commission to prepare legislation for a new revised monetary system. McKinley was very much in favor of the proposal, signaling Rockefeller agreement, and on July 24 he sent a message to Congress urging the creation of a special monetary commission. The bill for a national monetary commission passed the House of Representatives but died in the Senate.[7]

Disappointed but intrepid, the executive committee, failing a presidentially appointed commission, decided in August 1897 to go ahead and select its own. The leading role in appointing this commission was played by George Foster Peabody, who

[6]Ibid., pp. 231, 233. See also Louise Ware, *George Foster Peabody* (Athens: University of Georgia Press, 1951), pp. 161–67.

[7]See Kolko, *Triumph*, pp. 147–48.

served as liaison between the Indianapolis members and the New York financial community. To select the commission members, Peabody arranged for the executive committee to meet in the Saratoga Springs summer home of his investment banking partner, Spencer Trask. By September, the executive committee had selected the members of the Indianapolis Monetary Commission.

The members of the new Indianapolis Monetary Commission were as follows:[8]

Chairman was former Senator George F. Edmunds, Republican of Vermont, attorney, and former director of several railroads.

C. Stuart Patterson, dean of University of Pennsylvania Law School, and a top official of the Morgan-controlled Pennsylvania Railroad.

Charles S. Fairchild, a leading New York banker, president of the New York Security and Trust Company, former partner in the Boston Brahmin investment banking firm of Lee, Higginson and Company, and executive and director of two major railroads. Fairchild, a leader in New York state politics, had been secretary of the Treasury in the first Cleveland administration. In addition, Fairchild's father, Sidney T. Fairchild, had been a leading attorney for the Morgan-controlled New York Central Railroad.

Stuyvesant Fish, scion of two longtime aristocratic New York families, was a partner of the Morgan-dominated New York investment bank of Morton, Bliss and Company, and then president of Illinois Central Railroad and a trustee of Mutual Life. Fish's father had been a senator, governor, and secretary of state.

Louis A. Garnett was a leading San Francisco businessman.

Thomas G. Bush of Alabama was a director of the Mobile and Birmingham Railroad.

J.W. Fries was a leading cotton manufacturer from North Carolina.

[8]See Livingston, *Origins*, pp. 106–07.

William B. Dean was a merchant from St. Paul, Minnesota, and a director of the St. Paul–based transcontinental Great Northern Railroad, owned by James J. Hill, ally with Morgan in the titanic struggle over the Northern Pacific Railroad with Harriman, Rockefeller, and Kuhn, Loeb.

George Leighton of St. Louis was an attorney for the Missouri Pacific Railroad.

Robert S. Taylor was an Indiana patent attorney for the Morgan-controlled General Electric Company.

The single most important working member of the commission was James Laurence Laughlin, head professor of political economy at the new Rockefeller-founded University of Chicago and editor of its prestigious *Journal of Political Economy.* It was Laughlin who supervised the operations of the commission's staff and the writing of the reports. Indeed, the two staff assistants to the commission who wrote reports were both students of Laughlin's at Chicago: former student L. Carroll Root, and his current graduate student Henry Parker Willis.

The impressive sum of $50,000 was raised throughout the nation's banking and corporate community to finance the work of the Indianapolis Monetary Commission. New York City's large quota was raised by Morgan bankers Peabody and Orr, and heavy contributions to fill the quota came promptly from mining magnate William E. Dodge; cotton and coffee trader Henry Hentz, a director of the Mechanics National Bank; and J.P. Morgan himself.

With the money in hand, the executive committee rented office space in Washington, D.C., in mid-September, and set the staff to sending out and collating the replies to a detailed monetary questionnaire, sent to several hundred selected experts. The monetary commission sat from late September into December 1897, sifting through the replies to the questionnaire collated by Root and Willis. The purpose of the questionnaire was to mobilize a broad base of support for the commission's recommendations, which they could claim represented hundreds of expert views. Second, the questionnaire served as an important public relations device, making the commission and its work highly visible to the public, to the business community throughout the country, and to members of Congress. Furthermore, through this device, the commission could be seen as speaking for the business community throughout the country.

To this end, the original idea was to publish the Indianapolis Monetary Commission's preliminary report, adopted in mid-December, as well as the questionnaire replies in a companion volume. Plans for the questionnaire volume fell through, although it was later published as part of a series of publications on political economy and public law by the University of Pennsylvania.[9]

Undaunted by the slight setback, the executive committee developed new methods of molding public opinion using the questionnaire replies as an organizing tool. In November, Hugh Hanna hired as his Washington assistant financial journalist Charles A. Conant, whose task was to propagandize and organize public opinion for the recommendations of the commission. The campaign to beat the drums for the forthcoming commission report was launched when Conant published an article in the December 1 issue of *Sound Currency* magazine, taking an advanced line on the report, and bolstering the conclusions not only with his own knowledge of monetary and banking history, but also with frequent statements from the as-yet-unpublished replies to the staff questionnaire.

Over the next several months, Conant worked closely with Jules Guthridge, the general secretary of the commission; they first induced newspapers throughout the country to print abstracts of the questionnaire replies. As Guthridge wrote some commission members, he thereby stimulated "public curiosity" about the forthcoming report, and he boasted that by "careful manipulation" he was able to get the preliminary report "printed in whole or in part—principally in part—in nearly

[9]See Livingston, *Origins*, pp. 107–08.

7,500 newspapers, large and small." In the meanwhile, Guthridge and Conant orchestrated letters of support from prominent men across the country, when the preliminary report was published on January 3, 1898. As soon as the report was published, Guthridge and Conant made these letters available to the daily newspapers. Quickly, the two built up a distribution system to spread the gospel of the report, organizing nearly 100,000 correspondents "dedicated to the enactment of the commission's plan for banking and currency reform."[10]

The prime and immediate emphasis of the preliminary report of the Indianapolis Monetary Commission was to complete the promise of the McKinley victory by codifying and enacting what was already in place de facto: a single gold standard, with silver reduced to the status of subsidiary token currency. Completing the victory over Bryanism and free silver, however, was just a mopping-up operation; more important in the long run was the call raised by the report for banking reform to allow greater elasticity. Bank credit could then be increased in recessions and whenever seasonal pressure for redemption by agricultural country banks forced the large central reserve banks to contract their loans. The actual measures called for by the commission were of marginal importance. (More important was that the question of banking reform had been raised at all.)

The public having been aroused by the preliminary report, the executive committee decided to organize a second and final meeting of the Indianapolis Monetary Convention, which duly met at Indianapolis on January 25, 1898. The second convention was a far grander affair than the first, bringing together 496 delegates from 31 states. Furthermore, the gathering was a cross-section of America's top corporate leaders. While the state of Indiana naturally had the largest delegation, of 85 representatives of boards of trade and chambers of commerce, New York sent 74 delegates, including many from the Board of Trade and

[10]Ibid., pp. 109–10.

Transportation, the Merchants' Association, and the Chamber of Commerce in New York City.

Such corporate leaders attended as Cleveland iron manufacturer Alfred A. Pope, president of the National Malleable Castings Company; Virgil P. Cline, legal counsel to Rockefeller's Standard Oil Company of Ohio; and C.A. Pillsbury of Minneapolis-St. Paul, organizer of the world's largest flour mills. From Chicago came such business notables as Marshall Field and Albert A. Sprague, a director of the Chicago Telephone Company, subsidiary of the Morgan-controlled telephone monopoly, American Telephone and Telegraph Company. Not to be overlooked was delegate Franklin MacVeagh, a wholesale grocer from Chicago, and an uncle of a senior partner in the Wall Street law firm of Bangs, Stetson, Tracy and MacVeagh, counsel to J.P. Morgan and Company. MacVeagh, who was later to become secretary of the Treasury in the Taft administration, was wholly in the Morgan ambit. His father-in-law, Henry F. Eames, was the founder of the Commercial National Bank of Chicago, and his brother Wayne was soon to become a trustee of the Morgan-dominated Mutual Life Insurance Company.

The purpose of the second convention, as former Secretary of the Treasury Charles S. Fairchild candidly explained in his address to the gathering, was to mobilize the nation's leading businessmen into a mighty and influential reform movement. As he put it, "If men of business give serious attention and study to these subjects, they will substantially agree upon legislation, and thus agreeing, their influence will be prevailing." He concluded, "My word to you is, pull all together." Presiding officer of the convention, Iowa Governor Leslie M. Shaw, was, however, a bit disingenuous when he told the gathering, "You represent today not the banks, for there are few bankers on this floor. You represent the business industries and the financial interests of the country." There were plenty of bankers there, too.[11] Shaw

[11]Ibid., pp. 113–15.

himself, later to be secretary of the Treasury under Theodore Roosevelt, was a small-town banker in Iowa, and president of the Bank of Denison who continued as bank president throughout his term as convention governor. More important in Shaw's outlook and career was the fact that he was a longtime close friend and loyal supporter of the Des Moines Regency, the Iowa Republican machine headed by the powerful Senator William Boyd Allison. Allison, who was to obtain the Treasury post for his friend, was in turn tied closely to Charles E. Perkins, a close Morgan ally, president of the Chicago, Burlington and Quincy Railroad, and kinsman of the powerful Forbes financial group of Boston, long tied in with the Morgan interests.[12]

Also serving as delegates to the second convention were several eminent economists, each of whom, however, came not as academic observers but as representatives of elements of the business community. Professor Jeremiah W. Jenks of Cornell, a proponent of trust cartelization by government and soon to become a friend and adviser of Theodore Roosevelt as governor, came as delegate from the Ithaca Business Men's Association. Frank W. Taussig of Harvard University represented the Cambridge Merchants' Association. Yale's Arthur Twining Hadley, soon to be the president of Yale, represented the New Haven Chamber of Commerce, and Frank M. Taylor of the University of Michigan came as representative of the Ann Arbor Business Men's Association. Each of these men held powerful posts in the organized economics profession, Jenkins, Taussig, and Taylor serving on the currency committee of the American Economic Association. Hadley, a leading railroad economist, also served on the boards of directors of Morgan's New York, New Haven and Hartford and Atchison, Topeka and Santa Fe Railroads.[13]

[12]See Rothbard, "Federal Reserve," pp. 95–96.

[13]On Hadley, Jenks, and especially Conant, see Carl P. Parrini and Martin J. Sklar, "New Thinking about the Market, 1896–1904: Some American Economists on Investment and the Theory of Surplus Capital," *Journal of Economic History* 43 (September 1983): 559–78. The authors point

Both Taussig and Taylor were monetary theorists who, while committed to a gold standard, urged reform that would make the money supply more elastic. Taussig called for an expansion of national bank notes, which would inflate in response to the "needs of business." As Taussig[14] put it, the currency would then "grow without trammels as the needs of the community spontaneously call for increase." Taylor, too, as one historian puts it, wanted the gold standard to be modified by "a conscious control of the movement of money" by government "in order to maintain the stability of the credit system." Taylor justified governmental suspensions of specie payment to "protect the gold reserve."[15]

On January 26, the convention delegates duly endorsed the preliminary report with virtual unanimity, after which Professor J. Laurence Laughlin was assigned the task of drawing up a more elaborate final report, which was published and distributed a few months later. Laughlin's—and the convention's—final report not only came out in favor of a broadened asset base for a greatly increased amount of national bank notes, but also called explicitly for a central bank that would enjoy a monopoly of the issue of bank notes.[16]

---

out that Conant's and Hadley's major works of 1896 were both published by G.P. Putnam's Sons of New York. President of Putnam's was George Haven Putnam, a leader in the new banking reform movement. Ibid., p. 561, n. 2.

[14]Frank W. Taussig, "What Should Congress Do About Money?" *Review of Reviews* (August 1893): 151, quoted in Joseph Dorfman, *The Economic Mind in American Civilization* (New York: Viking Press, 1949), 3, p. xxxvii. See also ibid., p. 269.

[15]Ibid., pp. 392–93.

[16]The final report, including its recommendations for a central bank, was hailed by F.M. Taylor, in his "The Final Report of the Indianapolis Monetary Commission," *Journal of Political Economy* 6 (June 1898): 293–322. Taylor also exulted that the convention had been "one of the most notable movements of our time—the first thoroughly organized movement of the business classes in the whole country directed to the bringing about of a radical change in national legislation." Ibid., p. 322.

The convention delegates took the gospel of banking reform to the length and breadth of the corporate and financial communities. In April 1898, for example, A. Barton Hepburn, president of the Chase National Bank of New York, at that time a flagship commercial bank for the Morgan interests and a man who would play a large role in the drive to establish a central bank, invited Indianapolis Monetary Commissioner Robert S. Taylor to address the New York State Bankers Association on the currency question, since "bankers, like other people, need instruction upon this subject." All the monetary commissioners, especially Taylor, were active during the first half of 1898 in exhorting groups of businessmen throughout the nation for monetary reform.

Meanwhile, in Washington, the lobbying team of Hanna and Conant was extremely active. A bill embodying the suggestions of the monetary commission was introduced by Indiana Congressman Jesse Overstreet in January, and was reported out by the House Banking and Currency Committee in May. In the meantime, Conant met almost continuously with the banking committee members. At each stage of the legislative process, Hanna sent letters to the convention delegates and to the public, urging a letter-writing campaign in support of the bill.

In this agitation, McKinley Secretary of the Treasury Lyman J. Gage worked closely with Hanna and his staff. Gage sponsored similar bills, and several bills along the same lines were introduced in the House in 1898 and 1899. Gage, a friend of several of the monetary commissioners, was one of the top leaders of the Rockefeller interests in the banking field. His appointment as Treasury secretary had been gained for him by Ohio's Mark Hanna, political mastermind and financial backer of President McKinley, and old friend, high-school classmate, and business associate of John D. Rockefeller, Sr. Before his appointment to the cabinet, Gage was president of the powerful First National Bank of Chicago, one of the major commercial banks in the Rockefeller ambit. During his term in office, Gage tried to operate the Treasury as a central bank, pumping in money during recessions by purchasing government bonds on the open market, and depositing large funds with pet commercial banks. In 1900, Gage called vainly for the establishment of regional central banks.

Finally, in his last annual report as secretary of the Treasury in 1901, Lyman Gage let the cat completely out of the bag, calling outright for a government central bank. Without such a central bank, he declared in alarm, "individual banks stand isolated and apart, separated units, with no tie of mutuality between them." Unless a central bank established such ties, Gage warned, the panic of 1893 would be repeated.[17] When he left office early the next year, Lyman Gage took up his post as president of the Rockefeller-controlled U.S. Trust Company in New York City.[18]

The Gold Standard Act of 1900 and After

Any reform legislation had to wait until after the elections of 1898, for the gold forces were not yet in control of Congress. In the autumn, the executive committee of the Indianapolis Monetary Convention mobilized its forces, calling on no less than 97,000 correspondents throughout the country through whom it had distributed the preliminary report. The executive committee urged its constituency to elect a gold-standard Congress; when the gold forces routed the silverites in November, the results of the election were hailed by Hanna as eminently satisfactory.

The decks were now cleared for the McKinley administration to submit its bill, and the Congress that met in December 1899 quickly passed the measure; Congress then passed the conference report of the Gold Standard Act in March 1900.

The currency reformers had gotten their way. It is well known that the Gold Standard Act provided for a single gold

[17]Livingston, *Origins*, p. 153.

[18]Rothbard, "Federal Reserve," pp. 94–95.

standard, with no retention of silver money except as tokens. Less well known are the clauses that began the march toward a more "elastic" currency. As Lyman Gage had suggested in 1897, national banks, previously confined to large cities, were now made possible with a small amount of capital in small towns and rural areas. And it was made far easier for national banks to issue notes. The object of these clauses, as one historian put it, was to satisfy an "increased demand for money at crop-moving time, and to meet popular cries for 'more money' by encouraging the organization of national banks in comparatively undeveloped regions."[19]

The reformers exulted over the passage of the Gold Standard Act, but took the line that this was only the first step on the much-needed path to fundamental banking reform. Thus, Professor Frank W. Taussig of Harvard praised the act, and greeted the emergence of a new social and ideological alignment, caused by "strong pressure from the business community" through the Indianapolis Monetary Convention. He particularly welcomed the fact that the Gold Standard Act "treats the national banks not as grasping and dangerous corporations but as useful institutions deserving the fostering care of the legislature." But such tender legislative care was not enough; fundamental banking reform was needed. For, Taussig declared, "The changes in banking legislation are not such as to make possible any considerable expansion of the national system or to enable it to render the community the full service of which it is capable." In short, the changes allowed for more and greater expansion of bank credit and the supply of money. Therefore, Taussig concluded, "It is well nigh certain that eventually Congress will have to consider once more the further remodeling of the national bank system."[20]

In fact, the Gold Standard Act of 1900 was only the opening gun of the banking reform movement. Three friends and financial

[19]Livingston, *Origins*, p. 123.

[20]Frank W. Taussig, "The Currency Act of 1900," *Quarterly Journal of Economics* 14 (May 1900): 415.

journalists, two from Chicago, were to play a large role in the development of that movement. Massachusetts-born Charles A. Conant (1861–1915), a leading historian of banking, wrote *A History of Modern Banks of Issue* in 1896, while still a Washington correspondent for the *New York Journal of Commerce* and an editor of *Bankers Magazine*. After his stint of public relations work and lobbying for the Indianapolis convention, Conant moved to New York in 1902 to become treasurer of the Morgan-oriented Morton Trust Company. The two Chicagoans, both friends of Lyman Gage, were, along with Gage, in the Rockefeller ambit: Frank A. Vanderlip was picked by Gage as his assistant secretary of the Treasury, and when Gage left office, Vanderlip came to New York as a top executive at the flagship commercial bank of the Rockefeller interests, the National City Bank of New York. Meanwhile, Vanderlip's close friend and mentor at the *Chicago Tribune*, Joseph French Johnson, had also moved east to become professor of finance at the Wharton School of the University of Pennsylvania. But no sooner had the Gold Standard Act been passed when Joseph Johnson sounded the trump by calling for more fundamental reform.

Professor Johnson stated flatly that the existing bank note system was weak in not "responding to the needs of the money market," that is, not supplying a sufficient amount of money. Since the national banking system was incapable of supplying those needs, Johnson opined, there was no reason to continue it. Johnson deplored the U.S. banking system as the worst in the world, and pointed to the glorious central banking system as existed in Britain and France.[21] But no such centralized banking system yet existed in the United States:

[21]Joseph French Johnson, "The Currency Act of March 14, 1900," *Political Science Quarterly* 15 (1900): 482–507. Johnson, however, deplored the one fly in the Bank of England ointment—the remnant of the hard-money Peel's Bank Act of 1844 that placed restrictions on the quantity of bank note issue. Ibid., p. 496.

> In the United States, however, there is no single business institution, and no group of large institutions, in which self-interest, responsibility, and power naturally unite and conspire for the protection of the monetary system against twists and strains.

In short, there was far too much freedom and decentralization in the system. In consequence, our massive deposit credit system "trembles whenever the foundations are disturbed," that is, whenever the chickens of inflationary credit expansion came home to roost in demands for cash or gold. The result of the inelasticity of money, and of the impossibility of interbank cooperation, Johnson opined, was that we were in danger of losing gold abroad just at the time when gold was needed to sustain confidence in the nation's banking system.[22]

After 1900, the banking community was split on the question of reform, the small and rural bankers preferring the status quo. But the large bankers, headed by A. Barton Hepburn of Morgan's Chase National Bank, drew up a bill as head of a commission of the American Bankers Association, and presented it in late 1901 to Representative Charles N. Fowler of New Jersey, chairman of the House Banking and Currency Committee, who had introduced one of the bills that had led to the Gold Standard Act. The Hepburn proposal was reported out of committee in April 1902 as the Fowler Bill.[23]

The Fowler Bill contained three basic clauses. One allowed the further expansion of national bank notes based on broader assets than government bonds. The second, a favorite of the big banks, was to allow national banks to establish branches at home and abroad, a step illegal under the existing system due to fierce opposition by the small country bankers. While branch banking is consonant with a free market and provides a sound and efficient system for calling on other banks for redemption, the big banks had little interest in branch banking unless accom-

[22]Ibid., pp. 497f.

[23]Kolko, *Triumph*, pp. 149–50.

panied by centralization of the banking system. Thus, the Fowler Bill proposed to create a three-member board of control within the Treasury Department to supervise the creation of the new bank notes and to establish clearinghouse associations under its aegis. This provision was designed to be the first step toward the establishment of a full-fledged central bank.[24]

Although they could not control the American Bankers Association, the multitude of country bankers, up in arms against the proposed competition of big banks in the form of branch banking, put fierce pressure upon Congress and managed to kill the Fowler Bill in the House during 1902, despite the agitation of the executive committee and staff of the Indianapolis Monetary Convention.

With the defeat of the Fowler Bill, the big bankers decided to settle for more modest goals for the time being. Senator Nelson W. Aldrich of Rhode Island, perennial Republican leader of the U.S. Senate and Rockefeller's man in Congress,[25] submitted the Aldrich Bill the following year, allowing the large national banks in New York to issue "emergency currency" based on municipal and railroad bonds. But even this bill was defeated.

Meeting setbacks in Congress, the big bankers decided to regroup and turn temporarily to the executive branch. Foreshadowing a later, more elaborate collaboration, two powerful representatives each from the Morgan and Rockefeller banking interests met with Comptroller of the Currency William B. Ridgely in January 1903, to try to persuade him, by administrative fiat, to restrict the volume of loans made by the country

[24]See Livingston, *Origins*, pp. 150–54.

[25]Nelson W. Aldrich, who entered the Senate a moderately wealthy wholesale grocer and left years later a multimillionaire, was the father-in-law of John D. Rockefeller, Jr. His grandson and namesake, Nelson Aldrich Rockefeller, later became vice president of the United States, and head of the "corporate liberal" wing of the Republican Party.

banks in the New York money market. The two Morgan men at the meeting were J.P. Morgan and George F. Baker, Morgan's closest friend and associate in the banking business.[26] The two Rockefeller men were Frank Vanderlip and James Stillman, longtime chairman of the board of the National City Bank.[27] The close Rockefeller-Stillman alliance was cemented by the marriage of the two daughters of Stillman to the two sons of William Rockefeller, brother of John D. Rockefeller, Sr., and longtime board member of the National City Bank.[28]

The meeting with the comptroller did not bear fruit, but the lead instead was taken by the secretary of the Treasury himself, Leslie Shaw, formerly presiding officer at the second Indianapolis Monetary Convention, whom President Roosevelt appointed to replace Lyman Gage. The unexpected and sudden shift from McKinley to Roosevelt in the presidency meant more than just a turnover of personnel; it meant a fundamental shift from a Rockefeller-dominated to a Morgan-dominated administration. In the same way, the shift from Gage to Shaw was one of the many Rockefeller-to-Morgan displacements.

On monetary and banking matters, however, the Rockefeller and Morgan camps were as one. Secretary Shaw attempted to continue and expand Gage's experiments in trying to make the Treasury function like a central bank, particularly in making open market purchases in recessions, and in using Treasury deposits to bolster the banks and expand the money supply. Shaw violated the statutory institution of the independent Trea-

[26]Baker was head of the Morgan-dominated First National Bank of New York, and served as a director of virtually every important Morgan-run enterprise, including: Chase National Bank, Guaranty Trust Company, Morton Trust Company, Mutual Life Insurance Company, AT&T, Consolidated Gas Company of New York, Erie Railroad, New York Central Railroad, Pullman Company, and United States Steel. See Burch, *Elites*, pp. 190, 229.

[27]On the meeting, see Livingston, *Origins*, p. 155.

[28]Burch, *Elites*, pp. 134–35.

sury, which had tried to confine government revenues and expenditures to its own coffers. Instead, he expanded the practice of depositing Treasury funds in favored big national banks. Indeed, even banking reformers denounced the deposit of Treasury funds to pet banks as artificially lowering interest rates and leading to artificial expansion of credit. Furthermore, any government deficit would obviously throw a system dependent on a flow of new government revenues into chaos. All in all, the reformers agreed increasingly with the verdict of economist Alexander Purves, that "the uncertainty as to the Secretary's power to control the banks by arbitrary decisions and orders, and the fact that at some future time the country may be unfortunate in its chief Treasury official . . . [has] led many to doubt the wisdom" of using the Treasury as a form of central bank.[29] In his last annual report of 1906, Secretary Shaw urged that he be given total power to regulate all the nation's banks. But the game was up, and by then it was clear to the reformers that Shaw's as well as Gage's proto–central bank manipulations had failed. It was time to undertake a struggle for a fundamental legislative overhaul of the American banking system to bring it under central banking control.[30]

Charles A. Conant, Surplus Capital, and Economic Imperialism

The years shortly before and after 1900 proved to be the beginnings of the drive toward the establishment of a Federal Reserve System. It was also the origin of the gold-exchange standard, the fateful system imposed upon the world by the British in the 1920s and by the United States after World War II at Bretton Woods. Even more than the case of a gold standard

[29]Livingston, *Origins*, p. 156. See also ibid., pp. 161–62.

[30]On Gage's and Shaw's manipulations, see Rothbard, "Federal Reserve," pp. 94–96; and Milton Friedman and Anna Jacobson Schwartz, *A Monetary History of the United States, 1867–1960* (Princeton, N.J.: National Bureau of Economic Research, 1963), pp. 148–56.

with a central bank, the gold-exchange standard establishes a system, in the name of gold, which in reality manages to install coordinated international inflationary paper money. The idea was to replace a genuine gold standard, in which each country (or, domestically, each bank) maintains its reserves in gold, by a pseudo-gold standard in which the central bank of the client country maintains its reserves in some key or base currency, say pounds or dollars. Thus, during the 1920s, most countries maintained their reserves in pounds, and only Britain purported to redeem pounds in gold. This meant that these other countries were really on a pound rather than a gold standard, although they were able, at least temporarily, to acquire the prestige of gold. It also meant that when Britain inflated pounds, there was no danger of losing gold to these other countries, who, quite the contrary, happily inflated their own currencies on top of their expanding balances in pounds sterling. Thus, there was generated an unstable, inflationary system—all in the name of gold—in which client states pyramided their own inflation on top of Great Britain's. The system was eventually bound to collapse, as did the gold-exchange standard in the Great Depression and Bretton Woods by the late 1960s. In addition, the close ties based on pounds and then dollars meant that the key or base country was able to exert a form of economic imperialism, joined by its common paper and pseudo-gold inflation, upon the client states using the key money.

By the late 1890s, groups of theoreticians in the United States were working on what would later be called the "Leninist" theory of capitalist imperialism. The theory was originated, not by Lenin but by advocates of imperialism, centering around such Morgan-oriented friends and brain trusters of Theodore Roosevelt as Henry Adams, Brooks Adams, Admiral Alfred T. Mahan, and Massachusetts Senator Henry Cabot Lodge. The idea was that capitalism in the developed countries was "overproducing," not simply in the sense that more purchasing power was needed in recessions, but more deeply in that the rate of profit was therefore inevitably falling. The ever lower rate of profit from the "surplus capital" was in danger of crippling capitalism, except that salvation loomed in the form of foreign markets and especially foreign investments. New and expanded foreign markets would increase profits, at least temporarily, while investments in undeveloped countries would be bound to bring a high rate of profit. Hence, to save advanced capitalism, it was necessary for Western governments to engage in outright imperialist or neo-imperialist ventures, which would force other countries to open their markets for American products and would force open investment opportunities abroad.

Given this doctrine—based on the fallacious Ricardian view that the rate of profit is determined by the stock of capital investment, instead of by the time preferences of everyone in society—there was little for Lenin to change except to give an implicit moral condemnation instead of approval and to emphasize the necessarily temporary nature of the respite imperialism could furnish for capitalists.[31]

Charles Conant set forth the theory of surplus capital in his *A History of Modern Banks of Issue* (1896) and developed it in subsequent essays. The existence of fixed capital and modern technology, Conant claimed, invalidated Say's Law and the concept of equilibrium, and led to chronic "oversavings," which he defined as savings in excess of profitable investment outlets, in the developed Western capitalist world. Business cycles, opined Conant, were inherent in the unregulated activity of modern industrial capitalism. Hence the importance of government-encouraged monopolies and cartels to stabilize markets and the

[31]Indeed, the adoption of this theory of the alleged necessity for imperialism in the "later stages" of capitalism went precisely from pro-imperialists like the *U.S. Investor*, Charles A. Conant, and Brooks Adams in 1898–99, read and adopted by the Marxist H. Gaylord Wilshire in 1900–01, in turn read and adopted by the English left-liberal anti-imperialist John A. Hobson, who in turn influenced Lenin. See in particular Norman Etherington, *Theories of Imperialism: War, Conquest, and Capital* (Totowa, N.J.: Barnes and Noble, 1984). See also Etherington, "Reconsidering Theories of Imperialism," *History and Theory* 21, no. 1 (1982): 1–36.

business cycle, and in particular the necessity of economic imperialism to force open profitable outlets abroad for American and other Western surplus capital.

The United States's bold venture into an imperialist war against Spain in 1898 galvanized the energies of Conant and other theoreticians of imperialism. Conant responded with his call for imperialism in "The Economic Basis of Imperialism" in the September 1898 *North American Review*, and in other essays collected in *The United States in the Orient: The Nature of the Economic Problem* and published in 1900. S.J. Chapman, a distinguished British economist, accurately summarized Conant's argument as follows: (1) "In all advanced countries there has been such excessive saving that no profitable investment for capital remains," (2) since all countries do not practice a policy of commercial freedom, "America must be prepared to use force if necessary" to open up profitable investment outlets abroad, and (3) the United States possesses an advantage in the coming struggle, since the organization of many of its industries "in the form of trusts will assist it greatly in the fight for commercial supremacy."[32]

The war successfully won, Conant was particularly enthusiastic about the United States keeping the Philippines, the gateway to the great potential Asian market. The United States, he opined, should not be held back by "an abstract theory" to adopt "extreme conclusions" on applying the doctrines of the Founding Fathers on the importance of the consent of the governed. The Founding Fathers, he declared, surely meant that self-government could only apply to those competent to exercise it, a requirement that clearly did not apply to the backward people of the Philippines. After all, Conant wrote, "Only by the firm hand of the responsible governing races . . . can the assurance of

[32]Review of Charles A. Conant's *The United States in the Orient*, by S.J. Chapman in *Economic Journal* 2 (1901): 78. See Etherington, *Theories of Imperialism*, p. 24.

uninterrupted progress be conveyed to the tropical and undeveloped countries."[33]

Conant also was bold enough to derive important domestic conclusions from his enthusiasm for imperialism. Domestic society, he claimed, would have to be transformed to make the nation as "efficient" as possible. Efficiency, in particular, meant centralized concentration of power. "Concentration of power, in order to permit prompt and efficient action, will be an almost essential factor in the struggle for world empire." In particular, it was important for the United States to learn from the magnificent centralization of power and purpose in Czarist Russia. The government of the United States would require "a degree of harmony and symmetry which will permit the direction of the whole power of the state toward definite and intelligent policies." The U.S. Constitution would have to be amended to permit a form of czarist absolutism, or at the very least an enormously expanded executive power in foreign affairs.[34]

An interesting case study of business opinion energized and converted by the lure of imperialism was the Boston weekly, the *U.S. Investor*. Before the outbreak of war with Spain in 1898, the *U.S. Investor* denounced the idea of war as a disaster to business. But after the United States launched its war, and Commodore Dewey seized Manila Bay, the *Investor* totally changed its tune. Now it hailed the war as excellent for business, and as bringing about recovery from the previous recession. Soon the *Investor* was happily advocating a policy of "imperialism" to make U.S. prosperity permanent. Imperialism conveyed marvelous benefits to the country. At home, a big army and navy would be valuable in curbing the tendency of democracy to enjoy "a too great freedom from restraint, both of action and of thought." The *Investor* added that "European experience demonstrates that the

[33]David Healy, *U.S. Expansionism: The Imperialist Urge in the 1890s* (Madison: University of Wisconsin Press, 1970), pp. 200–01.

[34]Ibid., pp. 202–03.

army and navy are admirably adopted to inculcate orderly habits of thought and action."

But an even more important benefit from a policy of permanent imperialism is economic. To keep "capital . . . at work," stern necessity requires that "an enlarged field for its product must be discovered." Specifically, "a new field" had to be found for selling the growing flood of goods produced by the advanced nations, and for investment of their savings at profitable rates. The *Investor* exulted in the fact that this new "field lies ready for occupancy. It is to be found among the semi-civilized and barbarian races," in particular the beckoning country of China.

Particularly interesting was the colloquy that ensued between the *Investor,* and the *Springfield (Mass.) Republican*, which still propounded the older theory of free trade and laissez-faire. The *Republican* asked why trade with undeveloped countries was not sufficient without burdening U.S. taxpayers with administrative and military overhead. The *Republican* also attacked the new theory of surplus capital, pointing out that only two or three years earlier, businessmen had been loudly calling for more European capital to be invested in American ventures.

To the first charge, the *Investor* fell back on "the experience of the race for, perhaps ninety centuries, [which] has been in the direction of foreign acquisitions as a means of national prosperity." But, more practically, the *Investor* delighted over the goodies that imperialism would bring to American business in the way of government contracts and the governmental development of what would now be called the "infrastructure" of the colonies. Furthermore, as in Britain, a greatly expanded diplomatic service would provide "a new calling for our young men of education and ability."

To the *Republican's* second charge, on surplus capital, the *Investor*, like Conant, developed the idea of a new age that had just arrived in American affairs, an age of large-scale and hence overproduction, an age of a low rate of profit, and consequent formation of trusts in a quest for higher profits through suppression of competition. As the *Investor* put it,

"The excess of capital has resulted in an unprofitable competition. To employ Franklin's witticism, the owners of capital are of the opinion they must hang together or else they will all hang separately." But while trusts may solve the problem of specific industries, they did not solve the great problem of a general "congestion of capital." Indeed, wrote the *Investor*, "finding employment for capital . . . is now the greatest of all economic problems that confront us."

To the *Investor*, the way out was clear:

> [T]he logical path to be pursued is that of the development of the natural riches of the tropical countries. These countries are now peopled by races incapable on their own initiative of extracting its full riches from their own soil. . . . This will be attained in some cases by the mere stimulus of government and direction by men of the temperate zones; but it will be attained also by the application of modern machinery and methods of culture to the agricultural and mineral resources of the undeveloped countries.[35]

By the spring of 1901, even the eminent economic theorist John Bates Clark of Columbia University was able to embrace the new creed. Reviewing pro-imperialist works by Conant, Brooks Adams, and the Reverend Josiah Strong in a single celebratory review in March 1901 in the *Political Science Quarterly*, Clark emphasized the importance of opening foreign markets and particularly of investing American capital "with an even larger and more permanent profit."[36]

J.B. Clark was not the only economist ready to join in apologia for the strong state. Throughout the land by the turn of the twentieth century, a legion of economists and other social scientists had arisen, many of them trained in graduate schools in Germany to learn of the virtues of the inductive method, the German Historical School, and a collectivist, organicist state.

[35]*The Investor*, 19 January 1901, pp. 65–66, cited in Etherington, *Theories of Imperialism*, p. 17. Also ibid., pp. 7–23.

[36]Parrini and Sklar, "New Thinking," p. 565, n. 16.

Eager for positions and power commensurate with their graduate training, these new social scientists, in the name of professionalism and technical expertise, prepared to abandon the old laissez-faire creed and take their places as apologists and planners in a new, centrally planned state. Professor Edwin R.A. Seligman of Columbia University, of the prominent Wall Street investment banking family of J. and W. Seligman and Company, spoke for many of these social scientists when, in a presidential address before the American Economic Association in 1903, he hailed the "new industrial order."[37] Seligman prophesied that in the new, twentieth century, the possession of economic knowledge would grant economists the power "to control . . . and mold" the material forces of progress. As the economist proved able to forecast more accurately, he would be installed as "the real philosopher of social life," and the public would pay "deference to his views."

In his 1899 presidential address, Yale President Arthur Twining Hadley also saw economists developing as society's philosopher-kings. The most important application of economic knowledge, declared Hadley, was leadership in public life, becoming advisers and leaders of national policy. Hadley opined,

> I believe that their [economists'] largest opportunity in the immediate future lies not in theories but in practice, not with students but with statesmen, not in the education of individual citizens, however widespread and salutary, but in the leadership of an organized body politic.[38]

Hadley perceptively saw the executive branch of the government as particularly amenable to access of position and influence

[37]Seligman was also related by marriage to the Loebs and to Paul Warburg of Kuhn, Loeb. Specifically, E.R.A. Seligman's brother, Isaac N., was married to Guta Loeb, sister of Paul Warburg's wife, Nina. See Stephen Birmingham, *Our Crowd: The Jewish Families of New York* (New York: Pocket Books, 1977), app.

[38]Quoted in Edward T. Silva and Sheila A. Slaughter, *Serving Power: The Making of the Academic Social Science Expert* (Westport, Conn.: Greenwood Press, 1984), p. 103.

to economic advisers and planners. Previously, executives were hampered in seeking such expert counsel by the importance of political parties, their ideological commitments, and their mass base in the voting population. But now, fortunately, the growing municipal reform (soon to be called the Progressive) movement was taking power away from political parties and putting it into the hands of administrators and experts. The "increased centralization of administrative power [was giving] . . . the expert a fair chance." And now, on the national scene, the new American leap into imperialism in the Spanish-American War was providing an opportunity for increased centralization, executive power, and therefore for administrative and expert planning. Even though Hadley declared himself personally opposed to imperialism, he urged economists to leap at this great opportunity for access to power.[39]

The organized economic profession was not slow to grasp this new opportunity. Quickly, the executive and nominating committees of the American Economic Association (AEA) created a five-man special committee to organize and publish a volume on colonial finance. As Silva and Slaughter put it, this new, rapidly put-together volume permitted the AEA to show the power elite

> how the new social science could serve the interests of those who made imperialism a national policy by offering technical solutions to the immediate fiscal problems of colonies as well as providing ideological justifications for acquiring them.[40]

Chairman of the special committee was Professor Jeremiah W. Jenks of Cornell, the major economic adviser to New York Governor Theodore Roosevelt. Another member was Professor E.R.A. Seligman, another key adviser to Roosevelt. A third colleague was Dr. Albert Shaw, influential editor of the *Review of Reviews*, progressive reformer and social scientist, and longtime crony of Roosevelt's. All three were longtime leaders of the

[39]Ibid., pp. 120–21.

[40]Ibid., p. 133.

American Economic Association. The other two, non-AEA leaders, on the committee were Edward R. Strobel, former assistant secretary of state and adviser to colonial governments, and Charles S. Hamlin, wealthy Boston lawyer and assistant secretary of the Treasury who had long been in the Morgan ambit, and whose wife was a member of the Pruyn family, longtime investors in two Morgan-dominated concerns: the New York Central Railroad and the Mutual Life Insurance Company of New York.

Essays in Colonial Finance, the volume quickly put together by these five leaders, tried to advise the United States how best to run its newly acquired empire. First, just as the British government insisted when the North American states were its colonies, the colonies should support their imperial government through taxation, whereas control should be tightly exercised by the United States imperial center. Second, the imperial center should build and maintain the economic infrastructure of the colony: canals, railroads, communications. Third, where—as was clearly anticipated—native labor is inefficient or incapable of management, the imperial government should import (white) labor from the imperial center. And, finally, as Silva and Slaughter put it,

> the committee's fiscal recommendations strongly intimated that trained economists were necessary for a successful empire. It was they who must make a thorough study of local conditions to determine the correct fiscal system, gather data, create the appropriate administrative design and perhaps even implement it. In this way, the committee seconded Hadley's views in seeing as an opportunity for economists by identifying a large number of professional positions best filled by themselves.[41]

With the volume written, the AEA cast about for financial support for its publication and distribution. The point was not simply to obtain the financing, but to do so in such a way as to

[41]Ibid., p. 135. The volume in question is *Essays in Colonial Finance* (Publications of the American Economic Association, 3rd series, August 1900).

gain the imprimatur of leading members of the power elite on this bold move for power to economists as technocratic expert advisers and administrators in the imperial nation-state.

The American Economic Association found five wealthy businessmen to put up $125, two-fifths of the full cost of publishing *Essays in Colonial Finance*. By compiling the volume and then accepting corporate sponsors, several of whom had an economic stake in the new American empire, the AEA was signaling that the nation's organized economists were (1) wholeheartedly in favor of the new American empire; and (2) willing and eager to play a strong role in advising and administering the empire, a role which they promptly and happily filled, as we shall see in the following section.

In view of the symbolic as well as practical role for the sponsors, a list of the five donors for the colonial finance volume is instructive. One was Isaac N. Seligman, head of the investment banking house of J. and W. Seligman and Company, a company with extensive overseas interests, especially in Latin America. Isaac's brother, E.R.A. Seligman, was a member of the special committee on colonial finance and an author of one of the essays in the volume. Another was William E. Dodge, a partner of the copper mining firm of Phelps, Dodge, and Company and member of a powerful mining family allied to the Morgans. A third donor was Theodore Marburg, an economist who was vice president of the AEA at the time, and also an ardent advocate of imperialism as well as heir to a substantial American Tobacco Company fortune. Fourth was Thomas Shearman, a single-taxer and an attorney for powerful railroad magnate Jay Gould. And last but not least, Stuart Wood, a manufacturer who had a Ph.D. in economics and had been a vice president of the AEA.

Conant, Monetary Imperialism, and the Gold-Exchange Standard

The leap into political imperialism by the United States in the late 1890s was accompanied by economic imperialism, and one key to economic imperialism was monetary imperialism. In brief, the developed Western countries by this time were on the gold standard, while most of the Third World nations were on the silver standard. For the past several decades, the value of silver in relation to gold had been steadily falling, due to (1) an increasing world supply of silver relative to gold, and (2) the subsequent shift of many Western nations from silver or bimetallism to gold, thereby lowering the world's demand for silver as a monetary metal.

The fall of silver value meant monetary depreciation and inflation in the Third World, and it would have been a reasonable policy to shift from a silver-coin to a gold-coin standard. But the new imperialists among U.S. bankers, economists, and politicians were far less interested in the welfare of Third World countries than in foisting a monetary imperialism upon them. For not only would the economies of the imperial center and the client states then be tied together, but they would be tied in such a way that these economies could pyramid their own monetary and bank credit inflation on top of inflation in the United States. Hence, what the new imperialists set out to do was to pressure or coerce Third World countries to adopt, not a genuine gold-coin standard, but a newly conceived "gold-exchange" or dollar standard.

Instead of silver currency fluctuating freely in terms of gold, the silver-gold rate would then be fixed by arbitrary government price-fixing. The silver countries would be silver in name only; a country's monetary reserve would be held, not in silver, but in dollars allegedly redeemable in gold; and these reserves would be held, not in the country itself, but as dollars piled up in New York City. In that way, if U.S. banks inflated their credit, there would be no danger of losing gold abroad, as would happen under a genuine gold standard. For under a true gold standard, no one and no country would be interested in piling up claims to dollars overseas. Instead, they would demand payment of dollar claims in gold. So that even though these American bankers and economists were all too aware, after many decades of experience, of the fallacies and evils of bimetallism, they were willing to impose a form of bimetallism upon client states in order to tie them into U.S. economic imperialism, and to pressure them into inflating their own money supplies on top of dollar reserves supposedly, but not de facto redeemable in gold.

The United States first confronted the problem of silver currencies in a Third World country when it seized control of Puerto Rico from Spain in 1898 and occupied it as a permanent colony. Fortunately for the imperialists, Puerto Rico was already ripe for currency manipulation. Only three years earlier, in 1895, Spain had destroyed the full-bodied Mexican silver currency that its colony had previously enjoyed and replaced it with a heavily debased silver "dollar," worth only 41¢ in U.S. currency. The Spanish government had pocketed the large seigniorage profits from that debasement. The United States was therefore easily able to substitute its own debased silver dollar, worth only 45.6¢ in gold. Thus, the United States silver currency replaced an even more debased one and also the Puerto Ricans had no tradition of loyalty to a currency only recently imposed by the Spaniards. There was therefore little or no opposition in Puerto Rico to the U.S. monetary takeover.[42]

The major controversial question was what exchange rate the American authorities would fix between the two debased coins: the old Puerto Rican silver peso and the U.S. silver dollar. This was the rate at which the U.S. authorities would compel the Puerto Ricans to exchange their existing coinage for the new American coins. The treasurer in charge of the currency reform for the U.S. government was the prominent Johns Hopkins economist Jacob H. Hollander, who had been special commissioner to revise Puerto Rican tax laws, and who was one of the new breed of academic economists repudiating laissez-faire for comprehensive statism. The heavy debtors in Puerto Rico—mainly the large sugar planters—naturally wanted to pay their

[42]See the illuminating article by Emily S. Rosenberg, "Foundations of United States International Financial Power: Gold Standard Diplomacy, 1900–1905," *Business History Review* 59 (Summer 1985): 172–73.

peso obligations at as cheap a rate as possible; they lobbied for a peso worth 50¢ American. In contrast, the Puerto Rican banker-creditors wanted the rate fixed at 75¢. Since the exchange rate was arbitrary anyway, Hollander and the other American officials decided in the time-honored way of governments: more or less splitting the difference, and fixing a peso equal to 60¢.[43]

The Philippines, the other Spanish colony grabbed by the United States, posed a far more difficult problem. As in most of the Far East, the Philippines was happily using a perfectly sound silver currency, the Mexican silver dollar. But the United States was anxious for a rapid reform, because its large armed forces establishment suppressing Filipino nationalism required heavy expenses in U.S. dollars, which it of course declared to be legal tender for payments. Since the Mexican silver coin was also legal tender and was cheaper than the U.S. gold dollar, the U.S. military occupation found its revenues being paid in unwanted and cheaper Mexican coins.

Delicacy was required, and in 1901, for the task of currency takeover, the Bureau of Insular Affairs (BIA) of the War Department—the agency running the U.S. occupation of the Philippines—hired Charles A. Conant. Secretary of War Elihu Root was a redoubtable Wall Street lawyer in the Morgan ambit who sometimes served as J.P. Morgan's personal attorney. Root took a personal hand in sending Conant to the Philippines. Conant,

[43]Also getting their start in administering imperialism in Puerto Rico were economist and demographer W.H. Willcox of Cornell, who conducted the first census on the island as well as in Cuba in 1900, and Roland P. Falkner, statistician and bank reformer first at the University of Pennsylvania, and then head of the Division of Documents at the Library of Congress. Faulkner became commissioner of education in Puerto Rico in 1903, then went on to head the U.S. Commission to Liberia in 1909 and to be a member of the Joint Land Commission of the U.S. and Chinese governments. Harvard economist Thomas S. Adams served as assistant treasurer to Hollander in Puerto Rico. Political scientist William F. Willoughby succeeded Hollander as treasurer (Silva and Slaughter, *Serving Power*, pp. 137–38).

fresh from the Indianapolis Monetary Commission and before going to New York as a leading investment banker, was, as might be expected, an ardent gold-exchange-standard imperialist as well as the leading theoretician of economic imperialism.

Realizing that the Filipino people loved their silver coins, Conant devised a way to impose a gold U.S. dollar currency upon the country. Under his cunning plan, the Filipinos would continue to have a silver currency; but replacing the full-bodied Mexican silver coin would be an American silver coin tied to gold at a debased value far less than the market exchange value of silver in terms of gold. In this imposed, debased bimetallism, since the silver coin was deliberately overvalued in relation to gold by the U.S. government, Gresham's Law inexorably went into effect. The overvalued silver would keep circulating in the Philippines, and undervalued gold would be kept sharply out of circulation.

The seigniorage profit that the Treasury would reap from the debasement would be happily deposited at a New York bank, which would then function as a "reserve" for the U.S. silver currency in the Philippines. Thus, the New York funds would be used for payment outside the Philippines instead of as coin or specie. Moreover, the U.S. government could issue paper dollars based on its new reserve fund.

It should be noted that Conant originated the gold-exchange scheme as a way of exploiting and controlling Third World economies based on silver. At the same time, Great Britain was introducing similar schemes in its colonial areas in Egypt, in Straits Settlements in Asia, and particularly in India.

Congress, however, pressured by the silver lobby, balked at the BIA's plan. And so the BIA again turned to the seasoned public relations and lobbying skills of Charles A. Conant. Conant swung into action. Meeting with editors of the top financial journals, he secured their promises to write editorials pushing for the Conant plan, many of which he obligingly wrote himself. He was already backed by the American banks of Manila. Recalcitrant U.S. bankers were warned by Conant that they could no longer expect large government deposits from the War Department if they continued to oppose the plan. Furthermore, Conant won the support of the major enemies of his plan, the American silver companies and pro-silver bankers, promising them that if the Philippine currency reform went through, the federal government would buy silver for the new U.S. coinage in the Philippines from these same companies. Finally, the tireless lobbying, and the mixture of bribery and threats by Conant, paid off: Congress passed the Philippine Currency Bill in March 1903.

In the Philippines, however, the United States could not simply duplicate the Puerto Rican example and coerce the conversion of the old for the new silver coinage. The Mexican silver coin was a dominant coin not only in the Far East but throughout the world, and the coerced conversion would have been endless. The U.S. tried; it removed the legal tender privilege from the Mexican coins, and decreed the new U.S. coins be used for taxes, government salaries, and other government payments. But this time the Filipinos happily used the old Mexican coins as money, while the U.S. silver coins disappeared from circulation into payment of taxes and transactions to the United States.

The War Department was beside itself: How could it drive Mexican silver coinage out of the Philippines? In desperation, it turned to the indefatigable Conant, but Conant couldn't join the colonial government in the Philippines because he had just been appointed to a more far-flung presidential commission on international exchange for pressuring Mexico and China to go on a similar gold-exchange standard. Hollander, fresh from his Puerto Rican triumph, was ill. Who else? Conant, Hollander, and several leading bankers told the War Department they could recommend no one for the job, so new then was the profession of technical expertise in monetary imperialism. But there was one more hope, the other pro-cartelist and financial imperialist, Cornell's Jeremiah W. Jenks, a fellow member with Conant of President Roosevelt's new Commission on International Exchange (CIE). Jenks had already paved the way for Conant by visiting English and Dutch colonies in the Far East in 1901 to gain information about running the Philippines. Jenks finally came up with a name, his former graduate student at Cornell, Edwin W. Kemmerer.

Young Kemmerer went to the Philippines from 1903 to 1906 to implement the Conant plan. Based on the theories of Jenks and Conant, and on his own experience in the Philippines, Kemmerer went on to teach at Cornell and then at Princeton, and gained fame throughout the 1920s as the "money doctor," busily imposing the gold-exchange standard on country after country abroad.

Relying on Conant's behind-the-scenes advice, Kemmerer and his associates finally came out with a successful scheme to drive out the Mexican silver coins. It was a plan that relied heavily on government coercion. The United States imposed a legal prohibition on the importation of the Mexican coins, followed by severe taxes on any private Philippine transactions daring to use the Mexican currency. Luckily for the planners, their scheme was aided by a large-scale demand at the time for Mexican silver in northern China, which absorbed silver from the Philippines or that would have been smuggled into the islands. The U.S. success was aided by the fact that the new U.S. silver coins, perceptively called "conants" by the Filipinos, were made up to look very much like the cherished old Mexican coins. By 1905, force, luck, and trickery had prevailed, and the conants (worth 50¢ in U.S. money) were the dominant currency in the Philippines. Soon the U.S. authorities were confident enough to add token copper coins and paper conants as well.[44]

[44]See Rosenberg, "Foundations," pp. 177–81. Other economists and social scientists helping to administer imperialism in the Philippines were: Carl C. Plehn of the University of California, who served as chief statistician to the Philippine Commission in 1900–01, and Bernard Moses,

By 1903, the currency reformers felt emboldened enough to move against the Mexican silver dollar throughout the world. In Mexico itself, U.S. industrialists who wanted to invest there pressured the Mexicans to shift from silver to gold, and they found an ally in Mexico's powerful finance minister, Jose Limantour. But tackling the Mexican silver peso at home would not be an easy task, for the coin was known and used throughout the world, particularly in China, where it formed the bulk of the circulating coinage. Finally, after three-way talks between United States, Mexican, and Chinese officials, the Mexicans and Chinese were induced to send identical notes to the U.S. secretary of state, urging the United States to appoint financial advisers to bring about currency reform and stabilized exchange rates with the gold countries.[45]

These requests gave President Roosevelt, upon securing congressional approval, the excuse to appoint in March 1903 a three-man Commission on International Exchange to bring about currency reform in Mexico, China, and the rest of the silver-using world. The aim was "to bring about a fixed relationship between the moneys of the gold-standard countries and the present silver-using countries," in order to foster "export trade

---

historian, political scientist, and economist at the University of California, an ardent advocate of imperialism who served on the Philippine Commission from 1901 to 1903, and then became an expert in Latin American affairs, joining in a series of Pan American conferences. Political scientist David P. Barrows became superintendent of schools in Manila and director of education for eight years, from 1901 to 1909. This experience ignited a lifelong interest in the military for Barrows, who, while a professor at Berkeley and a general in the California National Guard in 1934, led the troops that broke the San Francisco longshoremen's strike. During World War II, Barrows carried over his interest in coercion to help in the forced internment of Japanese Americans in concentration camps. On Barrows, see Silva and Slaughter, *Serving Power*, pp. 137–38. On Moses, see Dorfman, *Economic Mind*, pp. 96–98.

[45]Parrini and Sklar, "New Thinking," pp. 573–77; Rosenberg, "Foundations," p. 184.

and investment opportunities" in the gold countries and economic development in the silver countries.

The three members of the CIE were old friends and like-minded colleagues. Chairman was Hugh H. Hanna, of the Indianapolis Monetary Commission; the others were his former chief aide at that commission, Charles A. Conant, and Professor Jeremiah W. Jenks. Conant, as usual, was the major theoretician and finagler. He realized that major opposition to Mexico's and China's going off silver would come from the important Mexican silver industry, and he devised a scheme to get European countries to purchase large amounts of Mexican silver to ease the pain of the shift.

In a trip to European nations in the summer of 1903, however, Conant and the CIE found the Europeans less than enthusiastic about making Mexican silver purchases as well as subsidizing U.S. exports and investments in China, a land whose market they too were coveting. In the United States, on the other hand, major newspapers and financial periodicals, prodded by Conant's public relations work, warmly endorsed the new currency scheme.

In the meanwhile, however, the United States faced similar currency problems in its two new Caribbean protectorates, Cuba and Panama. Panama was easy. The United States occupied the Canal Zone, and would be importing vast amounts of equipment to build the canal, so it decided to impose the American gold dollar as the currency in the nominally independent Republic of Panama. While the gold dollar was the official currency of Panama, the United States imposed as the actual medium of exchange a new debased silver peso worth 50¢. Fortunately, the new peso was almost the same in value as the old Colombian silver coin it forcibly displaced, and so, like Puerto Rico, the takeover could go without a hitch.

Among the U.S. colonies or protectorates, Cuba proved the toughest nut to crack. Despite all of Conant's ministrations, Cuba's currency remained unreformed. Spanish gold and silver coins, French coins, and U.S. currency all circulated side by side, freely fluctuating in response to supply and demand. Furthermore, similar to the pre-reformed Philippines, a fixed bimetallic exchange rate between the cheaper U.S., and the more valuable Spanish and French coins, led the Cubans to return cheaper U.S. coins to the U.S. customs authorities in fees and revenues.

Why then did Conant fail in Cuba? In the first place, strong Cuban nationalism resented U.S. plans for seizing control of their currency. Conant's repeated request in 1903 for a Cuban invitation for the CIE to visit the island met stern rejections from the Cuban government. Moreover, the charismatic U.S. military commander in Cuba, Leonard Wood, wanted to avoid giving the Cubans the impression that plans were afoot to reduce Cuba to colonial status.

The second objection was economic. The powerful sugar industry in Cuba depended on exports to the United States, and a shift from depreciated silver to higher-valued gold money would increase the cost of sugar exports, by an amount Leonard Wood estimated to be about 20 percent. While the same problem had existed for the sugar planters in Puerto Rico, American economic interests, in Puerto Rico and in other countries such as the Philippines, favored forcing formerly silver countries onto a gold-based standard so as to stimulate U.S. exports into those countries. In Cuba, on the other hand, there was increasing U.S. investment capital pouring into the Cuban sugar plantations, so that powerful and even dominant U.S. economic interests existed on the other side of the currency reform question. Indeed, by World War I, American investments in Cuban sugar reached the sum of $95 million.

Thus, when Charles Conant resumed his pressure for a Cuban gold-exchange standard in 1907, he was strongly opposed by the U.S. governor of Cuba, Charles Magoon, who raised the problem of a gold-based standard crippling the sugar planters. The CIE never managed to visit Cuba, and ironically, Charles Conant died in Cuba, in 1915, trying in vain to convince the Cubans of the virtues of the gold-exchange standard.[46]

The Mexican shift from silver to gold was more gratifying to Conant, but here the reform was effected by Foreign Minister Limantour and his indigenous technicians, with the CIE taking a back seat. However, the success of this shift, in the Mexican Currency Reform Act of 1905, was assured by a world rise in the price of silver, starting the following year, which made gold coins cheaper than silver, with Gresham's Law bringing about a successful gold-coin currency in Mexico. But the U.S. silver coinage in the Philippines ran into trouble because of the rise in the world silver price. Here, the U.S. silver currency in the Philippines was bailed out by coordinated action by the Mexican government, which sold silver in the Philippines to lower the value of silver sufficiently so that the conants could be brought back into circulation.[47]

The big failure of Conant-CIE monetary imperialism was in China. In 1900, Britain, Japan, and the United States intervened in China to put down the Boxer Rebellion. The three countries thereupon forced defeated China to agree to pay them and all major European powers an indemnity of $333 million. The United States interpreted the treaty as an obligation to pay in gold, but China, on a depreciated silver standard, began to pay in silver in 1903, an action that enraged the three treaty powers. The U.S. minister to China reported that Britain might declare China's payment in silver a violation of the treaty, which would presage military intervention.

Emboldened by United States success in the Philippines, Panama, and Mexico, Secretary of War Root sent Jeremiah W. Jenks on a mission to China in early 1904 to try to transform

[46]See Rosenberg, "Foundations," pp. 186–88.

[47]It is certainly possible that one of the reasons for the outbreak of the nationalist Mexican Revolution of 1910, in part a revolution against U.S. influence, was reaction against the U.S.-led currency manipulation and the coerced shift from silver to gold. Certainly, research needs to be done into this possibility.

China from a silver to a gold-exchange standard. Jenks also wrote to President Roosevelt from China urging that the Chinese indemnity to the United States from the Boxer Rebellion be used to fund exchange professorships for 30 years. Jenks's mission, however, was a total failure. The Chinese understood the CIE currency scheme all too well. They saw and denounced the seigniorage of the gold-exchange standard as an irresponsible and immoral debasement of Chinese currency, an act that would impoverish China while adding to the profits of U.S. banks where seigniorage reserve funds would be deposited. Moreover, the Chinese officials saw that shifting the indemnity from silver to gold would enrich the European governments at the expense of the Chinese economy. They also noted that the CIE scheme would establish a foreign controller of the Chinese currency to impose banking regulations and economic reforms on the Chinese economy. We need not wonder at the Chinese outrage. China's reaction was its own nationalistic currency reform in 1905, to replace the Mexican silver coin with a new Chinese silver coin, the tael.[48]

Jenks's ignominious failure in China put an end to any formal role for the Commission on International Exchange.[49] An immediately following fiasco blocked the U.S. government's use of economic and financial advisers to spread the gold-exchange standard abroad. In 1905, the State Department hired Jacob Hollander to move another of its Latin American client states, the Dominican Republic, onto the gold-exchange standard. When Hollander accomplished this task by the end of the year, the State Department asked the Dominican government to

[48]See Rosenberg, "Foundations," pp. 189–92.

[49]The failure, however, did not diminish the U.S. government's demand for Jenks's services. He went on to advise the Mexican government, serve as a member of the Nicaraguan High Commission under President Wilson's occupation regime, and also headed the Far Eastern Bureau of the State Department. See Silva and Slaughter, *Serving Power*, pp. 136–37.

hire Hollander to work out a plan for financial reform, including a U.S. loan, and a customs service run by the United States to collect taxes for repayment of the loan. Hollander, son-in-law of prominent Baltimore merchant Abraham Hutzler, used his connection with Kuhn, Loeb and Company to place Dominican bonds with that investment bank. Hollander also engaged happily in double-dipping for the same work, collecting fees for the same job from the State Department and from the Dominican government. When this peccadillo was discovered in 1911, the scandal made it impossible for the U.S. government to use its own employees and its own funds to push for gold-exchange experts abroad. From then on, there was more of a public-private partnership between the U.S. government and the investment bankers, with the bankers supplying their own funds, and the State Department supplying good will and more concrete resources.

Thus, in 1911 and 1912, the United States, over great opposition, imposed a gold-exchange standard on Nicaragua. The State Department formally stepped aside but approved Charles Conant's hiring by the powerful investment banking firm of Brown Brothers to bring about a loan and the currency reform. The State Department lent not only its approval to the project, but also its official wires, for Conant and Brown Brothers to conduct the negotiations with the Nicaraguan government.

By the time he died in Cuba in 1915, Charles Conant had made himself the chief theoretician and practitioner of the gold-exchange and the economic imperialist movements. Aside from his successes in the Philippines, Panama, and Mexico, and his failures in Cuba and China, Conant led in pushing for gold-exchange reform and gold-dollar imperialism in Liberia, Bolivia, Guatemala, and Honduras. His magnum opus in favor of the gold-exchange standard, the two-volume *The Principles of Money and Banking* (1905), as well as his pathbreaking success in the Philippines, was followed by a myriad of books, articles, pamphlets, and editorials, always backed up by his personal propaganda efforts.

Particularly interesting were Conant's arguments in favor of a gold-exchange standard, rather than a genuine gold-coin standard. A straight gold-coin standard, Conant believed, did not provide a sufficient amount of gold to provide for the world's monetary needs. Hence, by tying the existing silver standards in the undeveloped countries to gold, the "shortage" of gold could be overcome, and also the economies of the undeveloped countries could be integrated into those of the dominant imperial power. All this could only be done if the gold-exchange standard were "designed and implemented by careful government policy," but of course Conant himself and his friends and disciples always stood ready to advise and provide such implementation.[50]

In addition, adopting a government-managed gold-exchange standard was superior to either genuine gold or bimetallism because it left each state the flexibility of adapting its currency to local needs. As Conant asserted,

> It leaves each state free to choose the means of exchange which conform best to its local conditions. Rich nations are free to choose gold, nations less rich silver, and those whose financial methods are most advanced are free to choose paper.

It is interesting that for Conant, paper was the most "advanced" form of money. It is clear that the devotion to the gold standard of Conant and his colleagues, was only to a debased and inflationary standard, controlled and manipulated by the U.S. government, with gold really serving as a façade of allegedly hard money.

And one of the critical forms of government manipulation and control in Conant's proposed system was the existence and active functioning of a central bank. As a founder of the "science" of financial advising to governments, Conant, followed by his colleagues and disciples, not only pushed a gold-exchange standard wherever he could do so, but also advocated a central bank

[50]Rosenberg, "Foundations," p. 197.

to manage and control that standard. As Emily Rosenberg points out:

> Conant thus did not neglect . . . one of the major revolutionary changes implicit in his system: a new, important role for a central bank as a currency stabilizer. Conant strongly supported the American banking reform that culminated in the Federal Reserve System . . . and American financial advisers who followed Conant would spread central banking systems, along with gold-standard currency reforms, to the countries they advised.[51]

Along with a managed gold-exchange standard would come, as replacement for the old free-trade, nonmanaged, gold-coin standard, a world of imperial currency blocs, which "would necessarily come into being as lesser countries deposited their gold stabilization funds in the banking systems of more advanced countries."[52] New York and London banks, in particular, shaped up as the major reserve fund-holders in the developing new world monetary order.

It is no accident that the United States' major financial and imperial rival, Great Britain, which was pioneering in imposing gold-exchange standards in its own colonial area at this time, built upon this experience to impose a gold-exchange standard, marked by all European currencies pyramiding on top of British inflation, during the 1920s. That disastrous inflationary experiment led straight to the worldwide banking crash and the general shift to fiat paper moneys in the early 1930s. After World War II, the United States took up the torch of a world gold-exchange standard at Bretton Woods, with the dollar replacing the pound sterling in a worldwide inflationary system that lasted approximately 25 years.

Nor should it be thought that Charles A. Conant was the purely disinterested scientist he claimed to be. His currency reforms directly benefited his investment banker employers.

[51]Ibid., p. 198.

[52]Ibid.

Thus, Conant was treasurer, from 1902 to 1906, of the Morgan-run Morton Trust Company of New York, and it was surely no coincidence that Morton Trust was the bank that held the reserve funds for the governments of the Philippines, Panama, and the Dominican Republic, after their respective currency reforms. In the Nicaragua negotiations, Conant was employed by the investment bank of Brown Brothers, and in pressuring other countries he was working for Speyer and Company and other investment bankers.

After Conant died in 1915, there were few to pick up the mantle of foreign financial advising. Hollander was in disgrace after the Dominican debacle. Jenks was aging, and lived in the shadow of his China failure, but the State Department did appoint Jenks to serve as a director of the Nicaraguan National Bank in 1917, and also hired him to study the Nicaraguan financial picture in 1925.

But the true successor of Conant was Edwin W. Kemmerer, the "money doctor." After his Philippine experience, Kemmerer joined his old Professor Jenks at Cornell, and then moved to Princeton in 1912, publishing his book *Modern Currency Reforms* in 1916. As the leading foreign financial adviser of the 1920s, Kemmerer not only imposed central banks and a gold-exchange standard on Third World countries, but he also got them to levy higher taxes. Kemmerer, too, combined his public employment with service to leading international bankers. During the 1920s, Kemmerer worked as banking expert for the U.S. government's Dawes Commission, headed special financial advisory missions to more than a dozen countries, and was kept on a handsome retainer by the distinguished investment banking firm of Dillon, Read from 1922 to 1929. In that era, Kemmerer and his mentor Jenks were the only foreign currency reform experts available for advising. In the late 1920s, Kemmerer helped establish a chair of international economics at Princeton, which he occupied, and from which he could train students like Arthur N. Young and William W. Cumberland. In the mid-1920s, the money doctor served as president of the American Economic Association.[53]

Jacob Schiff Ignites the Drive for a Central Bank

The defeat of the Fowler Bill for a broader asset currency and branch banking in 1902, coupled with the failure of Treasury Secretary Shaw's attempts of 1903–1905 to use the Treasury as a central bank, led the big bankers and their economist allies to adopt a new solution: the frank imposition of a central bank in the United States.

The campaign for a central bank was kicked off by a fateful speech in January 1906 by the powerful Jacob H. Schiff, head of the Wall Street investment bank of Kuhn, Loeb and Company, before the New York Chamber of Commerce. Schiff complained that in the autumn of 1905, when "the country needed money," the Treasury, instead of working to expand the money supply, reduced government deposits in the national banks, thereby precipitating a financial crisis, a "disgrace" in which the New York clearinghouse banks had been forced to contract their loans drastically, sending interest rates sky-high. An "elastic currency" for the nation was therefore imperative, and Schiff urged the New York chamber's committee on finance to draw up a comprehensive plan for a modern banking system to provide for an elastic currency.[54] A colleague who had already been agitating for a central bank behind the scenes was Schiff's partner, Paul Moritz Warburg, who had suggested the plan to Schiff as early as 1903. Warburg had emigrated from the German investment firm of M.M. Warburg and Company in 1897, and before long his major

[53]For an excellent study of the Kemmerer missions in the 1920s, see Robert N. Seidel, "American Reformers Abroad: The Kemmerer Missions in South America, 1932–1931," *Journal of Economic History* 32 (June 1972): 520–45.

[54]On Schiff's speech, see *Bankers Magazine* 72 (January 1906): 114–15.

function at Kuhn, Loeb was to agitate to bring the blessings of European central banking to the United States.[55]

It took less than a month for the finance committee of the New York chamber to issue its report, but the bank reformers were furious, denouncing it as remarkably ignorant. When Frank A. Vanderlip, of Rockefeller's flagship bank, the National City Bank of New York, reported on this development, his boss, James Stillman, suggested that a new five-man special commission be set up by the New York chamber to come back with a plan for currency reform.

In response, Vanderlip proposed that the five-man commission consist of himself; Schiff; J.P. Morgan; George Baker of the First National Bank of New York, Morgan's closest and longest associate; and former Secretary of the Treasury Lyman Gage, now president of the Rockefeller-controlled U.S. Trust Company. Thus, the commission would consist of two Rockefeller men (Vanderlip and Gage), two Morgan men (Morgan and Baker), and one representative from Kuhn, Loeb. Only Vanderlip was available to serve, however, so the commission had to be redrawn. In addition to Vanderlip, beginning in March 1906, there sat, instead of Schiff, his close friend Isidore Straus, a director of R.H. Macy and Company. Instead of Morgan and Baker there now served two Morgan men: Dumont Clarke, president of the American Exchange National Bank and a personal adviser to J.P. Morgan, and Charles A. Conant, treasurer of Morton and Company. The fifth man was a veteran of the Indianapolis Monetary Convention, John Claflin, of H.B. Claflin

[55]Schiff and Warburg were related by marriage. Schiff, from a prominent German banker family himself, was a son-in-law of Solomon Loeb, cofounder of Kuhn, Loeb; and Warburg, husband of Nina Loeb, was another son-in-law of Solomon Loeb's by a second wife. The incestuous circle was completed when Schiff's daughter Frieda married Paul Warburg's brother Felix, another partner of Schiff's and Paul Warburg's. See Birmingham, *Our Crowd*, pp. 21, 209–10, 383, and appendix. See also Jacques Attali, *A Man of Influence: Sir Siegmund Warburg, 1902–82* (London: Weidenfeld and Nicholson, 1986), p. 53.

and Company, a large integrated wholesaling concern. Coming on board as secretary of the new currency committee was Vanderlip's old friend Joseph French Johnson, now of New York University, who had been calling for a central bank since 1900.

The commission used the old Indianapolis questionnaire technique: acquiring legitimacy by sending out a detailed questionnaire on currency to a number of financial leaders. With Johnson in charge of mailing and collating the questionnaire replies, Conant spent his time visiting and interviewing the heads of the central banks in Europe.

The special commission delivered its report to the New York Chamber of Commerce in October 1906. To eliminate instability and the danger of an inelastic currency, the commission called for the creation of a "central bank of issue under the control of the government." In keeping with other bank reformers, such as Professor Abram Piatt Andrew of Harvard University, Thomas Nixon Carver of Harvard, and Albert Strauss, partner of J.P. Morgan and Company, the commission was scornful of Secretary Shaw's attempt to use the Treasury as central bank. Shaw was particularly obnoxious because he was still insisting, in his last annual report of 1906, that the Treasury, under his aegis, had constituted a "great central bank." The commission, along with the other reformers, denounced the Treasury for overinflating by keeping interest rates excessively low; a central bank, in contrast, would have much larger capital and undisputed control over the money market, and thus would be able to manipulate the discount rate effectively to keep the economy under proper control. The important point, declared the committee, is that there be "centralization of financial responsibility." In the meantime, short of establishing a central bank, the committee urged that, at the least, the national banks' powers to issue notes should be expanded to include being based on general assets as well as government bonds.[56]

[56]See Livingston, *Origins*, pp. 159–64.

After drafting and publishing this "Currency Report," the reformers used the report as the lever for expanding the agitation for a central bank and broader note-issue powers to other corporate and financial institutions. The next step was the powerful American Bankers Association (ABA). In 1905, the executive council of the ABA had appointed a currency committee which, the following year, recommended an emergency assets currency that would be issued by a federal commission, resembling an embryonic central bank. In a tumultuous plenary session of the ABA convention in October 1906, the ABA rejected this plan, but agreed to appoint a 15-man currency commission that was instructed to meet with the New York chamber's currency committee and attempt to agree on appropriate legislation.

Particularly prominent on the ABA currency commission were:

• Arthur Reynolds, president of the Des Moines National Bank, close to the Morgan-oriented Des Moines Regency, and brother of the prominent Chicago banker, George M. Reynolds, formerly of Des Moines and then president of the Morgan-oriented Continental National Bank of Chicago and the powerful chairman of the executive council of the ABA;

• James B. Forgan, president of the Rockefeller-run First National Bank of Chicago, and close friend of Jacob Schiff of Kuhn, Loeb, as well as of Vanderlip;

• Joseph T. Talbert, vice president of the Rockefeller-dominated Commercial National Bank of Chicago, and soon to become vice president of Rockefeller's flagship bank, the National City Bank of New York;

• Myron T. Herrick, one of the most prominent Rockefeller politicians and businessmen in the country. Herrick was the head of the Cleveland Society of Savings, and was part of the small team of close Rockefeller business allies who, along with Mark Hanna, bailed out Governor William McKinley from bankruptcy in 1893. Herrick was a previous president of the ABA, had just finished a two-year stint as governor of Ohio, and was later to become ambassador to France under his old friend and political ally William Howard Taft as well as later under President Warren G. Harding, and a recipient of Herrick's political support and financial largesse; and

• Chairman of the ABA commission, A. Barton Hepburn, president of one of the leading Morgan commercial banks, the Chase National Bank of New York, and author of the well-regarded *History of Coinage and Currency in the United States*.

After meeting with Vanderlip and Conant as the representatives from the New York Chamber of Commerce committee, the ABA commission, along with Vanderlip and Conant, agreed on at least the transition demands of the reformers. The ABA commission presented proposals to the public, the press, and the Congress in December 1906 for a broader asset currency as well as provisions for emergency issue of bank notes by national banks.

But just as sentiment for a broader asset currency became prominent, the bank reformers began to worry about an uncontrolled adoption of such a currency. For that would mean that national bank credit and notes would expand, and that, in the existing system, small state banks would be able to pyramid and inflate credit on top of the national credit, using the expanded national bank notes as their reserves. The reformers wanted a credit inflation controlled by and confined to the large national banks; they most emphatically did *not* want uncontrolled state bank inflation that would siphon resources to small entrepreneurs and "speculative" marginal producers. The problem was aggravated by the accelerated rate of increase in the number of small Southern and Western state banks after 1900. Another grave problem for the reformers was that commercial paper was a different system from that of Europe. In Europe, commercial paper, and hence bank assets, were two-name notes endorsed by a small group of wealthy acceptance banks. In contrast to this acceptance paper system, commercial paper in the United States was unendorsed single-name paper, with the bank taking a chance on the creditworthiness of the business borrower. Hence, a decentralized financial system in the United States was not subject to big-banker control.

Worries about the existing system and hence about uncontrolled asset currency were voiced by the top bank reformers. Thus, Vanderlip expressed concern that "there are so many state banks that might count these [national bank] notes in their reserves." Schiff warned that "it would prove unwise, if not dangerous, to clothe six thousand banks or more with the privilege to issue independently a purely credit currency." And, from the Morgan side, a similar concern was voiced by Victor Morawetz, the powerful chairman of the board of the Atchison, Topeka and Santa Fe Railroad.[57]

Taking the lead in approaching this problem of small banks and decentralization was Paul Moritz Warburg, of Kuhn, Loeb, fresh from his banking experience in Europe. In January 1907, Warburg began what would become years of tireless agitation for central banking with two articles: "Defects and Needs of our Banking System" and "A Plan for a Modified Central Bank."[58] Calling openly for a central bank, Warburg pointed out that one of the important functions of such a bank would be to restrict the eligibility of bank assets to be used for expansion of bank deposits. Presumably, too, the central bank could move to require banks to use acceptance paper or otherwise try to create an acceptance market in the United States.[59]

[57]Livingston, *Origins*, pp. 168–69.

[58]See the collection of Warburg's essays in Paul M. Warburg, *The Federal Reserve System*, 2 vols. (New York: Macmillan, 1930). See also Warburg, "Essays on Banking Reform in the United States," *Proceedings of the Academy of Political Science* 4 (July 1914): 387–612.

[59]When the Federal Reserve System was established, Warburg boasted of his crucial role in persuading the Fed to create an acceptance market in the U.S. by agreeing to purchase all acceptance paper available from a few large acceptance banks at subsidized rates. In that way, the Fed provided an unchecked channel for inflationary credit expansion. The acceptance program helped pave the way for the 1929 crash.

It was surely no accident that Warburg himself was the principal beneficiary of this policy. Warburg became chairman of the board, from its founding in 1920, of the International Acceptance Bank, the world's

By the summer of 1907, *Bankers Magazine* was reporting a decline in influential banker support for broadening asset currency and a strong move toward the "central bank project." *Bankers Magazine* noted as a crucial reason the fact that asset currency would be expanding bank services to "small producers and dealers."[60]

The Panic of 1907 and Mobilization for a Central Bank

A severe financial crisis, the panic of 1907, struck in early October. Not only was there a general recession and contraction, but the major banks in New York and Chicago were, as in most other depressions in American history, allowed by the government to suspend specie payments, that is, to continue in operation while being relieved of their contractual obligation to redeem their notes and deposits in cash or in gold. While the Treasury had stimulated inflation during 1905–1907, there was nothing it could do to prevent suspensions of payment, or to alleviate "the competitive hoarding of currency" after the panic, that is, the attempt to demand cash in return for increasingly shaky bank notes and deposits.

Very quickly after the panic, banker and business opinion consolidated on behalf of a central bank, an institution that could regulate the economy and serve as a lender of last resort to bail banks out of trouble. The reformers now faced a twofold task: hammering out details of a new central bank, and more important, mobilizing public opinion on its behalf. The first step in such mobilization was to win the support of the

---

largest acceptance bank, as well as director of the Westinghouse Acceptance Bank and of several other acceptance houses. In 1919, Warburg was the chief founder and chairman of the executive committee of the American Acceptance Council, the trade association of acceptance houses. See Murray N. Rothbard, *America's Great Depression*, 4th ed. (New York: Richardson and Snyder, 1983), pp. 119–23.

[60]*Bankers Magazine* 75 (September 1907): 314–15.

nation's academics and experts. The task was made easier by the growing alliance and symbiosis between academia and the power elite. Two organizations that proved particularly useful for this mobilization were the American Academy of Political and Social Science (AAPSS) of Philadelphia, and the Academy of Political Science (APS) of Columbia University, both of which included in their ranks leading corporate liberal businessmen, financiers, attorneys, and academics. Nicholas Murray Butler, the highly influential president of Columbia University, explained that the Academy of Political Science "is an intermediary between . . . the scholars and the men of affairs, those who may perhaps be said to be amateurs in scholarship." Here, he pointed out, was where they "come together."[61]

It is not surprising, then, that the American Academy of Political and Social Science, the American Association for the Advancement of Science, and Columbia University held three symposia during the winter of 1907–1908, each calling for a central bank, and thereby disseminating the message of a central bank to a carefully selected elite public. Not surprising, too, was that E.R.A. Seligman was the organizer of the Columbia conference, gratified that his university was providing a platform for leading bankers and financial journalists to advocate a central bank, especially, he noted, because "it is proverbially difficult in a democracy to secure a hearing for the conclusions of experts." Then in 1908 Seligman collected the addresses into a volume, *The Currency Problem*.

Professor Seligman set the tone for the Columbia gathering in his opening address. The panic of 1907, he alleged, was moderate because its effects had been tempered by the growth of industrial trusts, which provided a more controlled and "more correct adjustment of present investment to future needs" than would a "horde of small competitors." In that way, Seligman displayed no comprehension of how competitive markets

[61]Livingston, *Origins*, p. 175, n. 30.

facilitate adjustments. One big problem, however, still remained for Seligman. The horde of small competitors, for whom Seligman had so much contempt, still prevailed in the field of currency and banking. The problem was that the banking system was still decentralized. As Seligman declared,

> Even more important than the inelasticity of our note issue is its decentralization. The struggle which has been victoriously fought out everywhere else [in creating trusts] must be undertaken here in earnest and with vigor.[62]

The next address was that of Frank Vanderlip. To Vanderlip, in contrast to Seligman, the panic of 1907 was "one of the great calamities of history"—the result of a decentralized, competitive American banking system, with 15,000 banks all competing vigorously for control of cash reserves. The terrible thing is that "each institution stands alone, concerned first with its own safety, and using every endeavor to pile up reserves without regard" to the effect of such actions on other banking institutions. This backward system had to be changed, to follow the lead of other great nations, where a central bank is able to mobilize and centralize reserves, and create an elastic currency system. Putting the situation in virtually Marxian terms, Vanderlip declared that the alien external power of the free and competitive market must be replaced by central control following modern, allegedly scientific principles of banking.

Thomas Wheelock, editor of the *Wall Street Journal*, then rung the changes on the common theme by applying it to the volatile call loan market in New York. The market is volatile, Wheelock claimed, because the small country banks are able to lend on that market, and their deposits in New York banks then rise and fall in uncontrolled fashion. Therefore, there must be central corporate control over country bank money in the call loan market.

A. Barton Hepburn, head of Morgan's Chase National Bank, came next, and spoke of the great importance of having a central

[62]Ibid., p. 177.

bank that would issue a monopoly of bank notes. It was particularly important that the central bank be able to discount the assets of national banks, and thus supply an elastic currency.

The last speaker was Paul Warburg, who lectured his audience on the superiority of European over American banking, particularly in (1) having a central bank, as against decentralized American banking, and (2)—his old hobby horse—enjoying "modern" acceptance paper instead of single-name promissory notes. Warburg emphasized that these two institutions must function together. In particular, tight government central bank control must replace competition and decentralization: "Small banks constitute a danger."

The other two symposia were very similar. At the AAPSS symposium in Philadelphia, in December 1907, several leading investment bankers and Comptroller of the Currency William B. Ridgely came out in favor of a central bank. It was no accident that members of the AAPSS's advisory committee on currency included A. Barton Hepburn; Morgan attorney and statesman Elihu Root; Morgan's longtime personal attorney, Francis Lynde Stetson; and J.P. Morgan himself. Meanwhile the AAAS symposium in January 1908 was organized by none other than Charles A. Conant, who happened to be chairman of the AAAS's social and economic section for the year. Speakers included Columbia economist J.B. Clark, Frank Vanderlip, Conant, and Vanderlip's friend George E. Roberts, head of the Rockefeller-oriented Commercial National Bank of Chicago, who would later wind up at the National City Bank.

All in all, the task of the bank reformers was well summed up by J.R. Duffield, secretary of the Bankers Publishing Company, in January 1908: "It is recognized generally that before legislation can be had there must be an educational campaign carried on, first among the bankers, and later among commercial organizations, and finally among the people as a whole." That strategy was well under way.

During the same month, the legislative lead in banking reform was taken by the formidable Senator Nelson W.

Aldrich (R-R.I.), head of the Senate Finance Committee, and, as the father-in-law of John D. Rockefeller, Jr., Rockefeller's man in the U.S. Senate. He introduced the Aldrich Bill, which focused on a relatively minor interbank dispute about whether and on what basis the national banks could issue special emergency currency. A compromise was finally hammered out and passed, as the Aldrich-Vreeland Act, in 1908.[63] But the important part of the Aldrich-Vreeland Act, which got very little public attention, but was perceptively hailed by the bank reformers, was the establishment of a National Monetary Commission that would investigate the currency question and suggest proposals for comprehensive banking reform. Two enthusiastic comments on the monetary commission were particularly perceptive and prophetic. One was that of Sereno S. Pratt of the *Wall Street Journal*. Pratt virtually conceded that the purpose of the commission was to swamp the public with supposed expertise and thereby "educate" them into supporting banking reform:

> Reform can only be brought about by educating the people up to it, and such education must necessarily take much time. In no other way can such education be effected more thoroughly and rapidly than by means of a commission . . . [that] would make an international study of the subject and present an exhaustive report, which could be made the basis for an intelligent agitation.

The results of the "study" were of course predetermined, as would be the membership of the allegedly impartial study commission.

Another function of the commission, as stated by Festus J. Wade, St. Louis banker and member of the currency commission of the American Bankers Association, was to "keep the financial issue out of politics" and put it squarely in the safe custody of

[63]The emergency currency provision was only used once, shortly before the provision expired, in 1914, and after the establishment of the Federal Reserve System.

carefully selected "experts."[64] Thus, the National Monetary Commission (NMC) was the apotheosis of the clever commission concept, launched in Indianapolis a decade earlier.

Aldrich lost no time setting up the NMC, which was launched in June 1908. The official members were an equal number of senators and representatives, but these were mere window dressing. The real work would be done by the copious staff, appointed and directed by Aldrich, who told his counterpart in the House, Cleveland Republican Theodore Burton: "My idea is, of course, that everything shall be done in the most quiet manner possible, and without any public announcement." From the beginning, Aldrich determined that the NMC would be run as an alliance of Rockefeller, Morgan, and Kuhn, Loeb people. The two top expert posts advising or joining the commission were both suggested by Morgan leaders. On the advice of J.P. Morgan, seconded by Jacob Schiff, Aldrich picked as his top adviser the formidable Henry P. Davison, Morgan partner, founder of Morgan's Bankers Trust Company, and vice president of George F. Baker's First National Bank of New York. It would be Davison who, on the outbreak of World War I, would rush to England to cement J.P. Morgan and Company's close ties with the Bank of England, and to receive an appointment as monopoly underwriter for all British and French government bonds to be floated in the United States for the duration of the war. For technical economic expertise, Aldrich accepted the recommendation of President Roosevelt's close friend and fellow Morgan man, Charles Eliot, president of Harvard University, who urged the appointment of Harvard economist A. Piatt Andrew. And an ex officio commission member chosen by Aldrich himself was George M. Reynolds, president of the Rockefeller-oriented Continental National Bank of Chicago.

The NMC spent the fall touring Europe and conferring on information and strategy with heads of large European banks

[64]Livingston, *Origins*, pp. 182–83.

and central banks. As director of research, A. Piatt Andrew began to organize American banking experts and to commission reports and studies. The National City Bank's foreign exchange department was commissioned to write papers on bankers' acceptances and foreign debt, while Warburg and Bankers Trust official Fred Kent wrote on the European discount market.

Having gathered information and advice in Europe in the fall of 1908, the NMC was ready to go into high gear by the end of the year. In December, the commission hired the inevitable Charles A. Conant for research, public relations, and agitprop. Behind the façade of the congressmen and senators on the commission, Senator Aldrich began to form and expand his inner circle, which soon included Warburg and Vanderlip. Warburg formed around him a subcircle of friends and acquaintances from the currency committee of the New York Merchants' Association, headed by Irving T. Bush, and from the top ranks of the American Economic Association, to whom he had delivered an address advocating central banking in December 1908. Warburg met and corresponded frequently with leading academic economists advocating banking reform, including E.R.A. Seligman; Thomas Nixon Carver of Harvard; Henry R. Seager of Columbia; Davis R. Dewey, historian of banking at MIT, longtime secretary-treasurer of the AEA and brother of the progressive philosopher John Dewey; Oliver M.W. Sprague, professor of banking at Harvard, of the Morgan-connected Sprague family; Frank W. Taussig of Harvard; and Irving Fisher of Yale.

During 1909, however, the reformers faced an important problem: they had to bring such leading bankers as James B. Forgan, head of the Rockefeller-oriented First National Bank of Chicago, solidly into line in support of a central bank. It was not that Forgan objected to centralized reserves or a lender of last resort—quite the contrary. It was rather that Forgan recognized that, under the national banking system, large banks such as his own were already performing quasi–central banking functions with their own country bank depositors; and he didn't want his bank deprived of such functions by a new central bank.

The bank reformers therefore went out of their way to bring such men as Forgan into enthusiastic support for the new scheme. In his presidential address to the powerful American Bankers Association in mid-September 1909, George M. Reynolds not only came out flatly in favor of a central bank in America, to be modeled after the German Reichsbank; he also assured Forgan and others that such a central bank would act as depository of reserves only for the large national banks in the central reserve cities, while the national banks would continue to hold deposits for the country banks. Mollified, Forgan held a private conference with Aldrich's inner circle and came fully on board for the central bank. As an outgrowth of Forgan's concerns, the reformers decided to cloak their new central bank in a spurious veil of "regionalism" and "decentralism" through establishing regional reserve centers, that would provide the appearance of virtually independent regional central banks to cover the reality of an orthodox European central bank monolith. As a result, noted railroad attorney Victor Morawetz made his famous speech in November 1909, calling for regional banking districts under the ultimate direction of one central control board. Thus, reserves and note issue would be supposedly decentralized in the hands of the regional reserve banks, while they would really be centralized and coordinated by the central control board. This, of course, was the scheme eventually adopted in the Federal Reserve System.[65]

On September 14, at the same time as Reynolds's address to the nation's bankers, another significant address took place.

[65]Victor Morawetz was an eminent attorney in the Morgan ambit who served as chairman of the executive committee of the Morgan-run Atchison, Topeka and Santa Fe Railway, and member of the board of the Morgan-dominated National Bank of Commerce. In 1908, Morawetz, along with J.P. Morgan's personal attorney, Francis Lynde Stetson, had been the principal drafter of an unsuccessful Morgan-National Civic Federation bill for a federal incorporation law to regulate and cartelize American corporations. Later, Morawetz was to be a top consultant to another "progressive" reformer of Woodrow Wilson's, the Federal Trade Commission. On Morawetz, see Rothbard, "Federal Reserve," p. 99.

President William Howard Taft, speaking in Boston, suggested that the country seriously consider establishing a central bank. Taft had been close to the reformers—especially his Rockefeller-oriented friends Aldrich and Burton—since 1900. But the business press understood the great significance of this public address, that it was, as the *Wall Street Journal* put it, a crucial step "toward removing the subject from the realm of theory to that of practical politics."[66]

One week later, a fateful event in American history occurred. The banking reformers moved to escalate their agitation by creating a virtual government-bank-press complex to drive through a central bank. On September 22, 1909, the *Wall Street Journal* took the lead in this development by beginning a notable, front-page, 14-part series on "A Central Bank of Issue." These were unsigned editorials by the *Journal*, but they were actually written by the ubiquitous Charles A. Conant, from his vantage point as salaried chief propagandist of the U.S. government's National Monetary Commission. The series was a summary of the reformers' position, also going out of the way to assure the Forgans of this world that the new central bank "would probably deal directly only with the larger national banks, leaving it for the latter to rediscount for their more remote correspondents."[67] To the standard arguments for a central bank—"elasticity" of the money supply, protecting bank reserves by manipulating the discount rate and the international flow of gold, and combating crisis by bailing out individual banks—Conant added a Conant twist: the importance of regulating interest rates and the flow of capital in a world marked by surplus capital. Government debt would, for Conant, provide the important function of sopping up surplus capital; that is, providing profitable outlets for savings by financing government expenditures.

[66]*Wall Street Journal,* 16 September 1909, p. 1. Cited in Livingston, *Origins*, p. 191.

[67]Ibid.

The *Wall Street Journal* series inaugurated a shrewd and successful campaign by Conant to manipulate the nation's press and get it behind the idea of a central bank. Building on his experience in 1898, Conant, along with Aldrich's secretary, Arthur B. Shelton, prepared abstracts of commission materials for the newspapers during February and March of 1910. Soon Shelton recruited J.P. Gavitt, head of the Washington bureau of the Associated Press, to scan commission abstracts, articles, and forthcoming books for "newsy paragraphs" to catch the eye of newspaper editors.

The academic organizations proved particularly helpful to the NMC, lending their cloak of disinterested expertise to the endeavor. In February, Robert E. Ely, secretary of the APS, proposed to Aldrich that a special volume of its *Proceedings* be devoted to banking and currency reform, to be published in cooperation with the NMC, in order to "popularize in the best sense, some of the valuable work of [the] Commission."[68] And yet, Ely had the gall to add that, even though the APS would advertise the NMC's arguments and conclusions, it would retain its "objectivity" by avoiding its own specific policy recommendations. As Ely put it, "We shall not advocate a central bank, but we shall only give the best results of your work in condensed form and untechnical language."

The AAPSS, too, weighed in with its own special volume, *Banking Problems* (1910), featuring an introduction by A. Piatt Andrew of Harvard and the NMC and articles by veteran bank reformers such as Joseph French Johnson, Horace White, and Morgan Bankers Trust official Fred I. Kent. But most of the articles were from leaders of Rockefeller's National City Bank of New York, including George E. Roberts, a former Chicago banker and U.S. Mint official about to join National City.

Meanwhile, Paul M. Warburg capped his lengthy campaign for a central bank in a famous speech to the New York YMCA on March 23, on "A United Reserve Bank for the United States."

[68]Ibid., p. 194.

Warburg basically outlined the structure of his beloved German Reichsbank, but he was careful to begin his talk by noting a recent poll in the *Banking Law Journal* that 60 percent of the nation's bankers favored a central bank provided it was "not controlled by 'Wall Street or any monopolistic interest.' " To calm this fear, Warburg insisted that, semantically, the new reserve bank *not* be called a central bank, and that the reserve bank's governing board be chosen by government officials, merchants and bankers—with bankers, of course, dominating the choices. He also provided a distinctive Warburg twist by insisting that the reserve bank replace the hated single-name paper system of commercial credit dominant in the United States by the European system whereby a reserve bank provided a guaranteed and subsidized market for two-named commercial paper endorsed by acceptance banks. In this way, the united reserve bank would correct the "complete lack of modern bills of exchange" (that is, acceptances) in the United States. Warburg added that the entire idea of a free and self-regulating market was obsolete, particularly in the money market. Instead, the action of the market must be replaced by "the best judgment of the best experts." And guess *who* was slated to be one of the best of those best experts?

The greatest cheerleader for the Warburg plan, and the man who introduced the APS's *Reform of the Currency* (1911), the volume on banking reform featuring Warburg's speech, was Warburg's kinsman and member of the Seligman investment banking family, Columbia economist E.R.A. Seligman.[69]

So delighted was the Merchants' Association of New York with Warburg's speech that it distributed 30,000 copies during the spring of 1910. Warburg had paved the way for this support by regularly meeting with the currency committee of the Merchants' Assocation since October 1908, and his efforts were aided by the fact that the resident expert for that committee was none other than Joseph French Johnson.

[69]See Rothbard, "Federal Reserve," pp. 98–99. Also, on Warburg's speech, see Livingston, *Origins*, pp. 194–98.

At the same time, in the spring of 1910, the numerous research volumes published by the NMC poured onto the market. The object was to swamp public opinion with a parade of impressive analytic and historical scholarship, all allegedly "scientific" and "value-free," but all designed to aid in furthering the common agenda of a central bank. Typical was E.W. Kemmerer's mammoth statistical study of seasonal variations in the demand for money. Stress was laid on the problem of the "inelasticity" of the supply of cash, in particular the difficulty of expanding that supply when needed. While Kemmerer felt precluded from spelling out the policy implications—establishing a central bank—in the book, his acknowledgments in the preface to Fred Kent and the inevitable Charles Conant were a tip-off to the cognoscenti, and Kemmerer himself disclosed them in his address to the Academy of Political Science the following November.

Now that the theoretical and scholarly groundwork had been laid, by the latter half of 1910, it was time to formulate a concrete practical plan and put on a mighty *putsch* on its behalf. In *Reform of the Currency,* published by the APS, Warburg made the point with crystal clarity: "Advance is possible only by outlining a tangible plan" that would set the terms of the debate from then on.[70]

The tangible plan phase of the central bank movement was launched by the ever pliant APS, which held a monetary conference in November 1910, in conjunction with the New York Chamber of Commerce and the Merchants' Association of New York. The members of the NMC were the guests of honor at this conclave, and delegates were chosen by governors of 22 states, as well as presidents of 24 chambers of commerce. Also attending were a large number of economists, monetary analysts, and representatives of most of the top banks in the country. Attendants at the conference included Frank Vanderlip, Elihu Root, Thomas W. Lamont of the Morgans, Jacob Schiff, and J.P. Morgan. The formal sessions of the conference were organized

[70]Livingston, *Origins*, p. 203.

around papers by Kemmerer, Laughlin, Johnson, Bush, Warburg, and Conant, and the general atmosphere was that bankers and businessmen were to take their general guidance from the attendant scholars. As James B. Forgan, Chicago banker who was now solidly in the central banking camp, put it: "Let the theorists, those who . . . can study from past history and from present conditions the effect of what we are doing, lay down principles for us, and let us help them with the details." C. Stuart Patterson pointed to the great lessons of the Indianapolis Monetary Commission, and the way in which its proposals triumphed in action because "we went home and organized an aggressive and active movement." Patterson then laid down the marching orders of what this would mean concretely for the assembled troops:

> That is just what you must do in this case, you must uphold the hands of Senator Aldrich. You have got to see that the bill which he formulates . . . obtains the support of every part of this country.[71]

With the New York monetary conference over, it was now time for Aldrich, surrounded by a few of the topmost leaders of the financial elite, to go off in seclusion and hammer out a detailed plan around which all parts of the central bank movement could rally. Someone in the Aldrich inner circle, probably Morgan partner Henry P. Davison, got the idea of convening a small group of top leaders in a super-secret conclave to draft the central bank bill. On November 22, 1910, Senator Aldrich, with a handful of companions, set forth in a privately chartered railroad car from Hoboken, New Jersey, to the coast of Georgia, where they sailed to an exclusive retreat, the Jekyll Island Club on Jekyll Island, Georgia. Facilities for their meeting were arranged by club member and co-owner J.P. Morgan. The cover story released to the press was that this was a simple duck-hunting expedition, and the conferees took elaborate precautions on the trips there and back to preserve their secrecy. Thus,

[71]Ibid., pp. 205–07.

the attendees addressed each other only by first name, and the railroad car was kept dark and closed off from reporters or other travelers on the train. One reporter apparently caught on to the purpose of the meeting, but was in some way persuaded by Henry P. Davison to maintain silence.

The conferees worked for a solid week at Jekyll Island to hammer out the draft of the Federal Reserve bill. In addition to Aldrich, the conferees included Henry P. Davison, Morgan partner; Paul Warburg, whose address in the spring had greatly impressed Aldrich; Frank A. Vanderlip, vice president of the National City Bank of New York; and finally, A. Piatt Andrew, head of the NMC staff, who had recently been made assistant secretary of the Treasury by President Taft. After a week of meetings, the six men had forged a plan for a central bank, which eventually became the Aldrich Bill. Vanderlip acted as secretary of the meeting, and contributed the final writing.

The only substantial disagreement was tactical, with Aldrich attempting to hold out for a straightforward central bank on the European model, while Warburg and the other bankers insisted that the reality of central control be cloaked in the politically palatable camouflage of "decentralization." It is amusing that the bankers were the more politically astute, while the politician Aldrich wanted to waive political considerations. Warburg and the bankers won out, and the final draft was basically the Warburg plan with a decentralized patina taken from Morawetz.

The financial power elite now had a bill. The significance of the composition of the small meeting must be stressed: two Rockefeller men (Aldrich and Vanderlip), two Morgans (Davison and Norton), one Kuhn, Loeb person (Warburg), and one economist friendly to both camps (Andrew).[72]

[72]See Rothbard, "Federal Reserve," pp. 99–101; and Frank A. Vanderlip, *From Farm Boy to Financier* (New York: D. Appleton-Century, 1935), pp. 210–19.

After working on some revisions of the Jekyll Island draft with Forgan and George Reynolds, Aldrich presented the Jekyll Island draft as the Aldrich Plan to the full NMC in January 1911. But here an unusual event occurred. Instead of quickly presenting this Aldrich Bill to the Congress, its drafters waited for a full year, until January 1912. Why the unprecedented year's delay?

The problem was that the Democrats swept the congressional elections in 1910, and Aldrich, disheartened, decided not to run for re-election to the Senate the following year. The Democratic triumph meant that the reformers had to devote a year of intensive agitation to convert the Democrats, and to intensify propaganda to the rest of banking, business, and the public. In short, the reformers needed to regroup and accelerate their agitation.

The Final Phase: Coping with the Democratic Ascendancy

The final phase of the drive for a central bank began in January 1911. At the previous January's meeting of the National Board of Trade, Paul Warburg had put through a resolution setting aside January 18, 1911, as a "monetary day" devoted to a "Business Men's Monetary Conference." This conference, run by the National Board of Trade, and featuring delegates from metropolitan mercantile organizations from all over the country, had C. Stuart Patterson as its chairman. The New York Chamber of Commerce, the Merchants' Association of New York, and the New York Produce Exchange, each of which had been pushing for banking reform for the previous five years, introduced a joint resolution to the monetary conference supporting the Aldrich Plan, and proposing the establishment of a new "businessmen's monetary reform league" to lead the public struggle for a central bank. After a speech in favor of the plan by A. Piatt Andrew, the entire conference adopted the resolution. In response, C. Stuart Patterson appointed none other than Paul M. Warburg to head a committee of seven to establish the reform league.

The committee of seven shrewdly decided, following the lead of the old Indianapolis convention, to establish the National Citizens' League for the Creation of a Sound Banking System in Chicago rather than in New York, where the control really resided. The idea was to acquire the bogus patina of a "grassroots" heartland operation and to convince the public that the league was free of dreaded Wall Street control. As a result, the official heads of the league were Chicago businessmen John V. Farwell and Harry A. Wheeler, president of the U.S. Chamber of Commerce. The director was University of Chicago monetary economist J. Laurence Laughlin, assisted by his former student, Professor H. Parker Willis.

In keeping with its Midwestern aura, most of the directors of the Citizens' League were Chicago nonbanker industrialists: men such as B.E. Sunny of the Chicago Telephone Company, Cyrus McCormick of International Harvester (both companies in the Morgan ambit), John G. Shedd of Marshall Field and Company, Frederic A. Delano of the Wabash Railroad Company (Rockefeller-controlled), and Julius Rosenwald of Sears, Roebuck. Over a decade later, however, H. Parker Willis frankly conceded that the Citizens' League had been a propaganda organ of the nation's bankers.[73]

The Citizens' League swung into high gear during the spring and summer of 1911, issuing a periodical, *Banking and Reform*, designed to reach newspaper editors, and subsidizing pamphlets by such pro-reform experts as John Perrin, head of the American National Bank of Indianapolis, and George E. Roberts of the National City Bank of New York. Consultant on the newspaper campaign was H.H. Kohlsaat, former executive committee member of the Indianapolis Monetary Convention. Laughlin

[73]Henry Parker Willis, *The Federal Reserve System* (New York: Ronald Press, 1923), pp. 149–50. Willis's account, however, conveniently overlooks the dominating operational role that both he and his mentor Laughlin played in the Citizens' League. See Robert Craig West, *Banking Reform and the Federal Reserve, 1863–1923* (Ithaca, N.Y.: Cornell University Press, 1977), p. 82.

himself worked on a book on the Aldrich Plan, to be similar to his own report of 1898 for the Indianapolis convention.

Meanwhile, a parallel campaign was launched to bring the nation's bankers into camp. The first step was to convert the banking elite. For that purpose, the Aldrich inner circle organized a closed-door conference of 23 top bankers in Atlantic City in early February, which included several members of the currency commission of the American Bankers Association (ABA), along with bank presidents from nine leading cities of the country. After making a few minor revisions, the conference warmly endorsed the Aldrich Plan.

After this meeting, Chicago banker James B. Forgan, president of the Rockefeller-dominated First National Bank of Chicago, emerged as the most effective banker spokesman for the central bank movement. Not only was his presentation of the Aldrich Plan before the executive council of the ABA in May considered particularly impressive, it was especially effective coming from someone who had been a leading critic (if on relatively minor grounds) of the plan. As a result, the top bankers managed to get the ABA to violate its own bylaws and make Forgan chairman of its executive council.

At the Atlantic City conference, James Forgan had succinctly explained the purpose of the Aldrich Plan and of the conference itself. As Kolko sums up:

> the real purpose of the conference was to discuss winning the banking community over to government control directly by the bankers for their own ends. . . . It was generally appreciated that the [Aldrich Plan] would increase the power of the big national banks to compete with the rapidly growing state banks, help bring the state banks under control, and strengthen the position of the national banks in foreign banking activities.[74]

By November 1911, it was easy pickings to have the full American Bankers Association endorse the Aldrich Plan. The

[74]Kolko, *Triumph*, p. 186.

nation's banking community was now solidly lined up behind the drive for a central bank.

However, 1912 and 1913 were years of some confusion and backing and filling, as the Republican Party split between its insurgents and regulars, and the Democrats won increasing control over the federal government, culminating in Woodrow Wilson's gaining the presidency in the November 1912 elections. The Aldrich Plan, introduced into the Senate by Theodore Burton in January 1912, died a quick death, but the reformers saw that what they had to do was to drop the fiercely Republican partisan name of Aldrich from the bill, and with a few minor adjustments, rebaptize it as a Democratic measure. Fortunately for the reformers, this process of transformation was eased greatly in early 1912, when H. Parker Willis was appointed administrative assistant to Carter Glass, the Democrat from Virginia who now headed the House Banking and Currency Committee. In an accident of history, Willis had taught economics to the two sons of Carter Glass at Washington and Lee University, and they recommended him to their father when the Democrats assumed control of the House.

The minutiae of the splits and maneuvers in the banking reform camp during 1912 and 1913, which have long fascinated historians, are fundamentally trivial to the basic story. They largely revolved around the successful efforts by Laughlin, Willis, and the Democrats to jettison the name Aldrich. Moreover, while the bankers had preferred the Federal Reserve Board to be appointed by the bankers themselves, it was clear to most of the reformers that this was politically unpalatable. They realized that the same result of a government-coordinated cartel could be achieved by having the president and Congress appoint the board, balanced by the bankers electing most of the officials of the regional Federal Reserve Banks, and electing an advisory council to the Fed. However, much would depend on whom the president would appoint to the board. The reformers did not have to wait long. Control was promptly handed to Morgan men, led by Benjamin Strong of Bankers

Trust as all-powerful head of the Federal Reserve Bank of New York. The reformers had gotten the point by the end of congressional wrangling over the Glass bill, and by the time the Federal Reserve Act was passed in December 1913, the bill enjoyed overwhelming support from the banking community. As A. Barton Hepburn of the Chase National Bank persuasively told the American Bankers Association at its annual meeting of August 1913: "The measure recognizes and adopts the principles of a central bank. Indeed . . . it will make all incorporated banks together joint owners of a central dominating power."[75] In fact, there was very little substantive difference between the Aldrich and Glass bills: the goal of the bank reformers had been triumphantly achieved.[76, 77]

Conclusion

The financial elites of this country, notably the Morgan, Rockefeller, and Kuhn, Loeb interests, were responsible for putting through the Federal Reserve System, as a governmentally created and sanctioned cartel device to enable the nation's banks to inflate the money supply in a coordinated fashion, without suffering quick retribution from depositors or noteholders demanding cash. Recent researchers, however, have also highlighted the vital supporting role of the growing number of technocratic experts and academics, who were happy to lend the

[75]Ibid., p. 235.

[76]On the essential identity of the two plans, see Friedman and Schwartz, *A Monetary History of the United States*, p. 171, n. 59; Kolko, *Triumph*, p. 235; and Paul M. Warburg, *The Federal Reserve System, Its Origins and Growth* (New York: Macmillan, 1930), 1, chaps. 8 and 9. On the minutiae of the various drafts and bills and the reactions to them, see West, *Banking Reform*, pp. 79–135; Kolko, *Triumph*, pp. 186–89, 217–47; and Livingston, *Origins*, pp. 217–26.

[77]On the capture of banking control in the new Federal Reserve System by the Morgans and their allies, and on the Morganesque policies of the Fed during the 1920s, see Rothbard, "Federal Reserve," pp. 103–36.

patina of their allegedly scientific expertise to the elites' drive for a central bank. To achieve a regime of big government and government control, power elites cannot achieve their goal of privilege through statism without the vital legitimizing support of the supposedly disinterested experts and the professoriat. To achieve the Leviathan state, interests seeking special privilege, and intellectuals offering scholarship and ideology, must work hand in hand.

Part 3

From Hoover to Roosevelt: The Federal Reserve and the Financial Elites

From Hoover to Roosevelt: The Federal Reserve and the Financial Elites

This chapter is grounded on the insight that American politics, from the turn of the twentieth century until World War II, can far better be comprehended by studying the interrelationship of major financial groupings than by studying the superficial and often sham struggles between Democrats and Republicans. In particular, American politics in this period was marked by a fierce struggle between two major financial-industrial groupings: the interests clustered around the House of Morgan on the one hand, and an alliance of Rockefeller (oil), Harriman (railroad), and Kuhn, Loeb (investment banking) interests on the other. The Morgans began in investment banking, and moved out into railroads, commercial banking, and then manufacturing; the Rockefeller–Harriman–Kuhn, Loeb alliance began in their three respective original spheres, and moved into commercial banking. In most instances, the two mighty combines clashed: for example, in whether or not Theodore Roosevelt (always closely allied to the Morgans) should use the antitrust weapon to smash Standard Oil, or whether, in his turn, President Taft (allied with the Ohio-based Rockefellers) should try to break up Morgan trusts such as International Harvester or United States Steel. In other areas, the interests of the two mammoths coincided and they were allies: thus, both groups were heavily represented in the drive for measures cartelizing industry that were sought and lobbied for by the National Civic Federation during the Progressive Era; and both groups joined to push through the Federal Reserve System.[1]

The Early Fed, 1914–1928: The Morgan Years

In their joining together to draft, and then to lobby for, the new Federal Reserve System, the House of Morgan was clearly very much the senior partner in the enterprise. The secret meeting of a handful of top bankers at the Jekyll Island Club in November 1910 that framed the prototype of the Federal Reserve Act was held at a resort facility provided by J.P. Morgan himself. The Federal Reserve, in its first two decades, contained two loci of power: the main one was the head, then called the governor, of the Federal Reserve Bank of New York; of lesser importance was the Federal Reserve Board in Washington. The governor of the New York Fed from the beginning until his death in 1928, was Benjamin Strong, who had spent his entire working life in the Morgan ambit. He was a vice president of the Bankers Trust Company, established by the Morgans to engage in the new and lucrative trust business; and his best friends in the world were his mentor and neighbor, the powerful Morgan partner Henry P. Davison, as well as two other Morgan partners, Dwight Morrow and Thomas W. Lamont. So highly trusted was Strong in the Morgan circle that he was brought in to be the personal auditor of J. Pierpont Morgan, Sr., during the panic of 1907. When he was offered the post of governor of the New York Fed in the new Federal Reserve System, the reluctant Strong was convinced by Davison that he could operate the Fed as a "real central bank . . . run from New York."[2]

[1]On the National Civic Federation, see James Weinstein, *The Corporate Ideal in the Liberal State, 1900–1918* (Boston: Beacon Press, 1968).

[2]So close were Strong and Davison that, when Strong's wife committed suicide after childbirth, Davison took the three surviving children into his home. On Strong and the Morgans, see Murray N. Rothbard, "The Federal

The Morgans were not nearly as dominant in the then-lesser institution of the Federal Reserve Board in Washington. On the original board, there were seven members, of whom two, the secretary of the Treasury and the comptroller of the currency, were ex officio. The Morgan bloc on the original board was led by Secretary of the Treasury William Gibbs McAdoo, son-in-law of President Wilson, whose Hudson and Manhattan Railroad Company in New York had been bailed out personally by J.P. Morgan, who then proceeded to staff the officers and board of Hudson and Manhattan with his closest business associates. From that point on, McAdoo was surrounded by a Morgan ambience.[3] Comptroller of the currency was John Skelton Williams, a protégé of McAdoo's who had also been a director of the Hudson and Manhattan Railroad. Another board member was McAdoo protégé Charles S. Hamlin, who came to the board from the post of assistant secretary of the Treasury. In addition to being a wealthy Boston lawyer—from a Boston financial group long affiliated with the Morgan interests—Hamlin had married into the wealthy Pruyn family of Albany, which had been associated with the Morgan-dominated New York Central Railroad.

If these three were solid Morgan men, the other four Reserve Board members were not nearly as reliable: Paul M. Warburg was partner and brother-in-law of Jacob Schiff of the investment banking house of Kuhn, Loeb; Frederic A. Delano, uncle of Franklin D. Roosevelt, was president of the Rockefeller-controlled Wabash Railway; William P.G. Harding was an Alabama

---

Reserve as a Cartelization Device," *Money in Crisis*, Barry Siegel, ed. (San Francisco: Pacific Institute for Public Policy, 1984), p. 109; Lester V. Chandler, *Benjamin Strong, Central Banker* (Washington, D.C.: Brookings Institution, 1958), pp. 23–41; and Ron Chernow, *The House of Morgan: An American Banking Dynasty and the Rise of Modern Finance* (New York: Atlantic Monthly Press, 1990), pp. 142–45, 182.

[3]Philip H. Burch, Jr., *Elites in American History*, vol. 2, *The Civil War to the New Deal* (New York: Holmes and Meier, 1981), pp. 207–09.

banker whose father-in-law's iron manufacturing company had prominent Morgan as well as rival Rockefeller men on its board; and Adolph C. Miller was an academic economist at Berkeley who had married into the wealthy Morgan-connected Sprague family of Chicago. Thus, of the seven members of the original board, three were Morgan men (but of whom two were ex officio); one was Kuhn, Loeb; one Rockefeller; one an independent banker with both Morgan and Rockefeller connections; and one was an economist with vague family ties to the Morgans. Hardly complete Morgan control of the board!

But the Morgans not only had by far the most powerful Federal Reserve banker, Benjamin Strong, in their corner, they also had the Republican administrations of the 1920s. Although there were various groups around President Warren G. Harding, as an Ohio Republican he was closest to the Rockefellers, and his secretary of state, Charles Evans Hughes, was a mentor of John D. Rockefeller, Jr.'s, New York Bible class, a leading Standard Oil attorney, and a trustee of the Rockefeller Foundation.[4] Harding's sudden death in August 1923, however, unexpectedly elevated Vice President Calvin Coolidge to the presidency.

Coolidge has been misleadingly described as a colorless small-town Massachusetts attorney. Actually, the new president was a member of a prominent Boston financial family, who were board members of leading Boston banks. One, T. Jefferson Coolidge, became prominent in the Morgan-affiliated United Fruit Company of Boston. Throughout his political career,

[4]Hughes was both counsel and chief foreign policy adviser to the Rockefellers' Standard Oil of New Jersey. On Hughes's close ties to the Rockefeller complex and their being overlooked even by Hughes's biographers, see the important but neglected article by Thomas Ferguson, "From Normalcy to New Deal: Industrial Structure, Party Competition, and American Public Policy in the Great Depression," *International Organization* 38 (Winter 1984): 67. On Hughes's and Rockefeller's men's Bible class, see Raymond B. Rosdick, *John D. Rockefeller, Jr.: A Portrait* (New York: Harper and Bros., 1956), p. 125.

moreover, Calvin Coolidge had two important mentors, both neglected by historians. One was Massachusetts Republican Party Chairman W. Murray Crane, who served as a director of three powerful Morgan-dominated institutions: the New Haven and Hartford Railroad, the Guaranty Trust Company of New York, and AT&T, on which he was also a member of the board's executive committee. The other was Amherst classmate and prominent Morgan partner Dwight Morrow. Morrow began to agitate for Coolidge for president as early as 1919, and continued his pressure at the Chicago Republican convention of 1920. Dwight Morrow and fellow Morgan partner Thomas Cochran lobbied strenuously for Coolidge at Chicago. Cochran, who was not an Amherst graduate, did not have the Amherst excuse for working for Coolidge, and so he kept in the background. Cochran and Morrow were happy, as prominent Morgan men, to confine their work to the background and to push forward as their front man for Coolidge the large, doughty Boston merchant Frank Stearns, who did have the virtue of being an Amherst graduate.[5]

Secretary of the Treasury throughout all three Republican administrations of the 1920s was the powerful multimillionaire tycoon Andrew Mellon, head of the Mellon interests, whose empire spread from the Mellon National Bank of Pittsburgh to encompass Gulf Oil, Koppers Company, and Aluminum Corporation of America. Mellon was generally allied to the Morgan interests. Furthermore, when Charles Evans Hughes returned to private law practice in the spring of 1925, Coolidge offered his crucial State Department post to longtime Wall Street attorney and former secretary of state and of war, Elihu Root, who might be called the veteran head of the "Morgan bar." At one critical time in Morgan's affairs, Root had served as

[5]Stearns, however, had not met Coolidge before being introduced to him by Morrow. Cochran was a leading Morgan partner, and board member of Bankers Trust Company, Chase Securities Corporation, and Texas Gulf Sulphur Company. Burch, *Elites, 2*, pp. 274–75, 302–03; and Harold Nicolson, *Dwight Morrow* (New York: Harcourt Brace, 1935), p. 232.

Morgan's personal attorney. After Root refused the State Department post, Coolidge was forced to settle for a lesser Morgan light, Minnesota attorney Frank B. Kellogg. Undersecretary to Kellogg was Joseph C. Grew, who had family connections with the Morgans (J.P. Morgan, Jr., had married a Grew), while, in 1927, two highly placed Morgan men were asked to take over relations with troubled Mexico and Nicaragua.[6]

The year 1924 indeed saw the House of Morgan at the pinnacle of political power in the United States. President Calvin Coolidge, friend and protégé of Morgan partner Dwight Morrow, was deeply admired by J.P. "Jack" Morgan, Jr. Jack Morgan saw the president, perhaps uniquely, as a rare blend of deep thinker and moralist. Morgan wrote a friend: "I have never seen any president who gives me just the feeling of confidence in the country and its institutions, and the working out of our problems, that Mr. Coolidge does."

On the other hand, the House of Morgan faced the happy dilemma in the 1924 presidential election that the Democratic candidate was none other than John W. Davis, senior partner of the Wall Street firm of Davis, Polk and Wardwell, and chief attorney for J.P. Morgan and Company. Davis, a protégé of the legendary Morgan partner Harry Davison, was also a personal friend and a backgammon and cribbage partner of Jack Morgan's. It was an embarrassment of riches. Whoever won the 1924 election, the Morgans could not lose, although they decided to opt for Coolidge.[7]

[6]Morgan partner Dwight Morrow became ambassador to Mexico in 1927, while Nicaraguan affairs came under the direction of Henry L. Stimson, Wall Street lawyer and longtime leading disciple of Elihu Root, and a partner in Root's law firm. As for Frank Kellogg, in addition to being a director of the Merchants National Bank of St. Paul, he had been general counsel for the Morgan-dominated United States Steel Company for the Minnesota region, and most importantly, the top lawyer for railroad magnate James J. Hill, long closely allied with the Morgan interests. Burch, *Elites*, 2, pp. 277, 305.

[7]Chernow, *House of Morgan*, pp. 254–55.

However, 1928, saw inevitable changes in Morgan domination of monetary policy. Benjamin Strong, sickly all year, died in October, and was replaced by George L. Harrison, his handpicked successor. While Harrison was a devoted "Morgan loyalist," he did not quite carry the clout of Benjamin Strong.[8]

The Coolidge administration, too, was coming to an end. The Morgans, again facing an embarrassment of riches, were torn three ways. Their prime goal was to induce their beloved president to break precedent and run for a third term. Not being able to persuade Coolidge, the Morgans next turned to Vice President Charles G. Dawes, who had been connected with various Morgan railroads in Chicago. When Dawes dropped out of the race, the Morgans turned at last to Herbert Clark Hoover, who had been a powerful secretary of commerce during the two Republican administrations of the 1920s. While Hoover had not been as intimately connected with the Morgans as had Calvin Coolidge, he had long been close to the Morgan interests. Particularly influential over Hoover during his administration were two unofficial but powerful advisers—both Morgan partners: Thomas W. Lamont, and Dwight Morrow, whom Hoover consulted regularly three times a week.[9]

Herbert Hoover's Cabinet was also loaded with Morgan people. As secretary of state, Hoover chose the longtime Morgan lawyer, and disciple and partner of Elihu Root, Henry L. Stimson. Andrew Mellon continued as Treasury secretary, and his undersecretary, who was to replace Mellon in 1931 and was close to Hoover, was Ogden L. Mills, a former congressman and New York corporate lawyer whose father, Ogden L. Mills, Sr., had been a leader of such Morgan railroads as New

[8]Ibid., p. 382.

[9]Lamont was actually able to induce Hoover to conceal Lamont's influence by faking entries in a diary left to historians. Ferguson, "From Normalcy to New Deal," p. 79. See also ibid., p. 77; and Burch, *Elites*, 2, p. 280.

York Central.[10] Hoover's secretary of the Navy was Charles Francis Adams, III, from the famous Boston Brahmin family long associated with the Morgans. This particular Adams daughter had been fortunate enough to marry Jack Morgan.

Benjamin Strong's monetary policy, throughout his reign, was essentially a Morgan policy. The Morgans, through their subsidiary, Morgan, Grenfell in London, had long been intimately associated with the British government and with the Bank of England. Before World War I, the House of Morgan had been named a fiscal agent of the British Treasury and of the Bank of England. After the war began, the Morgans became the sole purchaser of all goods and supplies for the British and French war effort in the United States, as well as the monopoly underwriter in the United States of all British and French bonds. The Morgans played a substantial role in bringing the United States into the war on Britain's side, and, as head of the Fed, Benjamin Strong obligingly doubled the money supply to finance America's role in the war effort.[11]

After the end of the war, Strong's monetary policy was deliberately guided by the prime objective of helping Great Britain establish, and impose upon Europe, a new and disastrous gold-exchange standard. The idea was to restore "England"—which really meant the Morgans' English associates and allies—to her old position of financial dominance by helping her establish a phony gold standard. Ostensibly this was a return to the prewar "classical" gold standard. But the return, in the spring of 1925,

[10]Mills was a descendant of the highly aristocratic eighteenth-century Livingston family of New York, as well as related to the Reids, Morgan-oriented owners of the *New York Herald-Tribune*. Mills's first wife was a member of the longtime Morgan-connected Vanderbilt family. See Jordan A. Schwarz, *The Interregnum of Despair: Hoover, Congress, and the Depression* (Urbana: University of Illinois Press, 1970), p. 111.

[11]On the Morgan role in pressuring the United States into entering World War I, see the classic work by Charles Callan Tansill, *America Goes to War* (Boston: Little, Brown, 1938), pp. 67–133.

was at the prewar par, a rate that hopelessly overvalued the pound sterling, which Britain had inflated and depreciated during the fiat money era after 1914. Britain insisted on returning to gold at an overvalued par, a policy guaranteed to hobble British exports, and yet was determined to indulge in continued cheap money and inflation, instead of contracting its money supply to make the prewar par viable. To help Britain get away with this peculiar and contradictory policy, the United States helped to pretend that the post-1925 standard in Europe—this gold bullion-pound standard—was really a genuine gold-coin standard. The United States inflated its money and credit in order to prevent inflationary Britain from losing gold to the United States, a loss which would endanger the new, jerry-built "gold standard" structure. The result, however, was eventual collapse of money and credit in the U.S. and abroad, and a worldwide depression. Benjamin Strong was the Morgans' architect of a disastrous policy of inflationary boom that led inevitably to bust.

THE HOOVER FED: HARRISON AND YOUNG

While secretary of commerce, Herbert Hoover had been a severe critic of Strong's inflationary policies. Unfortunately, however, Hoover was in favor of a different form of easy money and cheap credit. When he became president, he tried, like King Canute, to hold back the tides by continuing to generate cheap bank credit, and then using "moral suasion" to exhort banks and other lenders *not* to lend money for the purchase of stock. Hoover suffered from the fallacious view that industrial credit was productive and "legitimate" while financial, stock market credit was "unproductive." Moreover, he believed that valuable capital funds somehow got lost, or "absorbed," in the stock market and therefore became lost to productive credit. Hoover employed methods of intimidation of business that had been honed when he was food czar in World War I and then secretary of commerce, now trying to get banks to restrain stock market loans and to induce the New York Stock Exchange to curb speculation. Roy Young, Hoover's new appointee as governor of the

Federal Reserve Board, suffered from the same fallacious view. Partly responsible for the Hoover administration's adopting this policy was the wily manipulator Montagu Norman, head of the Bank of England, and close friend of the late Benjamin Strong, who had persuaded Strong to inflate credit in order to help England's disastrous gold-exchange policy. Norman, it might be added, was very close to the Morgan, Grenfell bank.

By June 1929, it was clear that the absurd policy of moral suasion had failed. Seeing the handwriting on the wall, Norman switched, and persuaded the Fed to resume its old policy of inflating reserves through subsidizing the acceptance market by purchasing all acceptances offered at a subsidized rate—a policy the Fed had abandoned in the spring of 1928.[13]

Despite this attempt to keep the boom going, however, the money supply in the United States leveled off by the end of 1928, and remained more or less constant from then on. This ending of the massive credit expansion boom made a recession inevitable, and sure enough, the American economy began to turn down in July 1929. Feverish attempts to keep the stock market boom going, however, managed to boost stock prices while the economic fundamentals were turning sour, leading to the famous stock market crash of October 24.

This crash was an event for which Herbert Hoover was ready. For a decade, Herbert Hoover had urged that the United States break its age-old policy of not intervening in cyclical recessions. During the postwar 1920–1921 recession, Hoover, as secretary of commerce, had unsuccessfully urged President Harding to intervene massively in the recession, to "do something" to cure the depression, in particular to expand credit and

[13]See A. Wilfred May, "Inflation in Securities" in *The Economics of Inflation*, H. Parker Willis and John M. Chapman, eds. (New York: Columbia University Press, 1935), pp. 292–93; Benjamin H. Beckhart, "Federal Reserve Policy and the Money Market, 1923–1931," in *The New York Money Market* (New York: Columbia University Press, 1931), 4, pp. 127, 142 ff.; and Murray N. Rothbard, *America's Great Depression*, 4th ed. (New York: Richardson and Snyder, 1983), pp. 117–23, 142–43, 148, 151–52.

to engage in a massive public-works program. Although the United States got out of the recession on its own, without massive intervention, Hoover vowed that next time it would be different. In late 1928, after he was elected president, Hoover presented a public works scheme, the "Hoover Plan" for "permanent prosperity," for a pact to "outlaw depression," to the Conference of Governors. Hoover had adopted the scheme of the well-known inflationists Foster and Catchings, for a mammoth $3 billion public-works plan to "stabilize" business cycles. William T. Foster was the theoretician and Waddill Catchings the financier of the duo; Foster was installed as head of the Pollak Foundation for Economic Research by Catchings, iron and steel magnate and investment banker at the powerful Wall Street firm of Goldman, Sachs.[14]

When the stock market crash came in October 1929, therefore, President Hoover was ready for massive intervention to attempt to raise wage rates, expand credit, and embark on public works. Hoover himself recalls that he was the very first president to consider himself responsible for economic prosperity: "therefore, we had to pioneer a new field." Hoover's admiring biographers correctly state that "President Hoover was the first president in our history to offer federal leadership in mobilizing the economic resources of the people." Hoover recalls it was a "program unparalleled in the history of depressions."[15] The major opponent of this new statist dogma was Secretary of the Treasury Mellon, who, though one of the leaders in pushing the boom, now at least saw the importance of liquidating the malinvestments, inflated costs, prices, and wage rates of the inflationary boom. Mellon, indeed, correctly cited the successful application of such a laissez-faire policy in previous recessions

[14]William T. Foster and Waddill Catchings, "Mr. Hoover's Plan: What It Is and What It Is Not—The New Attack on Poverty," *Review of Reviews* (April 1929): 77–78. See also Foster and Catchings, *The Road to Plenty* (Boston: Houghton Mifflin, 1928); and Rothbard, *America's Great Depression*, pp. 167–78.

[15]Rothbard, *America's Great Depression*, p. 186.

and crises. But Hoover overrode Mellon, with the support of Treasury Undersecretary Ogden Mills.

If Hoover stood ready to impose an expansionist and interventionist New Deal, Morgan man George L. Harrison, head of the New York Fed and major power in the Federal Reserve, was all the more ready to inflate. During the week of the crash, the last week of October, the Fed doubled its holdings of government securities, adding $150 million to bank reserves, as well as discounting $200 million more for member banks. The idea was to prevent liquidation of the bloated stock market, and to permit the New York City banks to take over the loans to stockbrokers that the nonbank lenders were liquidating. As a result, member banks of the Federal Reserve expanded their deposits by $1.8 billion—a phenomenal monetary expansion of nearly 10 percent *in one week*! Of this increase, $1.6 billion were increased deposits of the New York City banks. In addition, Harrison drove down interest rates, lowering its discount rates to banks from 6 percent to 4.5 percent in a few weeks.

Harrison conducted these actions with a will, overriding the objections of Federal Reserve Board Governor Roy Young, proclaiming that "the Stock Exchange should stay open at all costs," and announcing, "Gentlemen, I am ready to provide all the reserve funds that may be needed."[16]

By mid-November, the great stock break was over, and the market, artificially buoyed and stimulated by expanding credit, began to move upward again. With the stock market emergency seemingly over, bank reserves were allowed to decline, by the end of November, by about $275 million, to just about the level before the crash. By the end of the year, total bank reserves at $2.35 billion were almost exactly the same as they had been the day before the crash, or at the end of November, with total bank deposits increasing slightly during this period. But while the aggregates of factors determining reserves were the same, their distribution was very different. Fed ownership of government

[16]Chernow, *House of Morgan*, p. 319.

securities had increased by $375 million during these two months, from the level of $136 million before the crash, but the expansion had been offset by lower bank loans from the Fed, by greater money in circulation, and by people drawing $100 million of gold out of the banking system. In short, the Fed tried its best to inflate a great deal more, but its expansionary policy was partially thwarted by increasing caution and by withdrawal of money from the banking system by the general public.

Here we see, at the very beginning of the Hoover era, the spuriousness of the monetarist legend that the Federal Reserve was responsible for the great contraction of money from 1929 to 1933. On the contrary, the Fed and the administration tried their best to inflate, efforts foiled by the good sense, and by the increasing distrust of the banking system, of the American people.

At any rate, even though the Fed had not managed to inflate the money supply further, President Hoover was proud of his experiment in cheap money, and of the Fed's massive open market purchases. In a speech to a conference of industrial leaders he had called together in Washington on December 5, the president hailed the nation's good fortune in possessing the splendid Federal Reserve System, which had succeeded in saving shaky banks, restoring confidence, and making capital more abundant by lowering interest rates. Hoover had personally done his part by urging banks to discount more at the Fed, while Secretary Mellon reverted to his old Pollyanna mode in assuring one and all that there was "plenty of credit available." Hoover admirer William Green, head of the American Federation of Labor, proclaimed that the "Federal Reserve System is operating, serving as a barrier against financial demoralization. Within a few months industrial conditions will become normal, confidence and stabilization in industry and finance will be restored."[17]

By the end of 1929, Roy Young and other Fed officials favored pursuing a laissez-faire policy "to let the money market

[17]Rothbard, *America's Great Depression*, pp. 192–93.

'sweat it out' and reach monetary ease by the wholesome process of liquidation."[18] Once again, however, Harrison and the New York Fed overruled Washington, and instituted a massive easy-money program. Discount rates of the New York Fed fell from 4.5 percent in February to 2 percent at the end of 1930. Other short-term interest rates fell similarly. Once again, the New York Fed led the inflationist parade by purchasing $218 million of government securities during the year; the resulting increase of $116 million in bank reserves, however, was offset by bank failures in the latter part of the year, and by enforced contraction on the part of the shaky banks remaining in business. As a result, total money supply remained constant throughout 1930. Expansion was also cut short by the fact that the stock market boomlet early in the year had collapsed by the spring.

During the year, however, Montagu Norman was able to achieve part of his long-standing wish for formal collaboration between the world's major central banks. Norman pushed through a new central bankers' bank, the Bank for International Settlements (BIS), to meet regularly at Basle, and to provide regular facilities for cooperation. While the suspicious Congress forbade the Fed from joining the BIS formally, the New York Fed and its allied Morgan interests were able to work closely with the new bank. The BIS, indeed, treated the New York Fed as if it were the central bank of the United States. Gates W. McGarrah resigned as chairman of the board of the New York Fed in February to assume the position of president of the BIS, while Jackson E. Reynolds, a director of the New York Fed particularly close to the Morgan interests, became chairman of the BIS's organizing committee.[19] Unsurprisingly, J.P. Morgan and Company supplied much of the capital for the new BIS. And even though there was no legislative sanction for U.S. participation in

[18]Benjamin M. Anderson, Jr., *Economics and the Public Welfare* (New York: D. Van Nostrand, 1949), pp. 222–23.

[19]Reynolds was affiliated with the First National Bank of New York, long a flagship of the Morgan interests.

the bank, New York Fed Governor George Harrison made a "regular business trip" abroad in the fall to confer with the other central bankers, and the New York Fed extended loans to the BIS during 1931.[20]

Late 1930 was perhaps the last stand of the laissez-faire, sound-money liquidationists. Professor H. Parker Willis, a tireless critic of the Fed's inflationism and credit expansion, attacked the current easy money policy of the Fed in an editorial in the *New York Journal of Commerce*.[21] Willis pointed out that the Fed's easy-money policy was actually bringing about the rash of bank failures, because of the banks' "inability to liquidate" their unsound loans and assets. Willis noted that the country was suffering from frozen wasteful malinvestments in plants, buildings, and other capital, and maintained that the depression could only be cured when these unsound credit positions were allowed to liquidate. Similarly, Albert Wiggin, head of Chase National Bank, clearly reflecting the courageous and uncompromising views of the Chase bank's chief economist, Dr. Benjamin M. Anderson, denounced the Hoover policy of propping up wage

[20]Rothbard, *America's Great Depression*, p. 332.

[21]Willis, professor of banking at Columbia University and editor of the *Journal of Commerce*, had been a student of the great hard-money economist J. Laurence Laughlin at the University of Chicago. Laughlin and Willis were leading proponents of the "real bills" doctrine, the erroneous view that fractional reserve banking is sound and never inflationary, provided that banks confine their lending to short-term business credit that would be "self-liquidating" because loaned for inventory ("real goods") that would be sold shortly. Laughlin and Willis played an influential role in drafting, and then agitating for, the Federal Reserve System, which they expected would be strictly confined to rediscounting short-term "real bills" held by the banks. Willis was a longtime assistant to, and theoretician for, the powerful Democratic Senator Carter Glass of Virginia, ruling figure on the Senate Banking and Currency Committee.

Upon seeing the Fed stray far from his expected policies, H. Parker Willis, in the 1920s and 1930s, was a tireless and perceptive critic of the inflationary policies of the Fed, whether in boom or depression. The criticism was particularly intense to the extent that the Fed engaged in open market

rates and prices in depressions, and of pursuing inflationary cheap money, saying, "Our depression has been prolonged and not alleviated by delay in making necessary readjustments."[22]

On the other hand, *Business Week,* then as now a spokesman for "enlightened" business opinion, thundered in late October 1930 that the "deflationists" were "in the saddle."[23]

In August 1930, however, President Hoover took another decisive step in favor of inflationism by replacing Roy Young as chairman of the Federal Reserve Board by the veteran speculator and government official Eugene Meyer, Jr.

THE ADVENT OF EUGENE MEYER, JR.

Eugene Meyer, Jr., differed from Strong and Harrison in not being totally in the Morgan camp. Meyer's father, an immigrant from France, had spent all his life in the employ of the French international banking house of Lazard Frères, finally rising to the post of partner of Lazard's New York branch. Eugene, Jr., early broke out from Lazard on his on and became a successful

---

operations on government securities, or discounted bank loans to corporate securities. On Willis, see Rothbard, *America's Great Depression.*

After resigning as editor of the *Journal of Commerce* in May 1931, Willis continued to slam the inflationist policies of the Fed in the pages of the *Commercial and Financial Chronicle* during 1931 and 1932. A Willis article in a French publication in January 1932 upset George Harrison so much that he went so far as to plead with Senator Carter Glass to help put an end to "Willis's rather steady flow of disturbing and alarming articles about the American position." Harrison to Glass, January 16, 1932, cited in Milton Friedman and Anna J. Schwartz, *A Monetary History of the United States* (Princeton, N.J.: National Bureau of Economic Research, 1963), pp. 408–09, n. 162.

[22]*Commercial and Financial Chronicle* 131 (August 2, 1930): 690–91; *Commercial and Financial Chronicle* 132 (January 17, 1931): 428–29. Even though the Chase Bank was still in Morgan control at the time, Benjamin Anderson had always pursued an independent course.

[23]*Business Week* (October 22, 1930). Rothbard, *America's Great Depression,* p. 213.

speculator, investor and financier, an associate of the Morgans, and even more closely an associate of Bernard Baruch and Baruch's patrons, the powerful Guggenheim family, in virtual control of the American copper industry. It is true, however, that Meyer's brother-in-law, George Blumenthal, had left this post at Lazard to be a high official in J.P. Morgan and Company, and that Meyer himself had once acted as a liaison between the Morgans and the French government.[24] By the 1920s, Meyer's major financial base was his control of the mighty integrated chemical firm, Allied Chemical and Dye Corporation.[25]

Before World War I, Meyer's major financial involvement had been with the Guggenheims and the copper industry. By 1910, he was so prominent in the copper industry that he was able to arrange a cartel agreement between his old patrons, the Guggenheims, and Anaconda Copper, each agreeing to cut its production by 7.5 percent. In the same year, Meyer discovered in London a highly productive and profitable new process for mining copper, and was quickly able to become its franchiser in the United States.[26]

[24]It is also true that Meyer was never particularly close to Blumenthal. Merlo J. Pusey, *Eugene Meyer* (New York: Alfred A. Knopf, 1974).

[25]The advent of World War I cut the American textile industry off from the dyes of the German dye cartel, which had supplied 90 percent of its dyes. Meyer was astute enough to discover and finance a new dye-making process invented by a struggling chemist and German dye salesman, Dr. William Beckers, and Meyer quickly set up the Beckers Aniline and Chemical Works to sell dyes to the woolen industry. In 1916, Meyer brought about a merger with another new dye firm selling to the cotton industry, and with the supplier of aniline oil to both companies, forming the National Aniline and Chemical Company. Meyer eventually seized control of National Aniline and Chemical, which made heavy profits during the war selling blue dyes to the Navy. After the war, Meyer engineered the merger of National Aniline with companies making acids, alkalis, coke ovens, chemical by-products, and coal-tars, to form the powerful and highly profitable Allied Chemical and Dye Corporation on January 1, 1921. Pusey, *Eugene Meyer*, pp. 117–25.

[26]Ibid., pp. 82–88.

It should not be surprising, then, that, under the regime of World War I collectivism, Meyer began, first, in early 1917, as head of the nonferrous metals unit of Bernard Baruch's Raw Materials Committee under the Advisory Commission of the Council of National Defense. The nonferrous metals unit included copper, lead, zinc, antimony, aluminum, nickel, and silver. When the War Industries Board took over the task of collectivist planning of industry in August 1917, Meyer assumed the same task there—and was also to become the virtual "czar" of the copper industry.[27]

More important for his eventual role in the Hoover administration was Meyer's crucial part in the War Finance Corporation (WFC). The WFC had been set up by Secretary of the Treasury McAdoo in May 1918, ostensibly to finance industries essential to the war effort. Meyer was named the WFC's managing director. The WFC massively subsidized American industry. During the war, it had two basic functions. One was acting as agent of the Treasury to prop up the market for U.S. government bonds. During the last six months of the war, Meyer spent $378 million to keep government bonds from falling by more than one-quarter point a day, and later resold the bonds to the Treasury at the cost of purchase.

The second and dominant function of the WFC was to subsidize and bail out firms and industries in trouble, allegedly "essential" to the war effort. The WFC began with an authorized capital of $500 million supplied by the Treasury, and with the power to borrow up to $3 billion through the issue of bonds. Its major focus was on utilities, railroads, and the banks that had financed them. Banks were also under strain because many of their savings deposits had been drawn down to help finance

[27]On the Council of National Defense and the War Industries Board, see Murray N. Rothbard, "War Collectivism in World War I," in *A New History of Leviathan: Essays on the Rise of the American State*, Ronald Radosh and Murray N. Rothbard, eds. (New York: E.P. Dutton, 1972), pp. 70–83. On Meyer's role, see Pusey, *Eugene Meyer*, pp. 137–49.

the federal deficit. All in all, during the war, the WFC made loans of $71 million, in addition to its bond-price operations.

It was clear that the essential mission of the WFC acted as a camouflage for a government subsidy operation. As Meyer's approving biographer writes: "The WFC had been created as a rescue mission for essential war-disrupted industries, and Meyer had shaped it into a powerful instrument of public policy."[28]

If the WFC, and for that matter the rest of the apparatus of war collectivism, had been strictly war-related, they all would have been dropped swiftly as soon as the Armistice was signed on November 11, 1918. But on the contrary, Baruch, Meyer, the War Industries Board, and most business leaders were anxious to continue the benefits of collectivism indefinitely after the war was over. The goals were twofold: price controls to keep prices up during the expected postwar recession; and a permanent peacetime cartelization of American industry enforced by the federal government. Permanent cartelization was endorsed by the U.S. Chamber of Commerce and by the National Association of Manufacturers. President Wilson, however, prompted by Secretary of War Newton D. Baker, insisted on scuttling the WIB by the end of 1918. Other aspects of wartime government interventionism continued on, however, not the least of which was the War Finance Corporation.[29]

The War Finance Corporation was a striking example of a wartime government agency that refused to die. After the war, the investment bankers were worried that Europeans, shorn of American aid, would no longer be able to keep up

[28]Pusey, *Eugene Meyer*, p. 163.

[29]Rothbard, "War Collectivism," pp. 100–05. On an abortive attempt to continue collectivist planning through the Industrial Board of the Department of Commerce, see ibid., pp. 105–08; and Robert F. Himmelberg, "Business, Antitrust Policy, and the Industrial Board of the Department of Commerce, 1919," *Business History Review* (Spring 1968): 1–23.

the bountiful wartime level of American exports. Hence, the Morgans urged their friends in the Treasury Department to use the WFC to provide credits to finance American exports, specifically to pay American exporters and then collect the money from foreign importers. While the Wilson administration did not want a permanent government loan program, it persuaded Congress to extend the WFC in March 1919 and to authorize it to lend up to $1 billion over five years to American exporters and to American banks that made export loans.[30] Particularly ardent in pressuring Congress was WFC head Eugene Meyer, who had been gravely disappointed when the Wilson administration scuttled the War Industries Board.[31]

Meyer happily plunged into making and encouraging export loans and, while in Europe for the peace conference, he tried unsuccessfully to pressure British banks into issuing $600 million in loans to finance British imports, and to keep the overvalued pound from falling to its market levels. To counter the dangerously inflationary postwar boom, President Wilson shifted David F. Houston from the post of agriculture secretary to Treasury secretary, and Houston boldly set about shifting America to a more laissez-faire and deflationary course. Meyer worked feverishly to keep the inflationary boom going, the WFC approving loans totaling $150 million to finance the exports of cotton, tobacco, copper, coal, and steel. But Treasury Secretary Houston refused to give Meyer his required approval.

[30]Thomas W. Lamont, Morgan partner, made the proposal to Assistant Secretary of the Treasury Russell Leffingwell, and Secretary of the Treasury McAdoo pushed the measure through Congress. Not only was McAdoo solidly in the Morgan ambit, as we have seen, but Leffingwell, after he left the Treasury, became a leading partner of the Morgan bank. Burton I. Kaufman, *Efficiency and Expansion: Foreign Trade Organization in the Wilson Administration, 1913–1921* (Westport, Conn.: Greenwood Press, 1974), pp. 231–32; and Carl P. Parrini, *Heir to Empire: United States Economic Diplomacy, 1916–1923* (Pittsburgh: University of Pittsburgh Press, 1969), pp. 54–55.

[31]Pusey, *Eugene Meyer*, p. 164.

Houston declared, in fact, that he was proposing ending the WFC, in order to complete the government's withdrawal from all its wartime activities of government intervention in the economy. Houston pointed out that exports had already attained an unprecedented volume in 1919, and that it was important to bring down inflation. Meyer tried every device to persuade Houston, but he couldn't go over his head to the president because of Wilson's illness. Finally, Meyer threw in the towel and resigned his post in May 1920.[32]

Unfortunately, however, Eugene Meyer was soon back in the saddle. Recession always follows an inflationary boom. A recession hit in the fall of 1921, and the newly burgeoning farm bloc began its long-term drive to get the government to bring the farmer back to the unprecedented good times he had enjoyed from the artificial export boom created by World War I. During the presidential campaign of 1920, Secretary of Treasury Houston bravely resisted the farm bloc, maintaining that the federal government should do nothing to interfere with the inevitable postwar recession. Eugene Meyer, working for the Harding ticket, put himself at the head of the interventionist forces battling his old laissez-faire enemy. When Houston addressed the annual meeting of the American Bankers Association (ABA) in Washington, he refused to speak if the ABA succumbed to pressure by a group of Memphis bankers and businessmen to have Meyer address the group at the same meeting. When Houston's ploy was successful, the Memphis group of inflationist and interventionist bankers organized a rump meeting nearby featuring the address by Meyer, who led a fervent campaign for restoration of the WFC, this time stressing government financing of agricultural exports.

[32]Houston was a respected academic, who had been a political scientist and college president in Texas, and then served as chancellor of Washington University of St. Louis. It is refreshing to see a person of laissez-faire principle in this critical post. Ibid., pp. 169–70; and Burch, *Elites, 2*, pp. 210–11.

The defeat of the Democrats in November was a referendum on World War I, its aftermath, and the inflation and rationing of wartime, rather than against Houston, but Meyer used the victory to step up attacks on Secretary Houston. Organizing a nationwide campaign of demagogy, stressing especially the plight of the cotton farmer, Meyer personalized his assault on Houston's stalwart laissez-faire views. Combining hyperbole with alliteration, Meyer roasted Houston before the Joint Agricultural Committee of Congress. Meyer thundered,

> History records no precedent . . . for the wholesale sacrifices imposed upon the civilized world by the Secretary's [Houston's] present policies for the purpose of maintaining the petty platitudes of the outworn political economy which he professes.[33]

Congress duly passed the measure to revive the export lending of the WFC. When Wilson followed Houston's advice to veto the measure, asking Houston himself to write the veto message in December, Congress easily overrode the veto.

During the interregnum, Meyer and his friends angled for top jobs for him with the new Harding administration, but with Treasury and commerce closed off, Meyer turned down the post of assistant secretary of commerce under Herbert Hoover, correctly expecting Congress to re-enact the WFC. The new president duly reappointed Meyer to be head of the revived WFC, refurbished as an agricultural export aid bureau. In fact, exports were largely forgotten as the WFC was transformed into a simple agricultural relief agency. Under Meyer's aegis, and supported by Harding, Congress passed the Agricultural Credits Act of 1921, which increased the maximum authorized credits by the War Finance Corporation to $1 billion, and permitted it to lend directly to farmers' cooperatives and foreign importers, as well as exporters.

Meyer plunged in with a will, heavily financing farm co-ops, enabling them to buy and store crops, thereby raising

[33]Pusey, *Eugene Meyer*, p. 174.

farm prices, and presaging the more directly governmental farm price support policies of the Hoover and Roosevelt administrations. The WFC's first loan was to Aaron Sapiro's Staple Cotton Cooperative Association. Sapiro was a high-priced young attorney for several California farm co-ops who concocted grandiose plans for voluntary price-raising cartels in cotton, wheat, tobacco, and other crops, all of which turned out to be failures.[34] By the summer of 1923, the WFC had loaned $172 million to farm co-ops and another $182 million to rural banks, which in turn loaned money to farmers. The WFC, working closely with farm bloc leaders, appointed a Corn Belt Advisory Committee of farm leaders to pressure Midwestern rural bankers into lending more heavily to farmers in that region.

With banks providing a steady flow of short-term farm loans, and a vast Federal Farm Loan system, established in July 1916, supplying plentiful mortgage loans, the farm bloc still felt a gap in unsubsidized intermediate-term credit. Meyer and the co-op interests duly introduced a bill into Congress calling for a system of privately capitalized agricultural credit corporations, with the Federal Reserve empowered to extend credits and support these corporations. But the farm bloc, supported by Secretary of Commerce Hoover and Secretary of Agriculture Henry C. Wallace, went further, backing a competing bill establishing a large governmentally capitalized system of Federal Intermediate Credit Banks, patterned after the Federal Reserve System and governed by the Federal Farm Loan Board (FFLB), which had already been established to run the Farm Loan System. Congress passed both bills in one Agricultural Credits Act of 1923 in the summer of that year, but the Meyer system was in effect a dead letter; how could a privately financed albeit subsidized credit system compete with one financed by the U.S. Treasury?

[34]Rothbard, *America's Great Depression*, pp. 199–200.

With WFC duties now assumed by the new Federal Intermediate Credit system, Eugene Meyer allowed the War Finance Corporation's authority to make loans expire at the end of 1924. The WFC lingered on with no duties for five years, until Congress finally liquidated it in 1929. Meyer was cheerful about its demise, however, because he was able to use the virtually defunct post to meddle in, and eventually take over, the now-powerful Federal Farm Loan Board (FFLB). Meyer assumed control of the FFLB in March 1927, and continued to run it until the advent of the Hoover administration two years later.[35] His lengthy record in charge of inflationary government lending, in addition to his service in helping swing the New York Republican delegation to Hoover at the Republican convention of 1928, made Eugene Meyer eminently qualified to be Hoover's new governor of the Federal Reserve Board in the autumn of 1930.

Meyer in the Hoover Administration

In the midst of a German and the American bank crises, and a growing depression, Eugene Meyer battled the totally Morgan-run New York Fed for dominance over the Federal Reserve System. The Morgans were even more interested than Meyer in bailing out the European banking systems. In late June 1931, the New York Fed agreed to participate with the Bank of England, the Bank of France, and the Bank for International Settlements in a $100 million loan to try to bail out the German Reichsbank. Soon the Germans were asking for $500 million more to save their banking system. While Harrison was sympathetic, Meyer and the other bankers felt this was too much of a long-term commitment. The German government then asked the Fed, not only for the extra loan, but also

[35]Pusey, *Eugene Meyer*, pp. 183–92; Rothbard, *America's Great Depression*, pp. 196–98; and James Stuart Olson, *Herbert Hoover and the Reconstruction Finance Corporation, 1931–1933* (Ames: Iowa State University Press, 1977), p. 12.

for a reassuring statement—clearly mendacious—hailing the "fundamental soundness" of the German economy. Happening to be in New York in the midst of this German crisis on the weekend of July 12, Meyer found out by accident of a secret meeting at the New York Fed on the crisis with the top Morgan people in the administration, including Morgan partners Russell Leffingwell and S. Parker Gilbert; Albert Wiggin, head of the Morgan-run Chase National Bank; Acting Treasury Secretary Ogden Mills; Owen D. Young, chairman of the Morgan-run General Electric, and from the New York Fed, Governor George Harrison and Deputy Governor W. Randolph Burgess. The meeting had already persuaded President Hoover to issue a statement of sympathy for the German situation. Meyer, at this point, went ballistic, insisting that the president's statement, backed by a meeting of top banking worthies, would be taken by the Germans as well as everyone else as a "moral commitment to help the Germans," which would either lead to a disastrous blank-check support for German finance, or would make matters worse when that support was repudiated. Meyer also insisted that only the Federal Reserve Board in Washington could legally commit the Fed to such action. By his last-minute intervention, Meyer was fortunately able to block the Morgan cabal from getting Hoover to make the public endorsement. The following week, Hoover, aided by veteran Morgan-oriented lawyer and Secretary of State Henry L. Stimson, agitated again for direct loans to Germany, but Meyer was able to confine Hoover to engineering a Meyer-approved big power "standstill agreement" by which banks throughout the major countries of the world would continue to hold German and other Central European short-term debts without trying to get out of German marks and other shaky currencies of that region.

Generally, Meyer was able to overrule Harrison. Thus, when gold flowed out of U.S. banks after Britain's disastrous abandonment of the gold standard in late September, Meyer was able to force Harrison—wedded to cheap money—to raise the New York Fed's discount rate from 1.5 percent to 3.5 percent in

October, thereby reversing the gold drain by raising market confidence in the dollar.[36]

By early September 1931, even before Britain's abandonment of the gold standard, President Hoover, Eugene Meyer, and the nation's financial establishment all agreed that America required a massive infusion of more money and credit, under the direction of the federal government. There was one difference: whereas Meyer and the bankers wanted a revival of the War Finance Corporation for government to pour in the new money directly, Hoover first wanted to try a dab of his characteristic government-business partnership to encourage private bankers to contribute the necessary hundreds of millions of dollars to a federal agency. Hoover set up his National Credit Corporation (NCC) to attract $500 million from the banks in order to shore up shaky individual banks. But when the National Credit Corporation was only able to raise $150 million, Hoover quickly and cheerfully threw in the towel, and by the end of November, agreed to introduce a bill into Congress to revive the old WFC and expand it for peacetime uses into a new Reconstruction Finance Corporation (RFC).[37]

The RFC bill, which sailed through Congress by late January 1932, provided for the Treasury to pour $500 million of capital into the Reconstruction Finance Corporation, which was empowered to issue securities up to an additional $1.5 billion. The RFC could make loans to banks and financial institutions of all types. The theory was that, ensured of freedom from failing,

[36]Pusey, *Eugene Meyer*, pp. 209–15.

[37]Gerald D. Nash's story of a Hoover bitterly resisting the Reconstruction Finance Corporation until the last moment has now been replaced by a more accurate portrayal provided by James Olson: willing to give "voluntarism" a brief play, but then cheerfully falling back on pure statism. Gerald D. Nash, "Herbert Hoover and the Origins of the Reconstruction Finance Corporation," in *Mississippi Valley Historical Review* 46 (December 1959): 455–68; and James Olson, *Herbert Hoover*, pp. 24–29.

the timid banks would be emboldened to lend massively to business and industry, the money supply would dramatically rise, and prosperity would return. This was the doctrine trumpeted by President Hoover, Meyer, Mills, and Undersecretary of the Treasury Arthur A. Ballantine, a partner of the law firm headed by longtime Morgan attorney Elihu Root. Unsurprisingly, the representatives of groups expecting a massive infusion of federal money—commercial banks, savings banks, life insurance companies, and building and loan (in later years, savings and loan) associations—testifying before Congress "all praised the [RFC] bill in glowing terms, claiming that it was essential to the survival of the money market." In addition, the RFC was empowered to lend money to railroads, in order to relieve their indebtedness and revivify the railroad bond market. The railroad representatives were also delighted with the bill.

Hoover's original bill was even more sweeping, also allowing the RFC to make business loans to "bona fide institutions," but the Senate Democrats, suspicious of excessive executive power over business, killed this proposal. The Senate Democrats also reportedly extracted a promise from Hoover to make the beloved Eugene Meyer chairman of the new RFC. Meyer, doing double duty as governor of the Federal Reserve Board *and* head of the RFC, was now the most powerful single economic and financial force in the federal government.

The RFC, at the Democrats' insistence, was to have a board of directors consisting of four Republicans and three Democrats. Three of the Republicans were the ex officio heads of the Federal Reserve Board (Chairman Meyer), the secretary of the Treasury (Ogden Mills, who had replaced Mellon in January), and of the Federal Farm Loan Board (Paul Bestor, Meyer's protégé and successor). The fourth Republican appointee was former Vice President Charles G. Dawes, a Chicago railroad man in the Morgan ambit.

The RFC was not only patterned after the old War Finance Corporation in philosophy, but also aped its organizational structure and took over many of the WFC's actual personnel. The general counsel, and the three top examiners, of the WFC happily took up their old posts, while the first secretary of the RFC was George Cooksey, a former director of the WFC who had been a member of that outfit's remarkably leisurely liquidation committee from 1929 until he assumed his new position in the RFC. Like the War Finance Corporation, the RFC established eight divisions, as well as 33 local loan agencies.

Each of these loan agencies established an advisory committee consisting of the leading local bankers to scrutinize and pass on loan applications. This arrangement placed tremendous political and financial power into the hands of local bankers armed with federal power. Moreover, the Reconstruction Finance Corporation was not required to reveal the names of borrowers or the amounts of its loans to Congress or to the public. A tremendous political and economic power was thus placed in the RFC and bankers associated with it. Even progressive Senator George Norris of Nebraska lamented that he had never envisioned "putting the government into business as far as this bill would put it."

Hoover and his associates rationalized this power as being a temporary necessity to handle an emergency, supposedly much like World War I, when the prototype of the RFC had been established. Thus, Hoover repeatedly spoke of fighting the depression as the equivalent of fighting a war:

> We are engaged in a fight upon a hundred fronts just as positive, just as definite, and requiring just as greatly the moral courage, the organized action, the unity of strength, and the sense of devotion in every community as in war.

Eugene Meyer spoke repeatedly in military metaphors, and Secretary Mills spoke of the "great war against depression . . . being fought on many fronts," especially the "long battle . . . to carry our financial structure through the worldwide collapse."

And so too did business and financial leaders rationalize their hasty embrace of collectivism in the Reconstruction Finance Corporation. An illuminating article in the *Magazine of*

Wall Street, summarizing the congressional debate over the RFC bill, noted that big business, "always complaining of public intervention in economic matters," was now beating the drums for intervention, the RFC being supported by big bankers, industrialists, and railroad presidents. The article added:

> The answer made by representatives of business to the charge of socialism is that in all great emergencies, war for example, governments have always thrown themselves into the breach, because only they can organize and mobilize the whole strength of the nation. In war every country becomes practically a dictatorship and every man's resources are at its command; the country is now in an equally great emergency.[38]

The RFC certainly paid off for these favored business groups. The excuse for the secrecy was that public confidence would be weakened if the identity of the shaky business or bank receiving RFC loans became widely known. But of course these institutions, precisely because they were in weak and unsound shape, *deserved* to lose public confidence, and the sooner the better both for the public and for the health of the economy, which required the rapid liquidation of unsound investments and institutions. During the first five months of operation, from February to June 1932, the RFC made $1 billion of loans, of which 60 percent went to banks and 25 percent to railroads. The theory was that railroad bonds must be protected, since many of these securities were held by savings banks and insurance companies, alleged agents of the small investor. In practice, the bulk of these RFC railroad loans went

[38]Theodore Knappen, "The Irony of Big Business Seeking Government Management," in *Magazine of Wall Street* 49 (January 23, 1932): 386–88, cited in Olson, *Herbert Hoover*, pp. 45–46. See also ibid., pp. 39–46; and the excellent article by William E. Leuchtenburg, "The New Deal and the Analogue of War," in *Change and Continuity in Twentieth-Century America*, John Braeman, Robert H. Bremner, and Everett Walters, eds. (New York: Harper and Row, [1964] 1967), pp. 81–143.

to repaying debt. About a third of these loans went to repaying railroad debts to banks. Thus, one of the first RFC loans was $5.75 million to the Missouri Pacific Railroad to repay its debt to J.P. Morgan and Company, and an $8 million loan to the B and O Railroad to repay its debt to Kuhn, Loeb and Company. One of the main enthusiasts for this policy was Eugene Meyer, who touted it as "promoting recovery" by "putting more money into the banks." It certainly did the latter, at the expense of the taxpayers and of propping up inefficient banks and businesses. The loan to Missouri Pacific was a particularly egregious case, for as soon as Missouri Pacific performed its task of repaying its debt to Morgan, it was gently allowed to go into bankruptcy.

Another consequence of RFC bailout loans to railroads was to accelerate the socialization of the railroad industry, since the RFC, as a large-scale creditor, was able to place government directors on the board of the railroads reorganized after bankruptcy.[39]

While the Democrats in Congress had their way after August in forcing the RFC to report to Congress on its loans, President Hoover had *his* way in finally persuading Congress to transform the RFC into a bold, "positive" agency empowered to make new loans, to engage in capital loans, to finance sales of agriculture at home and abroad, and to make loans to states and cities, instead of being merely an agency defending indebted banks and railroads. This amendment to the RFC Act, the Emergency Relief and Construction Act of 1932, passed Congress at the end of July, and increased the RFC's authorized capital to $3.4 billion. Eugene Meyer, suffering from exhaustion, persuaded Hoover to include, in the amended bill, the separation of the ex officio members from

[39]Thus, see Arthur Stone Dewing, *The Financial Policy of Corporations*, 5th ed. (New York: Ronald Press, 1953), 2, p. 1263. On the Reconstruction Finance Corporation in this period, see Rothbard, *America's Great Depression*, pp. 261–65.

the RFC. But Meyer's double-duty work was greatly appreciated by Felix Frankfurter, soon to be one of the major gurus of the Roosevelt New Deal. Frankfurter telegraphed Meyer's wife that "Gene . . . has been the only brave and effective leader in [the Hoover] administration in dealing with depression."[40]

Free-market financial writer John T. Flynn had a very different assessment of the year of the Hoover-Meyer Reconstruction Finance Corporation. Flynn pointed out that RFC loans only prolonged the depression by maintaining the level of debt. Income "must be freed for purchasing by the extinguishment of excessive debts. . . . Any attempt to . . . save the weaker debtors necessarily prolongs the depression." Railroads should not be hampered from going into the "inevitable curative process" of bankruptcy.[41]

In the meantime, Eugene Meyer was promoting more inflationary damage as governor of the Federal Reserve. Meyer managed to persuade both Hoover and Virginia conservative Carter Glass, leading Democrat on the Senate Banking Committee, to push through the Glass-Steagall Act at the end of February, which allowed the Fed to use U.S. government securities in addition to gold as collateral for Federal Reserve notes, which were of course still redeemable in gold.[42] This act enabled the Federal Reserve to greatly expand credit and to lower interest rates. The Fed promptly went into an enormous

[40]Pusey, *Eugene Meyer*, p. 226.

[41]John T. Flynn, "Inside the RFC," *Harper's Magazine* 166 (1933): 161–69, quoted in Rothbard, *America's Great Depression*, pp. 263–64. See also J. Franklin Ebersole, "One Year in the Reconstruction Finance Corporation," *Quarterly Journal of Economics* (May 1933): 464–87.

[42]The Glass-Steagall Act of 1932 also contributed to inflation of bank credit by broadening the description of what assets were eligible for banks to rediscount at the Fed. Pusey, *Eugene Meyer*, pp. 227–31; and Susan Estabrook Kennedy, *The Banking Crisis of 1933* (Lexington: University Press of Kentucky, 1973), pp. 46–47.

binge of buying government securities, unprecedented at the time. The Fed purchased $1.1 billion of government securities from the end of February to the end of July, raising its holdings to $1.8 billion. Part of the reason for these vast open market operations was to help finance the then-huge federal deficit of $3 billion during fiscal year 1932.

Thus, we see the grave error of the familiar Milton Friedman-monetarist myth that the Federal Reserve either deliberately contracted the money supply after 1931 or at least passively allowed such contraction. The Fed, under Meyer, did its mightiest to inflate the money supply—yet despite its efforts, total bank reserves only rose by $212 million, while the total money supply *fell* by $3 billion. How could this be?

The answer to the mystery is that the inflationary policies of Hoover and Meyer proved to be counterproductive. American citizens lost confidence in the banks and demanded cash—Federal Reserve notes—for their deposits (currency in circulation rising by $122 million by the end of July), while foreigners lost confidence in the dollar and demanded gold (the gold stock in the United States falling by $380 million in this period). In addition, the banks, for the first time, did not fully lend out their new reserves, and accumulated excess reserves—these excess reserves rising to 10 percent of total reserves by mid-year. A common explanation claims that business, during a depression, lowered its demand for loans, so that pumping new reserves into the banks was only "pushing on a string." But this popular view overlooks the fact that banks can always use their excess reserves to buy existing securities; they don't have to wait for new loan requests. Why didn't they do so? Because the banks were whipsawed between two forces. On the one hand, bank failures had increased dramatically during the depression. Whereas during the 1920s, in a typical year 700 banks failed, with deposits totaling $170 million, since the depression struck, 17,000 banks had been failing per year, with a total of $1.08 billion in deposits. This increase in bank failures could give any bank pause, especially since all the banks knew in their hearts that, as fractional reserve banks, none of them could withstand determined and massive runs upon them by their depositors. Second, just at a time when bank loans were becoming risky, the cheap-money policy of the Fed had driven down interest returns from bank loans, thus weakening banks' incentive to bear risk. Hence the piling up of excess reserves. The more that Hoover and the Fed tried to inflate, the more worried the market and the public became about the dollar, the more gold flowed out of the banks, and the more deposits were redeemed for cash.

Professor Seymour Harris, writing at the time and years before he became one of America's leading Keynesians, concluded perceptively that the hard-money critics of the Hoover administration might have been right, and that it might be that the Fed's heavy open market purchases of government securities from 1930 to 1932 "retarded the process of liquidation and reduction of costs, and therefore have accentuated the depression."[43]

Herbert Hoover, of course, reacted quite differently to the abject failure of his inflationist program. Instead of blaming himself, he blamed the banks and the public. The banks were to blame by piling up excess reserves instead of making dangerous loans. By late May, Hoover was "disturbed at the apparent lack of cooperation of the commercial banks of the country in the credit expansion drive." Eugene Meyer's successor at the RFC, former Ohio Democratic Senator Atlee Pomerene, denounced the laggard banks bitterly: "I measure my words, the bank that is 75 percent liquid or more and refuses to make loans when proper security is offered, under present circumstances, is a parasite on the community." Hoover also went to the length of getting Treasury Secretary Ogden Mills to organize bankers and businessmen to lend or borrow the surplus

[43]Seymour E. Harris, *Twenty Years of Federal Reserve Policy* (Cambridge, Mass.: Harvard University Press, 1933), 2, p. 700. See also Rothbard, *America's Great Depression*, pp. 266–72.

credit piled up in the banks. Mills established a committee in New York City on May 19 headed by Owen D. Young, chairman of the board of Morgan's General Electric Corporation, and the Young Committee tried to organize a cartel to support bond prices, but the committee, despite its distinguished personnel, failed dismally to form a cartel that could defeat market forces.[44] The idea died quickly.

Not content with denouncing the banks, President Hoover also railed against the public for cashing in bank deposits for cash or gold. Stung by the public's redeeming $800 million of bank deposits for cash during 1931, Hoover organized a hue and cry against "traitorous hoarding." On February 3, 1932, Hoover established a new Citizens' Reconstruction Organization (CRO) headed by Colonel Frank Knox of Chicago. The cry went up from the CRO that the hoarder is unpatriotic because he restricts and destroys credit. (That is, by trying to redeem their own property and by trying to get the banks to redeem their false and misleading promises, the hoarders were exposing the unsound nature of the bank credit system.) On February 6, top-level antihoarding patriots met to coordinate the drive; they included General Charles Dawes, Eugene Meyer, Secretary of Commerce Robert P. Lamont, and Treasury Secretary Ogden Mills. A month later, Hoover delivered a public address on the evils of hoarding: "the battle front today is against the hoarding of currency," which prevents money from going into active circulation and thereby lifting us out of the depression.

President Hoover later took credit for this propaganda drive putting a check on hoarding, and it is true that cash in circulation reached a peak of $5.44 billion in July 1932, not rising above

[44]The Young Committee included Walter S. Gifford, head of AT&T (Morgan), Charles E. Mitchell of the National City Bank (Rockefeller), Alfred P. Sloan of General Motors (DuPont-Morgan), and Walter C. Teagle of Standard Oil of New Jersey (Rockefeller). Rothbard, *America's Great Depression*, pp. 271–72.

that until the culminating bank crisis in February 1933. But if true, so much the worse, for that means that bank liquidation was postponed for a year until the final banking crisis of 1933.

The New Deal: Going Off Gold

The international monetary system that the House of Morgan helped Great Britain cobble together in 1925 lay in ruins when Britain hastily abandoned the gold-exchange standard in late September 1931. The Morgans tried desperately to keep Britain on gold in 1931, and afterward tried to get their bearings in the newly chaotic monetary arena. By the time of Roosevelt's accession to power in the spring of 1933, the Morgans had thrown in the towel on the American gold-coin standard; indeed, the Morgan-oriented leadership at the Treasury, Mills and Ballantine, had been agitating for going off gold considerably earlier.[45] But the overriding Morgan concern was always their associates and colleagues in England, and they hoped for a rapid return to some kind of fixed-exchange-rate relation to Britain, and perhaps, by extension, to the other major European currencies as well. The Morgans wanted to reconstruct a regime of monetary internationalism as soon as possible.

But for the first time since the turn of the century, the Morgans were no longer dominant over the monetary thinking of American financial and business elites. In the midst of the cauldron of depression, a new economic and monetary nationalism, a desire for domestic inflation untrammelled by international monetary responsibilities, began to take hold. Backed by proto-monetarist and proto-Keynesian economists eager to spur inflationist federal policies to cure the depression, the shift of business groups toward inflation centered in farm and agribusiness groups, which had been agitating for higher farm prices since the early 1920s, and in industrialists making products for the retail market, who wanted government to pour new money into

[45]Chernow, *House of Morgan*, pp. 330–36, 358–59; Rothbard, *America's Great Depression*, p. 289.

consumption spending. Thus, in January 1933, powerful business groups formed The Committee for the Nation (more formally, The Committee for the Nation to Rebuild Prices and Purchasing Power), dedicated to getting the government to "reflate" prices back up to 1929 levels, and to get off the gold standard so that the government could issue fiat paper money for that purpose. The co-defenders of The Committee for the Nation were Vincent Bendix, head of Bendix Aviation, and General Robert E. Wood, head of the mighty retail combine of Sears, Roebuck. Others who soon joined them were Frank A. Vanderlip, former president of the National City Bank of New York—the flagship bank in the Rockefeller orbit; James H. Rand, Jr., president of Remington Rand Company, manufacturer of typewriters and other retail products; Lessing Rosenwald, major owner of Sears, Roebuck; Samuel S. Fels, producer of Fels Naptha; Philip K. Wrigley, head of William J. Wrigley Company; E.L. Cord of the Cord automobile company; William J. McAvenny, president of Hudson Motor Company; R.F. Wurlitzer, producer of Wurlitzer musical instruments; Frederic H. Frazier, chairman of the board of the General Baking Company; and a galaxy of farm leaders: Fred H. Sexauer, president of the Dairymen's League Cooperative Association; Edward A. O'Neal, head of the American Farm Bureau Federation; and Louis J. Taber, head of the National Grange. It should also be noted that Rockefeller's petroleum products were of course goods largely sold at retail.[46]

Another emboldened inflationist group was the silver mining interest, centered in the Mountain states, which seemingly had lost out permanently to the McKinley and Republican gold forces in the 1890s. Mountain-state senators led the silver bloc in Congress, and Senator Burton K. Wheeler (D-Mont.) introduced a bimetallic bill to reinstitute the silver-gold standard at

[46]Murray N. Rothbard, "The New Deal and the International Monetary System," in *The Great Depression and New Deal Monetary Policy* (San Francisco: Cato Institute, [1976] 1980), pp. 93–95.

the old nineteenth-century ratio of 16-to-1. Leading theoretician and lobbyist for the silver bloc was New York banker Rene Leon, who got himself appointed as adviser to the House Ways and Means Committee in unsuccessfully pressing for an international conference to raise silver prices.

More generally, the Rockefeller and Harriman forces had been allied against the Morgans since the turn of the century, and now they and other rising financial groups banded together avidly to overthrow and dethrone the financial and political dominance achieved by the House of Morgan during the Republican decade of the 1920s. Again influential in the new Democratic regime was the veteran speculator and political manipulator Bernard Baruch, who had been czar of the collectivized economy as head of the War Industries Board in World War I, and who yearned to re-establish a similar, collectivist cartelized regime in peacetime, using the depression as the means for achieving this goal. Baruch, since childhood, had been a protégé of the powerful Guggenheim family, who controlled the American copper industry, but who liked to keep a low political profile and operate through Baruch and his network of operatives.

Newer Jewish Wall Street investment banking houses, more anti-Morgan than Kuhn, Loeb, were also rising to help challenge Morgan: notably, Goldman, Sachs and Lehman Brothers, the Lehman family contributing New Deal governor of New York Herbert H. Lehman to the American political scene. Furthermore, Jewish retail interests, led by the Boston Filene brothers, were in favor of more inflation and consumer spending; and longtime Filene and retailer attorney Louis D. Brandeis had become powerful in the Democratic Party, and was helping run the New Deal surreptitiously from his seat on the U.S. Supreme Court. Brandeis was a longtime enemy of the Morgans, as attorney for opposing corporate interests, and a dedicated supporter of retail cartels supported by the government.

Moreover, all these financial and industrial groups were swinging notably leftward, not simply in monetary matters, but also in advocating far more government intervention, including promotion of labor unions, than the Morgans were willing to accept. Thus, these anti-Morgan groups, now gathered in the Democratic Party, were happy to form a coalition with left-wing intellectuals, technocrats, economists, and social workers who wished to staff the planning agencies, all to advance their common New Deal and ultra-statist agenda.

Particularly powerful in the New Deal and in the Democratic Party was the underrated W. Averell Harriman, scion of the great Harriman interests and longtime enemy of the Morgans. Harriman dominated a highly influential new agency set up in the New Deal, the Business Advisory Council (BAC) of the Department of Commerce, which transmitted the influence of the pro-New Deal wing of industry and finance. Also dominant in the BAC was Sidney J. Weinberg of Goldman, Sachs. The Franklin Roosevelt–Hyde Park–Democrat wing of the Roosevelt family had always been close to their Hudson Valley neighbors, the Astors and the Harrimans,[47] whereas the Oyster Bay–Theodore Roosevelt–Republican wing of the family had always been close to the Morgans.[48]

[47]In early 1933, Mary Harriman Rumsey, sister of Averell, decided to establish a major pro-New Deal newspaper to offset the Republican ownership of the bulk of the press. She, Averell, and their friend and associate Vincent Astor, tried to buy the near-bankrupt *Washington Post*, but were beaten out by Eugene Meyer, who was looking for a satisfying post after leaving the Federal Reserve Board in the early days of the Roosevelt administration. The trio then established the weekly news magazine *Today*, bringing in former New Deal brain truster Raymond Moley as editor, and, in a couple of years, merged with, and took control over, the influential weekly, *Newsweek*. Philip H. Burch, Jr., *Elites in American History*, vol. 3, *The New Deal to the Carter Administration* (New York: Holmes and Meier, 1980), p. 60.

[48]The unsung power of Harriman in the New Deal may be gauged by his neglected but vital role in the two most left-wing appointments to the Roosevelt Cabinet: Frances Perkins as secretary of labor and Harry Hopkins as secretary of commerce. How did these two social workers, without apparent ties to either labor or business, acquire these posts? Frances Perkins was a close, longtime friend of Mary Harriman Rumsey,

To return to monetary policy: Eugene Meyer, who, after all, had three years to go in a ten-year term as governor of the Federal Reserve Board, refused President Hoover's request to resign immediately upon the inauguration of President Roosevelt. But Meyer found out quickly that he could not agree to going off the gold standard and an inflationary higher gold price, and he tendered his resignation as Fed chief in early May 1933.

President Roosevelt's early monetary appointments sent an important signal of his new orientation and policies. To succeed Meyer, Roosevelt appointed his friend, the young Georgia banker Eugene R. Black, who had been governor of the Federal Reserve Bank of Atlanta. Black's orientation may be gauged by the fact that, when he left the Fed a year later, he was to spend 16 years climbing up the executive ladder at the powerful Chase National Bank, which by this time had shifted firmly from the Morgan to the Rockefeller camp (see "Banking and Financial Legislation: 1933–1935," p. 308). Indeed, for the rest of his working life, Eugene Black was to serve at Chase as protégé

---

and indeed lived in the same house as Mrs. Rumsey in Washington (the latter had been widowed since 1922) until her accidental death in 1934. Perkins was also a close friend of the New York banker Henry Bruere, who was president of the large Bowery Savings Bank, treasurer of the influential left-liberal Twentieth Century Fund, and a director of the Harriman-controlled Union Pacific Railroad. Bruere served as credit coordinator in the Roosevelt administration and as executive assistant to Secretary of the Treasury William Woodin.

As for Hopkins, he was a friend of Harriman's, who obtained the unanimous support of the BAC for Hopkins's Cabinet appointment. Hopkins chose as his No. 2 man at commerce Edward J. Noble, who had been a board member in the early 1930s of the ambitious but ill-fated Aviation Corporation, set up by Harriman, and by Robert Lehman of Lehman Brothers. In 1933, the Aviation Corporation was reorganized, and most of its assets sold to the newly formed Pan American Corporation, on whose board sat both Robert Lehman and FDR's cousin, Lyman Delano. It did not harm Hopkins that he was also a friend of John D. Hertz, partner in Lehman Brothers. Burch, *Elites*, 3, pp. 30–31, 59.

of none other than the eminent Winthrop W. Aldrich, chairman of the board at Chase and a close kinsman of the Rockefeller family.[49]

Roosevelt's first secretary of the Treasury was William H. Woodin, who received the appointment after it was turned down by Melvin Traylor, president of the First National Bank of Chicago, one of the main commercial banks in the Rockefeller orbit. Woodin had spent most of his career as a high official of the American Car and Foundry Company in New York, and was now chairman of the board of the American Locomotive Company. Woodin was also a director of such important enterprises as the Harriman-controlled American Ship and Commerce Corporation, as well as the Rockefeller-dominated Remington Arms Company. He had also been a founding director of the County Trust Company of New York, along with the influential Vincent Astor and Herbert H. Lehman. Woodin's financial associations in New York were therefore in the Harriman-Astor-Lehman-Rockefeller ambit rather than in the Morgan network.

Ill health forced Woodin to resign in December 1933, however, and his place was taken by Henry Morgenthau, Jr., who was to be an important and controversial Treasury secretary for the remainder of Roosevelt's reign in office. Morgenthau, who rose from undersecretary, was a longtime friend and neighbor of Roosevelt's, and a gentleman-farmer interested in agriculture. He was backed by his wealthy father, who had been ambassador to Turkey under Wilson, but more important was Henry Jr.'s close links to the powerful investment banking family of Lehman Brothers. Indeed, Henry Jr. was married to a

[49]Aldrich's father, Nelson W. Aldrich, had been a moderately wealthy wholesale grocer who became senator from Rhode Island. Nelson's daughter Abby married John D. Rockefeller, Jr., and from then on Nelson, a longtime Republican majority leader, was Rockefeller's man in government. Winthrop was therefore a brother-in-law of John D. Rockefeller, Jr., and uncle to the next generation of Rockefeller brothers.

Lehman (her mother was a sister of Herbert H. and Arthur Lehman), and Henry's nephew Jules Ehrich had married a sister of Philip Lehman. Moreover, Henry Sr. had long been a major stockholder of the Underwood Typewriter Company, and several of his fellow board members were Philip Lehman; Philip's cousin Arthur Lehman; Maurice Wertheim, who had married Henry Jr.'s sister, Alma; and Waddill Catchings, a top official of Goldman, Sachs.[50]

Two fateful monetary steps were taken in 1933 by the incoming Roosevelt administration. The first and most revolutionary deed, accomplished in April, was to go off the gold standard, to confiscate almost all the gold of American citizens and place it under the ownership of the Federal Reserve, to embargo the export of gold and to devalue the dollar to $35 a gold ounce. This swift policy carried out almost completely the program of The Committee for the Nation. But in March and April even the Morgans had been convinced by the banking crisis to go off gold. Democratic Morgan partner Russell Leffingwell was influential in urging Roosevelt to go off gold and devalue the dollar, and Jack Morgan himself applauded Roosevelt's decision to inflate and go off gold.

The major theoretician of the inflationists, who had liquidated the assets of his own prior Stable Money Association into The Committee for the Nation, was Yale Professor Irving Fisher, the intellectual forerunner of Milton Friedman (who has hailed Fisher as "the greatest economist of the twentieth century") and who mechanistically had believed that since the price level was not rising in the 1920s, there was no inflation to worry about and no coming crash. Fisher strongly urged the inflationist devaluation and fiat standard upon Roosevelt, who had asked him for advice. When Roosevelt cast the die against gold, Fisher exulted to his wife, "Now I *am* sure—as far as we ever can be sure of anything—that we are going to snap out of this depression fast. I am now one of the happiest men in the world."

[50]Burch, *Elites*, 3, pp. 26–27.

Fisher had a personal as well as an ideological stake in rapid inflation. Sure of a permanent prosperity and stock boom in the late 1920s, he had invested all of his wife's and most of his sister-in-law's substantial Hazard family fortune in the stock market, and he was desperately anxious for Roosevelt to reflate and to drive up stock prices. As Fisher added in the same letter to his wife: "I mean that if F.D.R. had followed Glass [who had urged him to stay on gold] we would have been pretty surely ruined." As it happened, the fiat money policy did *not* restore the stock market and Fisher's and his wife's and sister-in-law's fortune *was* ruined by his unwise speculations—a mute testimony to the unsoundness of Fisherine monetarism in explaining or counteracting business cycles.[51]

On the other side of the gold-standard decision were the bulk of the nation's economists, who signed a mass petition urging immediate return to gold. They were led by two doughty hard-money men: Dr. H. Parker Willis, who had staunchly opposed the Strong-Morgan inflationism of the 1920s and urged rapid liquidation of unsound assets to promote recovery; and Dr. Benjamin M. Anderson, longtime hard-money economist of Chase National Bank, who had influenced Chase President Albert Wiggin in favor of hard-money and laissez-faire policies. In the executive branch, the major opponent of the new fiat regime was Lewis W. Douglas, Arizona scion of the Phelps Dodge copper mining interests, and Roosevelt's head of the Bureau of Budget. The fiscally conservative Douglas had, in early 1933, persuaded Roosevelt to make severe cuts in the proposed appropriations of the executive agencies.

Even though monetary nationalism had triumphed, the Morgan interests and the other monetary internationalists were anxious to re-establish fixed exchange rates with Britain,

[51]See Rothbard, "The New Deal," pp. 93–97; Chernow, *House of Morgan*, pp. 357–59; and Jordan Schwarz, *1933: Roosevelt's Decision, the United States Leaves the Gold Standard* (New York: Chelsea House, 1969). Fisher was also a partner with James H. Rand, Jr., in a card-index manufacturing firm.

and to rebuild the special relationship with Morgan allies in Britain and western Europe. The ultra-inflationists, led by The Committee for the Nation, were strongly opposed to fixed exchange rates with Britain and wanted to press ahead with monetary or dollar nationalism, higher gold prices, and continued inflation.

Tensions within the administration, and within the industrial and financial communities, centered around the World Economic Conference set for London in June 1933, which had been prepared for a year by the British-dominated League of Nations, in a desperate attempt to restore some sort of fixed-exchange-rate, stabilized international monetary system. The World Economic Conference, with delegates from 64 nations, met on June 12. The gold bloc at the conference, led by the French, urged an immediate restoration of the full, classical gold standard; the British wanted fixed exchange rates, tied to gold or not, but emphasizing that the pound must be cheaper at $4.00, so as not to lose the export advantage Britain had built up in the past two years. The United States, on the other had, wanted to place prime emphasis on continued domestic inflation; currency stabilization, which should not put the pound below $4.25, could wait until some future date after domestic prices had risen.

From the beginning, however, there was great tension between the bulk of the American delegation to London and the Roosevelt administration in Washington. Chief economic adviser to the American delegation was James P. Warburg of Kuhn, Loeb, who took the Morgan line of favoring a new international gold standard at new and more realistic exchange rates. Morgan-oriented George L. Harrison of the New York Fed, and Professor O.M.W. Sprague, were sent by FDR to work on an agreement for temporary stabilization of exchange rates for the duration of the conference. When, however, Sprague and Harrison concluded an agreement on June 16 with the British and French for temporary stabilization of the three currencies, setting the dollar-sterling rate at $4.00 a pound, and pledging the United States not to inflate the currency in the meanwhile,

Roosevelt angrily rejected the agreement. Roosevelt gave two reasons to the chagrined Sprague and Harrison: the pound must be no cheaper than $4.25, and Roosevelt could accept no restraint on his freedom to inflate to raise domestic prices. Harrison quit in disgust and returned home—a harbinger of the fate of the Morgans in the years to come.

The World Economic Conference proceeded with lengthy discussions, both the Americans and British talking about an eventual "gold standard" which would enjoy no domestic gold coin or bullion circulation, with gold to be used only as a medium for settling international balances of payments—a foretaste of the eventual Bretton Woods system after World War II. The stubbornness of the United States finally forced the assembled delegates to agree on an innocuous final declaration at the end of June that committed the United States to very little more than its own resolution for eventual return to a sadly denatured gold standard, coupled with a vague agreement to cooperate in limiting exchange-rate speculation.

This declaration, weak as it was, seemed to offer hope of eventual stabilization, and so it was strongly supported by Sprague, Warburg, and by chief brain truster Raymond Moley, assistant secretary of state, who was head of the American delegation to London. Within the administration, the agreement was strongly supported by Douglas, Baruch, and by Undersecretary of the Treasury Dean G. Acheson. Acheson was a disciple of Morgan-oriented lawyer Henry L. Stimson, and one of his Washington law partners, J. Harry Covington, was a director of the Guggenheim-controlled Kennecott Copper Corporation. Sending the proposed declaration to Roosevelt on June 30, Moley pointed out that dollar depreciation during June had brought the pound-dollar rate up to $4.40, well above the $4.25 that Roosevelt had insisted on.

On July 1, however, FDR stunned Moley, the delegates, and the American supporters of the agreement by flatly rejecting the declaration, stating that the United States should be allowed the time "to permit . . . a demonstration of the value of price-lifting efforts which we have well in hand." But, adding insult to injury, Roosevelt followed up this rejection on July 3 with an arrogant and contemptuous message to the London conference, which became known as his famous "bombshell message." Here, Roosevelt denounced any idea of currency stabilization as a "specious fallacy." In particular, he thundered, "old fetishes of so-called international bankers are being replaced by efforts to plan national currencies" in order to obtain a fixed price level. In short, Roosevelt was now totally and publicly committed to the entire nationalist Fisher–Committee for the Nation program for fiat paper money, currency inflation, and a very steep "reflation" of prices. The idea of stable exchange rates or an international monetary order would fade away for the remainder of the 1930s, and monetary nationalism, currency blocs, and economic warfare would be the order of the day for the remainder of the decade.[52]

The chagrined supporters of the aborted London monetary agreement soon found it necessary to leave the Roosevelt administration. This included Acheson; Warburg, who had been offered the job of undersecretary of the Treasury before Acheson and who was close to his ancient Kuhn, Loeb allies, the Harriman interests; Lewis W. Douglas, who was soon to write a bitter book attacking the New Deal;[53] and Moley, who returned to the academy and who helped run *Today* and *Newsweek* with his friends the Astors and Harrimans.

The Committee for the Nation has long been known as the prime mover behind the fiat money and inflationist policy of the early New Deal; what has not been known until recently was the powerful behind-the-scenes role in the committee played by the Rockefeller empire, in conjunction with their

[52]Rothbard, "The New Deal," pp. 97–105. On the World Economic Conference, see Leo Pasvolsky, *Current Monetary Issues* (Washington, D.C.: Brookings Institution, 1933). The full text of the Roosevelt bombshell message can be found in ibid., pp. 83–84.

[53]Lewis W. Douglas, *The Liberal Tradition* (New York: D. Van Nostrand, 1935).

longtime international rival, the British Royal Dutch Shell Oil, financed by the Rothschild interests. Thus, a top financier of The Committee for the Nation was James A. Moffett, a longtime director and high official of the Rockefeller flagship company, the Standard Oil Company of New Jersey. Moffett, friend and early supporter of Roosevelt, coordinated his behind-the-scenes agitation for inflation and against the London Economic Conference with New York banker and leading silver-bloc agitator Rene Leon, who functioned as an agent for the powerful Sir Henri Deterding, head of Royal Dutch Shell, who was heading the international agitation for a worldwide cartelized increase in the price of silver. Deterding pressured Roosevelt for inflation, not so much in his capacity as an oil leader, as in a financier of silver production. It turns out that Moffett and Leon, working in tandem, were most influential in successfully pressuring Roosevelt to torpedo the London Economic Conference. Here was a startlingly clear case of Rockefeller (and Royal Dutch Shell) against Morgan.[54]

Banking and Financial Legislation: 1933–1935

The Rockefellers' and other financiers' war with the Morgans in 1933 had been building for several years. By the late 1920s, the Rockefellers, along with newly rising financial groups, increasingly resented the Morgan grip over both the Federal Reserve, especially the New York Fed, as well as the administration.

[54]Professor Thomas Ferguson, who has done particularly illuminating research on the Morgan-Rockefeller battle in the New Deal, had access to the Rene Leon papers, which, as well as oral testimony from Leon's widow, attests to the crucial Leon-Moffett role in persuading Roosevelt to make his decisive repudiation of the London agreement. Moffett was later to join the Rockefeller-controlled Standard Oil of California. Thomas Ferguson, "Industrial Conflict and the Coming of the New Deal: The Triumph of Multinational Liberalism in America," in *The Rise and Fall of the New Deal Order*, 1930–1980, Steve Fraser and Gary Gerstle, eds. (Princeton, N.J.: Princeton University Press, 1989), pp. 28–29.

Bankers enraged at Benjamin Strong and the New York Fed's low-interest policy on behalf of Britain in the 1920s, were led by Melvin A. Traylor, head of the Rockefeller-controlled First National Bank of Chicago. The Rockefellers had never been England-oriented. Traylor led the Chicago bankers in going to the Democratic convention in 1928 and supporting Al Smith, the Democratic nominee. Averell Harriman, of Brown Brothers, Harriman, solidified his support of the Democratic Party during the same year and for similar reasons. Also, brash new ethnic groups rose to challenge Morgan hegemony and were fiercely fought by the Morgans and their controlled New York Fed: these included the Bank of America, a huge new Italian-American-run commercial bank chain in the West; and the rising Irish-American buccaneer Joseph P. Kennedy of Boston, both of whom were Democrats and emphatically outside the WASP-Morgan-Republican structure.

The crucial event occurred within the Morgans' showcase New York institution, the Chase National Bank, a commercial bank with an investment banking arm, Chase Securities. As a result of the 1929 crash, the Rockefeller-controlled Equitable Trust Company was in vulnerable shape, and its new head, Winthrop W. Aldrich, engineered a merger into Chase in March 1930, making Chase the world's largest bank. Aldrich was the brother-in-law of John D. Rockefeller, and was destined to be for decades the key Rockefeller man in banking as well as in the manipulation of politicians.

A titanic three-year struggle immediately ensued for control of Chase between the Rockefeller and the Morgan forces, who had previously been in charge. The CEO of Chase had been Morgan man Albert H. Wiggin, with Wiggin ally Charles McCain as chairman of the board. The Rockefeller forces quickly mobilized to make Winthrop Aldrich president of the bank, a move fought desperately but unsuccessfully by Morgan partner Thomas W. Lamont. Aldrich was now president and subordinate to Wiggin and McCain, but the nose of the camel was now in the tent, as Aldrich strove to oust Wiggin and McCain and take over the bank. Supporting Aldrich in this struggle were board members Thomas M. Debevoise, fraternity brother and top counsel to John D. Rockefeller, Jr.;[55] Vincent Astor, of the famed Astor family and friend and cousin of Franklin Roosevelt; and Gordon Auchincloss, close friend of Winthrop Aldrich. As the conflict came to a climax in late 1932, Lamont found to his horror that several high Chase officials in the Aldrich camp were supporting Roosevelt. Cementing the closeness of Rockefeller and Chase National to Franklin D. Roosevelt was the crucial role of the shadowy, dominant adviser to President Woodrow Wilson, "Colonel" Edward Mandell House. House, a Democratic politician from Texas, had inherited railroads and other properties in Texas, and, during Wilson's day, was very close to the Morgans. Now, however, House, a key behind-the-scenes adviser to Roosevelt, had shifted to the Rockefeller orbit, impelled by the fact that his daughter was married to Gordon Auchincloss.[56]

At the end of 1932, Aldrich managed to oust Wiggin as chairman of the board of Chase; and he immediately began to use his perch as president to launch a multipronged and savage attack on the Morgan empire. In the first place, he collaborated fully and enthusiastically with the bitter and raucous Pecora–U.S. Senate Banking and Currency Committee assaults on Wall Street and particularly on the Morgan empire. Aldrich happily fed the Pecora committee data blackening the Wiggin-McCain regime at Chase, and Pecora was able to use such material to vilify demagogically the Morgan and other bankers for activities that were legal and legitimate. Thereby, Pecora could appeal both to the ignorance and to the envy of the bedazzled public. Thus, Pecora was able to hector the Morgan bankers for

[55]Debevoise served as the general counsel for all three top Rockefeller philanthropies: the Rockefeller Institute for Medical Research, the General Education Board, and the Rockefeller Foundation. John Ensor Harr and Peter J. Johnson, *The Rockefeller Century* (New York: Charles Scribner's Sons, 1988), p. 160.

[56]Ibid., pp. 312–15; Ferguson, "The Coming of the New Deal," pp. 14–15; and Chernow, *House of Morgan*, pp. 206–09, 362.

not paying income taxes during the depression—the public not being willing to understand the legitimacy of deducting severe stock losses from one's income. The Morgans were also pilloried for having a "preferred list" of financiers and politicians for purchasing new stock issues in advance of public sale. The list made juicy reading as a clear attempt to curry favor, and it was in vain that the Morgans remonstrated that this opportunity can only be profitable in a rising stock market.[57]

[57]The Roosevelt administration was embarrassed by the appearance on the Morgan preferred list of its secretary of the Treasury, William H. Woodin of the American Car and Foundry Company, and Vice President John Nance Garner led a campaign at a Cabinet meeting to fire Woodin. Roosevelt, however, refused to fire his friend, who resigned from the Cabinet in late 1933 on account of illness. The Cabinet was also disturbed by the appearance on the Morgan list of another of FDR's old friends, Norman H. Davis, a roving ambassador in the State Department. Davis, however, was able to retain his place in the administration, and used his post later to enable the Morgans to recoup their political fortunes in the later New Deal. Chernow, *House of Morgan*, pp. 369–74. Other notables on the Morgan preferred list included former President Calvin Coolidge; Charles Francis Adams of the famed Boston Adams family, secretary of the Navy under Hoover and father-in-law of Harry Morgan, son of J.P. Morgan, Jr.; John J. Raskob of DuPont, Democratic National Committee chairman; former Secretary of the Treasury William Gibbs McAdoo, a senator actually sitting on the Pecora committee; and many others.

Norman Davis, son of a successful Tennessee businessman and a millionaire from financial dealings in Cuba before World War I, was known, correctly, as a longtime friend of the Morgans. Davis had been a close friend of key Morgan partner Henry P. Davison, and was made Morgan's representative to Cuba in 1912, negotiating a $10 million Morgan loan to the Cuban government two years later. Davis became a financial adviser on foreign loans to Secretary of the Treasury McAdoo during World War I, and after the war worked with Morgan partner Thomas W. Lamont as a financial adviser to the American delegation to the Paris Peace Conference. During the Wilson administration, Davis had become undersecretary of state and was a director of the American Foreign Banking Corporation, headed by Albert Wiggin of Chase. See G. William Domhoff, *The Power Elite and the State: How Policy Is Made in America* (New York: Aldine de Gruyter, 1990), pp. 115–16.

Similarly, Pecora was able to put Wiggin in the dock for profitably short-selling Chase stock on a loan from Chase.[58] He badgered and ridiculed J. P. Morgan himself, and drove McCain into resigning from the bank. Aldrich used this crisis to become the dominant force at Chase, and to assume the post of chairman of the board in January 1934.

Ferdinand Pecora has received little but adulation from the media and historians. Ironically, his harassment and persecution of Wall Street originated with Herbert Hoover. As early as 1919, Hoover had called for government regulation of the stock market to eliminate "vicious speculation." In 1928 and 1929, Hoover had pioneered in the view that the problem of bank credit was that too much of it was going *to the stock market* rather than that there was too much bank credit, period. After the crash, President Hoover naturally segued into charging that the collapse of stock prices was caused by the vicious action of short-sellers, forgetting that for every short-seller there must be a buyer. Under threat of regulation, Hoover forced Morgan man Richard Whitney, head of the New York Stock Exchange, to agree "voluntarily" to withhold loans of stock for purposes of short-selling.

After forcing the stock exchange to restrict short-selling in the crisis of late 1931 and yet again in February 1932, but being dissatisfied with continuing declines in stock prices, President Hoover finally carried out his threat and pressured the U.S. Senate to investigate the New York Stock Exchange, even though he admitted that the federal government had no constitutional jurisdiction over the exchange, which was a New York institution. Hoover continually and hysterically denounced what he termed "sinister" and "systematic bear raids" on stocks, as well as "vicious pools . . . pounding down" security prices,

[58]The Rockefeller forces, noted their friendly biographers, had "thrown [Wiggin] to the wolves." Peter Collier and David Horowitz, *The Rockefellers: An American Dynasty* (New York: Holt, Rinehart and Winston, 1976), p. 161; and Burch, *Elites*, 3, p. 39.

"deliberately making a profit from the losses of other people"—which of course is what bulls and bears always do from each other. Angrily replying to the protest of New York bankers, Hoover used some crystal ball of his own to assert that current prices of securities did not represent "true values"; instead, he declared, the vicious "propaganda that values should be based on earnings at the bottom of a depression is an injury to the country and to the investing public." Mr. Hoover's preferred alternative criterion? The absurd one of the public being "willing to invest on the basis of the future of the United States."[59] Hoover, lacking any knowledge of the market, was foolishly convinced that all-powerful Democratic speculators, headed by John J. Raskob of DuPont and Bernard Baruch, were conducting bear raids to drive down the prices of stocks. It was in vain that Whitney and the Morgans tried to pooh-pooh these fantasies.

Hoover kept pressing the Senate Banking and Currency Committee to conduct hearings on "short-selling in the stock exchange," beginning his pressure in late February 1932. Sensing disaster from these bull-in-a-china-shop tactics, Thomas Lamont vainly pleaded with Hoover to suspend his campaign. Finally, the hearings got under way in April 1932, the first witness, Richard Whitney, terming Hoover's charges "purely ridiculous." When, in private, Hoover told Lamont that short-selling by bears was responsible for all economic ills, including business stagnation and falling prices, and that "real values" were being destroyed by bear raids, Lamont tartly replied: "But what can be called 'real value' if a security has no earnings and pays no dividends?"[60]

In late April, a new subcommittee broadened the Senate inquiry from the fruitless attempt to discover a Democratic bear conspiracy, to include pools and stock market manipulations in general. The short-selling emphasis seemed ridiculous when

[59]Rothbard, *America's Great Depression*, pp. 278–79; see also, pp. 170, 219, 241.

[60]Chernow, *House of Morgan*, pp. 352–53.

the Morgans stepped in to try to revive a crash in the bond market—a market where short-selling had been prohibited.

The Senate subcommittee hearings were suspended in late June, but they took on a very different, and fateful, aspect when they reopened in January 1933, with Ferdinand Pecora of New York as chief counsel. The aggressive Pecora, a former chief assistant district attorney in New York, proceeded to launch a savage and demagogic assault on Wall Street in general and on the Morgan interests in particular. Pecora had been born in Sicily, and emigrated as a child to New York. At first intending to enter the Episcopal ministry, Pecora instead became a lawyer and, at the age of 30, became a district leader of the Progressive Party in 1912, and soon became vice president of the New York State party. Joining the Wilson Democratic Party a few years later, Pecora rose in the district attorney's office during the 1920s. Politically ambitious, Pecora ran unsuccessfully for district attorney on the Democratic ticket in 1930, and repeated his effort and failure while basking in the public limelight during the Pecora stock market practices hearings in 1933.

Pecora cultivated a media image of feisty integrity, but more astute observers noted that his angry and glaring searchlight pilloried Republican bankers, but managed to overlook such leading Democratic and pro–New Deal investment bankers on Wall Street as Brown Brothers, Harriman and Lehman Brothers. We know now, too, that President Franklin D. Roosevelt, who, in his inaugural address had ranted against "unscrupulous money changers" and in his first fireside chat to the radio public had oddly blamed *investment* bankers for the commercial banking crisis, met secretly with Pecora and with Senate Banking Committee Chairman Duncan Fletcher to urge them to go after J.P. Morgan and Company. Ferdinand Pecora was only too happy to oblige.[61]

[61]Joel Seligman, *The Transformation of Wall Street: A History of the Securities and Exchange Commission and Modern Corporate Finance* (Boston: Houghton Mifflin, 1982), pp. 20–21, 29–30; Kennedy, *Banking*

It was the hysterical atmosphere deliberately generated by the Pecora hearings, particularly Pecora's assaults on Albert Wiggin's Chase National Bank and on the Morgans, that created the atmosphere that permitted the coalition of New Deal reformers and Winthrop W. Aldrich's Rockefeller forces to drive through fateful banking and financial legislation during the "First 100 Days" of 1933, legislation that overturned and destroyed the economic power of the Morgan empire. In particular, the Roosevelt administration managed to pass the Banking Act (Glass-Steagall Act) of 1933 and the Securities Act of 1933. In a thorough and illuminating analysis of the Pecora hearings, Professor George Benston has demonstrated both the legitimacy and the economic soundness of the maligned practices of the investment bankers, as well as their complete irrelevance to the major anti-Morgan thrust of the Banking Act of 1933: the compulsory separation of investment and commercial banking.[62] Benston shows that the charges were generally trumped-up, and the vaunted Pecora "findings" were usually only ad hoc speculation by individual senators.[63]

The Banking Act of 1933 had three major provisions: (1) the compulsory separation of commercial and investment banking; (2) the provision of federal "insurance" to guarantee all bank deposits; and (3) prohibiting commercial banks from paying interest on their demand deposits. The compulsory separation clauses (a) severely restricted commercial banks from buying

---

Crisis, pp. 106–28; Chernow, *House of Morgan*, pp. 362–74; and Ferguson, "Coming of the New Deal," p. 16.

[62]This Glass-Steagall Act of 1933 is not to be confused with the Glass-Steagall Act of 1932, which had broadened the eligibility of bank assets to be rediscounted by the Fed.

[63]Benston points out, for example, that Albert Wiggin's much-denounced practice of acquiring Chase stock helped align his managerial interests with that of the Chase bank, and was therefore economically helpful. See George J. Benston, *The Separation of Commercial and Investment Banking: The Glass-Steagall Act Revisited and Reconsidered* (New York: Oxford University Press, 1990), pp. 88–89, and, more largely, pp. 1–133.

securities—except, cleverly, that *government* securities were exempt from this restriction; (b) prohibited commercial banks from issuing, underwriting, selling, or distributing any securities (again, government securities were exempt); and (c) prohibited any investment bank, that is, a bank that does underwrite corporate securities, from ever accepting any deposits.

Provision (b), the divestment by commercial banks of underwriting, was a slap by Aldrich and the reformers against the security affiliates that large, commercial banks had developed for investment banking functions, in particular the two largest: Chase's Chase Securities Corporation and National City Bank's National City Company. These securities affiliates had been particularly active in the late 1920s, and it was therefore all too easy to blame them for the stock market crash.[64] Aldrich had been happy to repudiate the Wiggin-Morgan regime's Chase Securities Corporation, which was doing badly during the depression anyway, but his main thrust was provision (c), a direct death blow to J.P. Morgan and Company, a private investment bank which also accepted bank deposits. The Rockefeller commercial banks, not tied in much with investment banking anyway and content to use their allied investment banks, could happily strike at Morgan and its characteristic fusion of the two forms of banking.[65]

Indeed, not only did Winthrop Aldrich agitate for this latter clause, he actually drafted Section 21 of the Senate bill in Glass's behalf![66]

[64]Ibid., pp. 128–33. The banks set up these wholly owned affiliates by state charter because the National Banking Act, setting up national banks during the Civil War, had been interpreted as prohibiting underwriting operations carried out directly. Ibid., p. 25.

[65]The National City Bank, powerful rival of Chase in New York, was also unfairly pilloried at the Pecora hearings. See Bentson.

[66]Edward J. Kelly, III, "Legislative History of the Glass-Steagall Act," in *Deregulating Wall Street: Commercial Bank Penetration of the Corporate Securities Market*, Ingo Walter, ed. (New York: John Wiley and Sons, 1985), pp. 53–63.

The Morgans fought back bitterly, William Potter of the Morgan-dominated Guaranty Trust calling Aldrich's proposal "quite the most disastrous . . . ever heard from a member of the financial community." The opposition was to no avail, however, with President Roosevelt personally urging Senator Glass to retain Section 21. As Chernow writes, "This was the *coup de grâce* for the House of Morgan."[67] J.P. Morgan and Company delayed their final divestment decision, hoping for the passage of Carter Glass's amendment to the Banking Act of 1935, allowing some securities powers to deposit banks, but Roosevelt delivered the final blow to the Morgans by personally interceding in the House-Senate conference committee to kill the amendment. Upon this defeat, J.P. Morgan and Company made the fateful decision to keep its deposit business and to divest itself of its power center, the investment banking business. The Morgans set up a new Morgan, Stanley and Company to engage in investment banking.[68]

It is a tragic irony that Carter Glass and his theoretician H. Parker Willis were lured into this alliance with the Rockefellers and the New Dealers to clobber the Morgans by coercively divorcing commercial and investment banking. Willis, as noted above, was a trenchant critic of the Strong-Morgan credit inflation of the 1920s. Unfortunately, Willis's "real bills" approach, which led him to oppose the bank credit expansion, also led him to oppose it for the wrong reason. Contrary to Willis, the problem was not that the banks were buying corporate securities or lending money to the stock market; the problem was that the banks were inflating credit, period. But Willis and Glass, starting with the wrong reasoning, came to the wrong solution: to compel the commercial banks to stop purchasing or issuing securities, as a partial means of reaching the ultimate goal—forcing the banks and the Fed to return to the original concept of confining their credit to short-term self-liquidating "real" bills. Hence, the luring of the reluctant Glass

[67]Chernow, *House of Morgan*, pp. 362–63, 375.

[68]Ibid., pp. 384ff.

and Willis into uncongenial schemes of socializing and cartelizing Wall Street and helping the Rockefellers destroy the Morgans.

Professor Benston points out that all the provisions of the Banking Act of 1933 helped develop a coherent structure for government cartelization of the banking industry. In the first place, the separation sections, which we have been discussing, helped the commercial bankers get rid of unprofitable securities, and to eliminate the powerful competition of investment bankers for customers' deposits. As for investment bankers, one-third of them, including J.P. Morgan and Company, hived off that business to stick to deposit banking, leaving the remainder free of their competition. In particular, as we have seen, the Rockefellers rid the commercial banks of unwelcome investment banking competition.

Other Banking Act provisions reinforced the cartelization. Thus, federal deposit insurance guaranteed all bank deposits, thereby cartelizing the industry and supposedly guaranteeing every bank's success. The prohibition of bank payment of interest on demand deposits was a particularly cartelizing device, since it "forced" the banks collectively to keep payment of interest to their depositors at zero, policing any competing bank that would have liked to break the cartel by bidding for depositors' accounts.[69]

In addition to all this, the Banking Act of 1933 began the crucial process of stripping away the dominant power of the Federal Reserve Bank of New York (and hence of the Morgans) over the operations of the Federal Reserve System, and of transferring that power to political appointees in Washington. Previously, for example, each Federal Reserve Bank—and therefore the private bankers in that district—had total power over its own open-market operations—and therefore over the movement of bank reserves. In practice, this meant the New York

[69]Benston, *Separation of Commercial and Investment Banking*, pp. 136, 221–22.

Fed, since open market operations were in U.S. government securities, and the bond market is located in New York. The Banking Act of 1933 began a transfer of power by creating a statutory Federal Open Market Committee (FOMC). The FOMC, however, continued to be in private banker hands, since it consisted of one member from each Federal Reserve District, selected by the board of directors of each Federal Reserve Bank. In practice, these were the governors of each Federal Reserve Bank.

The new law required that every Federal Reserve bank's open market operation conform to Federal Reserve Board regulations, but each Federal Reserve bank retained the right to refuse to participate in the FOMC's recommended open market policies. The result of this hybrid system was that the Federal Reserve Board was ultimately responsible for Fed policy, but it could not initiate open market operations. The Federal Reserve Board could ratify or veto FOMC policies, but those policies had to be initiated by the FOMC. The Federal Open Market Committee, for its part, could initiate open market policies, but it could not execute them; execution remained in the hands of the New York Fed and the Federal Reserve banks. The Federal Reserve banks, for their part, could not initiate open market policies, but could obstruct them by failing to execute them.

All in all, the Federal Reserve Bank of New York, while losing much of its power over open market operations in the 1933 act, was able to live with the new arrangement. It was more annoyed over a neglected provision of the act, that forbade the New York Fed (or any other Federal Reserve bank) from conducting negotiations with foreign banks—a direct slap at the crucial New York Fed–Morgan role during the 1920s in making arrangements with the Bank of England and other European banks.[70]

[70]Sidney Hyman, *Marriner S. Eccles: Private Entrepreneur and Public Servant* (Stanford, Calif.: Stanford University Graduate School of Business, 1976), pp. 156–57; Kennedy, *Banking Crisis*, p. 210; and Chernow, *House of Morgan*, p. 383.

The demagogic eruption of the Pecora hearings also led to another New Deal 100 Days measure that both revolutionized and cartelized the securities industry and delivered another body blow to the House of Morgan. This was the Securities Act of 1933, passed in May, followed the next year by its more powerful successor, the Securities Exchange Act of June 1934. The first act imposed rigorous and expensive laws and procedures for any new securities issues, allegedly to protect the investing public. Its actual effect was to cartelize the sources of new capital, channeling the supply of savings into firms big enough to bear the substantial costs and freezing out smaller and more risky new capital ventures. Even more directly, the Securities Act cartelized the investment banking industry, keeping out any newer and smaller investment banks that might challenge the established giants. While many investment bankers were unhappy with specific provisions and urged amendments, they were on the whole delighted with the basic thrust of the regulation. Thus, testifying on the bill before the House Commerce Committee, George W. Bovenizer, partner in Kuhn, Loeb and Company, and a venerable Morgan enemy, declared that his firm was

> wholeheartedly in favor of the type of legislation . . . suggested by the President. We have stood by now for the past 12 years, or more, and have looked on with apprehension as the good name of investment banker has been put into jeopardy . . . by the actions of some people who should never have been in the business. . . . I believe that every honest banker today will look with great favor upon the principle of this legislation as the dawn of a new era.[71]

The enforcement of the Securities Act was put into the hands of the Federal Trade Commission, since the accession of Roosevelt in left-wing hands, but a new Securities and Exchange Commission created for this purpose was to take over the

[71]Vincent P. Carosso, *Investment Banking in America: A History* (Cambridge, Mass.: Harvard University Press, 1970), p. 357. See also Benston, *Separation of Commercial and Investment Banking*, pp. 136–37.

enforcement powers in July 1934. By that time, however, Congress had passed the Securities Exchange Act of June 1934, greatly expanding the powers of the Securities and Exchange Commission from compulsory registration of new issues to control over the practices of the exchange as well as to compulsory disclosure for existing securities.[72]

The securities legislation constituted a body blow to the Morgan empire because the Morgans dominated the New York Stock Exchange, especially through the exchange's president, Richard Whitney. Whitney, a scion of the prominent Morgan-oriented financial family, was the head of Richard Whitney and Company, the major bond broker for J.P. Morgan and Company. In addition, Richard's brother George was a senior partner at the House of Morgan, and was Morgan's man on such important boards as that of General Motors and of the giant Morgan-controlled public utility holding company, the United Corporation. Since Richard Whitney was the leader of fierce opposition to any government regulation of securities and in behalf of laissez-faire, his defeat by the New Dealers, and in particular his later disgrace, tended to discredit his free-market views.[73]

It had always been assumed that since the Stock Exchange was a New York institution, it could only be constitutionally regulated by the state of New York, rather than by the federal government. The New Dealers, however, considered states' rights an absurd obstacle in the path of centralizing the economy, and they treated it accordingly. Moreover, by imposing federal regulation

[72]Carosso, *Investment Banking*, pp. 356–68, 375–79.

[73]Chernow, *House of Morgan*, pp. 316, 421–29. The revelation, conviction, and imprisonment of Richard Whitney in 1938 for embezzlement of Stock Exchange funds to cover reckless personal debts was another horrific blow to Morgan power, especially since Morgan partners George Whitney and Thomas W. Lamont, by the end knew of (but did not condone) Whitney's criminal activities, but failed to report them to the authorities. Radical New Dealer William O. Douglas, then chairman of the SEC and out for Morgan blood, was able to use the scandal to dominate, alter, and dictate Stock Exchange procedures from then on.

and enforcement, they could at one and the same time dominate and cartelize the securities and investment banking industries, while delivering another body blow to the House of Morgan.

The two securities acts were written by New Dealers, many of them young and all eager to radicalize and transform American finance. Substantial roles were played by Federal Trade Commission Chairman Huston Thompson, a Washington State populist, and by the venerable New York trial lawyer Samuel Untermyer, scourge of the House of Morgan as chief counsel of the U.S. Senate's Pujo Committee in 1912, which had then helped to drive J.P. Morgan, Sr., to his grave. But the most important role in drafting and pushing through the securities acts was played by powerful left-liberal theorist, agitator, and shadowy manipulator Felix Frankfurter, a professor at Harvard Law School. An old friend and adviser to Franklin Roosevelt, Frankfurter specialized in seeding his former students and assistants, his "happy hot dogs," into powerful positions in the federal government. In particular, Frankfurter folded into the New Deal, and into drafting the securities acts, his disciples James M. Landis, Benjamin Cohen, and Thomas "Tommy the Cork" Corcoran. And standing behind Frankfurter, pulling the strings from his Supreme Court bench, was the even more shadowy master manipulator Louis D. Brandeis, Frankfurter's mentor from Harvard Law School. Brandeis was able to violate judicial ethics systematically while on the Court, by putting Frankfurter on permanent retainer on his secret payroll, and using Frankfurter as his agent in the political realm. Brandeis, who had been powerful in the Wilson administration, had been fiercely anti-Morgan for decades, and was a longtime legal representative for retail users of Morgan railroads and utilities, particularly for the Filine interests of Boston.[74, 75]

[74]For Frankfurter's role in the securities acts, see Seligman, *Transformation of Wall Street*, pp. 39–127. The sinister Brandeis-Frankfurter connection lasted for decades until 1937, when Frankfurter broke with his mentor and paymaster for opposing Roosevelt's plan to pack the Supreme Court. It was a case of Frankfurter, for the first time trapped

While the New Deal Left originally wanted security regulation in the hands of the left-dominated Federal Trade Commission (FTC), they were perfectly happy to "compromise" by setting up a specialized Securities and Exchange Commission (SEC). Indeed, Roosevelt cunningly threw a sop to conservatives and moderates by naming his old friend, the Irish-American stock speculator and buccaneer Joseph P. Kennedy, to be chairman of the five-man SEC, while the other commissioners were leftist ideologues from the FTC, including the leading New Dealer writing the legislation, James McCauley Landis. Rounding out the SEC was none other than that scourge of the Morgans and the Wall Street Republicans, Ferdinand Pecora. Landis was to succeed Kennedy when the latter left the SEC chairmanship in 1935.

While Joseph Kennedy was a bit more conservative than his colleagues, especially on the New Deal assault on public utility holding companies, his life as a speculator successfully bamboozled many moderates who did not realize the extent of Kennedy's

---

between Brandeis and FDR, choosing to serve the more powerful friend. It was also yet another case in history of one of the leaders of a revolution (in this case the New Deal Revolution), here the aging Brandeis, being left behind by a movement that had become too radical for him. On Brandeis and Frankfurter, see the illuminating Bruce Allen Murphy, *The Brandeis-Frankfurter Connection: The Secret Political Connection of Two Supreme Court Justices* (New York: Anchor Press, [1982] 1983), pp. 130–38 and passim.

[75]In recent years, historians have fortunately been able to shake off the hagiographical tradition, depicting Brandeis as a saintly "people's lawyer" and devotee of free competition—a tradition typified in Alpheus Thomas Mason, *Brandeis: A Free Man's Life* (New York: Viking, 1946). Instead, we are beginning to find a duplicitous statist and advocate of retail cartelization at the expense of consumers. For excellent revisionist works on Brandeis, in addition to Murphy, see Allon Gal, *Brandeis of Boston* (1980), and Thomas K. McCraw, "Brandeis and the Origins of the FTC," in *Prophets of Regulation* (Cambridge, Mass.: Harvard University Press, 1984), pp. 80–142. The later revisionist works were inspired by the publication of the letters and papers of Brandeis during the 1970s, a task completed in 1980.

collectivist views. Thus, Kennedy not only enthusiastically endorsed the New Deal, he went beyond it to advocate a general federal incorporation law, as well as the abolition of private investment banking. In addition, during his buccaneering period in the 1920s, he had repeatedly clashed with the Morgan interests. The extent of Kennedy's collectivism is seen by his assertion, similar to all collectivist planners:

> An organized functioning economy requires a planned economy. The more complex the society the greater the demand for planning. Otherwise there results a haphazard and inefficient method of social control, and in the absence of planning the law of the jungle prevails.[76]

Though Kennedy was a buccaneer, he was scarcely the lone ranger. In the late 1920s and the 1930s, Kennedy worked closely with various Hollywood film corporations, particularly those such as Paramount Pictures, dominated by Lehman Brothers.[77]

As for Landis, on the other hand, businessmen expecting a socialistic antibusiness force at the helm of the SEC were pleasantly surprised to find Landis a conscious and deliberate creator of governmental cartelization, of a government-business partnership in behalf of "industrial self-government" under the benign aegis of federal regulation. Landis charmed the financial groups by overcoming his personal dislike of bankers, brokers, and accountants in order to include them in his well of support and regulation. Thus, as early as 1934, Landis wrote in the *Yearbook of the Encyclopedia Britannica*:

[76]Seligman, *Transformation of Wall Street*, p. 105.

[77]Burch, *Elites,* 3, p. 32. Chernow writes of Joseph Kennedy as a Morgan "hobgoblin," who had been repeatedly snubbed by J.P. Morgan, Jr., in the late 1920s. In fact, Chernow sees the New Deal clash with Morgan in ethnic terms: "The money changers had indeed been chased from the Temple, by the Irish, the Italians, and the Jews—the groups excluded from WASP Wall Street in the 1920s." Chernow, *House of Morgan*, p. 379.

> In all its efforts the [Securities and Exchange] Commission has sought and obtained the cooperation not only of the exchanges, but also of brokerage houses, investment bankers, and corporation executives, who in turn recognize that their efforts to improve financial practices are now buttressed by the strong arm of the government.[78]

Landis also shrewdly won over the accounting profession, which had been fearful of New Deal attempts to dictate to and penalize the nation's accountants. Instead, Landis explicitly offered that profession, previously resentful of domination by corporate clients, the opportunity to cartelize and rule the securities roost, under the benevolent aegis of the SEC. As historian Thomas McCraw puts it,

> [I]t struck him [Landis] as far preferable to use their [the accountants'] existing expertise and to make their professional institutions the vehicle of change, rather than attempting to force results with direct government action.[79]

As a result, the accounting profession took to Landis and the SEC with alacrity. The American Institute of Accountants quickly formed a Special Committee on Cooperation with the Securities and Exchange Commission, and this group functioned as a permanent liaison with the SEC. A leading scholar of accountancy soon noted that, with the establishment of the SEC policy,

> the control function of accounts takes on a new and quite different form. Instead of being merely a tool of control by business enterprise they become a tool for the control of business enterprise itself.

[78]McCraw, "Landis and the Statecraft of the SEC," in *Prophets of Regulation*, p. 188. Ferdinand Pecora, however, resisted this new Landis dispensation, which he regarded as a sellout to Wall Street. After six months as an SEC commissioner, Pecora resigned to accept an appointment as a justice on the New York State Supreme Court.

[79]As McCraw puts it, "When the leaders of the profession realized that a unique opportunity to gain respect lay at hand, their hostility to regulation abruptly ceased." Ibid., p. 190.

In other words, the scholar, D.R. Scott, was noting the wondrous fact that whereas until the SEC, accountants were forced to subordinate themselves to their private business clients on the market, the SEC was enabling accountancy to enter a new era: where accountants could turn the tables by serving the central government to control and dominate their clients.[80]

In particular, Landis set up a special accounting subdivision headed by a chief accountant, who quickly became the most important auditing regulator in the United States. The chief accountant happily accepted the charge of driving toward more rigorous audits, cracking down against violators, and setting up compulsory uniform accounting standards. In 1937, the chief accountant began the practice of issuing much-vaunted "Accounting Series Releases," laying down a network of standardized accounting practices for the profession. Much of the SEC's power to enforce guidelines was deliberately delegated to the professional associations of accountants, thus further enlisting the organized profession as surrogate cartelists and enforcers.

One charm the SEC regulations had for the accountants is that the SEC acts required a large number of new financial statements by "an independent public or certified accountant"—provisions that created a welcome substantial increase in the demand for accountants. As a result, while the number of lawyers and physicians in the nation increased by about 71 percent between 1930 and 1970, the number of accountants swelled by no less than 271 percent.[81]

Finally, Landis's shrewd strategy induced the New York and other regional stock exchanges to collaborate and run their own regulation, under the wing, of course, of the federal government. In a series of addresses to the New York Stock Exchange Institute during 1935, Landis called for "self-government" as the crucial principle. Indeed, Landis carefully

[80]Ibid.

[81]Ibid., pp. 191–92.

worked out the SEC rules in a series of negotiations with the exchanges. In early 1937, Landis outlined his strategy candidly in a major address. Regulation, Landis noted,

> welded together existing self-regulation and direct control by government. In so doing, it followed lines of institutional development, buttressing existing powers by the force of government, rather than absorbing all authority and power to itself. In so doing, it made the loyalty of the institution to the broad objectives of government a condition of its continued existence, thus building from within as well as imposing from without.[82]

James M. Landis left the SEC in alleged triumph in 1938 to attain the coveted post of dean of Harvard Law School.[83] He was succeeded as SEC chairman by commission member William O. Douglas, an old friend of Roosevelt's, who had developed his own network at Yale Law School. Douglas, even more left-wing and anti-Morgan than Landis, felt that Landis had been lax in hounding Morgan's Richard Whitney out of his post as head of the New York Stock Exchange. Douglas proceeded to pursue this goal with vigor. But even Douglas was no simple antibusiness socialist, preferring to continue cartelization by working with dissident anti-Morgan groups within the stock exchange, led by the Rockefeller-oriented E.A. Pierce. Douglas was particularly able to work with the retail commission brokers, led by young St. Louis stockbroker William McChesney

[82]Ibid., p. 192

[83]In McCraw's worshipful account, Landis's brilliant achievement, achieving the status of a living "legend" before he was 40 (Landis was born in 1899) and apparently slated for the Supreme Court, was succeeded by tragic decline. Burnt out and unhappy in academia, Landis gradually but surely went into decline, marked by alcoholism. Finally, Landis was jailed for failure to file income tax returns for six years, and suspended from the practice of law for a year in July 1964. Shortly afterward, Landis died in his pool, either of heart attack or suicide. Landis's house and effects were promptly seized by the IRS, and sold to settle his tax claims. Some may call this denouement a terrible tragedy; others, poetic justice. McCraw, *Prophets of Regulation*, pp. 203–09.

Martin, Jr., who resented the elite floor traders led by Whitney and the Morgans. It was these dissidents who ousted Whitney and took over the stock exchange, and whose tough new disclosure rules unexpectedly turned up the financial irregularities of Richard Whitney, that were to send him to the penitentiary for embezzlement in 1938. As Douglas exclaimed at this stroke of good fortune: "The Stock Exchange was delivered into my hands."

Douglas cunningly used the Whitney crisis, coming on top of widespread denunciations of short-sellers allegedly causing a stock collapse during the 1938 recession, to complete the anti-Morgan and cartelizing coup at the New York Stock Exchange. William McChesney Martin was named head of the exchange in a new, full-time salaried post as president, and Douglas and Martin proceeded to conduct what Professor McCraw correctly terms a "carefully orchestrated" series of negotiations to hammer out a new cooperative SEC–Stock Exchange structure. Both men used time-honored tactics: Douglas employing severe pressure to force his desired changes; Martin pretending to oppose the changes, but "rais[ing] the specter of direct SEC intervention to persuade his recalcitrant colleagues to accept the new system." In the end, both men effected a cartelizing revolution, achieving their common goals. As McCraw concludes: "Again, the SEC had used the circumstances of an evanescent crisis to work permanent change, insisting all the while that the exchange itself propose and adopt the new rules as its own."[84, 85]

The New Dealers completed their financial revolution as well as their successful multipronged assault against the Morgans,

[84]McCraw, *Prophets of Regulation*, pp. 352–53. See also ibid., pp. 193–96.

[85]1938 saw the extension of federal regulation and cartelization to the once free, decentralized and unregulated over-the-counter market. In 1933, the elite investment bankers in the Investment Bankers' Association, eager to cartelize and regulate the over-the-counter market, seized the opportunity offered by the National Recovery Administration (NRA) to

with their most implacably radical piece of legislation: the Public Utility Holding Act of August 1935. Urged on by Roosevelt himself, the administration insisted on driving through the drastic "death sentence" clause, abolishing all holding company systems in the public utility industry. By 1932, the public utility industry, formerly mired in separate locations, had been producing almost 50 percent of its output in three efficient nationwide holding companies. One was Samuel Insull's independent

---

draft a very strict "Code of Fair Competition." The association then established an Investment Bankers Code Committee that could pursue stringent enforcement of the code using the powers of the federal government. There was one weakness of the cartel, however: it did not include the smaller but numerous noninvestment-bank over-the-counter dealers.

When the Supreme Court ruled the NRA unconstitutional in the *Schechter* decision in May 1935, Landis promptly stepped in to try to reconstitute the code under the aegis of the SEC. The code committee, now reconstituted in an Investment Bankers Conference Committee, engaged in lengthy negotiations with the SEC, to try to replicate the SEC structure for the organized stock exchanges. Finally, in early 1938, Senator Frank Maloney (D-Conn.), a friend of Chairman Douglas, pushed through the Maloney Act, which provided that the over-the-counter industry could establish its own private association that would be invested with the power, under SEC supervision, to fine, suspend, or expel those dealers found in violation of rules jointly worked out with the SEC. This new association, so reminiscent of the NRA, was specifically declared exempt from the antitrust laws.

The over-the-counter industry happily responded to the Maloney Act by creating the National Association of Securities Dealers (NASD), a private association invested with government power. The NASD promptly fixed a uniform dealer commission rate of 5 percent—an open measure of cartelization—and, while no broker or dealer was required to join the NASD, nonmembers were prohibited by law from engaging in any securities underwriting. In effect, membership was compulsory, and the NASD "assumed the functions and structure of a regulatory agency." At the SEC's insistence, the NASD strengthened this regulatory function by hiring its own professional staff of several hundred examiners and investigators, and the SEC habitually ratified stern disciplinary measures, including suspension and expulsion, meted out over the years by the NASD. McCraw, *Prophets of Regulation*, pp. 197–200.

Chicago-based utility empire, which collapsed with Insull fleeing to Europe in mid-1932; the other two were Morgan-oriented combines: J.P. Morgan's directly controlled United Corporation, and General Electric's Bond and Share Company, General Electric being from its inception in the Morgan ambit. For seven years until 1935, the Federal Trade Commission engaged in massive assaults on the utility holding companies, and Pecora did his snarling best with a retrospective series of blasts against Insull. Finally, Roosevelt set up a National Power Policy Committee in the summer of 1934 to draft legislation abolishing utility holding companies. Arch New Dealer, Interior Secretary Harold Ickes, was chairman of this committee, and general counsel was Benjamin V. Cohen, who drafted the fateful Public Utility Holding Act (PUHA), a measure so radical that Joseph Kennedy felt he had to resign as chairman of the SEC.

The public utility holding companies, led by the Morgans, waged a long ferocious political and constitutional battle against the PUHA. It was led by the Edison Electric Institute, the lobbying organization for the public utilities, and by its general counsel, longtime Morgan attorney and personal friend of Morgan's, John W. Davis. Also assisting the opposition effort was Wendell L. Willkie, head of the Commonwealth and Southern Corporation, a subsidiary of Morgan's United Corporation. Davis thundered that the act was "vicious . . . the last word in federal tyranny . . . the gravest threat to the liberties of the American citizen that has emanated from the halls of Congress in my lifetime." But all to no avail, as in 1938 the Supreme Court, tamed and denatured by the New Deal, upheld the constitutionality of the Public Utilities Holding Company.[86]

[86]Seligman, *Transformation of Wall Street*, pp. 127–38. Wendell Willkie's sudden surprise Republican nomination for president in 1940 was a cleverly engineered Morgan coup in the Republican Party. During that period, Willkie sat on the board of the Morgan-dominated First National Bank of New York. Willkie's close friends included the inevitable Thomas W. Lamont; Perry Hall, vice president of Morgan, Stanley and Company; George Howard, president of the United

Marriner S. Eccles and the Banking Act of 1935

The saga of Marriner Stoddard Eccles has been told many times, not only by his adoring biographer,[87] but also by numerous historians of the New Deal. How Marriner Eccles, young multimillionaire head of a Western banking and construction empire, had been led by the depression and by his reading of Foster and Catchings, to rethink his previous laissez-faire views, and to arrive, virtually on his own and therefore almost miraculously, at proto-Keynesian conclusions. How he came to impress the New Dealers, and was called first to the Treasury and then soon became the radical New Deal head of the Federal Reserve Board and of the entire Federal Reserve System, to remain chairman of the board until after World War II.

In truth, rediscovering ancient economic fallacies hardly qualifies as a notable achievement. Eccles read Foster and Catchings in early 1931, and adopted wholesale their view of

---

Corporation; and S. Sloan Colt, president of the Morgan-established and Morgan-dominated Bankers Trust Company. Moreover, the two young New York Republican leaders who actually engineered the nomination were Oren Root, Jr., of the top "Morgan" law firm of Davis (John W.), Polk, Wardwell, Gardiner and Reed; and Charlton MacVeagh. Not only was MacVeagh a former officer of J.P. Morgan and Company, but his father had been a longtime partner of the Davis Polk law firm, and his brother was still an officer there. Burch, *Elites*, 3, pp. 44–45, 66.

It is intriguing that one of Willkie's two main rivals for the nomination, New York's Thomas E. Dewey, was all his life virtually in the hip pocket of Winthrop W. Aldrich, the Rockefellers, and the Chase National Bank. Thus, see Harr and Johnson, *Rockefeller Century*, pp. 208–09, 405–06.

[87]Hyman, *Marriner Eccles*, passim. Hyman goes so far as to say that "Marriner Eccles *is* American economic history." For a good summary of Eccles's "remarkable intellectual accomplishment" from the hagiographical point of view, see L. Dwight Israelson, "Marriner S. Eccles, Chairman of the Federal Reserve Board," *American Economic Review* 75 (May 1985): 357–62.

underconsumption as cause of depression, and government deficit spending and stimulation of consumption as the way to recovery. Any intellectual acumen on Eccles's part would, on the contrary, have led him to realize that Foster and Catchings were writing during the boom of the 1920s, and would have led him to wonder what accounted for the sudden change from boom to depression—a change that can scarcely be explained by an alleged state of permanent underconsumption. Under the influence and assistance of proto-monetarist and radical New Dealer Lauchlin Currie, Eccles soon added governmental monetary inflation to his armamentarium, to make him a comprehensive inflationist and macro–New Dealer. Given such influences, it was easy to become a "Keynesian" slightly before Keynes's time.

Moreover, it is doubtful that Marriner Eccles's conversion to statism was purely intellectual. Marriner was the son of David Eccles, who, as a penniless lad and Morman convert, had emigrated from Glasgow to Utah, there to build up one of the largest fortunes in the West. Most of David's fortune was in banking and sugar manufacturing. When David died in 1912, Marriner, at age 22, managed to elbow aside competing Mormon families of David's, and assume control of his father's empire. By the early 1930s, Marriner had expanded the business empire greatly, a business empire centered in a network of bank holding companies throughout the West, and also including milk production and construction as well as sugar. Marriner Eccles's empire was centered in his bank holding company, the First Security Corporation, and indeed Marriner had pioneered in forming such holding companies in banking.[88] Eccles's conversion away from free markets was, indeed, micro as well as

[88]By the time of the depression, Marriner Eccles was president of: the First Security Corporation, the Eccles Investment Company, the First National Bank of Ogden (Utah), the First Savings Bank of Ogden, the Eccles Hotel Company, the Sego Milk Company, the Utah Construction Company, and the Amalgamated Sugar Company.

macro: as head of the important Amalgamated Sugar Company, Eccles led a vigorous effort to cartelize the sugar industry, and to unite all sugar producers, foreign and domestic, in an allotment plan to form rigorous maximum production quotas for each firm. Furthermore, as a large banker in a shaky banking environment, Eccles was understandably eager to push for federal guarantees of bank deposits, legislation that redounded to his direct benefit.

From the failure of the voluntary sugar cartel, it was an easy step for Eccles to advocate a compulsory cartel plan for all of agriculture: essentially the Agricultural Adjustment Administration's domestic allotment plan for the federal government to compel restriction of agricultural production in order to raise farm prices. It was also an easy step for Eccles to weave together his banking and sugar interests, to advocate the federal government's subsidy of farm mortgages, mortgages which of course had been and would continue to be purchased by Eccles's savings banks.[89]

There was another personal economic reason for Eccles to suddenly look benignly on massive federal public works spending. In 1930, President Hoover decided to build the mammoth Boulder Dam, which became one of the major public works projects of the early depression years. One of the major construction companies in the consortium that built the dam was Utah Construction, with Eccles putting up much of the capital and personally present at the San Francisco meeting where the consortium was formed.[90]

[89]Hyman, *Marriner Eccles*, p. 107. Israelson is therefore wrong to imply that Eccles confined his statism to the macro sphere. Israelson, "Marriner S. Eccles," pp. 358–59. Actually, this implication is belied by evidence on the same page of Israelson's article.

[90]Another major firm in this construction consortium was W.A. Bechtel Company. Eccles and Utah Construction had a close association with the Bechtels for many years, often subcontracting construction work to Bechtel in northern California. This association continues to the present day: Eccles's successor as chairman of Utah Construction, Edmund

By the time of his appearance at the Senate Finance Committee hearings at the end of February 1933, in testimony that would win him great notoriety, Eccles had worked out a complete collectivist program: not only for macro deficits, public works, and unemployment relief, not only for guaranteed bank deposits, and not only for taxing the rich and subsidizing the poor, but also a plea for agricultural cartels, for federal agencies which would have to approve all new capital issues, and all "means of transportation and all means of communication to ensure their operation in the public interest"; and, as a topper, "a national planning board to coordinate public and private economic activities."[91]

What was unusual about Eccles was not that he was a big businessman who had opted for collectivism—he was only one of many in this era—but that he was willing and eager to move to Washington to carry out these programs personally. Eccles had another personal economic and intellectual interest in serving in Washington in money and banking. Like the Bank of America's A.P. Giannini, Eccles was a Western outsider to the Morgan-dominated Federal Reserve System of the 1920s, and he had conceived a bitter hatred of the Morgan empire, as well as a crusading desire to transform American banking by shifting power in the Fed, once and for all, from

---

Littlefield, became a senior director of Bechtel Corporation in the early 1980s.

The construction of the Boulder Dam was also the occasion for Bechtel to save Stephen Bechtel's old college chum John A. McCone's Consolidated Steel from bankruptcy by awarding Consolidated a huge fabricated steel contract in constructing the dam. Bechtel and McCone soon began to collaborate closely with Standard Oil of California in worldwide construction contracts for refineries and oil complexes. McCone went on to become a high public official, including head of the Atomic Energy Commission and of the CIA. Laton McCartney, *Friends in High Places: The Bechtel Story* (New York: Simon and Schuster, 1988), pp. 34 and passim.

[91]Israelson, "Marriner S. Eccles," p. 358.

the Morgan- and Wall Street–dominated New York Federal Reserve Board to a non-Morgan politically appointed Federal Reserve Board in Washington.

Two channels have been charted for the way that Eccles's views became known to the New Dealers. Robert Hinckley, an old friend of Eccles's and nephew of Senator William King (D-Utah), and another young man, Dean Brimhall, a brother-in-law of Eccles's, had formed a bimonthly discussion club in Utah called the *Freidenkers*. On hearing of Eccles's new views, the *Freidenkers* became Eccles's disciples, and Hinckley used Senator King's influence to get Eccles a hearing at the Senate Finance Committee. Also Marriner was a regent of the University of Utah, and when radical New Dealer Stuart Chase spoke at the Chautauqua lecture series at the university, he was impressed with Eccles's views. Another, overlooked influence on the New Dealers is the fact that George Dern, Roosevelt's secretary of war and former governor of Utah, was a financial subaltern of Eccles's, being a director of two Salt Lake City banks, both part of Eccles's First Security Corporation holding company.

After a year, in February 1934, Eccles came to Washington as special assistant on monetary and credit matters to Secretary of the Treasury Henry Morgenthau. Eccles found himself frustrated at Treasury, however, since Morgenthau had old-fashioned pro-balanced-budget views. Morgenthau was heavily under the influence of Lewis W. Douglas, still in the administration as head of the Bureau of Budget (then in the Treasury Department), and of Undersecretary of the Treasury T. Jefferson Coolidge, of the Morgan-allied financial family in Boston, who had been placed in his spot on the urging of George Harrison. But Eccles did not waste his months at the Treasury, finding support and enthusiastic agreement in two young aides, former Fed economist Winfield W. Riefler and Lauchlin Currie, a young Ph.D. from Harvard. Currie, whose important monetarist work was in the process of being published by Harvard University Press, converted Eccles to the goal of total political control over the money supply, and of the alleged necessity for recovery to concentrate on open market operations for rapid inflation of the money supply.[92]

In early September 1934, Eccles was asked by administration aides to accept an appointment as governor of the Federal Reserve Board in Washington, Eugene Black having resigned to return to Georgia and later to move to the Chase National Bank. Eccles boldly replied that he would only accept the post if at the same time there was a fundamental structural change at the Fed, and power was shifted from the New York Fed to the Federal Reserve Board in Washington. Following up on this determined stance, Eccles submitted a memorandum to the White House on November 4, written in collaboration with Eccles's aide and theoretician, Lauchlin Currie. The memo stressed that the Federal Reserve Board must take full power from the New York Fed: that it must obtain "complete control over the timing, character and volume of open market purchases and sales of bills and securities by the Reserve banks." Until this point, wrote Eccles/Currie, private banker "interest, as represented by individual Reserve bank governors, has prevailed over the

[92]See Lauchlin Currie, *The Supply and Control of Money in the United States*, 2nd rev. ed. (Cambridge, Mass.: Harvard University Press, [1934] 1935). Currie's doctoral thesis proved to be perhaps the most important monetarist work of the pre–World War II period. Currie's thesis was simple:

> An ideal monetary system *from the standpoint of control* would be one in which expansions and contractions of the supply of money could be brought about easily and quickly to any required extent. . . . It appears to the writer that the most perfect control could be achieved by direct government issue of all money, both notes and deposits subject to check. (Ibid., p. 151)

A history of monetary theory by a leading early monetarist partially acknowledged the importance of Currie's influence on economic theory. Lloyd W. Mints, *A History of Banking Theory* (Chicago: University of Chicago Press, 1945). Currie's vital influence on Eccles and hence on banking legislation in the United States is shown in Hyman, *Marriner Eccles*, pp. 155 ff., and in Israelson, "Marriner S. Eccles," p. 358. It is therefore all the more astonishing that there is not a single mention of Currie in Friedman and Schwartz, *Monetary History*.

public interest, as represented at the [Federal Reserve] Board." From now on, the "public interest" must prevail. In particular, the Federal Reserve Board must gain complete control over the Open Market Committee, now composed of the 12 governors of the private Federal Reserve banks. Such changes were necessary, the memo concluded, in order for the Fed to become a genuine "central bank"; although, secure in such new powers, there would be no need to arouse intense political opposition by *calling* such a setup a "central bank."[93]

On November 10, FDR, impressed by the memo and emboldened by his smashing victory over the Republicans in the November 1934 congressional elections, announced the appointment of Marriner Eccles as governor of the Federal Reserve Board, and he was sworn in a week later. At the same time as his appointment was announced and submitted for confirmation to the Senate, the radical Banking Act of 1935, embodying the Eccles/Currie program, was scheduled to be submitted to Congress. Lined up against Eccles and the new banking act were powerful Senator Carter Glass, chairman of the Senate Finance Committee and of the crucial subcommittee of the Senate Banking and Currency Committee, as well as Glass's theoretician Professor H. Parker Willis, who denounced the banking act as the "worst and most dangerous measure that has made its appearance for a long time." In this particular battle, the opposition was a coalition of former enemies, the Willis-Glass hard-money qualitativists; and the Morgan empire, spearheaded by George L. Harrison, whose New York Fed stood to lose its dominating power over the banking system. In contrast, founding monetarist and veteran inflationist Irving Fisher of Yale, spiritual mentor to Milton Friedman, claimed that the banking bill "will represent a great step forward, probably the greatest in the president's administration."

With the fight now under way, Eccles moved quickly to establish his own total control over dissident institutions within

[93]Hyman, *Marriner Eccles*, pp. 157–58.

the Federal Reserve. He met with the Federal Advisory Council (FAC), a powerful voice of private bankers within the Federal Reserve. The FAC consisted of one private banker from each of the 12 Federal Reserve districts; almost always, they were representatives from large metropolitan banks in each district. The occasional publications of the FAC were often presented to the public as if they were the official views of the Federal Reserve Board. Thus, in September, strategically timed for the election, the FAC had publicly called for a balanced federal budget, incensing Eccles and the New Dealers. Eccles now cracked down, ordering the FAC to confine itself to an advisory role, and to issue no public statements without first submitting the recommendations to the Federal Reserve Board and notifying it in advance of any public pronouncement. The Federal Advisory Council promptly knuckled under.

Eccles then moved to completely control any legislative recommendations to emerge from the Federal Reserve System. He abolished the Fed's Committee on Legislative Programs, which had been headed by Harrison, and had consisted only of private or regional Fed bankers with the exception of one representative from the Federal Reserve Board. Eccles then created a new legislative committee, consisting solely of his own appointed professional staff. In addition to Eccles himself, members were Chester Morrill, Federal Reserve Board secretary; Walter Wyatt, the board's general counsel; Emanuel Goldenweiser, director of the Fed's Division of Research and Statistics; and Lauchlin Currie, the division's new assistant director. The committee was charged with drafting a new banking act. The committee draft would then go to a subcommittee on banking legislation of the administration's Interdepartmental Loan Committee, chaired by Secretary Morgenthau, and consisting of the heads Federal Advisory Council and Federal Deposit Insurance Corporation (FDIC), and the comptroller of the currency, as well as several representatives of the Treasury.

To gain support from the Treasury and other administration figures as well as from Congress and the nation's bankers, FDR devised a cunning strategy: he would present Eccles's radical reform as Title II of the new banking act, sandwiched in between two reforms the bankers desperately wanted: Title I, liberalizing assessment on banks for deposit insurance, a pet reform of FDIC head Leo T. Crowley; and Title III, which granted bankers a grace period beyond the statutory July 1, 1935, imposed by the Banking Act of 1933, before they had to repay loans granted to them by their own banks. Title III was a favorite project of Comptroller of the Currency J.R.T. O'Conner. It was no accident that both Crowley and O'Connor were members of the decisive Interdepartmental Loan subcommittee. While both Crowley and O'Connor fought to present their own bills separately from Eccles's, Morgenthau went along with Roosevelt's strategy and with Eccles's reforms, the banking act being hammered through the committee quickly and submitted to Congress on February 5.[94]

In Congress, Eccles's nomination sailed through, with struggles concentrated on the banking act. In the hearings, particularly interesting in opposition was James P. Warburg of Kuhn, Loeb, and chairman of the board of the Kuhn, Loeb–run Bank of Manhattan. Warburg, who as an old-line banker had been allied with the Morgans at the London Economic Conference, denounced the banking bill as "Curried Keynes."[95] In the course of the controversy, the highly influential *New York Times* and the *Washington Post* (owned and directed by Eugene

[94]Ibid., pp. 167–71.

[95]Lauchlin Currie, continuing as economist at the Fed, rose to the post of administrative assistant to President Roosevelt during World War II. There he was recruited as a valuable member of the Silvermaster group of Soviet espionage agents. The group was organized by Board of Economic Warfare official Nathan Gregory Silvermaster, and it included Treasury economist and later director of the International Monetary Fund, Harry Dexter White. After the defection of Soviet agent Elizabeth Bentley after World War II and his naming by Bentley, Lauchlin Currie found it expedient to emigrate to Colombia, spending the rest of his days as economic adviser to the Colombian government. Elizabeth Bentley,

Meyer) changed their initial opposition to support for the bill. Essentially, Eccles won almost all of his points: the shift of banking control from Morgan's New York Fed to the non-Morgan Washington politicians had been completed. In the Senate, Eccles only had to make one important concession to Glass: instead of the Federal Open Market Committee consisting solely of the governors of the Federal Reserve Board, it would be instead comprised of the seven members of the Federal Reserve Board plus five rotating representatives of the Federal Reserve banks (in practice, their presidents) and hence of private bankers.

But despite this compromise, the decisive act had taken place: open market policy would be initiated in, dominated by, and enforced by the Federal Reserve Board in Washington. Actual open market operations would be carried out, most conveniently, in New York, but strictly under the orders of the Federal Reserve Board–dominated FOMC. Individual Federal Reserve banks (in practice, the New York Fed) were prohibited from buying or selling government securities for their own account, except under the direction, or with the explicit permission, of the FOMC. To further reduce the power of the Federal Reserve banks, it was explicitly provided that the bank-elected members of the FOMC were *not* to serve in any way as agents of the banks that elected them; indeed, the banks were not to know what was going to happen but only to have a chance to be heard through an advisory committee. Indeed, the bank presidents serving on the FOMC were not even allowed to divulge actions taken at FOMC meetings to their own board of directors! Harrison fought unsuccessfully against this provision; and in a last-ditch and finally failing battle in 1937, Harrison tried to get the FOMC to allow

---

Out of Bondage (New York: Ballantine Books, 1988), particularly the "Afterword" by Hayden Peake; and Christopher Andrew and Oleg Gordievsky, *KGB: The Inside Story of Its Foreign Operations from Lenin to Gorbachev* (New York: Harper Collins, 1990), pp. 281–84, 369–70.

Reserve banks to conduct open market operations on their own in case of individual bank emergencies.

In addition, the Federal Reserve Board was given veto power over the election of the president and first vice president of each district Federal Reserve bank. And, in a symbolic gesture, all district Fed "governors," the hoary name for heads of the central banks, were demoted to "presidents," whereas the old "members" of the Federal Reserve Board in Washington were upgraded to "governors," while the previous "governor" of the Federal Reserve Board now became the board's august "chairman of the board of governors." Furthermore, cementing Chairman Eccles's power within Washington, the Treasury secretary and the comptroller of the currency were both removed as ex officio members of the Federal Reserve Board.

Finally, the last shred of qualitativist restraint upon the Fed's expansion of credit was removed, as bank assets deemed eligible for Fed rediscounting were broadened totally to include any paper whatever deemed "satisfactory" by the Fed—that is, any assets the Fed wished to declare eligible.[96]

The Banking Act of 1935 was important for being the final settled piece of New Deal banking legislation that consolidated all the revolutionary changes from the beginning of the Roosevelt administration. The Morgans tried desperately, for example, to alter the 1933 Glass-Steagall provision, compelling the separation of commercial and investment banking, but this reversion was successfully blocked by Winthrop Aldrich. Specifically, Senator Glass's amendment to the Banking Act of 1935, restoring limited securities power to deposit banks, was able to reach the congressional conference committee; for a while, it looked like this Morgan maneuver would succeed, but presumably at the behest of Aldrich, however, FDR

[96]Friedman and Schwartz, *Monetary History*, pp. 445–49.

personally interceded with the committee to kill the Glass amendment.[97]

For his part, Aldrich, as a Wall Street banker himself, was not very happy about the permanent shift of power from Wall Street to Washington, but he was content to go along with the overall result, as part of the anti-Morgan coalition with Western banking.

The centralization of power over the banking system in Washington was now complete. It is no wonder that the irrepressible H. Parker Willis, writing the following year, lamented the centralized monetary and banking tyranny that the Federal Reserve had become. Willis wisely perceived that the course of inflationary centralization to have begun in the 1920s as Morgan control in the hands of the New York Fed, and now, with the New Deal, was immeasurably accelerated and shifted to Washington:

> The Eccles group which advocated the Act of 1935 sought to obtain for themselves those powers which the more ambitious of the banking clique in New York and elsewhere had already arrogated to the Federal Reserve Bank of New York and to the small group by which the institution was practically directed [the House of Morgan]. There was no change in the conception or notion of centralization, but only in the agency or personnel through which such centralization should be put into effect.[98]

The New Deal, Willis went on, had passed various allegedly temporary and emergency measures in its first three years, which were now permanently consolidated into the Banking Act of 1935, and thus "was built up perhaps the most highly

[97]Chernow, *House of Morgan*, p. 384; Ferguson, "Coming of the New Deal," pp. 29–30.

[98]Henry Parker Willis, *The Theory and Practice of Central Banking: With Special Reference to American Experience 1913–1935* (New York: Harper and Brothers, 1936), p. 107.

centralized and irresponsible financial and banking machine of which the modern world holds record."

The result, Willis pointed out, was that the years of "tremendous deficit" from 1931 on were marked by a process of "gradually diverting the funds and savings of the community to the support of governmentally directed enterprises." It was "an extraordinary development—an extreme application of central banking which brought the system of the United States to a condition of even higher concentration" than in other countries. Willis ominously and prophetically concluded,

> Today, the United States thus stands out as a nation of despotically controlled central banking; one in which, as all now admit, moreover, business paper of every kind is gradually taking the form of government paper which is then financed through a governmentally controlled central banking organization.[99]

Epilogue: Return of the Morgans

It is well not to cry for the Morgans. Though permanently dethroned by the New Deal, they were able to make a comeback by the late 1930s. The great thrust for economic nationalism had subsided, and the Morgans were able to begin to work again for stabilization of exchange rates. In the fall of 1936, the United

[99]Ibid., p. 108. Marriner Eccles, too, ended up left behind by the New Deal revolution he had helped to lead. Specifically, Eccles could not understand why Truman's Fair Deal insisted on continuing deficits and monetary inflation even after the depression and World War II were over. Removed by Truman as chairman of the Federal Reserve Board in 1948, Eccles, as a continuing member of the board, was the principal figure in forcing an end, in 1951, to the disastrously inflationary Fed policy of supporting the price of Treasury securities, and hence providing a channel for perpetual monetization of the federal deficit. After leaving the Fed, Eccles went back into the conservative Republican camp. Such is the leftward drift of American politics that he could do so without repudiating any of his New Deal macro positions.

States entered into a tripartite agreement with Great Britain and France, the three countries agreeing—not exactly on fixed exchange rates—but on maneuvering to support each other's exchanges at least within any given 24-hour period. Soon, the agreement, which was to last until World War II, was expanded to include Belgium, Holland, and Switzerland.

As the nations moved toward World War II, the Morgans, who had long been closely connected with Britain and France, rose in importance in American foreign policy, while the Rockefellers, who had little connection with Britain and France and had patent agreements with I.G. Farben in Germany, fell in relative strength. Secretary of State Cordell Hull, a close longtime friend of FDR's roving ambassador and Morgan man Norman H. Davis, took the lead in exerting pressure against Germany for its bilateral rather than multilateral trade agreements and for its exchange controls, all put in place to defend a chronically overvalued mark.[100, 101]

[100]Rothbard, "New Deal and International Monetary System," pp. 105–11. Germany could not devalue the mark, because the German public erroneously blamed foreign exchange devaluation, instead of monetary expansion, for the disastrous runaway inflation of 1923, and devaluation would have been political suicide for any government, even Hitler's. For a valuable explanation of the workings of the German barter agreements of the 1930s, see Ludwig von Mises, *Human Action* (New Haven, Conn.: Yale University Press, 1949), pp. 796–99. Unfortunately, this section was removed in later editions. [*Mises's original text was reinstated in the scholar's edition (Auburn, Ala.: Ludwig von Mises Institute, 1998), pp. 796–799.*—Ed.]

[101]One incident almost marred the success of the Tripartite Agreement. In the fall of 1938, the British began pushing the pound below $4.80. Treasury officials promptly warned Morgenthau that if "sterling drops substantially below $4.80, our foreign and domestic business will be adversely affected." Morgenthau then successfully insisted that a new trade agreement then being worked out with Britain include a provision that the agreement would end should the British allow the pound to fall below $4.80. Lloyd C. Gardner, *Economic Aspects of New Deal Diplomacy* (Madison: University of Wisconsin Press, 1964), p. 107.

As the United States prepared to enter World War II, it made its economic war aims brutally simple: the ending of the economic and monetary nationalism of the 1930s, and their replacement by a new international economic order based upon the dollar instead of the pound. In the trade area, this meant vigorous U.S. promotion of exports and the reduction of tariffs and quotas against American products (the so-called "open door" for American commerce and investments), and in the monetary sphere, it meant the breakup of national currency blocs, and the restoration of multilateral exchanges with fixed parities based upon the dollar. Even as the United States prepared to enter the war to save Britain, its continuing conflict with the British proclivity for exchange controls and an Imperial Preference bloc remained unresolved.[102]

The resolution of the problem came after lengthy negotiations throughout World War II, culminating in the Bretton Woods Agreement in July 1944. Basically, the agreement was a compromise in which the United States won the main point: a new multilateral world of fixed exchange rates of currencies based on the dollar, while the Americans accepted the British

[102]At the Atlantic Conference with Churchill in August 1941, FDR revealingly told his son, Elliott:

> It's something that's not generally known, but British bankers and German bankers have had world trade pretty well sewn up in their pockets for a long time. . . . Well, that's not so good for world trade, is it? . . . If in the past German and British economic interests have operated to exclude us from world trade, kept our merchant shipping closed down, closed us out of this or that market, and now Germany and Britain are at war, what should we do? (Robert Freeman Smith, "American Foreign Relations, 1920–1942," in *Toward a New Past*, Barton J. Bernstein, ed. [New York: Pantheon, 1968], p. 252)

See also Gabriel Kolko, *The Politics of War: The World and United States Foreign Policy, 1943–45* (New York: Random House, 1968), pp. 248–49; and Rothbard, "New Deal and International Monetary System," pp. 111–15.

Keynesian insistence on jointly promoting permanent inflationary policies to ensure "full employment." The United States had achieved the objective expressed by Secretary Morgenthau: "to move the financial center of the world from London to the United States Treasury."[103] It is no wonder that, in January 1945, Lamar Fleming, Jr., president of Anderson, Clayton and Company, world's largest cotton export brokers, could write to his longtime colleague and boss William L. Clayton that the "British empire and British international influence is a myth already." The United States would soon become the protector of Britain against the emerging Russian landmass, prophesied Fleming, and this would mean "the absorption into the American empire of the parts of the British empire which we will be willing to accept."[104]

The dominant role in the critical wartime negotiations leading up to Bretton Woods was played not by the State Department, but secretly by the Council of Foreign Relations (CFR), a highly influential organization of businessmen and experts set up by the Morgans after World War I to promote an internationalist foreign political and economic policy. Private study groups set up by the CFR intermeshed and virtually dictated to parallel study groups established by the sometimes reluctant Department of State. President of the CFR from 1936 until 1944 and director of this effort was none other than Norman Davis, longtime Morgan affiliate and disciple of Morgan partner Henry P. Davison. The Morgans, indeed, were back.[105] During the war, many Morgan-oriented men who had strongly opposed the

[103]Richard N. Gardner, *Sterling-Dollar Diplomacy* (Oxford: Clarendon Press, 1956), p. 76.

[104]Kolko, *Politics of War,* p. 294. See also Rothbard, "New Deal and International Monetary System," pp. 112, 120.

[105]See the illuminating research of Domhoff, *Power Elite,* pp. 115ff.; and Laurence H. Shoup and William Minter, *Imperial Brain Trust: The Council on Foreign Relations and United States Foreign Policy* (New York: Monthly Review Press, 1977).

economic nationalism of the early New Deal happily came back to help run the World War II and postwar version of the new era: Lewis W. Douglas; Dean Acheson, who had left the New Deal because of its radical monetary measures, was back as assistant secretary of state for monetary affairs; Acheson's mentor, Henry L. Stimson, was secretary of war; and Stimson's other disciple, John J. McCloy, in effect ran the war effort as his deputy secretary. And when the ailing Cordell Hull retired in late 1944, he was replaced as secretary of state by Edward Stettinius, son of a Morgan partner and himself former president of Morgan-dominated United States Steel.[106]

After World War II, the Morgans were content to slide into a new role as junior partner to the Rockefellers. The new prominence of oil made the Rockefellers the dominant force in the political and financial Eastern Establishment. The Rockefellers assumed control of the Council of Foreign Relations, the entire shift being neatly symbolized by the new postwar role of John J. McCloy, who was to serve as chairman of the Council of Foreign Relations, of the Rockefeller Foundation, and of the Rockefeller flagship bank, the Chase National Bank.[107] The old verities and financial group conflicts of the pre–World War II era had disappeared, and had been transformed into a new world.

[106]Stettinius chose as his assistant secretary for economic affairs William L. Clayton, chairman and major partner of the cotton export firm, Anderson, Clayton and Company. Clayton had formerly been a leader of the fiercely anti-New Deal Liberty League. Clayton's major focus in the postwar era was the promotion of American exports, especially cotton; as undersecretary of state he was chiefly responsible for drafting and pushing through the Marshall Plan, which promptly awarded Anderson, Clayton and Company a major cotton export contract. His work in foreign policy accomplished, Clayton could return to private life. Rothbard, "New Deal and International Monetary System," p. 113.

[107]It is no wonder that, in the late 1950s, John Kenneth Galbraith and Richard Rovere dubbed McCloy "Chairman of the Establishment." Kai Bird, *The Chairman: John J. McCloy, the Making of the American Establishment* (New York: Simon and Schuster, 1992).

Part 4

The Gold-Exchange Standard in the Interwar Years

THE GOLD-EXCHANGE STANDARD IN THE INTERWAR YEARS

Great Britain emerged victorious from its travail in World War I, but its economy, and particularly its currency, lay in shambles. All the warring countries had financed their massive four-year war effort by monetizing their deficits, most of them doubling, tripling, or quadrupling their money supply, with equivalent impacts upon their prices.[1] The massive influx of government paper money forced these warring governments to go rapidly off the gold standard. The currencies depreciated in terms of gold, but the depreciation was masked by a network of exchange controls that marked the collectivized economies

[1]Germany, which multiplied its money supply eightfold during the war, would soon spiral into runaway inflation, propelled by accelerated monetization of government deficits and of private credit; France and Austria also went into hyperinflation after the war to a lesser extent than Germany. See Melchior Palyi, *The Twilight of Gold 1914–1936* (Chicago: Henry Regnery, 1972), p. 33. See also D.E. Moggridge, *British Monetary Policy, 1924–1931: The Norman Conquest of $4.86* (Cambridge: Cambridge University Press, 1972).

[*Previously published in an edited version as "The Gold-Exchange Standard in the Interwar Years," in* Money and the Nation State: The Financial Revolution, Government and the World Monetary System, *Kevin Dowd and Richard H. Timberlake, Jr., eds. (New Brunswick, N.J.: Transactions Publishers, 1998), pp. 105–63.*—Ed.]

during World War I. Only the United States, which entered the war two and a half years after the other countries and hence inflated its currency less, managed to remain de jure on its prewar gold standard. De facto, however, the U.S. barred export of gold during the war, and so was effectively off gold during that period. In March 1919, when foreign exchange markets became free once more, the bad news became evident: while the dollar, again de facto as well as de jure on gold, remained at its prewar par (approximately one-twentieth of a gold ounce), European fiat paper currencies were sadly depreciated. The once-mighty pound sterling, traditionally at approximately $4.86, now sold at approximately $3.50 and at one point, in February 1920, was down to $3.20.[2] Here was a 30- to 35-percent depreciation from its prewar par.

Thus, wartime and postwar Europe was thrown into a cauldron of inflation, depreciation, exchange-rate volatility, and the menace of warring currency blocs. For the first time since the Napoleonic Wars, the world lacked an international money, a medium of exchange that could be used throughout the world, and lacked the international harmony, the monetary stability and calculability, that a world money could generate. Europe, and the world, were plunged into the chaos of an international moneyless, or barter, system. All the countries therefore looked back with understandable nostalgia at the relative Eden that had existed before the Great War.

The Classical Gold Standard

The nineteenth-century monetary system has been referred to as the "classical" gold standard. It has become fashionable among economists to denigrate that system as only existent in the last decades of the nineteenth century, and as simply a form

[2]Precisely, British currency had traditionally been defined so that one ounce of gold was equal to 77s. 10½d. Comparing the prewar ratios of the dollar and the pound to gold, the pound sterling was therefore set at $4.86656. The gold ounce was also set equal to $20.67.

of pound sterling standard, since London was the great financial center during this period. This disparagement of gold, however, is faulty and misleading. It is true that London was the major financial center in that period, but the world was scarcely on a pound standard. Active competition from other financial centers—Berlin, Paris, Amsterdam, Brussels, New York—ensured that gold was truly the only standard money throughout the world.[3] Furthermore, to stress only the few decades before 1914 as the age of the gold standard ignores the fact that gold and silver have been the world's two monetary metals from time immemorial. Countries shifted to and from freely fluctuating parallel gold and silver standards, in attempts, self-defeating in the long run, to fix the rate of exchange between the two metals ("bimetallism"). The fact that countries stampeded from silver and toward gold monometallism in the late nineteenth century should not obscure the fact that gold and silver, for centuries, were the world's moneys, and that previous paper money experiments (the longest during the Napoleonic Wars) were considered to be both ephemeral and disastrously inflationary. Specie standards, whether gold or silver, have been virtually coextensive with the history of civilization.[4] Apart from a few calamitous

[3]See Palyi, *Twilight of Gold*, pp. 1–21, 118–19. See also David P. Calleo, "The Historiography of the Interwar Period: Reconsiderations," in *Balance of Power or Hegemony: The Interwar Monetary System*, Benjamin M. Rowland, ed. (New York: Lehrman Institute and New York University Press, 1976), pp. 227–60. Calleo shows that the pre-1914 gold standard was a genuine, multicentered gold standard, not a British sterling standard.

[4]Professor Timberlake misconstrues the historical research of Luigi Einaudi on "imaginary money" in the Middle Ages. Far from showing, as Timberlake believes, that moneys of account can be "imaginary" in relation to media of exchange, they simply reveal various countries' experiences with various relationships between gold and silver, both commodity moneys. See Luigi Einaudi, "The Theory of Imaginary Money from Charlemagne to the French Revolution," in *Enterprise and Secular Change*, F.C. Lane and J.C. Riemersma, eds. (Homewood, Ill.: Richard D. Irwin,

experiments, such as John Law's Mississippi Bubble and the South Sea Bubble in the 1710s, and apart from the generation-long experience in Britain during the Napoleonic War, until the twentieth century specie rather than paper had always been the standard money.

In the classical gold standard, every nation's currency was defined as a unit of weight of gold, and therefore the paper currency was redeemable by its issuer (the government or its central bank) in the defined weight of gold coin. While gold bullion, in the form of large bars, was used for international payment, gold coin was used in everyday transactions by the general public. For obvious reasons, it is the inherent tendency of every money-issuer to create as much money as it can get away with, but governments or central banks were, on the gold standard, restricted in their issue of paper or bank deposits by the iron necessity of immediate redemption in gold, and particularly in gold coin on demand. As in the familiar Hume-Cantillon international price-specie flow mechanism, an increase of bank notes or deposits in a country beyond its gold stock increases the supply of money, say francs in France. The increase of the supply of francs and incomes in francs leads to (a) an increase in both domestic and foreign spending, hence raising imports; and (b) a rise in domestic French prices, in turn making domestic goods less competitive abroad and lowering exports, and making foreign goods more attractive and raising imports. The result is an inexorable deficit in the balance of payments, putting pressure upon French banks to supply gold to English, American, or Dutch exporters. In short, since in fractional reserve banking, paper and bank notes pyramid as a multiple of gold reserves, this expansion of the already engorged top of the inverted

---

1953), pp. 229–61; Richard Timberlake, *Gold, Greenbacks, and the Constitution* (Berryville, Va.: George Edward Durell Foundation, 1991); and Murray N. Rothbard, "Aurophobia, or Free Banking on What Standard?" *Review of Austrian Economics* 6, no. 1 (1992): 97–108.

pyramid, must inexorably be followed by a loss in the bottom supporting the swollen liabilities. In addition, clients who are holders of French bank notes or deposits, are apt to become increasingly concerned, lose confidence in the viability of the French banks, and hence call on those banks to redeem in gold—putting those banks at risk for a devastating bank run. The result will be an often panicky and sudden contraction of bank notes, generating a recession to replace the previous inflationary boom, and leading to a contraction in notes and deposits, a drop in the French money supply, and a consequent fall in domestic French prices. The balance-of-payments deficit is reversed, and gold flows back into French coffers.

In short, the classical gold standard put a severe limit upon the inherent tendency of monopoly money-issuers to issue money without check. As Ludwig von Mises pointed out, this international specie-flow mechanism also described a correct, if primitive, model of the business cycle. While central banking and fractional reserve banking allowed play for a boom-bust cycle, the inflationary boom, and its compensating bust, was kept in strict bounds.[5] While scarcely perfect or lacking problems, the classical gold standard worked well enough for the world after World War I to look back upon it with understandable nostalgia.[6]

[5]Prices during the boom did not necessarily increase in historical terms. If a secular price fall was occurring due to increased production, as happened in much of the nineteenth century, the inflationary boom took the form of prices being higher than they would have been in the absence of the expansion of money and credit.

[6]While the United States was the only major power before 1914 to lack a central bank, the quasi-centralized national banking system performed a similar function in the years between the Civil War and 1914. Instead of the government conferring a monopoly note-issuing privilege upon the central bank, the federal government conferred that privilege upon a handful of large, federally chartered "national banks," located in New York and a few other Eastern financial centers.

Britain Faces the Postwar World

At the end of World War I, only the United States dollar remained on the old gold-coin standard, at the one-twentieth-of-an-ounce par. The other powers suffered from national fiat currencies; suddenly, their currencies were no longer units of weight of gold but independent names, such as pound, franc, mark, etc., their rates depreciating in relation to gold and volatile with respect to one another. Except for mavericks such as Cambridge's John Maynard Keynes, it was generally agreed that this system was intolerable, and that a way must be found to reconstruct a world monetary order, including restoration of a world money and medium of exchange. At the heart of the European monetary crisis was Great Britain, which would take the lead in trying to solve the problem. In the first place, London had been the major prewar financial center; and second, Britain dominated the postwar League of Nations, and in particular its powerful Economic and Financial Committee. Furthermore, though inflated and depreciated, the British pound was still in far better shape than the other major currencies of Europe. Thus, while the pound sterling in February 1920 was depreciated by 35 percent compared to its 1914 gold par, the French franc was depreciated by 64 percent, the Belgian franc by 62 percent, the Italian lira by 71 percent, and the German mark in terrible shape by 96 percent.[7] It was clear that Britain was in a position to guide the world to a new postwar monetary order, and it eagerly took up what turned out to be the last remnants of its old imperial task.

The British understandably decided that the fluctuating fiat money system inherited from the war was intolerable, and that it was vital to return to a sound international money, the gold standard. However, at the same time, they also decided that they would have to return to gold at the old prewar par of

[7]Palyi, *Twilight of Gold*, pp. 38–39.

$4.86. Apparently, few if any economists or statesmen at the time argued for cutting British losses, starting with the real world as it existed in the early 1920s, facing reality, and going back to gold at the realistic, depreciated $3.20 or $3.50 per pound sterling. In view of the enormous difficulties the decision to go back to gold at $4.86 entailed, it is difficult in hindsight to understand why there was so little support for going back at a realistic par or why there was so much drive to go back at the old one.[8] For going back to a pound 30 to 35 percent above the market rate, meant that English exports upon which the country depended to finance its exports, were now priced far above their competitive price in world markets. Coal, cotton textiles, iron and steel, and shipbuilding, in particular, the bulk of the export industries that had generated prewar prosperity, became permanently depressed in the 1920s, with accompanying heavy unemployment in those industries. In order to avoid export depression, Britain would have to have been willing to undergo a substantial monetary and price deflation, to make its goods once more competitive in foreign markets. But, in contrast to pre-World War I days, British wage rates had been made rigid downward by powerful trade-unionism, and particularly by a massive and extravagant system of national unemployment insurance. Rather than accept a rigorous deflationary policy, therefore, to accompany its return to gold, Britain insisted on just the opposite: a continuation of monetary inflation and a policy of low interest rates and cheap money. Thus, Great Britain, in the post-World War I world, committed itself to a monetary policy based on three rigidly firm but mutually self-contradictory axioms: (1) a return to gold; (2) returning at a sharply overvalued pound of $4.86; and (3) continuing a policy of inflation and cheap money. Given a program based on such grave inner self-contradiction, the

[8]For an early English critique of not going back at a realistic par, see Lionel Robbins, *The Great Depression* (New York: Macmillan, 1934), esp. pp. 77–87.

British maneuvered on the world monetary scene with brilliant tactical shrewdness; but it was a policy that was doomed to end in disaster.

Why did the British insist on returning to gold at the old, overvalued par? Partly it was a vain desire to recapture old glories, to bring back the days when London was the world's financial center. The British did not seem to realize fully that the United States had emerged from the war as the great creditor nation, and financially the strongest one, so that financial predominance was inexorably moving to New York or Washington. To recapture their financial predominance, the British believed that they would have to bring back the old, traditional, $4.86. Undoubtedly, the British also remembered that after two decades of war against the French Revolution and Napoleon, the pound had quickly recovered from its depreciated state, and the British had been able to restore the pound at its pre-fiat money par. This restoration was made possible by the fact that the post–Napoleonic War pound returned quickly to its prewar par, because of a sharp monetary and price deflation that occurred in the inevitable postwar recession.[9] The British after World War I apparently did not realize that (a) the restoration of the pre–Napoleonic War par had required a substantial deflation, and (b) their newly rigidified war structure could not easily afford or adapt to a deflationary policy. Instead, the British would insist on having their cake and eating it too: on enjoying the benefits of gold at a highly overvalued pound while still continuing to inflate and luxuriate in cheap money.

[9]The pound sterling was depreciated by 45 percent before the end of the Napoleonic War. When the war ended, the pound returned nearly to its prewar gold par. This appreciation was caused by (a) a general expectation that Britain would resume the gold standard, and (b) a monetary contraction of 17 percent in one year, from 1815 to 1816, accompanied by a price deflation of 63 percent. See Frank W. Fetter, *Development of British Monetary Orthodoxy, 1797–1875* (Cambridge, Mass.: Harvard University Press, 1965).

Another reason for returning at $4.86 was a desire by the powerful city of London—the financiers who held much of the public debt swollen during the war—to be repaid in pounds that would be worth their old prewar value in terms of gold and purchasing power. Since the British were now attempting to support more than twice as much money on top of approximately the same gold base as before the war, and the other European countries were suffering from even more inflated currencies, the British and other Europeans complained all during the 1920s of a gold "shortage," or shortage of "liquidity." These complaints reflected a failure to realize that, on the market, a "shortage" can only be the consequence of an artificially low price of a good. The "gold shortage" of the '20s reflected the artificially low "price" of gold, that is, the artificially overvalued rate at which pounds—and many other European currencies—returned to gold in the 1920s, and therefore the arbitrarily low rate at which gold was pegged in terms of those currencies.

More particularly, since the pound was pegged at an overvalued rate compared to gold, Britain would tend to suffer in the 1920s from gold flowing out of the country. Or, put another way, the swollen and inflated pounds would, in the classic price-specie-flow mechanism, tend to drive gold out of Britain to pay for a deficit in the balance of payments, an outflow that could put severe contractionary pressure upon the English banking system. But how could Britain, in the postwar world, cleave to these contradictory axioms and yet avoid a disastrous outflow of gold followed by a banking collapse and monetary contraction?

Return to Gold at $4.86: The Cunliffe Committee and After

Britain's postwar course had already been set during the war. In January 1918, the British Treasury and the Ministry of Reconstruction established the Cunliffe Committee, the Committee on Currency and Foreign Exchanges After the War, headed by the venerable Walter Lord Cunliffe, retiring governor of the Bank of England. As early as its first interim report in the summer of 1918, and confirmed by its final report the following year, the Cunliffe Committee called in no uncertain terms for return to the gold standard at the prewar par. No alternatives were considered.[10] This course was confirmed by the Vassar-Smith Committee on Financial Facilities in 1918, which was composed largely of representatives of industry and commerce, and which endorsed the Cunliffe recommendations. A minority of bankers, including Sir Brien Cockayne and incoming Bank of England Governor Montagu Norman, argued for an immediate return to gold at the old par, but they were overruled by the majority, led by their economic adviser, the distinguished Cambridge economist and chosen successor to Alfred Marshall's professorial chair, Arthur Cecil Pigou. Pigou argued for postponement of the return, hoping to ease the transition by loans from abroad and, particularly, by inflation in the United States. The hope for U.S. inflation became a continuing theme during the 1920s, since inflated and depreciated Britain was in danger of losing gold to the United States, a loss which could be staved off, and the new 1920s system sustained, by inflation in the United States. After exchange controls and most other wartime controls were lifted at the end of 1919, Britain, not knowing precisely when to return to gold, passed the Gold and Silver Export Embargo Act in 1920 for a five-year period, in effect continuing a fiat paper standard until the end of 1925, with an announced intention of returning to gold at that time. Britain was committed to doing something about gold in 1925.[11]

The United States and Great Britain both experienced a traditional immediate postwar boom, continuing the wartime

[10]Moggridge, *British Monetary Policy*, p. 18; and Palyi, *Twilight of Gold*, p. 75.

[11]R.S. Sayers, "The Return to Gold, 1925" (1960) in *The Gold Standard and Employment Policies Between the Wars*, Sidney Pollard, ed. (London: Metheun, 1970), p. 86.

inflation, in 1919 and 1920, followed by a severe corrective recession and deflation in 1921. The English deflation did not suffice to correct the overvaluation of the pound, since the United States, now the strongest country on gold, had deflated as well. The fact that sterling began to appreciate to the old par during 1924 misled the British into thinking that the pound would not be overvalued at $4.86; actually, the appreciation was the result of speculators betting on a nearly sure thing: the return to gold during 1925 of the pound at the old $4.86 par.

A crucial point: while prices and wage rates rose together in England during the wartime and postwar inflationary boom, they scarcely fell together. When commodity prices fell sharply in England in 1920 and 1921, wages fell much less, remaining high above prewar levels. This rise in real wage rates, bringing about high and chronic unemployment, reflected the severe downward wage rigidity in Britain after the war, caused by the spread of trade unionism and particularly by the massive new unemployment insurance program.[12]

The condition of the English economy, in particular the high rate of unemployment and depression of the export industries during the 1922–1924 recovery from the postwar recession, should have given the British pause. From 1851 to 1914, the unemployment rate in Great Britain had hovered consistently around 3 percent; during the boom of 1919–1920, it was 2.4 percent. Yet, during the postwar "recovery," British unemployment ranged between 9 and 15 percent. It should have been clear that something was very wrong.

It is no accident that the high unemployment was concentrated in the British export industries. Compared to the prewar year of 1913, most of the domestic economy in Britain was in

[12]Palyi, *Twilight of Gold*, p. 155; and Benjamin M. Anderson, *Economics and the Public Welfare: Financial and Economic History of the United States, 1914–1946* (Princeton, N.J.: D. Van Nostrand, 1949), p. 74.

fairly good shape in 1924. Setting 1913 as equal to 100, real gross domestic product was 92 in 1924, consumer expenditure was 100, construction was 114, and gross fixed investment was a robust 132. But while real imports were 100 in 1924, real exports were in sickly shape, at only 72. Or, in monetary terms, British imports were 111 in 1924, whereas British exports were only 80. In contrast, world exports were 107 as compared to 1913.

The sickness of British exports may be seen in the fate of the traditional, major export industries during the 1920s. Compared to 1913, iron and steel exports in 1924 were 77.5; cotton textile exports were 65; coal exports were 80; and shipbuilding exports a disastrous 35. Consequently, Britain was now in debt to such strong countries as the United States, while a creditor to such financially weak countries as France, Russia, and Italy.[13]

It should be clear that the export industries suffered particularly from depression because of the impact of the overvalued pound; and that furthermore the depression took the form of permanently high unemployment even in the midst of a general recovery because wage rates were kept rigidly downward by trade unions, and especially by the massive system of unemployment insurance.[14]

There were several anomalies and paradoxes in the conflicts and discussions over the Cunliffe Committee recommendations from 1918 until the actual return to gold in 1925. The critics of the committee were generally discredited for being ardent inflationists as well as opponents of the old par. These forces included J.M. Keynes; the Federation of British Industries, the powerful trade association; and Sir Reginald McKenna, a wartime chancellor of the Exchequer and after the war head of

[13]Moggridge, *British Monetary Policy*, pp. 28–29.

[14]It is unfortunate that Dr. Melchior Palyi, in his valuable perceptive and solidly anti-inflationary work on the interwar period, is blind to the problems generated by the insistence on going back to gold at the prewar par. Palyi dismisses all such considerations as "Keynesian." Palyi, *Twilight of Gold*, passim.

the huge Midland Bank. And yet, most of these inflationists and antideflationists (with the exception of Keynes and of W. Peter Rylands, Federation of British Industries president in 1921) were willing to go along with return at the prewar par. This put the critics of deflation and proponents of cheap money in the curiously anomalous position of being willing to accept return to an overvalued pound, while combating the logic of that pound—namely, deflation in order to attain English exports competitive in world markets. Thus McKenna, who positively desired a policy of domestic inflation and cheap money and cared little for exchange-rate stability or gold, was willing to go along with the return to gold at $4.86. The Federation of British Industries, which recognized the increasing rigidity of wage costs, was fearful of deflation, and its 1921 President Peter Rylands argued forcefully that stability of exchange "is of far greater importance than the re-establishment of any prewar ratio," and went so far as to advocate a return at the far more sensible rate of $4.00 to the pound:

> We have got accustomed to a relationship . . . of about four dollars to the pound, and I feel that the interests of the manufacturers would be best served if it could by some means be fixed at four dollars to the pound and remain there for all time.[15]

But apart from Rylands, the other antideflationists were willing to go along with the prewar par. Why?

The influential journal, the *Round Table,* one of their number, noted the anomaly:

> [W]hile there is a very large body of opinion which wants to see the pound sterling again at par with gold, there are very few so far as we know, who publicly advocate in order to

[15]In an address to the annual general meeting of the Federation of British Industries in November 1921. See L.J. Hume, "The Gold Standard and Deflation: Issues and Attitudes in the 1920s" (1963), in *The Gold Standard*, Pollard, ed., p. 141.

> secure such a result an actively deflationary policy at this particular moment, leading to a further fall in prices.[16]

There are several solutions to this puzzle, all centering around the view that deflationary adjustments from a return to the prewar par would be insignificant. In the first place, there was a confident expectation, echoing the original view of Pigou, that price inflation in the United States would set things right and validate the $4.86 pound. This was the argument used on behalf of $4.86 by the *Round Table*, by McKenna, and by his fellow dissident banker, F.C. Goodenough, chairman of Barclays Bank.

A second reason we have already alluded to: the inevitable rise in sterling to par as the return date approached misled many people into believing that the market action was justifying the choice of rate. But a third reason for optimism particularly needs exploring: that the British were subtly but crucially changing the rules of the game, and returning to a very different and far weaker "gold standard" than had existed before the war.

When the British government made its final decision to return to gold at $4.86 in the spring of 1925, Colonel F.V. Willey, head of the Federation of British Industries, was one of the few to register a perceptive warning note:

> The announcement made today . . . will rapidly bring the pound to parity with the dollar and will . . . increase the present difficulties of our export trade, which is already suffering from a greater rise in the value of the pound than is justified by the relative level of sterling and gold prices.[17]

The way was paved for the final decision to return to gold by the Committee on Currency and Bank of England Note Issues, appointed by Chancellor of the Exchequer Philip Snowden on May 5, 1924, at the suggestion of influential British Treasury official Sir Otto Niemeyer. The committee, known as the Chamberlain-Bradbury Committee, was co-chaired by former

[16]*Round Table* 14 (1923), p. 28, quoted in ibid., p. 136.

[17]*The Times* (London) April 29, 1925, cited in ibid., p. 144.

Chancellor Sir Austen Chamberlain and by Sir John Bradbury, a former member of the old Cunliffe Committee. Also on the new committee were Niemeyer and Professor Pigou of the Cunliffe group. We have a full account of the testimony before the Chamberlain-Bradbury Committee, and of the arguments used to induce Chancellor of the Exchequer Churchill to go back to gold the following year. It is clear from those accounts that the dominant theme was that deflation and export depression could be avoided because of expected rising prices in the United States, which would restore the British export position and avoid an outflow of gold from Britain to the United States. Thus, Sir Charles Addis, a member of the old Cunliffe Committee, a director of the Bank of England, and the director upon whom bank Governor Montagu Norman relied most for advice, called for a return to gold during 1925. Addis welcomed any deflation as a necessary sacrifice in order to restore London as the world's financial center, but he expected a rise in prices in the United States. After listening to a great deal of testimony, the committee leaned toward recommending not a return to gold but waiting until 1925 so as to allow American prices to rise. Bradbury wrote to Gaspard Farrer, a director of Barclays and a member of the Cunliffe Committee, that waiting a bit would be preferred: "Odds are that within the comparatively near future America will allow gold to depreciate to the value of sterling."[18] In early September 1924, Pigou stepped in again, reworking an early draft by the committee secretary to make his economist's report. Pigou once more asserted that an increase in U.S. prices was likely, thereby easing the path toward restoration of gold at $4.86 with little needed deflation. Acting on Pigou's recommendation, the Chamberlain-Bradbury Committee in its draft report in October urged a return to $4.86 at the end of 1925, expecting that the alleged gap of 10 to 12 percent in American and

[18]Bradbury to Farrer, July 24, 1924. Moggridge, *British Monetary Policy*, p. 47.

British price levels would be made up in the interim by a rise in American prices.[19]

Even influential Treasury official Ralph Hawtrey—a friend and fellow Cambridge apostle of Keynes, an equally ardent inflationist and critic of gold, and chief architect of the European gold-exchange standard of the 1920s—favored a return to gold at $4.86 in 1925. He differed in this conclusion from Keynes because he confidently expected a rise in American prices to bear the brunt of the adjustment.[20]

The British Labor government fell in early October 1924, and the general election in late October swept a conservative government into power. After carefully listening to Keynes, McKenna, and other critics, and after holding a now-famous dinner party of the major advocates on March 17, the new chancellor of the Exchequer, Winston Churchill, made the final decision to go back to gold on March 20, announcing and passing a gold standard act, returning to gold at $4.86 on

[19]Undoubtedly the most charming testimony before the committee was by the free-market, hard-money economist from the London School of Economics, Edwin Cannan. In contrast to the other partisans of $4.86, Cannan fully recognized that the return to gold would require considerable deflation, and that the needed reduction in wage rates would cause extensive difficulty and unemployment in view of the new system of widespread unemployment insurance which made the unemployed far "more comfortable than they used to be." The only thing to be done, counseled Cannan, was to return to gold immediately at $4.86, and get it over with. As Cannan wrote at the time, the necessary adjustments "must be regarded in the same light as those which a spendthrift or a drunkard is rightly exhorted by his friends to face like a man." Ibid., pp. 45–46; Edwin Cannan, *The Paper Pound: 1797–1821*, 2nd ed. (London: P.S. King, 1925), p. 105, cited in Murray Milgate, "Cannan, Edwin," in *The New Palgrave: A Dictionary of Economics*, Peter Newman, Murray Milgate, and John Eatwell, eds. (New York: Stockton Press, 1987), 1, p. 316.

Cannan's sentiment and passion for justice are admirable, but, in view of the antagonistic political climate of the day, it might have been the better part of valor to return to gold at a realistic, depreciated pound.

[20]Moggridge, *British Monetary Policy*, p. 72.

April 28, and putting the new gold standard into effect immediately.[21]

It cannot be stressed too strongly that the British decision to return to gold at $4.86 was not made in ignorance of deflationary problems or export depression, but rather in the strong and confident expectation of imminent American inflation. This dominant expectation was clear from the assurances of Sir John Bradbury to Churchill; from the anticipation of even such cautious men as Sir Otto Niemeyer and Montagu Norman; from the optimism of Ralph Hawtrey; and above all in the official Treasury memorandum attached to the Gold Standard Act of 1925.[22, 23]

[21]Actually, the old Gold Embargo Act remained in force until allowed to expire on December 31, 1925. Since gold exports were prohibited until then, the gold standard was really not fully restored until the end of the year. Palyi, *Twilight of Gold,* p. 71. The Churchill dinner party included Prime Minister Stanley Baldwin, Foreign Secretary Austen Chamberlain, Keynes, McKenna, Niemeyer, Bradbury, and Sir Percy Grigg, principal private secretary to the chancellor of the Exchequer. Sir Percy James Grigg, *Prejudice and Judgment* (London: Hutchinson, 1948), pp. 182–84. On Churchill's early leaning to Keynes, see Moggridge, *British Monetary Policy,* p. 76.

[22]Moggridge, *British Monetary Policy,* pp. 84ff.

[23]In a memorandum to Churchill, Sir Otto Niemeyer delivered an eloquent critique of the Keynesian view that inflation would serve as a cure for the existing unemployment. Niemeyer declared:

> You can by inflation (a most vicious form of subsidy) enable temporary spending power to cope with large quantities of products. But unless you increase the dose continually there comes a time when having destroyed the credit of the country you can inflate no more, money having ceased to be acceptable as a value. Even before this, as your inflated spending creates demand, you have had claims for increased wages, strikes, lockouts, etc. I assume it will be admitted that with Germany and Russia before us [that is, runaway inflation] we do not think plenty can be found on this path.

Niemeyer concluded that employment can only be provided by thrift and accumulation of capital, facilitated by a stable currency, and not by doles

American Support for the Return to Gold at $4.86: The Morgan Connection

Why were the British so confident that American prices would rise sufficiently to support their return to gold at the overinflated $4.86? Because of the power of the new United States central bank, the Federal Reserve System, installed in 1914, and because of the close and friendly relationship between the British government, its Bank of England, and the Federal Reserve. The Fed, they were sure, would do what was necessary to help Britain reconstruct the world monetary order.

To understand these expectations, we must explore the Federal Reserve–Bank of England connection, and particularly the crucial tie that bound them together: their mutual relationship with the House of Morgan. The powerful J.P. Morgan and Company took the lead in planning, drafting the legislation, and mobilizing the agitation for the Federal Reserve System that brought the dubious benefits of central banking to the United States in 1914. The purpose of the Federal Reserve was to cartelize the nation's banking system, and to enable the banks to inflate together, centralizing and economizing reserves, with the Federal Reserve as "lender of last resort." The Federal Reserve's new monopoly of note issue took the de facto place of gold as the nation's currency. Not only were the majority of Federal Reserve Board directors in the Morgan orbit, but the man who was able to become the virtually absolute ruler of the Fed from its inception to his death in 1928, Benjamin Strong, was a man who had spent his entire working life as a leading Morgan banker.[24]

Benjamin Strong was a protégé of the most powerful of the partners of the House of Morgan after Morgan himself, Henry

---

and palliatives. Unfortunately, Niemeyer neglected to consider the crucial role of excessively high wage rates in causing unemployment. Ibid., p. 77.

[24]See Murray N. Rothbard, "The Federal Reserve as a Cartelization Device: The Early Years, 1913–1930," in *Money in Crisis*, Barry Siegel, ed. (San Francisco: Pacific Institute for Public Policy, 1984), pp. 93–117.

"Harry" Pomeroy Davison. Strong was also a neighbor and close friend of Davison and of two other top Morgan partners in the then-wealthy New York suburb of Englewood, New Jersey, Dwight Morrow and Thomas W. Lamont. In 1904, Davison offered Strong the post of secretary of the new Morgan-created Bankers Trust Company, designed to compete in the burgeoning trust business. So close were Davison and Strong that, when Strong's wife committed suicide after childbirth, Davison took the three surviving Strong children into his home. Strong later married the daughter of the president of Bankers Trust, and rose quickly to the posts of vice president and finally president. So highly trusted was Strong in the Morgan circle that he was brought in to be J. Pierpont Morgan's personal auditor during the panic of 1907. When Strong was offered the crucial post of governor of the New York Fed in the new Federal Reserve System, Strong, at first reluctant, was convinced by Davison that he could run the Fed as "a real central bank . . . run from New York."[25]

The House of Morgan had always enjoyed strong connections with England. The original Morgan banker, J. Pierpont Morgan's father Junius, had been a banker in England; and the Morgan's London branch, Morgan, Grenfell and Company, was headed by the powerful Edward C. "Teddy" Grenfell (later Lord St. Just). Grenfell's father and grandfather had both been directors of the Bank of England as well as members of Parliament, and Grenfell himself had become a director of the Bank of England in 1904. Assisting Grenfell as leading partner at Morgan, Grenfell was Teddy's cousin, Vivian Hugh Smith, later Lord Bicester, a personal friend of J.P. Morgan, Jr.'s. Not only

[25]Rothbard, "Federal Reserve," p. 109; Lester V. Chandler, *Benjamin Strong, Central Banker* (Washington, D.C.: Brookings Institution, 1958), pp. 23–41; Ron Chernow, *The House of Morgan: An American Banking Dynasty and the Rise of Modern Finance* (New York: Atlantic Monthly Press, 1990), pp. 142–45, 182; and Lawrence E. Clark, *Central Banking Under the Federal Reserve System* (New York: Macmillan, 1935), pp. 64–82.

was Smith's father a governor of the Bank of England, but he came from the so-called "City Smiths," the most prolific banking family in English history, originating in seventeenth-century banking. Due to the good offices of Grenfell and Smith, J.P. Morgan and Company, before the war, had been named a fiscal agent of the English Treasury and of the Bank of England. In addition, the House of Morgan had long been closely associated with British and French wars, its London branch having helped England finance the Boer, and its French bank the Franco-Prussian War of 1870–1871.[26]

As soon as war in Europe began, Harry Davison rushed to England and got the House of Morgan a magnificent deal: Morgan was made the monopoly purchaser of all goods and supplies for the British and French in the United States for the duration of the war. In this coup, Davison was aided and abetted by the British ambassador to Washington, Sir Cecil Arthur Spring-Rice, a personal friend of J.P. Morgan, Jr. These war-based purchases eventually amounted to an astronomical $3 billion, out of which the House of Morgan was able to earn a direct commission of $30 million. In addition, the House of Morgan was able to steer profitable British and French war contracts to those firms which it dominated, such as General Electric, DuPont, Bethlehem Steel, and United States Steel, or to those firms with which it was closely allied, such as DuPont Company and the Guggenheims' huge copper companies, Kennecott and American Smelting and Refining.

To pay for these massive purchases, Britain and France were obliged to float huge bond issues in the United States, and they made the Morgans virtually the sole underwriter for these bonds. Thus, the Morgans benefited heavily once more: from the bond issues, as well as from the fees and contracts from war purchases by the Allies.

[26]France also appointed the House of Morgan as its fiscal agent, having long had close connections through the Paris branch, Morgan Harjes. Chernow, *House of Morgan*, pp. 104–05, 186, 195. Sir Henry Clay, *Lord Norman* (London: Macmillan, 1957), p. 87.

In this way, the House of Morgan, which had been suffering financially before the outbreak of war, profited greatly from and was deeply committed to, the British and French cause. It is no wonder that the Morgans did their powerful best to maneuver the United States into World War I on the side of the English and French.

After the United States entered the war in the spring of 1917, Benjamin Strong, as head of the Fed, obligingly doubled the money supply to finance the war effort, and the U.S. government took over the task of financing the Allies.[27] Strong was able to take power in the Fed with the help of and close cooperation from Secretary of the Treasury William Gibbs McAdoo after U.S. entry into the war. McAdoo, for the first time, made the Fed the sole fiscal agent for the Treasury, abandoning the Independent Treasury System that had required it to deposit and disburse funds only from its own subtreasury vaults. The New York Fed sold nearly half of all Treasury securities offered during the war; it handled most of the Treasury's foreign exchange business, and acted as a central depository of funds from other Federal Reserve banks. Because of this Treasury support, Strong and the New York Fed emerged from the U.S. experience in World War I as the dominant force in American finance. McAdoo himself came to Washington as secretary of the Treasury after having been befriended and bailed out of his business losses by J.P. Morgan, Jr., personally, and by Morgan's closest associates.[28]

[27]On the interconnections among the Morgans, the Allies, foreign loans, and the Federal Reserve, and on the role of the Morgans in bringing the United States into the war, see Charles C. Tansill, *America Goes to War* (Boston: Little, Brown, 1938), pp. 32–143. See also Chernow, *House of Morgan*, pp, 186–204. It is instructive that the British exempted the House of Morgan from its otherwise extensive mail censorship in and out of Britain, granting J.P. Morgan, Jr., and his key partners special code names. Ibid., pp. 189–90.

[28]Rothbard, "Federal Reserve," pp. 107–08, 111–12; Henry Parker Willis, *The Theory and Practice of Central Banking* (New York: Harper and

Scarcely had Benjamin Strong been appointed when he began to move strongly toward "international central bank cooperation," a euphemism for coordinated, or cartelized, inflation, since the classical gold standard had no need for such cooperation. In February 1916, Strong sailed to England and worked out an agreement of close collaboration between the New York Fed and the Bank of England, with both central banks maintaining an account with each other, and the Bank of England regularly purchasing sterling bills on account for the New York bank. In his usual high-handed manner, Strong bluntly told the Federal Reserve Board in Washington that he would go ahead with such an agreement with or without board approval; the cowed Federal Reserve Board then finally decided to endorse the scheme. A similar agreement was made with the Bank of France.[29]

Brothers, 1936), pp. 90–91; and Chandler, *Benjamin Strong*, p. 105. The massive U.S. deficits to pay for the war, were financed by Liberty Bond drives headed by a Wall Street lawyer who was a neighbor of McAdoo's in Yonkers, New York. This man, Russell C. Leffingwell, would become a leading Morgan partner after the war. Chernow, *House of Morgan*, p. 203.

[29]Rothbard, "The Federal Reserve," p. 114; Chandler, *Benjamin Strong*, pp. 93–98. While some members of the Federal Reserve Board had heavy Morgan connections, its complexion was scarcely as Morgan-dominated as Benjamin Strong. Of the five Federal Reserve Board members, Paul M. Warburg was a leading partner of Kuhn, Loeb, an investment bank rival of Morgan, and during the war suspected of being pro-German; Governor William P.G. Harding was an Alabama banker whose father-in-law's iron manufacturing company had prominent Morgan as well as rival Rockefeller men on its board; Frederic A. Delano, uncle of Franklin D. Roosevelt, was president of the Rockefeller-controlled Wabash Railway; Charles S. Hamlin, an assistant secretary to McAdoo, was a Boston attorney married into a family long connected with the Morgan-dominated New York Central Railroad and an assistant secretary to McAdoo. Finally, economist Adolph C. Miller, professor at Berkeley, had married into the wealthy, Morgan-connected Sprague family of Chicago. At that period, Secretary of Treasury McAdoo and his longtime associate, John Skelton Williams, comptroller of the currency, were automatically

Strong made his agreement with the governor of the Bank of England, Lord Cunliffe, but his most fateful meeting was with the man who was then the bank's deputy governor, Montagu Norman. This meeting proved to be the beginning of the momentous Strong-Norman close friendship and collaboration that was a dominant feature of the international financial world in 1920. Norman became governor of the Bank of England in 1920 and the two men continued their momentous collaboration until Strong's death in 1928.

Montagu Collet Norman was born to banking on both sides of his family. His father was a banker and related to the great banking family of Barings, while his uncle was a partner of Baring Brothers. Norman's mother was the daughter of Mark W. Collet, a partner in the London banking firm of Brown, Shipley and Company, the London branch of the great Wall Street banking firm of Brown Brothers. Collet's father had been governor of the Bank of England in the 1880s. As a young man, Montagu Norman began working at his father's bank, and then at Brown, Shipley; in the late 1890s, Norman worked for three years at the New York office of Brown Brothers, making many Wall Street banking connections, and then he returned to London to become a partner of Brown, Shipley.

Intensely secretive, Montagu Norman habitually gave the appearance, in the words of an admiring biographer, "of being engaged in a perpetual conspiracy." A lifelong bachelor, he declared that "the Bank of England is my sole mistress, I think

---

Federal Reserve Board members, but only ex officio. Thus, setting aside the two ex officio members, the Federal Reserve Board began its existence with one Kuhn, Loeb member, one Morgan man, one Rockefeller person, a prominent Alabama banker with both Morgan and Rockefeller connections, and an economist with family ties to Morgan interests. When we realize that the Rockefeller and Kuhn, Loeb interests were allied during this era, we can see that the Federal Reserve Board scarcely could be considered under firm Morgan control. Rothbard, "The Federal Reserve," p. 108.

only of her, and I've dedicated my life to her."[30] Two of Norman's oldest and closest friends were the two main directors of Morgan, Grenfell: Teddy Grenfell and particularly Vivian Hugh Smith. Smith had buoyed Norman's confidence when the latter had been reluctant to become a director of the Bank of England in 1907; more particularly, one of Norman's best friends was the vivacious and high-spirited wife of Vivian, Lady Sybil. Norman would disappear for long, platonic weekends with Lady Sybil, who inducted him into the mysteries of theosophy and the occult, and Norman became a godfather to the numerous Smith children.

Strong, who had been divorced by his second wife, and Norman, formed a close friendship that lasted until Strong's death. They would engage in long vacations together, registering under assumed names, sometimes at Bar Harbor or Saratoga but more often in southern France. The pair would, in addition, visit each other at length, and also write a steady stream of correspondence, personal as well as financial.

While the close personal relations between Strong and Norman were of course highly important for the collaboration that formed the international monetary world of the 1920s, it should not be overlooked that both were intimately bound to the House of Morgan. "Monty Norman," writes a historian of the Morgans, "was a natural denizen of the secretive Morgan world." He continues:

> The House of Morgan formed an indispensable part of Norman's strategy for reordering European economies. . . . Imperial to the core, he [Norman] wanted to preserve London as a financial center and the bank [of England] as arbiter of the world monetary system. Aided by the House of Morgan, he would manage to exercise a power in the 1920s that far outstripped the meager capital at his disposal.

[30]Clay, *Lord Norman*, p. 487; and Andrew Boyle, *Montagu Norman* (London: Cassell, 1967), p. 198.

As for Benjamin Strong, he

> was solidly in the Morgan mold. . . . Hobbled by a regulation that he couldn't lend directly to foreign governments, Strong needed a private bank as his funding vehicle. He turned to the House of Morgan, which benefited incalculably from his patronage. In fact, the Morgan-Strong friendship would mock any notion of the new Federal Reserve System as a curb on private banking power.[31]

Let us now turn specifically to the aid that Benjamin Strong delivered to Great Britain to permit its return to gold at $4.86 in 1925. A key as we have seen, to permit Britain to inflate rather than declare, was to induce the United States to inflate dollars so as to keep it from losing gold to the U.S. Before the return to gold, the United States was supposed to inflate so as to persuade the exchange markets that $4.86 would be viable and thereby lift the pound from its postwar depreciated state to the $4.86 figure.

Benjamin Strong and the Fed began their postwar inflationary policy from November 1921 until June 1922, when the Fed tripled its holdings of U.S. government securities and happily discovered the expansion of reserves and inflation of the money supply. Fed authorities hailed the inflation as helping to get the nation out of the 1920–21 recession, and Montagu Norman lauded the easy credit in the U.S. and urged upon Strong a further inflationary fall in interest rates.[32]

[31]Chernow, *House of Morgan*, pp. 246, 244.

[32]Too much has been made of the fact that this discovery of the inflationary power of open market purchases by the Fed was the accidental result of a desire to increase Fed earnings. The result was not *wholly* unexpected. Thus, Strong, in April 1922, wrote to Undersecretary of the Treasury S. Parker Gilbert that one of his major reasons for these open market purchases was "to establish a level of interest rates . . . which would facilitate foreign borrowing in this country . . . and facilitate business improvement." Strong to Gilbert, April 18, 1922. Gilbert went on to become a leading partner of the House of Morgan. See Murray N. Rothbard,

During 1922 and 1923, Norman continued to pepper Strong with pleas to inflate the dollar further, but Strong resisted these blandishments for a time. Instead of rising further toward $4.86, the pound began to fall in the foreign exchange markets in response to Britain's inflationary policies, the pound slipping to $4.44 and reaching $4.34 by mid-1924. Since Strong was ill through much of 1923, the Federal Reserve Board was able to take command during his absence, and to sell off most of the Fed's holdings of government securities. Strong returned to his desk in November, however, and by January his rescue of Norman and of British inflationary policy was under way. During 1924 the Fed purchased nearly $500 million in government securities, driving up the U.S. money supply by 8.3 percent during that year.[33]

Benjamin Strong outlined the reasoning for his inflationary policy in the spring of 1924 to other high U.S. officials. To New York Fed official Pierre Jay, he explained that it was in the U.S. interest to facilitate Britain's earliest possible return to the gold standard, and that in order to do so, the U.S. had to inflate, so that its prices were a bit higher than England's, and its interest rates a bit lower. At the proper moment, credit inflation, "secret at first," would only be made public, "when the pound is fairly close to par." To Secretary of the Treasury Andrew Mellon, Strong explained that in order to enable Britain to return to gold, the U.S. would have to bring about a "gradual readjustment" of price levels so as to raise U.S. prices relative to Britain. The higher U.S. prices, added Strong, "can be facilitated by cooperation between the Bank of England and the Federal

---

America's Great Depression, 4th ed. (New York: Richardson and Snyder, [1963] 1983), p. 321, n. 2. See also ibid., pp. 123–24, 135; Chandler, *Benjamin Strong*, pp. 210–11; and Harold L. Reed, *Federal Reserve Policy, 1921–1930* (New York: McGraw-Hill, 1930), pp. 14–41.

[33]In terms of currency plus total adjusted deposits. If savings and loan shares are added, the money supply rose by 9 percent during 1924. Rothbard, *America's Great Depression*, pp. 88, 102–05.

Reserve System in the maintaining of lower interest rates in this country and higher interest rates in England." Strong declared that "the burden of this readjustment must fall more largely upon us than upon them." Why? Because

> it will be difficult politically and socially for the British government and the Bank of England to force a price liquidation in England beyond what they have already experienced in face of the fact that their trade is poor and they have a million unemployed people receiving government aid.[34]

Or, to put it in blunter terms, the American people would have to pay the penalties of inflation in order to enable the British to pursue a self-contradictory policy of returning to gold at an overvalued pound, while continuing an inflationary policy, so that they would not have to confront the consequences of their own actions, including the system of massive unemployment insurance.

Moreover, to ease the British return to gold, the New York Fed extended a line of credit for gold of $200 million to the Bank of England in early January 1925, bolstered by a similar $100 million line of credit by J.P. Morgan and Company to the British government, a credit instigated by Strong and guaranteed by the Federal Reserve. It must be added that these large $300 million credits were warmly approved by Secretary Mellon and unanimously approved by the Federal Reserve Board.[35]

American monetary inflation, backed by the heavy line of credit to Britain, temporarily accomplished its goal. American interest rates were down by 1.5 percent by the autumn of 1924, and these interest rates were now below those in Britain. The

[34]Strong to Pierre Jay, April 23 and April 28, 1924. Strong to Andrew Mellon, May 27, 1924. Moggridge, *British Monetary Policy*, pp. 51–53; Rothbard, *America's Great Depression*, pp. 133–34; Chandler, *Benjamin Strong*, pp. 283–84, 293ff.

[35]Rothbard, *America's Great Depression*, p. 133; Chandler, *Benjamin Strong*, pp. 284, 308ff., 312ff.; and Moggridge, *British Monetary Policy*, pp. 60–62.

inflow of gold from Britain was temporarily checked. As Lionel Robbins explained in mid-1924:

> Matters took a decisive turn. American prices began to rise. . . . In the foreign exchange markets a return to gold at the old parity was anticipated. The sterling-dollar exchange appreciated from $4.34 to $4.78. In the spring of 1925, therefore, it was thought that the adjustment between sterling and gold prices was sufficiently close to warrant a resumption of gold payments at the old parity.[36]

Just as Montagu Norman was the master manipulator in England, he himself was being manipulated by the Morgans, in what has been called "their holy cause" of returning England to gold. Teddy Grenfell was the Morgan manipulator in London, writing Morgan that "as I have explained to you before, our dear friend Monty works in his own peculiar way. He is masterful and very secretive." In late 1924, when Norman got worried about the coming return to gold, he sailed to New York to have his confidence bolstered by Strong and J.P. Morgan, Jr. "Jack" Morgan gave Norman a pep talk, saying that if Britain faltered on returning to gold, "centuries of goodwill and moral authority would have been squandered."[37]

It should not be thought that Benjamin Strong was the only natural ally of the Morgans in the administrations of the 1920s. Andrew Mellon, the powerful tycoon and head of the Mellon interests, whose empire spread from the Mellon National Bank of Pittsburgh to encompass Gulf Oil, Koppers Company, and ALCOA, was generally allied to the Morgan interests. Mellon was secretary of the Treasury for the entire decade. Although there were various groups around President Warren Harding, as

[36]Robbins, *Great Depression*, p. 80; Rothbard, *America's Great Depression*, p. 133; and Benjamin H. Beckhard, "Federal Reserve Policy and the Money Market, 1923–1931," in *The New York Money Market*, Beckhart, et al. (New York: Columbia University Press, 1931), 4, p. 45.

[37]Grenfell to J.P. Morgan, Jr., March 23, 1925; Chernow, *House of Morgan*, pp. 274–75.

an Ohio Republican, he was closest to the Rockefellers, and his secretary of state, Charles Evans Hughes, was a leading Standard Oil attorney and a trustee of the Rockefeller Foundation.[38] Harding's sudden death in August 1923, however, elevated Vice President Calvin Coolidge to the presidency.

Coolidge has been misleadingly described as a colorless small-town Massachusetts attorney. Actually, the new president was a member of a prominent Boston financial family, who were board members of leading Boston banks, and one, T. Jefferson Coolidge, became prominent in the Morgan-affiliated United Fruit Company of Boston. Throughout his political career, furthermore, Coolidge had two important mentors, neglected by historians. One was Massachusetts Republican chairman W. Murray Crane, who served as a director of three powerful Morgan-dominated institutions: the New Haven and Hartford Railroad, AT&T, and the Guaranty Trust Company of New York. He was also a member of the executive committee of the board of AT&T. The other was Amherst classmate and Morgan partner Dwight Morrow. Morrow began to agitate for Coolidge for president in 1919, and at the Chicago Republican convention of 1920, Dwight Morrow and fellow Morgan partner Thomas Cochran lobbied strenuously, though discreetly behind the scenes, for Coolidge, allowing fellow Amherst graduate and Boston merchant Frank W. Stearns to take the foreground.[39]

[38]Hughes was both attorney and chief foreign policy adviser to Rockefellers' Standard Oil of New Jersey. On Hughes's close ties to the Rockefeller complex and their being overlooked even by Hughes's biographers, see the important but neglected article by Thomas Ferguson, "From Normalcy to New Deal: Industrial Structure, Party Competition, and American Public Policy in the Great Depression," *International Organization* 38 (Winter 1984): 67.

[39]"Morrow and Thomas Cochran, although moving spirits in the whole drive, remained in the background. The foreground was filled by the large, the devoted, the imperturbable figure of Frank Stearns." Harold Nicolson, *Dwight Morrow* (New York: Harcourt, Brace, 1935), p. 232. Cochran, a leading Morgan partner, and board member of Bankers

Furthermore, when Secretary of State Charles Evans Hughes returned to private law practice in the spring of 1925, Coolidge offered his post to then-veteran Wall Street attorney and former Secretary of State and of War Elihu Root, who might be called the veteran leader of the "Morgan bar." Root was at one critical time in Morgan affairs, J.P. Morgan, Sr.'s, personal attorney. After Root refused the secretary of state position, Coolidge was forced to settle for a lesser Morgan light, Minnesota attorney Frank B. Kellogg.[40] Undersecretary of state to Kellogg was Joseph C. Grew, who had family connections with the Morgans (J.P. Morgan, Jr., had married a Grew), while, in 1927, two highly placed Morgan men were asked to take over relations with troubled Mexico and Nicaragua.[41]

The year 1924 saw the Morgans at the pinnacle of their political power in the United States. President Calvin Coolidge, friend and protégé of Morgan partner Dwight Morrow, was deeply admired by Jack Morgan, who saw the president as a rare blend of deep thinker and moralist. Morgan wrote a friend: "I have never seen any President who gives me just the feeling of confidence in the Country and its

---

Trust Company, Chase Securities Corporation, and Texas Gulf Sulphur Company, was, by the way, a Midwesterner and not an Amherst graduate and therefore had no reasons of friendship to work strongly for Coolidge. Stearns, incidentally, had not met Coolidge before being introduced to him by Morrow. Philip H. Burch, Jr., *Elites in American History*, vol. 2, *The Civil War to the New Deal* (New York Holmes and Meier, 1981), pp. 274–75, 302–03.

[40]In addition to being a director of the Merchants National Bank of St. Paul, Kellogg had been general counsel for the Morgan-dominated U.S. Steel Corporation for the Minnesota region, and most importantly, the top lawyer for the railroad magnate James J. Hill, long closely allied with Morgan interests.

[41]Morgan partner Dwight Morrow became ambassador to Mexico that year, and Nicaraguan affairs came under the direction of Henry L. Stimson, Wall Street lawyer and longtime leading disciple of Elihu Root, and a partner in Root's law firm. Burch, *Elites*, pp. 277, 305.

institutions, and the working out of our problems, that Mr. Coolidge does."

On the other hand, the Democratic presidential candidate that year was none other than John W. Davis, senior partner of the Wall Street law firm of Davis Polk and Wardwell, and the chief attorney for J.P. Morgan and Company. Davis, a protégé of the legendary Harry Davison, was also a personal friend and backgammon and cribbage partner of Jack Morgan's. Whoever won the 1924 election, the Morgans couldn't lose.[42]

The Establishment of the New Gold Standard of the 1920s

Bullion, Not Coin

One of the reasons the British were optimistic that they could succeed in their basic maneuver in the 1920s is that they were not really going back to the gold standard at all. They were attempting to clothe themselves in the prestige of gold while trying to avoid its anti-inflationary discipline. They went back, not to the classical gold standard, but to a bowdlerized and essentially sham version of that venerable standard.

In the first place, under the old gold standard, the nominal currency, whether issued by government or bank, was redeemable in gold coin at the defined weight. The fact that people were able to redeem in and use gold for their daily transactions kept a strict check on the overissue of paper. But in the new gold standard, British pounds would not be redeemable in gold coin at all: only in "bullion" in the form of bars worth many thousands of pounds. Such a gold standard meant that gold could not be redeemed domestically at all; bars could hardly circulate for daily transactions, so that they could only be used by wealthy international traders.

[42]Chernow, *House of Morgan*, pp. 254–55.

The decision of the British Cabinet on March 20, 1925, to go back to gold was explicitly predicated on three conditions. First was the attainment of a $300 million credit line from the United States. Second was that the bank rate would not increase upon announcement of the decision, so that there would be no contractionary or anti-inflationary pressure exercised by the Bank of England. And third and perhaps most important was that the new standard would be gold bullion and not gold coin. The chancellor of the Exchequer would persuade the large "clearing banks" to "use every effort . . . to discourage the use of gold for internal circulation in this country." The bankers were warned that if they could not provide satisfactory assurances that they would not redeem in gold coin, "it would be necessary to introduce legislation on this point." The Treasury, in short, wanted to avoid "psychologically unfortunate and controversial legislation" barring gold redemption within the country, but at the same time wanted to guard against the risk of "internal drain" (that is, redemption in the property to which they were entitled) from foreign agents, the irresponsible public, or "sound currency fanatics."[43] The bankers, headed by Reginald McKenna, were of course delighted not to have to redeem in gold, but wanted legislation to formalize this desired condition.

Finally, the government and the bankers agreed happily on the following: the bankers would not hold gold, or acquire gold coins or bullion for themselves, or for any customers residing in the United Kingdom. The Treasury, for its part, redrafted its banking report to allow for legislation to prevent any internal redemption if necessary, and "enforce" such a ban on the all-too-willing bankers.

Under the Gold Standard Act of 1925, then, pounds were convertible into gold, not in coin, but in bars of no less than 400 gold ounces, that is $1,947. The new gold standard was not even a full gold bullion standard, since there was to be no redemption

[43]The latter phrase is in a letter from Sir Otto Niemeyer to Winston Churchill, February 25, 1925. Moggridge, *British Monetary Policy*, p. 83.

at all in gold to British residents; gold bullion was only due to pound-holders outside Great Britain. Britain was now only on an "international gold bullion standard."[44]

The purpose of redemption in gold bullion only, and only to foreigners, was to take control of the money supply away from the public, and place it in the hands of the governments and central bankers, permitting them to pyramid monetary inflation upon gold centralized into their hands. Thus, Norman, when asked by the governor of the Bank of Norway for his advice about returning to gold, urged Norway to return only in gold bars, and only for international payments. Norman's reasoning is revealing:

> [I]n Norway the convenience of paper currency is appreciated, and confidence in the value of money does not depend upon the existence of gold coin. . . . Demand is rendered more inelastic wherever the principle of gold circulation, for currency or for hoarding, is accepted, and any inelasticity may be dangerous. . . . I do not believe that gold in circulation can safely be regarded as a reserve that can be made available in case of need, and I think that even in times of abundance hoarding is bad, because it weakens the command of the Central Bank over the monetary circulation and hence over the purchasing power of the monetary unit.
>
> For these reasons, I suggest that your best course would be to establish convertibility of notes into gold bars only and in amounts which will ensure that the use of monetary gold can be limited, in case of need, to the settlement of international balances.[45, 46]

[44]Ibid., pp. 79–83.

[45]Clay, *Lord Norman*, pp. 153–54; and Palyi, *Twilight of Gold*, pp. 121–23.

[46]Contrast to Norman these insights of pro-gold-coin-standard economist Walter Spahr:

> A gold-coin standard provides the people with direct control over the government's use and abuse of the public purse. . . . When governments or banks issue money or other promises to pay in a manner that raises doubts as to their

Norway, and indeed all the countries returning to gold, heeded Norman's advice. The way was paved for this development by the fact that, during World War I, the European countries had systematically taken gold coins out of circulation and replaced them with paper notes and deposits. During the 1920s, virtually the only country still on the classical gold-coin standard was the United States.

Despite this tradition, it was still necessary for Monty Norman and the Bank of England to exert considerable pressure to force many European nations to return to gold bullion rather than gold coin. Thus, Dr. William Adams Brown, Jr., writes:

> In some countries the reluctance to adopt the gold bullion standard was so great that some outside pressure was needed to overcome it . . . [that is] strong representations on the part of the Bank of England that such action would be a contribution to the general success of the stabilization effort as a whole. Without the informal pressure . . . several efforts to return in one step to the full gold standard would undoubtedly have been made.[47]

The Gold-Exchange Standard, Not Gold

The major twist, the major deformation of a genuine gold standard perpetrated by the British in the 1920s, was not the gold bullion standard, unfortunate though that was. The major

---

> value as compared with gold, those people entertaining such doubts will demand gold in lieu of . . . paper money, or bank deposits. . . . The gold-coin standard thus places in the hands of every individual who uses money some power to express his approval or disapproval of the government's management of the people's monetary and fiscal affairs. (Walter E. Spahr, *Monetary Notes* [December 1, 1947], p. 5, cited in Palyi, *Twilight of Gold*, p. 122)

[47]Williams Adams Brown, Jr., *The International Gold Standard Reinterpreted, 1914–1934* (New York: National Bureau of Economic Research, 1940), 1, p. 355.

inflationary camouflage was to return, not to a gold standard at all, but to a "gold-exchange" standard. In a gold-exchange standard, only one country, in this case Great Britain, is on a gold standard in the sense that its currency is actually redeemable in gold, albeit only gold bullion for foreigners. All other European countries, even though nominally on a gold standard, were actually on a pound-sterling standard. In short, a typical European country, say, "Ruritania," would hold as reserves for its currency, not gold but British pounds sterling, in practice, bills or deposits payable in sterling at London. Anyone who demanded redemption for Ruritanian "rurs," then, would receive British pounds rather than gold.

The gold-exchange standard, then, cunningly broke the classical gold standard's stringent limits on monetary and credit expansion, not only for the other European countries, but also for the base or key currency country, Great Britain itself. Under the genuine gold standard, inflating the number of pounds in circulation would cause pounds to flow into the hands of other countries, which would demand gold in redemption. Thereby gold would move out of British bank and currency reserves, and pressure would be put on Britain to end its inflation and to contract credit. But, under the gold-exchange standard, the process was very different. If Britain inflated the number of pounds in circulation, the result, again, was a deficit in the balance of trade and sterling balances piling up in the accounts of other nations. But now that these nations have been induced to use pounds as their reserves rather than gold, these nations, instead of redeeming the pounds in gold, would inflate, and pyramid a multiple of their currency on top of their increased stock of pounds. Thus, instead of checking inflation, a gold-exchange standard encourages all countries to inflate on top of their increased supply of pounds. Britain, too, is now able to "export" her inflation to other nations without paying a price. Thus, in the name of sound money and a check against inflation, a pseudo gold standard was instituted, designed to induce a double-inverted pyramid of inflation, all on top of British pounds, the whole process supported by a gold stock that does not dwindle.

Since all other countries were sucked into the inflationary gold-exchange trap, it seemed that the only nation Britain had to worry about was the United States, the only country to continue on a genuine gold standard. That was the reason it became so vitally important for Britain to get the United States, through the Morgan connection, to go along with this system and to inflate, so that Britain would not lose gold to the United States.

For the other nations of Europe, it became an object of British pressure and maneuvering to induce these countries themselves to return to a gold standard, with several vital provisions: (a) that *their* currencies too be overvalued, so that British exports would not suffer, and British imports would not be overstimulated—in other words, so that *they* join Britain in overvaluing their currencies; (b) that each of these countries adopt their own central bank, with the help of Britain, which would inflate their currencies in collaboration with the Bank of England; and (c) that they return, not to a genuine gold standard, but to a gold-exchange standard, keeping their balances in London and refraining from exercising their legal right to redeem those sterling balances in gold.

In this way, for a few years Britain could have its cake and eat it too. It could enjoy the prestige of going back to gold, going back at a highly overvalued pound, and yet continue to pursue an inflationary, cheap-money policy instead of the opposite. It could inflate pounds and see other countries keep their sterling balances and inflate on top of them; it could induce other countries to go back to gold at overvalued currencies and to inflate their money supplies;[48] and it could also try to prop up its flagging

[48]When the gold-exchange standard broke down in 1931, the economist H. Parker Willis noted that "the ease with which the gold-exchange standard can be instituted, especially with borrowed money, has led a good many nations during the past decade to 'stabilize' . . . at too high a rate." H. Parker Willis, "The Breakdown of the Gold Exchange Standard and its Financial Imperialism," *The Annalist* (October 16, 1931): 626ff.

exports by using cheap credit to lend money to European nations so that they could purchase British goods.

Not that *every* country was supposed to return to gold at the overvalued, prewar par. The rule of thumb imposed in the 1920s was that (a) currencies, such as that of Britain herself, that had depreciated up to 60 percent from prewar (for example, the Netherlands and the Scandinavian countries) would return at the prewar par; (b) currencies that had depreciated from 60 to 90 percent were to return to gold within that zone, but at a rate substantially above their lowest rate (for example, Belgium, Italy, Czechoslovakia, and France). The French franc, which had depreciated to 240 to the pound due to massive inflation, returned to gold at the doubled rate of 124 to the pound. And (c) only those currencies that had been wiped out by devastating hyperinflation, like Austria, Bulgaria, and especially Germany, were allowed to return to gold at a realistic rate, and even they were stabilized at a little bit above their lowest point. As a result, virtually every European currency suffered from the requirement to raise the value of its currency artificially above its depreciated level.[49]

The gold-exchange standard was not created *de novo* by Great Britain in the interwar period. It is true that a number of European central banks before 1914 had held foreign exchange reserves in addition to gold, but these were strictly limited, and they were held as earning assets—these after all were privately owned central banks in need of earnings—not as instruments of monetary manipulation. But in a few cases, particularly where the pyramiding countries were from the Third World, they did function as a gold-exchange standard: that is, the Third World currency pyramided its currency on top of a key country's reserves (pounds or dollars) instead of on gold. This system began in India, after the late 1870s, as a historical accident. The plan of the British imperial center was to shift India which, like

[49]Palyi, *Twilight of Gold*, pp. 73–74. See also p. 185.

many Third World countries, had been on a silver standard, onto a seemingly sounder gold, following the imperial nations. India's reserves in pound sterling balances in London were supposed to be only a temporary transition to gold. But, as in so many cases of seeming transition, the Indian gold-exchange standard lingered on, and received great praise for its modern inflationary potential from John Maynard Keynes, then in his first economic post at the India Office. It was Keynes, after leaving the India Office and going to Cambridge, who trumpeted the new form of monetary system as a "limping" or imperfect gold standard but as a "more scientific and economic system," which he dubbed the gold-exchange standard. As Keynes wrote in February 1910, "it is cheaper to maintain a credit at one of the great financial centres of the world, which can be converted with great readiness to gold when it is required." In a paper delivered the following year to the Royal Economic Society, Keynes proclaimed that out of this new system would evolve "the ideal currency of the future."

Elaborating his views into his first book, *Indian Currency and Finance* (London, 1913), Keynes emphasized that the gold-exchange standard was a notable advance because it "economized" on gold internally and internationally, thus allowing greater "elasticity" of money (a longtime code word for ability to inflate credit) in response to business needs. Looking beyond India, Keynes prophetically foresaw the traditional gold standard as giving way to a more "scientific" system based on one or two key reserve centers. "A preference for a tangible reserve currency," Keynes declared blithely, "is . . . a relic of a time when governments were less trustworthy in these matters than they are now."[50] He also believed that Britain was the natural center of the

[50]Robert Skidelsky, *John Maynard Keynes*, vol. 1, *1883–1920* (New York: Viking Press, 1986), p. 275. See also ibid., pp 272–74; and Palyi, *Twilight of Gold*, pp. 155–57. While Keynes's book was largely an apologia for the existing system in India, he also gently chided the British government for not going far enough in managed inflation by failing to establish a central bank. Skidelsky, *Keynes*, pp. 276–77.

new reformed monetary order. While his book was still in proofs, Keynes was appointed a member of the Royal Commission on Indian Finance and Currency, to study and make recommendations for the basic institutions of the Indian monetary system. Keynes dominated the commission proceedings, and while he got his way on maintaining the gold-exchange standard, he was not able to convince the commission to adopt a central bank. However, he managed to bully it into including his annex favoring the state bank in its report, completed in early 1914. In addition, in his work on the commission, Keynes managed to enchant his doting mentor, Alfred Marshall, the unquestioned ruler of academic economists in Britain.[51]

While Montagu Norman was the field marshal of the gold-exchange standard of the 1920s, its major theoretician was long-time Treasury official Ralph Hawtrey. When Hawtrey rose to the position of director of Financial Enquiries at the Treasury in 1919, he delivered a speech before the British Association on "The Gold Standard." The speech presaged the gold-exchange standard of the 1920s. Hawtrey sought not only a system of stable exchange rates as before the war, but also a monetary system that would stabilize the world purchasing power of

[51]Skidelsky, *Keynes*, pp. 374–83. Meanwhile, in the United States, the government, investment bankers, and economists such as Charles A. Conant, Jeremiah W. Jenks, and Jacob Hollander, collaborated in imposing or attempting to impose gold-exchange standards and central banks in Latin America and Asia, beginning with the U.S. acquisition of a colonial empire after the Spanish-American War. During the 1920s, Edwin W. Kemmerer, the "money doctor," a student of Jenks and disciple of Conant, continued this task throughout the Third World. See Edward T. Silva and Sheila Slaughter, *Serving Power: The Making of the Academic Social Science Expert* (Westport, Conn.: Greenwood Press, 1984), pp. 103–38; Emily S. Rosenberg, "Foundations of United States International Financial Power: Gold Standard Diplomacy, 1900–1905," *Business History Review* 59 (Summer 1985): 172–98; and Robert N. Seidel, "American Reformers Abroad: The Kemmerer Missions in South America, 1923–1931," *Journal of Economic History* 32 (June 1972): 520–45.

gold, or world price levels. Hawtrey recommended international cooperation to stabilize price levels, and urged the use of an index number of world prices, a proposal reminiscent of Yale Professor Irving Fisher's suggestion for a "tabular" gold-exchange standard made in 1911. In practice, such calls for price-level stabilization, which were pursued by Benjamin Strong in the 1920s, were really calls for price inflation, to combat the dominant secular trend in a progressing free-market economy of falling prices.

In the post–World War I world, this attempt at dual stabilization meant that the governments would have to salvage the high postwar price levels from the threat of deflation, and in particular to alleviate the "shortage" of gold compared to the swollen totals of paper currencies existing in Europe. As Professor Eric Davis writes:

> There had been concern in official circles that a return to the Gold Standard would be inhibited by a shortage of gold. Prices were much higher than before the war, and thus if there was a general return to the old parities there might be insufficient gold. . . . Hawtrey picked up on the idea that the Gold Exchange Standard could be widely introduced to economise on the use of gold for monetary purposes. Since countries would hold foreign exchange, much presumably in sterling balances as a substitute for gold, there was a special advantage for Britain: the demand for the pound would be increased at the same time the demand for gold lessened.[52]

The central instrument for imposing the new gold-exchange standard on Europe was the international financial conference called by the League of Nations at Genoa in the spring of 1922.

[52]Eric G. Davis, "R.G. Hawtrey, 1879–1975," in *Pioneers of Modern Economics in Britain*, D.P. O'Brien and J.R. Presley, eds. (Totowa, N.J.: Barnes and Noble, 1981), p. 219. Hawtrey's speech was published as "The Gold Standard," *Economic Journal* 29 (1919): 428–42. Fisher's proposal was in Irving Fisher, *The Purchasing Power of Money* (New York: Macmillan, 1911), pp. 332–46.

At a previous international financial conference at Brussels in September 1920, the league had established a powerful financial and economic committee, which from the very beginning was dominated by Montagu Norman through his allies on the committee. Head of the committee was British Treasury official Sir Basil Blackett, and also dominant on the committee were two of Norman's closest associates, Sir Otto Niemeyer and Sir Henry Strakosch. All of these men were ardent price-level stabilizationists. Moreover, Norman's chief adviser in international monetary affairs, Sir Charles S. Addis, was also a dedicated stabilizationist.[53]

Prodded by Norman, British Prime Minister Lloyd George successfully urged the British Cabinet, in mid-December 1921, to call for a broad economic conference on the postwar reconstruction of Europe, to include discussions of German reparations, Soviet Russian reconstruction, the public debt, and the monetary system. At a meeting of the Allied Supreme Council at Cannes in early January 1922, Lloyd George got the delegates to propose an all-European economic and financial conference for the reconstruction of Central and Eastern Europe. Promptly the British set up an interdepartmental committee on economics and finance to prepare for the conference. Head of the committee was the permanent secretary of the Board of Trade, Sir Sidney Chapman. The aim of the Chapman Committee was to return to a gold standard, restore international credit, and establish cooperation between the various central banks. On March 7, 1922, the Chapman Committee issued its report for a draft agreement, which included currency stabilization, central bank cooperation, and adoption of a gold-exchange rather than a straight gold standard, with

[53]Rothbard, *America's Great Depression*, p. 161. See also Paul Einzig, *Montagu Norman* (London: Kegan Paul, 1932), pp. 67, 78; Clay, *Lord Norman*, p. 138; and Anne Orde, *British Policy and European Reconstruction After the First World War* (Cambridge: Cambridge University Press, 1990), pp. 105–18.

each country deciding on the rate at which it would return to gold.

The European economic conference occurred at Genoa from April 10 to May 19, 1922. The conference divided itself into several commissions, including economic and transportation commissions. The relevant commission for our concerns was the Financial Commission, headed by British Chancellor of the Exchequer Sir Robert Horne. The Financial Commission divided itself into three subcommissions, on credits, exchanges, and currency. Credit resolutions dealt with intergovernmental loans, and exchanges was an attempt to eliminate exchange controls. Currency was the subcommission dealing with the international monetary system. The crucial committee, however, was a large Committee of Experts covering all three subcommissions, and which actually drew up the resolutions finally passed by the conference. The Committee of Experts was appointed solely by Sir Robert Horne, and it met in London during the early stages of the Genoa Conference. This large committee, consisting of government officials and financial authorities, was headed by the ubiquitous Sir Basil Blackett.

Ralph Hawtrey drew up the Treasury plans for international money, after having "extended discussions" with Montagu Norman, and presented them to the Committee of Experts. After a temporary setback, the Hawtrey plan was reintroduced and substantially passed, in the form of 12 currency resolutions, by the Financial Commission and then ratified by the plenary of the Genoa Conference.[54] Having gotten his plan approved by the nations of Europe, Hawtrey became

[54]Davis, "R.G. Hawtrey," pp. 219–20, 232; Carole Fink, *The Genoa Conference: European Diplomacy, 1921–1922* (Chapel Hill: University of North Carolina Press, 1984), pp. 158, 232; and Dan P. Silverman, *Reconstructing Europe After the Great War* (Cambridge, Mass.: Harvard University Press, 1982), pp. 282ff.

the leading fugleman and interpreter of the Genoa resolutions.[55]

The currency resolutions of the Genoa Conference, which formed the European monetary system of the 1920s, called for a stable currency value in each country, and for the establishment of central banks everywhere: "in countries where there is no central bank of issue, one should be established." These central banks, not only in Europe but elsewhere (particularly the United States) should practice "continuous cooperation" in order to bring about and maintain "currency reform." The conference suggested an early formal meeting of central banks and an international convention to launch this coordination. The currencies of Europe should be on a common standard, which at present would have to be gold. After expressing a desire for balanced budgets in each nation, the conference declared that some countries would need foreign loans to attain stabilization. Fixing the value of the currency unit in gold was left, by the conference, to each country, and the resolutions were vague on the criteria to be used.

Resolution 9 looked specifically to a new form of gold standard, which would

> centralize and coordinate the demand for gold, and so . . . avoid those wide fluctuations in the purchasing power of gold which might otherwise result from the simultaneous and competitive efforts of a number of countries to secure metallic reserves.

In other words, to fix and *raise* price levels above the free market, and in particular to try to avoid redemption in gold and

[55]See Ralph G. Hawtrey, "The Genoa Resolutions on Currency," *Economic Journal* 32 (1922): 290–304, included in Ralph G. Hawtrey, *Monetary Reconstruction* (London: Longmans, Green, 1923), pp. 131–47. The text of the Genoa resolutions themselves can be found in the *Federal Reserve Bulletin* (June 1922): 678–79, reprinted in Joseph Stagg Lawrence, *Stabilization of Prices* (New York: Macmillan, 1928), pp. 162–65.

subsequent contraction of overexpanded paper currencies. Resolution 9 then became specific: the point was to economize "the use of gold by maintaining reserves in the form of foreign balances, such, for example, as the gold-exchange standard or an international clearing system." Resolution 11 spelled out the gold-exchange system in detail, and also declares that credit will be regulated not only to keep the various currencies at par, "but also with a view of preventing undue fluctuations in the purchasing power of gold," that is, the stabilizationist program of fixing (and raising) prices higher than free-market levels.

In particular, in Resolution 11, "the maintenance of the currency at its gold value must be assured by the provision of an adequate reserve of approved assets, not necessarily gold." In more detail:

> A participating country, in addition to any gold reserve held at home, may maintain in any other participating country reserves of approved assets in the form of bank balances, bills, short-term securities, or other suitable liquid resources.

And:

> The ordinary practice of a participating country will be to buy and sell exchange on other participating countries within a prescribed fraction of parity of exchange for its own currency on demand.

The *gold* aspect of this scheme is covered in the clause: "When progress permits, certain of the participating countries (i.e., Great Britain, and the U.S., if it participates) will establish a free market in gold and thus become gold centers." The upshot, the currency resolution concludes, is that "the convention will thus be based on a gold exchange standard."[56]

Ralph Hawtrey's essay on behalf of the Genoa system is instructive in many ways. Most of it is devoted to defending the idea of coordinated central bank action, that is, essentially

[56]Lawrence, *Stabilization of Prices*, p. 164.

monetary expansion, to stabilize the price level. Hawtrey asks the crucial question:

> It may be asked, why is any international agreement on the subject of the gold standard necessary at all? When we have once got a currency based on commodity like gold, why should we not rely on free market conditions, as we did before the war?[57]

Why indeed? Why can't the new pseudo gold standard be like the old? Hawtrey makes it clear that his reason is a phobia about deflation. The paper money stock had multiplied since 1914, and therefore there "has been a great fall in the commodity value of gold." Even in late 1922, after the price fall of the 1921 recession, the value of the gold dollar was "only two-thirds of what it was before the war." Hence, the "danger" of a scramble to secure gold, and a contraction of money and prices. But what is so terrible about deflation? Here, Hawtrey avoids even mentioning the wage rigidity and the unemployment insurance system that had changed the economic face of Britain. He simply points to the "notorious . . . chronic state of depression which prevailed during the spread of the gold standard in the period 1873–1896." This is really his only horrible example.

But, in the first place, Hawtrey is wrong in attributing falling prices during the late nineteenth century to a shift from silver to gold. The falling prices were due to the industrial revolution, and the phenomenal advance of productivity, and hence a drop in price levels, during this period. But a more important error is that Hawtrey has made the all-too-common modern error of identifying falling prices with "depression." In reality, production and living standards were progressing, in Britain and the United States, during this period, costs were falling and therefore there was no squeeze on profits. The era of falling prices was not a "depression" at all, and was only

[57]Hawtrey, *Monetary Reconstruction*, pp. 134–35.

experienced as such decades later by historians who fail to understand the social benefits of falling prices.[58]

Second, in his exegesis Hawtrey lets the cat out of the bag. He virtually concedes that his ideal is to abandon gold altogether, and remain with only managed fiat money. Thus, in discussing the key currency countries, Hawtrey states wistfully, "At the gold centres some gold reserves must be maintained." But if the gold standard becomes worldwide, "if all the gold standard countries adhere to it, gold will nowhere be needed as a means of remittance, and gold will only be withdrawn from the reserves for use as a raw material of industry."[59] In short, Hawtrey looked forward to dispensing with gold as a monetary metal altogether, and to have the world solely on a fiat paper standard.

Hawtrey concludes his essay by conceding that there was only one defect in the Genoa resolutions: that there was no mention of how long it would take to return to gold. Even the strongest countries, he emphasized, would have to wait until their currencies rose on the exchange market to equal their designated rates. To induce a rise in pound sterling to meet the high fixed rate, Britain would either have to deflate, or else foreign countries, especially the United States, would have to inflate to correct the international discrepancy. "Further deflation," declaimed Hawtrey, "is out of the question." Therefore the only hope was to "stabilize our currency at its existing purchasing power," and wait for the increased gold supply in the United States to lead to a substantial inflation in the United States.[60] Like the other British leaders, Hawtrey was pinning his faith on Uncle Sam's inflating enough to "help Britain."[61]

[58]Thus, see the illuminating work by S.B. Saul, *The Myth of the Great Depression, 1873–1896* (London: Macmillan, 1969).

[59]Hawtrey, *Monetary Reconstruction*, p. 136.

[60]Ibid., p. 147.

[61]For contemporaneous critiques of Hawtrey's stabilizationism as a mask for inflationism, see Lawrence, *Stabilization of Prices*, pp. 326, 432–33;

Many historians have written off the Genoa Conference as a "failure" and dismissed its influence on the international money of the twentieth century. It is true that the formal institutions of central bank cooperation called for at Genoa were not established, largely because of the reluctance of the United States. But the critical point is that Genoa triumphed anyway, since Benjamin Strong was willing to perform the same tasks in informal but highly effective central bank cooperation to establish and prop up Britain's pseudo gold standard. Strong's reluctance stemmed from two sources: an understandable fear that isolationist and antibank sentiment would raise a firestorm against any formal collaboration with European central banks—especially in an America that had reacted against the formal foreign interventionism of the League of Nations. And second, Strong actually preferred the full gold standard, and was queasy about the inflationary unsoundness of a gold-exchange standard. But his reluctance did not prevent him from collaborating closely in support of his friend Montagu Norman and of their common Morgan connection. Their collaboration constituted, in the words of Michael Hogan, an "informal entente."[62] Actually, what Strong preferred was close "key currency" collaboration between, say, the central banks of the United States, England, and France, rather than to be outvoted at formal international conventions.[63]

In fact, after international commodity prices began to decline in 1926, Norman became more frantic in pursuing formal meetings of central bankers, and more insistent on continuing and

---

and Patrick Deutscher, *R.G. Hawtrey and the Development of Macroeconomics* (Ann Arbor: University of Michigan Press, 1990), pp. 211–15.

[62]Michael J. Hogan, *Informal Entente: The Private Structure of Cooperation in Anglo-American Economic Diplomacy, 1918–1928* (Columbia: University of Missouri Press, 1977). On Strong's misgivings on the gold-exchange system, see Stephen V.O. Clarke, *Central Bank Cooperation, 1924–31* (New York: Federal Reserve Bank of New York, 1967), pp. 36–40.

[63]Clarke, *Central Bank Cooperation*, pp. 40–41.

intensifying the inflationary thrust of the gold-exchange standard. Finally, with the establishment of the Bank for International Settlements at Geneva in 1930, Norman at least succeeded in having regular monthly meetings of central bankers.[64]

Far from Genoa being merely a flash in the pan, the 1922 conference placed its decisive stamp upon the postwar monetary world. In the words of Professor Davis, "the widespread adoption of the Gold Exchange Standard can be seen as the legacy of Genoa."[65]

Following the Genoa model, Great Britain, as we have seen, set up the gold-exchange system by returning to its new version of gold in 1925; the other European countries, as well as other nations, followed, each at its own pace. By early 1926, some form of gold standard was established, at least de facto, in 39 countries. By 1928, 43 nations were de jure on the gold standard. Of these, even the few allegedly on the gold bullion standard such as France, kept most of their reserves in sterling balances in London, and the same is true of officially gold-coin nations such as the Netherlands. Apart from the United States, the only officially gold-coin countries were minor nations on the world periphery, such as Mexico, Colombia, Cuba, and the Union of South Africa.[66] It should be noted that Norway and Denmark, who insisted in following the Genoa path of struggling back to gold at a highly overvalued currency, suffered, like Britain, from an export depression throughout the 1920s; whereas Finland, acting on better advice, went back at a realistically devalued rate, and avoided chronic depression during this period.[67]

[64]Ibid., p. 36.

[65]Davis, "R.G. Hawtrey," p. 232, n. 74.

[66]Palyi, *Twilight of Gold*, pp. 116–17, 107.

[67]Finland acted on the advice of the great classical liberal Swedish economic historian, Professor Eli Heckscher of the University of Stockholm. See Richard A. Lester, "The Gold Parity Depression in Norway and Denmark, 1924–1928," *Journal of Political Economy* (August 1937): 433–67; and Palyi, *Twilight of Gold*, pp. 73, 107.

Throughout Europe, Great Britain, wielding its control of the Finance Committee of the League of Nations, engineered the stabilization of currencies on a gold-exchange, that is, a sterling-exchange standard: in Germany, Austria, Hungary, Estonia, Bulgaria, Greece, Belgium, Poland, and Latvia. New central banks were established in the nations of Eastern Europe, basing themselves on reserves in sterling, with British supervisors and directors installed in those banks.[68]

Emile Moreau, the shrewd governor of the Bank of France, recorded his analysis of this British monetary power play in his diary:

> England having been the first European country to reestablish a stable and secure money has used that advantage to establish a basis for putting Europe under a veritable financial domination. The Financial Committee [of the League of Nations] at Geneva has been the instrument of that policy. The method consists of forcing every country in monetary difficulty to subject itself to the Committee at Geneva, which the British control. The remedies prescribed always involve the installation in the central bank of a foreign supervisor who is British or designated by the Bank of England, and the deposit of a part of the reserve of the central bank at the Bank of England, which serves both to support the pound and to fortify British influence. To guarantee against possible failure they are careful to secure the cooperation of the Federal Reserve Bank of New York. Moreover, they pass on to America the task of making some of the foreign loans if they seem too heavy, always retaining the political advantages of these operations.[69]

[68]Judith L. Kooker, "French Financial Diplomacy: The Interwar Years," in Rowland, *Balance of Power*, pp. 86–90.

[69]Entry of February 6, 1928. Chandler, *Benjamin Strong*, pp. 379–80. Rothbard, *America's Great Depression*, p. 139. See also the entry in October 1926, in which Moreau comments on a report of Pierre Quesnay, general manager of the Bank of France, on the "doctrinaire, and without doubt somewhat Utopian or even Machiavellian" schemes of Montagu Norman and his financier associates such as Sir Otto Niemeyer, Sir Arthur Salter,

The Gold-Exchange Standard in Operation: 1926–1929

By the end of 1925, Montagu Norman and the British Establishment were seemingly monarch of all they surveyed. Backed by Strong and the Morgans, the British had had everything their way: they had saddled the world with a new form of pseudo gold standard, with other nations pyramiding money and credit on top of British sterling, while the United States, though still on a gold-coin standard, was ready to help Britain avoid suffering the consequences of abandoning the discipline of the classical gold standard.

But it took little time for things to go very wrong. The crucial British export industries, chronically whipsawed between an overvalued pound and rigidly high wage rates kept up by strong, militant unions and widespread unemployment insurance, kept slumping during an era when worldwide trade and exports were prospering. Unemployment remained chronically high. The unemployment rate had hovered around 3 percent from 1851 to 1914. From 1921 through 1926 it had averaged 12 percent; and unemployment did little better after the return to gold. In April 1925, when Britain returned to gold, the unemployment rate stood at 10.9 percent. After the return, it fluctuated sharply, but always at historically very high levels. Thus, in the year after return, unemployment climbed above 12 percent, fell back to 9 percent, and jumped to over 14 percent during most of 1926. Unemployment fell back to 9 percent by the summer of 1927, but hovered around 10 to 11 percent for the next two years. In other words, unemployment in Britain, during the entire 1920s, lingered around severe recession levels.[70]

---

and Sir Henry Strakosch, aided and abetted by Benjamin Strong, to establish and dominate the "economic and financial organization of the world by Norman and his fellow-central bankers." Palyi, *Twilight of Gold*, pp. 134–45.

[70]Peter Clarke, "The Treasury's Analytical Model of the British Economy Between the Wars," in *The State and Economic Knowledge: The*

The unemployment was concentrated in the older, previously dominant, and heavily unionized industries in the north of England. The pattern of the slump in British exports may be seen by some comparative data. If 1924 is set equal to 100, world exports had risen to 132 by 1929, while Western European exports had similarly risen to 134. United States exports had also risen to 130. Yet, amid this worldwide prosperity, Great Britain lagged far behind, exports rising only to 109. On the other hand, British imports *rose* to 113 in the same period. After the 1929 crash until 1931, all exports fell considerably, world exports to 113, Western European to 107, and the United States, which had taken the brunt of the 1929 crash, to 91; and yet, while British imports rose slightly from 1929 to 1931 to 114, its exports drastically fell to 68. In this way, the overvalued pound combined with rigid downward wage rates to work their dire effects in both boom and recession. Overall, whereas, in 1931, Western European and world exports were considerably higher than in 1924, British exports were very sharply lower.

Within categories of British exports, there was a sharp and illuminating separation between two sets of industries: the old, unionized export staples in the north of England, and the newer, relatively nonunion, lower-wage industries in the south. These newer industries were able to flourish and provide plentiful employment because they were permitted to hire workers at a lower hourly wage than the industries of the north.[71] Some of these industries, such as public utilities, flourished because they were not dependent on exports. But even the exports from these new, relatively nonunionized industries did very well during this period. Thus from 1924 to 1928–29, the volume of

---

American and British Experiences, Mary Furner and Barry Supple, eds. (Cambridge: Cambridge University Press, 1990), p. 177. See also Palyi, *Twilight of Gold,* p. 109.

[71]Anderson, *Economics and Public Welfare,* p. 166; Moggridge, *British Monetary Policy,* p. 117.

automobile exports rose by 95 percent, exports of chemical and machinery manufactures rose by 24 percent, and of electrical goods by 23 percent. During the 1929–31 recession, exports of these new industries did relatively better than the old: machinery and electrical exports falling to 28 percent and 22 percent respectively below the 1924 level, while chemical exports fell only to 5 percent below and automobile exports remained comfortably in 1931 at fully 26 percent *above* 1924.

On the other hand, the older, staple export industries, the traditional mainstays of British prosperity, fared very badly in both these periods of boom and recession. The nonferrous metal industry rose only slightly by 14 percent by 1928–29 and then fell to 55 percent of 1924 in the next two years. In even worse shape were the once-mighty cotton and woolen textile industries, the bellwethers of the Industrial Revolution in England. From 1924 to 1929, cotton exports fell by 10 percent, and woolens by 20 percent, and then, in the two years to 1931, they plummeted phenomenally, cottons to 50 percent of 1924 and woolens to 46 percent. Remarkably, cotton and woolen exports were at this point their lowest in volume since the 1870s.

Perhaps the worst problem was in the traditionally prominent export, coal. Coal exports had declined to 69 percent of 1924 volume in 1931; but perhaps more ominously, they had fallen to 88 percent in 1928–29, slumping, like textiles, in the midst of worldwide prosperity.

So high were British price levels compared to other countries, in both of these periods, that Britain's imports, remarkably, rose in every category during boom and recession. Thus, imports of manufactured goods into Britain rose by 32.5 percent from 1924 to 1928–29, and then rose another 5 percent until 1931. So costly, too, was the once-proud British iron and steel industry that, after 1925, the British, for the first time in their history, became *net importers* of iron and steel.

The relative rigidity of wage costs in Britain may be seen by comparing their unit wage costs with the U.S., setting 1925 in each country equal to 100. In the United States, as prices fell about 10 percent in response to increased productivity and output, wage rates also declined, falling to 93 in 1928, and to 90 in 1929. Swedish wages were even more flexible in those years, enabling Sweden to surmount without export depression and return to gold at the prewar par. Swedish wage rates fell to 88 in 1928, 80 in 1929, and 70 in 1931. In Great Britain, on the other hand, wage rates remained stubbornly high, in the face of falling prices, being 97 in 1928, 95 the following year, and down to only 90 in 1931.[72] In contrast, wholesale prices in England fell by 8 percent in 1926 and 1927, and more sharply still thereafter.

The blindness of British officialdom to the downward rigidity of wage rates was quite remarkable. Thus, the powerful deputy controller of finance for the Treasury, Frederick W. Leith-Ross, the major architect of what became known as the "Treasury view," wrote in bewilderment to Hawtrey in early August 1928, wondering at Keynes's claim that wage rates had remained stable since 1925. In view of the substantial decline in prices in those years, wrote Leith-Ross, "I should have thought that the average wage rate showed a substantial decline during the past four years." Leith-Ross could only support his view by challenging the wage index as inaccurate, citing his own figures that aggregate payrolls had declined. Leith-Ross doesn't seem to have realized that this was precisely the problem: that keeping wage rates up in the face of declining money may indeed lower payrolls, but by creating unemployment and the lowering of hours worked. Finally, by the spring of 1929, Leith-Ross was forced to face reality, and conceded the point. At last, Leith-Ross admitted that the problem was rigidity of labor costs:

> If our workmen were prepared to accept a reduction of 10 percent in their wages or increase their efficiency by 10 percent, a large proportion of our present unemployment could be overcome. But in fact organized labor is so attached to the maintenance of the present standard of wages and hours of

[72]Moggridge, *British Monetary Policy*, pp. 117–25.

> labor that they would prefer that a million workers should remain in idleness and be maintained permanently out of the Employment Fund, than accept any sacrifice. The result is to throw on to the capital and managerial side of industry a far larger reorganization than would be necessary: and until labor is prepared to contribute in larger measure to the process of reconstruction, there will inevitably be unemployment.[73]

Leith-Ross might have added that the "preference" for unemployment was made not by the unemployed themselves but by the union leadership on their alleged behalf, a leadership which itself did not have to face the unemployment dole. Moreover, the willingness of the workers to accept this deal might have been very different if there were no generous Employment Fund for them to tap.

It was in fact the highly militant coal miners' union, led by the prominent leftist Aneurin "Nye" Bevan, that was the first to stir up grave doubt about the glory of the British return to gold. Not only was coal a highly unionized export industry located in the north, but already overinflated coal-mining wages had been given an extra boost during the first Labor government of Ramsay MacDonald, in 1924. In addition to the high wage rates, the miners' union insisted on numerous cost-raising restrictive, featherbedding practices, some of them resurrected from the defunct postmedieval guilds. These obstructionist tactics helped rigidify the British economy, preventing changes and adaptations of occupation and location, and hampering rationalizing and innovative managerial practices. As Professor Benham trenchantly pointed out:

> Employers who wished to make changes had to face the powerful opposition of organized labor. The introduction of new methods, such as the "more looms to a weaver" system,

[73]Draft memorandum to Chancellor of Exchequer Churchill, April 1929. Clarke, "Treasury's Analytical Model," p. 186. See also ibid., pp. 179–80, 184–87.

> was resisted. Strict lines of demarcation between occupations were maintained in engineering and elsewhere. A plumber could repair a pipe conveying cold water; if it conveyed hot water, he had to call in a hot water engineer. Entry into certain occupations was rendered difficult. A man can become an efficient building operative in a few months; an apprenticeship of four years was required. British railways could not have their labour force as they chose. A host of restrictions, insisted upon by the Trade Unions, made this impossible.[74]

By 1925, the year of the return to gold, British coal was already facing competition of rehabilitated, newly modernized, low-cost coal mines in France, Belgium, and Germany. British coal was no longer competitive, and its exports were slumping badly. The Baldwin government appointed a royal commission, headed by Sir Herbert Samuel, to study the vexed coal question. The Samuel Commission reported in March 1926, urging that miners accept a moderate cut in wages, and an increase in working hours at current pay, and suggesting that a substantial number of miners move to other areas, such as the south, where employment opportunities were greater. But this was not the sort of rational solution that would appeal to the spoiled, militant unions, who rejected those proposals and went on strike, thereby generating the traumatic and abortive general strike of 1926.

The strike was broken, and coal-mining wages fell slightly, but the victory for rationality was all too pyrrhic. Keynes was able to convince the inflationist press magnate, Lord Beaverbrook, that the miners were victims of a Norman–Churchill–international

[74]Palyi, *Twilight of Gold*, p. 79. Frederic C. Benham, *British Monetary Policy* (London: P.S. King, 1932), pp. 27f. A manifestation of this obstructive and restrictive trade-union spirit circulated to the members of the union of Building Trade Workers in 1926: "You should keep a keen control of overtime. Adopt a militant policy against all forms of piece work; be watchful and limit apprentices; remember the power you now occupy is conditioned by the scarcity of your labor."

banker conspiracy to profit at the expense of the British working class. But instead of identifying the problem as inflationism, cheap money, and the gold bullion–gold-exchange standard in the face of an overvalued pound, Beaverbrook and British public opinion pointed to "hard money" as the villain responsible for recession and unemployment. Instead of tightening the money supply and interest rates in order to preserve its own created gold standard, the British Establishment was moved to follow its own inclinations still further: to step up its disastrous commitment to inflation and cheap money.[75]

During the general strike, Britain was forced to import coal from Europe instead of exporting it. In olden times, the large fall in export income would have brought about a severe liquidation of credit, contracting the money supply and lowering prices and wage rates. But the British banks, caught up as they were in the ideology of inflationism, instead expanded credit on a lavish scale, and sterling balances piled up on the continent of Europe. "Instead of a readjustment of prices and costs in England and a breaking up of the rigidities, England by credit expansion held the fort and continued the rigidities."[76]

The massive monetary inflation in Britain during 1926 caused gold to flow out of the country, especially to the United States, and sterling balances to accumulate in foreign countries, especially in France. In the true gold-standard days, Britain would have taken all this as a furious signal to contract and tighten up; instead it persisted in continuing inflationism and cheap money, lowering its crucial "bank rate" (Bank of England discount rate) from 5 percent to 4.5 percent in April 1927. This action further weakened the pound sterling, and Britain lost $11 million in gold during the next two months.

France's important role during the gold-exchange era has served as a convenient whipping boy for the British and for the

[75]Palyi, *Twilight of Gold*, pp. 102–04.

[76]Anderson, *Economics and Public Welfare*, p. 167.

Establishment ever since. The legend has it that France was the spoiler, by returning to gold at an *under*valued franc (pegging the franc first in 1926, and then officially returning to gold two years later), consequently piling up sterling balances, and then breaking the gold-exchange system by insisting that Britain pay in gold. The reality was very different. France, during and after World War I, suffered severe hyperinflation, fueled by massive government deficits. As a result, the French franc, classically set at 19.3¢ under the old gold standard, had plunged down to 5¢ in May 1925, and accelerated its decline to 1.94¢ in late July 1926. By June 1926, Parisian mobs protesting the runaway inflation and depreciation surrounded the Chamber of Deputies, threatening violence if former Premier Raymond Poincaré, known as a staunch monetary and fiscal conservative, was not returned to his post. Poincaré was returned to office July 2, pledging to cut expenses, balance the budget, and save the franc.

Armed with a popular mandate, Poincaré was prepared to drive through any necessary monetary and fiscal reforms. Poincaré's every instinct urged him to return to gold at the prewar par, a course that would have been disastrous for France, being not only highly deflationary but also saddling French taxpayers with a massive public debt. Furthermore, returning to gold at the prewar par would have left the Bank of France with a very low (8.6-percent) gold reserve to bank notes in circulation. Returning at par, of course, would have gladdened the hearts of French bondholders as well as of Montagu Norman and the British Establishment. Poincaré was talked out of this path, however, by the knowledgeable and highly perceptive Emile Moreau, governor of the Bank of France, and by Moreau's deputy governor, distinguished economist Charles Rist. Moreau and Rist were well aware of the chronic export depression and unemployment that the British were suffering because of their stubborn insistence on the prewar par. Finally, Poincaré reluctantly was persuaded by Moreau and Rist to go back to gold at a realistic par.

When Poincaré presented his balanced budget and his monetary and financial reform package to Parliament on August 2, 1926, and drove them through quickly, confidence in the franc dramatically rallied, pessimistic expectations in the franc were changed to optimistic ones, and French capital, which had understandably fled massively into foreign currencies, returned to France, quickly doubling its value on the foreign exchange market to almost 4¢ by December. To avoid any further rise, the French government quickly stabilized the franc de facto at 3.92¢ on December 26, and then returned de jure to gold at the same rate on June 25, 1928.[77]

At the end of 1926, while the franc was now pegged, France was not yet on a genuine gold standard. Officially, and de jure, the franc was still set at the prewar par, when one gold ounce had been set at approximately 100 francs. But now, at the new pegged value, the gold ounce, in foreign exchange, was worth 500 francs. Obviously, no one would now deposit gold at a French bank in return for 100 paper francs, thereby wiping out 80 percent of his assets. Also, the Bank of France (which was a privately owned firm) could not buy gold at the current expensive rate, for fear that the French government might decide, after all, to go back to gold de jure at a higher rate, thereby inflicting a severe loss on its gold holdings. The government, however, did agree to indemnify the bank for any losses it might incur in foreign exchange transactions; in that way, Bank of France stabilization operations could only take place in the foreign exchange market.

The French government and the Bank of France were now committed to pegging the franc at 3.92¢. At that rate, francs were purchased in a mighty torrent on the foreign exchange

[77]Dr. Anderson estimates that it would have been "safer" for France to have gone back at 3.5¢ (which it could have done at the market rate in November). Anderson, *Economics and Public Welfare*, p. 158. On the saga of France and the French franc in this period, see ibid., pp. 154–61, 168–73; and Palyi, *Twilight of Gold*, pp. 185–90. For the influence of Moreau and Rist, see Kooker, "French Financial Diplomacy," pp. 91–93.

market, forcing the Bank of France to keep the franc at 3.92¢ by selling massive quantities of newly issued francs for foreign exchange. In that way, foreign exchange holdings of the Bank of France skyrocketed rapidly, rising from a minuscule sum in the summer of 1926 to no less than $1 billion in October of the following year. Most of these balances were in the form of sterling (in bank deposits and short-term bills), which had piled up on the continent during the massive British monetary inflation of 1926 and now moved into French hands with the advent of upward speculation in the franc, and with continued inflation of the pound. Willy-nilly, and against their will, therefore, the French found themselves in the same boat as the rest of Europe: on the gold-exchange or gold-sterling standard.[78]

If France had gone onto a genuine gold standard at the end of 1926, gold would have flowed out of England to France, forcing contraction in England and forcing the British to raise interest rates. The inflow of gold into France and the increased issue of francs for gold by the Bank of France would also have temporarily lowered interest rates there. As it was, French interest rates were sharply lowered in response to the massive issue of francs, but no contraction or tightening was experienced in England; quite the contrary.[79]

Moreau, Rist, and the other Bank of France officials were alert to the dangers of their situation, and they tried to act in lieu of the gold standard by reducing their sterling balances, partly by demanding gold in London, and partly by exchanging sterling for dollars in New York.

This situation put considerable pressure upon the pound, and caused a drain of gold out of England. In the classical gold-standard era, London would have responded by raising the bank rate and tightening credit, stemming or even reversing the

[78]See the lucid exposition in Anderson, *Economics and Public Welfare,* pp. 168–70.

[79]The open market discount rate in Paris fell from 7 percent in August 1926 to 2 percent in August of the following year. Ibid., p. 172.

gold outflow. But England was committed to an unsound, inflationist policy, in stark contrast to the old gold system. And so, Norman tried his best to use muscle to prevent France from exercising its own property rights and redeeming sterling in gold, and absurdly urged that sterling was beneficial for France, and that they could not have too much sterling. On the other hand, he threatened to go off gold altogether if France persisted—a threat he was to make good four years later. He also invoked the spectre of France's World War I debts to Britain.[80] He tried to get various European central banks to put pressure on the Bank of France not to take gold from London. The Bank of France found that it could sell up to £3 million a day without attracting the angry attention of the Bank of England; but any more sales than that would call forth immediate protest. As one official of the Bank of France said bitterly in 1927, "London is a free gold market, and that means that anybody is free to buy gold in London except the Bank of France."[81]

Why did France pile up foreign exchange balances? The anti-French myth of the Establishment charges that the franc was undervalued at the new rate of 3.92¢, and that therefore the ensuing export surplus brought foreign exchange balances into France. The facts of the case were precisely the reverse. Before World War I, France traditionally had a deficit in its balance of trade. During the post–World War I inflation, as usually occurs with fiat money, the foreign exchange rate rose more rapidly than domestic prices, since the highly liquid foreign exchange market is particularly quick to anticipate and discount the future. Therefore, during the French hyperinflation, exports were consistently greater than imports.[82] Then, when France

[80]Kooker, "French Financial Diplomacy," p. 100.

[81]Anderson, *Economics and Public Welfare*, pp. 172–73.

[82]Thus, in 1925, the last full year of the hyperinflation, French exports were 103.8 percent of imports; the surplus was concentrated in manufactured goods, which had an export surplus of 23.8 billion francs, partially offset by a net import deficit of 5.4 billion in food and 16.8 billion in industrial raw materials. Palyi, *Twilight of Gold*, p. 185.

pegged the franc to gold at the end of 1926, the balance of trade reversed itself again to the original pattern. Thus, in 1928, French exports were only 96.1 percent of imports. On the simplistic-trade, or relative-purchasing-power criterion, then, we would have to say that the post-1926 franc was *over*- rather than *under*valued. Why didn't gold or foreign exchange flow out of France? For the same reason as before World War I; the chronic trade deficits were covered by perennial "invisible" net revenues into France, in particular the flourishing tourist trade.

What then accounted for the amassing of sterling by France? The inflow of capital into France. During the French hyperinflation, capital had left France in droves to escape the depreciating franc, much of it finding a haven in London. When Poincaré put his monetary and budget reforms into effect in 1926, capital happily reversed its flow, and left London for France, anticipating a rising or at least a stable franc.

In fact, rather than being obstreperous, the French, succumbing to the blandishments and threats of Montagu Norman, were overly cooperative, much against their better judgment. Thus, Norman warned Moreau in December 1927 that if he persisted in trying to redeem sterling in gold, Norman would devalue the pound. In fact, Poincaré prophetically warned Moreau in May 1927 that sterling's position had weakened and that England might all too readily give up on its own gold standard. And when France stabilized the franc de jure at the end of June 1928, foreign exchange constituted 55 percent of the total reserves of the Bank of France (with gold at 45 percent), an extraordinarily high proportion of that in sterling. Furthermore, much of the funds deposited by the Bank of France in London and New York were used for stock market loans and fueled stock speculation; worse, much of the sterling balances were recycled to repurchase French francs, which continued the accumulation of sterling balances in France. It is no wonder that Dr. Palyi concludes that

> [i]t was at Norman's urgent request that the French central bank carried a weak sterling on its back well beyond the

> limit of what a central bank could reasonably afford to do under the circumstances. No other major central bank took anything like a similar risk (percentage-wise).[83, 84]

Monty Norman could neutralize the French, at least temporarily. But what of the United States? The British, we remember, were counting heavily on America's continuing price inflation, to keep British gold out of American shores. But instead, American prices were falling slowly but steadily during 1925 and 1926, in response to the great outpouring of American products. The gold-exchange standard was being endangered by one of its crucial players before it had scarcely begun!

So, Norman decided to fall back on his trump card, the old magic of the Norman-Strong connection. Benjamin Strong must, once more, rush to the rescue of Great Britain! After Norman turned for help to his old friend Strong, the latter invited the world's four leading central bankers to a top-secret conference in New York in July 1927. In addition to Norman and Strong, the conference was attended by Deputy Governor Rist of the Bank of France and Dr. Hjalmar Schacht, governor of the German Reichsbank. Strong ran the American side with an iron hand, keeping the Federal Reserve Board in Washington in the dark, and even refusing to let Gates McGarrah, chairman of the board of the Federal Reserve Bank of New York, attend the meeting. Strong and Norman tried their best to have the four nations embark on a coordinated policy of monetary inflation and cheap money. Rist demurred,

[83]Ibid., p. 187. The recycling of pounds and francs was pointed out by a leading French banker, Raymont Philippe, *Le'Drame Financier de 1924–1928*, 4th ed. (Paris: Gallimard, 1931), p. 134; cited in Palyi, *Twilight of Gold*, p. 194.

[84]Moreau did resist Norman's pressure to inflate the franc further, and he repeatedly urged Norman to meet Britain's gold losses by tightening money and raising interest rates in England, thereby checking British purchase of francs and attracting capital at home. All this urging was to no avail, Norman being committed to a cheap-money policy. Rothbard, *America's Great Depression*, p. 141.

although he agreed to help England by buying gold from New York instead of London, (that is, drawing down dollar balances instead of sterling). Strong, in turn, agreed to supply France with gold at a subsidized rate: as cheap as the cost of buying it from England, despite the far higher transportation costs.[85]

Schacht was even more adamant, expressing his alarm at the extent to which bank credit expansion had already gone in England and the United States. The previous year, Schacht had acted on his concerns by reducing his sterling holdings to a minimum and increasing the holdings of gold in the Reichsbank. He told Strong and Norman: "Don't give me a low [interest] rate. Give me a true rate. Give me a true rate, and then I shall know how to keep my house in order."[86] Thereupon, Schacht and Rist sailed for home, leaving Strong and Norman to plan the next round of coordinated inflation themselves. In particular, Strong agreed to embark on a mighty inflationary push in the United States, lowering interest rates and expanding credit—an agreement which Rist, in his memoirs, maintains had already been privately concluded before the four-power conference began. Indeed, Strong gaily told Rist during their meeting that he was going to give "a little *coup de whiskey* to the stock market."[87] Strong also agreed to buy $60 million more of sterling from England to prop up the pound.

Pursuant to the agreement with Norman, the Federal Reserve promptly launched its greatest burst of inflation and cheap credit in the second half of 1927. This period saw the

[85]Ibid.

[86]Anderson, *Economics and Public Welfare,* p. 181. Schacht had stabilized the German mark in a new Rentenmark after the old mark had been destroyed by a horrendous runaway inflation by the end of 1923. The following year, he put the mark on the gold-exchange standard.

[87]Charles Rist, "Notice Biographique," *Revue d'Economie Politique* (November–December, 1955): 1006ff.

largest rate of increase of bank reserves during the 1920s, mainly due to massive Fed purchases of U.S. government securities and of bankers' acceptances, totaling $445 million in the latter half of 1927. Rediscount rates were also lowered, inducing an increase in bills discounted by the Fed. Benjamin Strong decided to sucker the suspicious regional Federal Reserve banks by using Kansas City Fed Governor W.J. Bailey as the stalking horse for the rate-cut policy. Instead of the New York Fed initiating the rediscount rate cut from 4 percent to 3.5 percent, Strong talked the trusting Bailey into taking the lead on July 29, with New York and the other regional Feds following a week or two later. Strong told Bailey that the purpose of the rate cuts was to help the farmers, a theme likely to appeal to Bailey's agricultural region. He made sure *not* to tell Bailey that the major purpose was to help England pursue its inflationary gold-exchange policy.

The Chicago Fed, however, balked at lowering its rates, and Strong got the Federal Reserve Board in Washington to force it to do so in September. The isolationist *Chicago Tribune* angrily called for Strong's resignation, charging correctly that discount rates were being lowered in the interests of Great Britain.[88]

After generating the burst of inflation in 1927, the New York Fed continued, over the next two years, to do its best: buying heavily in prime commercial bills of foreign countries, bills endorsed by foreign central banks. The purpose was to bolster foreign currencies, and to prevent an inflow of gold into the U.S. The New York Fed also bought large amounts of sterling bills in 1927 and 1929. It frankly described its policy as follows:

> We sought to support exchange by our purchases and thereby not only prevent the withdrawal of further amounts

[88]Anderson, *Economics and Public Welfare*, pp. 182–83. See also Rothbard, *America's Great Depression*, pp. 140–42; Beckhard, "Federal Reserve Policy," pp. 67ff.; and Lawrence E. Clark, *Central Banking Under the Federal Reserve System* (New York: Macmillan, 1935), p. 314.

> of gold from Europe but also, by improving the position of the foreign exchanges, to enhance or stabilize Europe's power to buy our exports.[89]

If Strong was the point man for the monetary inflation of the late 1920s, the Coolidge administration was not far behind. Pittsburgh multimillionaire Andrew W. Mellon, secretary of the Treasury throughout the Republican era of the 1920s, was long closely allied with the Morgan interests. As early as March 1927, Mellon assured everyone that "an abundant supply of easy money" would continue to be available, and he and President Coolidge repeatedly acted as the "*capeadores* of Wall Street," giving numerous newspaper interviews urging stock prices upward whenever prices seemed to flag. And in January 1928, the Treasury announced that it would refund a 4.5-percent Liberty Bond issue, falling due in September, in 3.5-percent notes. Within the administration, Mellon was consistently Strong's staunchest supporter. The only sharp critic of Strong's inflationism within the administration was Secretary of Commerce Herbert C. Hoover, only to be met by Mellon's denouncing Hoover's "alarmism" and interference.[90]

The motivation for Benjamin Strong's expansionary policy of the late 1920s was neatly summed up in a letter by one of his top aides to one of Montagu Norman's top henchmen, Sir Arthur Salter, then director of Economic and Financial Organization for the League of Nations. The aide noted that Strong, in the spring of 1928, "said that very few people indeed realized that we were now paying the penalty for the decision which was reached early in 1924 to help the rest of the world back to

[89]Clark, *Central Banking Under the Federal Reserve*, p. 198.

[90]Unfortunately, Hoover shortsightedly attacked only credit expansion *in the stock market* rather than credit expansion per se. Rothbard, *America's Great Depression*, pp. 142–43; Anderson, *Economics and Public Welfare*, p. 182; Ralph W. Robey, "The *Capeadores* of Wall Street," *Atlantic Monthly* (September 1928); and Harold L. Reed, *Federal Reserve Policy, 1921–1930* (New York: McGraw-Hill, 1930), p. 32.

a sound financial and monetary basis."[91] Similarly, a prominent banker admitted to H. Parker Willis in the autumn of 1926 that bad consequences would follow America's cheap-money policy, but that "that cannot be helped. It is the price we must pay for helping Europe." Of course, the price paid by Strong and his allies was not so "onerous," at least in the short run, when we note, as Dr. Clark pointed out, that the cheap credit aided especially those speculative, financial, and investment banking interests with whom Strong was allied—notably, of course, the Norman complex.[92] The British, as early as mid-1926, knew enough to be appreciative. Thus, the influential London journal, *The Banker*, wrote of Strong that "no better friend of England" existed. *The Banker* praised the "energy and skillfulness that he has given to the service of England," and exulted that "his name should be associated with that of Mr. [Walter Hines] Page as a friend of England in her greatest need."[93]

On the other hand, Morgan partner Russell C. Leffingwell was not nearly as sanguine about the Strong-Norman policy of joint credit expansion. When, in the spring of 1929, Leffingwell heard reports that Monty was getting "panicky" about the speculative boom in Wall Street, he impatiently told fellow Morgan partner Thomas W. Lamont, "Monty and Ben sowed the wind. I expect we shall all have to reap the whirlwind. . . . I think we are going to have a world credit crisis."[94]

[91]O. Ernest Moore to Sir Arthur Salter, May 25, 1928. In Chandler, *Benjamin Strong*, pp. 280–81.

[92]Willis was a leading and highly perceptive critic of America's inflationary policies in the interwar period. H. Parker Willis, "The Failure of the Federal Reserve," *North American Review* (May 1929): 553. Clark's study was written as a doctoral thesis under Willis. Clarke, *Central Banking Under the Federal Reserve*, p. 344.

[93]Page was the Anglophile ambassador to Great Britain under Wilson and played a large role in getting the United States in the war. Clark, *Central Banking Under the Federal Reserve*, p. 315.

[94]Chernow, *House of Morgan*, p. 313.

Unfortunately, Benjamin Strong was not destined personally to reap the whirlwind. A sickly man, Strong in effect was not running the Fed throughout 1928, finally dying on October 16 of that year. He was succeeded by his handpicked choice, George L. Harrison, also a Morgan man but lacking the personal and political clout of Benjamin Strong.

At first, as in 1924, Strong's monetary inflation was temporarily successful in accomplishing Britain's goals. Sterling was strengthened, and the American gold inflow from Britain was sharply reversed, gold flowing outward. Farm produce prices, which had risen from an index of 100 in 1924 to 110 the following year, and had then slumped back to 100 in 1926 and 99 in 1927, now jumped up to 106 the following year. Farm and food exports spurted upward, and foreign loans in the United States were stimulated to new heights, reaching a peak in mid-1928. But, once again, the stimulus was only temporary. By the summer of 1928, the pound sterling was sagging again. American farm prices fell slightly in 1929, and agricultural exports fell in the same year. Foreign lending slumped badly, as both domestic and foreign funds poured into the booming American stock market.

The stock market had already been booming by the time of the fatal injection of credit expansion in the latter half of 1927. The Standard and Poor's industrial common stock index, which had been 44.4 at the beginning of the 1920s boom in June 1921, had more than doubled to 103.4 by June 1927. Standard and Poor's rail stocks had risen from 156.0 in June 1921 to 316.2 in 1927, and public utilities from 66.6 to 135.1 in the same period. Dow Jones industrials had doubled from 95.1 in November 1922 to 195.4 in November 1927. But now, the massive Fed credit expansion in late 1927 ignited the stock market fire. In particular, throughout the 1920s, the Fed deliberately and unwisely stimulated the stock market by keeping the "call rate," that is, the interest rate on bank call loans to the stock market, artificially low. Before the establishment of the Federal Reserve System, the call rate frequently had risen far above 100 percent, when a stock market boom became severe; yet in the historic and virtually runaway stock market boom of 1928–29, the call rate never went above 10 percent. The call rates were controlled at these low levels by the New York Fed, in close collaboration with, and at the advice of, the Money Committee of the New York Stock Exchange.[95] The stock market, during 1928 and 1929, went into overdrive, virtually doubling these two years. The Dow went up to 376.2 on August 29, 1929, and Standard and Poor's industrials rose to 195.2, rails to 446.0, and public utilities to 375.1 in September. Credit expansion always concentrates its booms in titles to capital, in particular stocks and real estate, and in the late 1920s, bank credit propelled a massive real estate boom in New York City, in Florida, and throughout the country. These included excessive mortgage loans and construction from farms to Manhattan office buildings.[96]

The Federal Reserve authorities, now concerned about the stock market boom, tried feebly to tighten the money supply during 1928, but they failed badly. The Fed's sales of government securities were offset by two factors: (a) the banks shifting their depositors from demand deposits to "time" deposits, which required a much lower rate of reserves, and which were really savings deposits redeemable de facto on demand, rather than genuine time loans, and (b) more important, the fruit of the disastrous Fed policy of virtually creating a market in bankers' acceptances, a market which had existed in Europe but not in the United States. The Fed's policy throughout the 1920s was to subsidize and in effect create an acceptance market by standing

[95]Rothbard, *America's Great Depression*, p. 116; Clarke, *Central Banking Under the Federal Reserve*, p. 382; Adolph C. Miller, "Responsibilities for Federal Reserve Policies, 1927–1929," *American Economic Review* (September 1935).

[96]On the real estate boom of the 1920s, see Homer Hoyt, "The Effect of Cyclical Fluctuations upon Real Estate Finance," *Journal of Finance* (April 1947): 57.

ready to buy any and all acceptances sold by certain favored acceptance houses at an artificially cheap rate. Hence, when bank reserves tightened as the Fed sold securities in 1928, the banks simply shifted to the acceptance market, expanding their reserves by selling acceptances to the Fed. Thus, the Fed's selling of $390 million of securities was partially offset, during latter 1928, by its purchase of nearly $330 million of acceptances.[97] The Fed's sticking to this inflationary policy in 1928 was now made easier by adopting the fallacious "qualitativist" view, held as we have seen also by Herbert Hoover, that the Fed could dampen down the boom by restricting loans to the stock market while merrily continuing to inflate in the acceptance market.

In addition to pouring in funds through acceptances, the Fed did nothing to tighten its rediscount market. The Fed discounted $450 million of bank bills during the first half of 1928; it finally tightened a bit by raising its rediscount rates from 3.5 percent at the beginning of the year to 5 percent in July. After that, it stubbornly refused to raise the rediscount rate any further, keeping it there until the end of the boom. As a result, Fed discounts to banks rose slightly until the end of the boom instead of declining. Furthermore, the Fed failed to sell any more of its hoard of $200 million of government securities after July 1928; instead, it bought some securities on balance during the rest of the year.

Why was Fed policy so supine in late 1928 and in 1929? A crucial reason was that Europe, and particularly England, having lost the benefit of the inflationary impetus by mid-1928, was clamoring against any tighter money in the U.S. The easing in late 1928 prevented gold inflows from the U.S. from getting very large. Britain was again losing gold; sterling was again weak; and the United States once again bowed to its wish to see Europe avoid the consequences of its own inflationary policies.

[97]On the unfortunate Fed acceptance policy of the 1920s, see Rothbard, *America's Great Depression*, pp. 117–23.

Leading the inflationary drive within the administration were President Coolidge and Treasury Secretary Mellon, eagerly playing their roles as the *capeadores* of the bull market on Wall Street. Thus, when the stock market boom began to flag, as early as January 1927, Mellon urged it onward. Another relaxing of stock prices in March spurred Mellon to call for and predict lower interest rates; again, a weakening of stock prices in late March induced Mellon to make his statement assuring "an abundant supply of easy money which should take care of any contingencies that might arise." Later in the year, President Coolidge made optimistic statements every time the rising stock market fell slightly. Repeatedly, both Coolidge and Mellon announced that the country was in a "new era" of permanent prosperity and permanently rising stock prices. On November 16, the *New York Times* declared that the administration in Washington was the source of most of the bullish news and noted the growing "impression that Washington may be depended upon to furnish a fresh impetus for the stock market." The administration continued these bullish statements for the next two years. A few days before leaving office in March 1929, Coolidge called American prosperity "absolutely sound" and assured everyone that stocks were "cheap at current prices."[98, 99]

[98]Rothbard, *America's Great Depression*, p. 148. See also ibid., pp. 116–17; and Robey, "*Capeadores*." The leading "bull" speculator of the era, former General Motors magnate William Crapo Durant, who was to get wiped out in the crash, hailed Coolidge and Mellon as the leaders of the boom. *Commercial and Financial Chronicle* (April 20, 1929): 2557ff.

[99]Some of Strong's apologists claim that, if Strong had been at the helm, he would have imposed tight money in 1928. For an example, see Carl Snyder, *Capitalism, the Creator: The Economic Foundations of Modern Industrial Society* (New York: Macmillan, 1940), pp. 227–28. Snyder worked under Strong as head of the statistical department of the New York Fed. But we now know the contrary: that Strong protested against even the feeble restrictive measures during 1928 as being too severe, in a letter from Strong to Walter W. Stewart, August 3, 1928. Stewart, formerly head of the Fed's research division, had a few years

The clamor from England against any tighter money in the U.S. was driven by England's loss of gold and the pressure on sterling. France, having unwillingly piled up $450 million in sterling by the end of June 1928, was anxious to redeem sterling for gold, and indeed sold $150 million of sterling by mid-1929. In deference to Norman's threats and pleas, however, the Bank of France sold that sterling for dollars rather than for gold in London. Indeed, so cowed were the French that (a) French sales of sterling in 1929–31 were offset by sterling purchases by a number of minor countries, and (b) Norman managed to persuade the Bank of France to sell no more sterling until after the disastrous day in September 1931 when Britain abandoned its own gold-exchange standard and went on to a fiat pound standard.[100]

Meanwhile, despite the great inflation of money and credit in the U.S., the massive increase in the supply of goods in the U.S. continued to lower prices gradually, wholesale prices falling from 104.5 (1926=100) in November 1925 to 100 in 1926, and then to 95.2 in June 1929. Consumer price indices in the U.S. also fell gradually in the late 1920s. Thus, despite Strong's loose money policies, Norman could not count on price inflation in the U.S. to bail out his gold-exchange system. Montagu Norman, in addition to pleading with the U.S. to keep inflating, resorted to dubious short-run devices to try to keep gold from flowing out to the U.S. Thus, in 1928 and 1929, he would sell gold for sterling to raise the sterling rate a bit, in sales timed to coincide with the departure of fast boats from London to New York, thus inducing gold holders to keep the precious metal in London. Such short-run tricks were hardly adequate substitutes for tight money or for raising bank rate in England, and weakened long-run confidence in the pound sterling.[101]

---

earlier shifted to become economic adviser of the Bank of England, and had written to Strong warning of unduly tight restriction on American bank credit. Chandler, *Benjamin Strong*, pp. 459–65.

[100]Palyi, *Twilight of Gold*, pp. 187, 194.

[101]Anderson, *Economic and Public Welfare*, p. 201.

In March 1929, Herbert Clark Hoover, who had been a powerful secretary of commerce during the Republican administrations of the 1920s, became president of the United States. While not as intimately connected as Calvin Coolidge, Hoover long had been close to the Morgan interests. Mellon continued as secretary of the Treasury, with the post of secretary of state going to the longtime top Wall Street lawyer in the Morgan ambit, Henry L. Stimson, disciple and partner of J.P. Morgan's personal attorney, Elihu Root.[102] Perhaps most important, Hoover's closest, but unofficial adviser, whom he regularly consulted three times a week, was Morgan partner Dwight Morrow.[103]

Hoover's method of dealing with the inflationary boom was to try not to tighten the money supply, but to keep bank loans out of the stock market by a jawbone method then called "moral suasion." This too was the preferred policy of the new governor of the Federal Reserve Board in Washington, Roy A. Young. The fallacy was to try to restrict credit to the stock market while keeping it abundant to "legitimate" commerce and

[102]Undersecretary of the Treasury Ogden Mills, Jr., who was to replace Mellon in 1931 and who was close to Hoover, was a New York corporate lawyer from a family long associated with the Morgan interests. Hoover's secretary of the Navy was Charles F. Adams, from a Boston Brahmin family long associated with the Morgans, and whose daughter married J.P. Morgan, Jr.

[103]Burch, *Elites in American History*, p. 280. For the important but private influence on President Hoover by Morgan partner Thomas W. Lamont, including Lamont's inducing Hoover to conceal his influence by faking entries in a diary that Hoover left to historians, see Ferguson, "From Normalcy to New Deal," p. 79.

The Morgans, in the 1928 Republican presidential race, were torn three ways: between inducing, unsuccessfully, President Coolidge to run for a third term; Vice President Charles G. Dawes, who had been a Morgan railroad lawyer and who dropped out of the 1928 race; and Herbert Hoover. On Hoover's worries before the nomination about the position of the Morgans, and on Lamont's assurances to him, see the illuminating letter from Thomas W. Lamont to Dwight Morrow, December 16, 1927, in Ferguson, "From Normalcy to New Deal," p. 77.

industry. Using methods of intimidation of business honed when he was secretary of commerce, Hoover attempted to restrain stock loans by New York banks, tried to induce the president of the New York Stock Exchange to curb speculation, and warned leading editors and publishers about the dangers of high stock prices. None of these superficial methods could be effective.

Professor Beckhart added another reason for the adoption of the ineffective policy of moral suasion: that the administration had been persuaded to try this tack by the old manipulator, Montagu Norman. Finally, by June 1929, the moral suasion was at last abandoned, but discount rates were still not raised, so that the stock market boom continued to rage, even as the economy in general was quietly but inexorably turning downward. Secretary Mellon once again trumpeted our "unbroken and unbreakable prosperity." In August, the Federal Reserve Board finally agreed to raise the rediscount rate to 6 percent, but any tightening effect was more than offset by the Fed's simultaneously lowering its acceptance rate, thereby once again giving an inflationary fillip to the acceptance market. One reason for this resumption of acceptance inflation, after it had been previously reversed in March, was, yet again, "another visit of Governor Norman."[104] Thus, once more, the cloven hoof of Montagu Norman was able to give its final impetus to the boom of the 1920s. Great Britain was also entering upon a depression, and yet its inflationary policies resulted in a serious outflow of gold in June and July. Norman was able to get a line of credit of $250 million from a New York banking consortium, but the outflow continued through September, much of it to the United States. Continuing to help England, the New York Fed bought heavily in sterling bills from August through October. The new subsidization of the acceptance market, mostly foreign acceptances, permitted further aid to Britain through the purchase of sterling bills.

[104]Beckhart, "Federal Reserve Policy," pp. 142ff. See also ibid., p. 127.

A perceptive epitaph on the qualitative-credit politics of 1928–29 was pronounced by A. Wilfred May:

> Once the credit system had become infected with cheap money, it was impossible to cut down particular outlets of this credit without cutting down all credit, because it is impossible to keep different kinds of money separated in water-tight compartments. It was impossible to make money scarce for stock-market purposes, while simultaneously keeping it cheap for commercial use. . . . When Reserve credit was created, there was no possible way that its employment could be directed into specific uses, once it had flowed through the commercial banks into the general credit stream.[105]

Depression and the End of the Gold-Sterling-Exchange Standard: 1929–1931

The depression, or what nowadays would be called the "recession," that struck the world economy in 1929 could have been met in the same way the U.S., Britain, and other countries had faced the previous severe contraction of 1920–21, and the way in which all countries met recessions under the classical gold standard. In short: they could have recognized the folly of the preceding inflationary boom and accepted the recession mechanism needed to return to an efficient free-market economy. In other words, they could have accepted the liquidation of unsound investments and the liquidation of egregiously unsound banks, and have accepted the contractionary deflation of money, credit, and prices. If they had done so, they would, as

[105]A. Wilfred May, "Inflation in Securities," in *The Economics of Inflation*, H. Parker Willis and John M. Chapman, eds. (New York: Columbia University Press, 1935), pp. 292–93; Charles O. Hardy, *Credit Policies of the Federal Reserve System* (Washington, D.C.: Brookings Institution, 1932), pp. 124–77; Oskar Morgenstern, "Developments in the Federal Reserve System," *Harvard Business Review* (October 1930): 2–3; and Rothbard, *America's Great Depression*, pp. 151–52.

in the previous cases, have encountered a recession-adjustment period that would have been sharp, severe, but mercifully short. Recessions unhampered by government almost invariably work themselves into recovery within a year or 18 months.

But the United States, Britain, and the rest of the world had been permanently seduced by the siren song of cheap money. If inflationary bank credit expansion had gotten the world into this mess, then more, more of the same would be the only way out. Pursuit of this inflationist, "proto-Keynesian" folly, along with other massive government interventions to prevent price deflation, managed to convert what would have been a short, sharp recession into a chronic, permanent, stagnation with an unprecedented high unemployment that only ended with World War II.

Great Britain tried to inflate its way out of the recession, as did the United States, despite the monetarist myth that the Federal Reserve deliberately contracted the money supply from 1929 to 1933. The Fed inflated partly to help Britain and partly for its own sake. During the week of the great stock market crash—the final week of October 1929—the Federal Reserve, specifically George Harrison, doubled its holding of government securities, and discounted $200 million for member banks. During that one week, the Fed added $300 million to bank reserves, the expansion being generated to prevent stock market liquidation and to permit the New York City banks to take over brokers' loans being liquidated by nonbank lenders. Over the objections of Roy Young of the Federal Reserve Board, Harrison told the New York Stock Exchange that "I am ready to provide all the reserve funds that may be needed."[106] By December, Secretary Mellon issued one of his traditionally optimistic pronouncements that there was "plenty of credit available," and President Hoover, addressing a business conference on December 5, hailed the nation's good fortune in possessing

[106]Chernow, *House of Morgan*, p. 319.

the splendid Federal Reserve System, which had succeeded in saving shaky banks, had restored confidence, and had made capital more abundant by reducing interest rates.

In early 1930, the Fed launched a massive cheap-money program, lowering rediscount rates during the year from 4.5 percent to 2 percent, with acceptance rates and call loan rates falling similarly. The Fed purchased $218 million in government securities, increasing total member bank reserves by over $100 million. The money supply, however, remained stable and did not increase, due to the bank failures of late 1930. The inflationists were not satisfied, however, *Business Week (*then as now a voice for "enlightened" business opinion) thundering in late October that the "deflationists" were "in the saddle." In contrast, H. Parker Willis, in an editorial in the *New York Journal of Commerce*, trenchantly pointed out that the easy-money policy of the Fed was actually bringing about the bank failures, because of the banks' "inability to liquidate." Willis noted that the country was suffering from frozen and wasteful malinvestments in plants, buildings, and other capital, and that the depression could only be cured when these unsound credit positions were allowed to liquidate.[107]

In 1930, Montagu Norman got part of his wish to achieve a formal intercentral bank collaboration. Norman was able to push through a new "central bankers' bank," the Bank for

[107]*Business Week* (October 22, 1930); *Commercial and Financial Chronicle* 131 (August 2, 1930): 690–91. In addition, Albert Wiggin, head of the Chase National Bank, then clearly reflecting the views of the bank's chief economist, Dr. Benjamin M. Anderson, denounced the new Hoover policies of propping up wage rates and prices in depressions, and of pursuing cheap money. "When wages are kept higher than the market situation justifies," wrote Wiggin in the Chase annual report for January 1931, "employment and the buying power of labor fall off. . . . Our depression has been prolonged and not alleviated by delay in making necessary readjustments." *Commercial and Financial Chronicle* 132 (January 17, 1931): 428–29; Rothbard, *America's Great Depression*, pp. 191–93, 212–13, 217, 220–21.

International Settlements (BIS), to meet regularly at Basle, to provide clearing facilities for German reparations payments, and to provide regular facilities for meeting and cooperation. While Congress forbade the Fed from formally joining the BIS, the New York Fed and the Morgan interests worked closely with the new bank. The BIS, indeed, treated the New York Fed as if it were the central bank of the United States. Gates W. McGarrah resigned his post as chairman of the board of the New York Fed in February 1930 to assume the position of president of the BIS, and Jackson E. Reynolds, a director of the New York Fed, was chairman of the BIS's first organizing committee. J.P. Morgan and Company unsurprisingly supplied much of the capital for the BIS. And even though there was no legislative sanction for U.S. participation in the bank, New York Fed Governor George Harrison made a "regular business trip" abroad in the fall to confer with the other central bankers, and the New York Fed extended loans to the BIS during 1931.

During 1931, many of the European banks, swollen by unsound credit expansion, met their comeuppance. In October 1929, the important Austrian bank, the Boden-Kredit-Anstalt, was headed for liquidation. Instead of allowing the bank to fold and liquidate, international finance, headed by the Rothschilds and the Morgans, bailed the bank out. The Boden bank was merged into the older and stronger Österreichische-Kredit-Anstalt, now by far the largest commercial bank in Austria, capital being provided by an international financial syndicate including J.P. Morgan and Rothschild of Vienna. Moreover, the Austrian government guaranteed some of the Boden bank's assets.

But the now-huge Kredit-Anstalt was weakened by the merger, and, in May 1931, a run developed on the bank, led by French bankers angered by the announced customs union between Germany and Austria. Despite aid to the Kredit-Anstalt by the Bank of England, Rothschild of Vienna, and the BIS (aided by the New York Fed and other central banks), to a total of over $31 million, and the Austrian government's guarantee of

Kredit-Anstalt liabilities up to $150 million, bank runs, once launched, are irresistible, and so Austria went off the gold standard, in effect, declaring national bankruptcy in June 1931. At that point, a fierce run began on the German banks, the Bank for International Settlements again trying to shore up Germany by arranging a $100 million loan to the Reichsbank, a credit joined in by the Bank of England, the Bank of France, the New York Fed, and several other central banks. But the run on the German banks, both from the German people as well as from foreign creditors, proved devastating. By mid-July, the German banking system collapsed from internal runs, and Germany went off the gold standard. Since the German public feared runaway inflation above all else and identified the cause of the inflation as exchange-rate devaluation, the German government felt it had to maintain the par value of the mark, now highly overvalued relative to gold. To do so, while at the same time resuming inflationary credit expansion, the German government had to "protect" the mark by severe and thoroughgoing exchange controls.

With the successful runs on Austria and Germany, it was clear that England would be the next to suffer a worldwide lack of confidence in its currency, including runs on gold. Sure enough, in mid-July, sterling redemption in gold became severe, and the Bank of England lost $125 million in gold in nine days in late July.

The remedy to such a situation under the classical gold standard was very clear: a sharp rise in bank rate to tighten English money and to attract gold and foreign capital to stay or flow back into England. In classical gold standard crises, the bank had raised its bank rate to 9 or 10 percent until the crises passed. And yet, so wedded was England to cheap money, that it entered the crisis in mid-July at the absurdly low bank rate of 2.5 percent, and grudgingly raised the rate only to 4.5 percent by the end of July, keeping the rate at this low level until it finally threw in the towel and, on the black Sunday of September 20, went off the very gold-exchange standard that it recently had foisted upon the rest of the world. Indeed, instead of tightening money, the Bank of England made the pound shakier still by inflating credit further. Thus, in the last two weeks of July, the Bank of England purchased nearly $115 million in government securities.

England disgracefully threw in the towel even as foreign central banks tried to prop the Bank of England up and save the gold-exchange standard. Answering Norman's pleas, the Bank of France and the New York Fed each loaned the Bank of England $125 million on August 1, and then, later in August, another $400 million provided by a consortium of French and American bankers. All this aid was allowed to go down the drain on the altar of inflationism and a 4.5-percent bank rate. As Dr. Anderson concluded,

> England went off the gold standard with Bank Rate at 4.5 percent. To a British banker in 1913, this would have been an incredible thing. . . . The collapse of the gold standard in England was absolutely unnecessary. It was the product of prolonged violation of gold standard rules, and, even at the end, it could have been averted by the return to orthodox gold standard methods.[108]

England betrayed not only the countries that aided the pound, but also the countries it had cajoled into adopting the gold-exchange standard in the 1920s. It also specifically betrayed those banks it had persuaded to keep huge sterling balances in London: specifically, the Netherlands Bank and the Bank of France. Indeed, on Friday, September 18, Dr. G. Vissering, head of the Netherlands Bank, phoned Monty Norman and asked him about the crisis of sterling. Vissering, who was poised to withdraw massive sterling balances from London, was assured without qualification by his old friend Norman that, England would, at all costs, remain on the gold standard. Two days later, England betrayed its word. The Netherlands Bank suffered severe

[108]Anderson, *Economics and Public Welfare*, p. 248. See also ibid., pp. 245–50; Benham, *British Monetary Policy*, pp. 9–10.

losses.[109] The Netherlands Bank was strongly criticized by the Dutch government for keeping its balances in sterling until it was too late. In its own defense, the bank quoted repeated assurances from the Bank of England about the safety of foreign funds in London. The bank made it clear that it was betrayed and deceived by the Bank of England.[110]

The Bank of France also suffered severely from the British betrayal, losing about $95 million. Despite its misgivings, it had loyally supported the English gold-standard system by allowing sterling balances to pile up. The Bank of France sold no sterling until after England went off gold; by September 1931, it had amassed a sterling portfolio of $300 million, one-fifth of France's monetary reserves. In fact, during the period of 1928–31, the sterling portfolio of the Bank of France was at times equal to two-thirds of the entire gold reserve of the Bank of England.

Despite Montagu Norman, who began to blame the French government for his own egregious failure, it was not the French authorities who put pressure on sterling in 1931. On the contrary, it was the shrewd private French investors and commercial banks, who, correctly sensing the weakness of sterling and the British refusal to employ orthodox measures in its support, decided to make a run on the pound in exchange for gold.[111] The run was aggravated by the glaring fact that Britain had a chronic import deficit, and also was scarcely in a position to save the gold standard through tight money when the British government, at the end of July, projected a massive fiscal 1932–33 deficit of £120 million, the largest since 1920. Attempts in September to cut the budget were overridden by union strikes, and even by a short-lived sit-down strike by British naval personnel, which convinced

[109]Anderson, *Economics and Public Welfare*, pp. 246–47, 253.

[110]Palyi, *Twilight of Gold*, pp. 276–78.

[111]Ibid., pp. 187–90. Kooker, "French Financial Diplomacy," pp. 105–06, 113–17.

foreigners that Britain would not take sufficient measures to defend the pound.

In his memoirs, the economist Moritz J. Bonn neatly summed up the significance of England's action in September 1931:

> September 20, 1931, was the end of an age. It was the last day of the age of economic liberalism in which Great Britain had been the leader of the world. . . . Now the whole edifice had crashed. The slogan "safe as the Bank of England" no longer had any meaning. The Bank of England had gone into default. For the first time in history a great creditor country had devalued its currency, and by so doing had inflicted heavy losses on all those who had trusted it.[112]

As soon as England went off the gold standard, the pound fell by 30 percent. It is ironic that, after all the travail Britain had put the world through, the pound fell to a level, $3.40, that might have been viable if she had originally returned to gold at that rate. Twenty-five countries followed Britain off gold and onto floating, and devaluating, exchange rates. The era of the gold-exchange standard was over.

EPILOGUE

The world was now plunged into a monetary chaos of fiat money, competing devaluation, exchange controls, and warring monetary and trade blocs, accompanied by a network of protectionist restrictions. These warring blocs played an important though neglected part in paving the way for World War II. This trend toward monetary and other economic nationalism was accentuated when the United States, the last bastion of the gold-coin standard, devalued the dollar and went off that standard in 1933. The Franklin Roosevelt branch of the family had always been close to its neighbors the Astors and Harrimans, and

[112]Moritz J. Bonn, *Wandering Scholar* (New York: John Day, 1948) p. 278.

American politics, since the turn of the twentieth century, had been marked by an often bitter financial and political rivalry between the House of Morgan on the one hand, and an alliance of the Harrimans, the Rockefellers, and Kuhn, Loeb on the other. Accordingly, the early years of the Roosevelt New Deal were marked by a comprehensive and successful assault on the House of Morgan, that is, in the Glass-Steagall Act, outlawing Morgan-type integration of commercial and investment banking. In contrast to the Morgan dominance during the Republican era of the 1920s, the early New Deal was dominated by an alliance of the Harrimans, Rockefellers, and various retailers, farm groups, the silver bloc, and industries producing for retail sales (for example, automobiles and typewriters), all of whom were now backing an inflationist and economic nationalist program. When the British, backed by the Morgans, convened a World Economic Conference in London in June 1933, to try to restabilize exchange rates, the plan was scuttled at the last minute by President Roosevelt, under the influence of the inflationist-economic nationalist bloc. The Morgans were taking a shellacking at home and abroad.

It was only in 1936, by the good offices of leading Morgan banker Norman Davis, a longtime friend of Roosevelt's, and of Democrat Morgan partner Russell Leffingwell, that the Morgans would begin to recoup their political losses. The beginning of the return of the Morgans was symbolized by the September 1936 Tripartite Monetary Agreement, partially stabilizing the exchange rates of the currencies of Britain, France, and the U.S., a collaboration that was soon extended to Belgium, Holland, and Switzerland. These agreements, in addition to the dollar's still remaining on an international (but not domestic) gold bullion standard at $35 an ounce, set the stage for the Morgan drive organized by Norman Davis, head of Morgan's Council of Foreign Relations, to bring a new world gold-exchange standard out of the cauldron of World War II. The difference is that this inflationary "Bretton Woods" system would be a dollar, not a sterling, gold-exchange standard. Moreover, this inflationary system under the cloak of the prestige of gold, was destined to last a great deal longer than the British venture, finally collapsing at the end of the 1960s.[113]

[113]For an overview of the monetary struggles and policies of the New Deal, see Murray N. Rothbard, "The New Deal and the International Monetary System," in *The Great Depression and New Deal Monetary Policy* (San Francisco: Cato Institute, [1976] 1980), pp. 79–129. Some of the details in this account of the economic and financial interests involved have been superseded by Ferguson, "From Normalcy to New Deal," pp. 41–93; Thomas Ferguson, "Industrial Conflict and the Coming of the New Deal: The Triumph of Multinational Liberalism in America," in *The Rise and Fall of the New Deal Order, 1930–1980,* Steve Fraser and Gary Gerstle, eds. (Princeton, N.J.: Princeton University Press, 1989), pp. 3–31. On the road to Bretton Woods, see G. William Domhoff, *The Power Elite and the State* (New York: Aldine de Gruyter, 1990), pp. 114–81. On the Harriman influence in the New Deal, see Philip H. Burch, Jr., *Elites in American History,* vol. 3, *The New Deal to the Carter Administration* (New York: Holmes and Meier, 1980), pp. 20–31.

Part 5

The New Deal and the International Monetary System

THE NEW DEAL AND THE INTERNATIONAL MONETARY SYSTEM

The international monetary policies of the New Deal may be divided into two decisive and determining actions, one at the beginning of the New Deal and the other at its end. The first was the decision, in early 1933, to opt for domestic inflation and monetary nationalism, a course that helped steer the entire world onto a similar path during the remainder of the decade. The second was the thrust, during World War II, to reconstitute an international monetary order, this time built on the dollar as the world's "key" and crucial currency. If we wished to use lurid terminology, we might call these a decision for dollar nationalism and dollar imperialism respectively.

THE BACKGROUND OF THE 1920S

It is impossible to understand the first New Deal decision for dollar nationalism without setting that choice in the monetary world of the 1920s, from which the New Deal emerged. Similarly, it is impossible to understand the monetary system of the 1920s without reference to the pre–World War I monetary order and its breakup during the war; for the world of the 1920s was an attempt to reconstitute an international monetary order,

[*Originally published in* Watershed of Empire: Essays on New Deal Foreign Policy, *Leonard P. Liggio and James J. Martin, eds. (Colorado Springs, Colo.: Ralph Myles, 1976).*—Ed.]

seemingly one quite similar to the *status quo ante*, but actually based on very different principles and institutions.

The prewar monetary order was genuinely "international"; that is, world money rested not on paper tickets issued by one or more governments but on a genuine economic commodity—gold—whose supply rested on market supply-and-demand principles. In short, the international gold standard was the monetary equivalent and corollary of international free trade in commodities. It was a method of separating money from the State just as enterprise and foreign trade had been so separated. In short, the gold standard was the monetary counterpart of laissez-faire in other economic areas.

The gold standard in the prewar era was never "pure," no more than was laissez-faire in general. Every major country, except the United States, had central banks which tried their best to inflate and manipulate the currency. But the system was such that this intervention could only operate within narrow limits. If one country inflated its currency, the inflation in that country would cause the banks to lose gold to other nations, and consequently the banks, private and central, would before long be brought to heel. And while England was the world financial center during this period, its predominance was market rather than political, so it too had to abide by the monetary discipline of the gold standard. As H. Parker Willis described it:

> Prior to the World War the distribution of the metallic money of gold standard countries had been directed and regulated by the central banks of the world in accordance with the generally known and recognized principles of international distribution of the precious metals. Free movement of these metals and freedom on the part of the individual to acquire and hold them were general. Regulation of foreign exchange . . . existed only sporadically . . . and was so conducted as not to interfere in any important degree with the disposal of holding of specie by individuals or by banks.[1]

[1]H. Parker Willis, *The Theory and Practice of Central Banking* (New York: Harper and Bros., 1936), p. 379.

The advent of the World War disrupted and rended this economic idyll, and it was never to return. In the first place, all of the major countries financed the massive war effort through an equally massive inflation, which meant that every country except the United States, even including Great Britain, was forced to go off the gold standard, since they could no longer hope to redeem their currency obligations in gold. The international order not only was sundered by the war, but also split into numerous separate, competing, and warring currencies, whose inflation was no longer subject to the gold restraint. In addition, the various governments engaged in rigorous exchange control, fixing exchange rates and prohibiting outflows of gold; monetary warfare paralleled the broader economic and military conflict.

At the end of the war, the major powers sought to reconstitute some form of international monetary order out of the chaos and warring economic blocs of the war period. The crucial actor in this drama was Great Britain, which was faced with a series of dilemmas and difficulties. On the one hand, Britain not only aimed at re-establishing its former eminence, but it meant to use its victorious position and its domination of the League of Nations to work its will upon the other nations, many of them new and small, of post-Versailles Europe. This meant its monetary as well as its general political and economic dominance. Furthermore, it no longer felt itself bound by old-fashioned laissez-faire restraints from exerting frankly political control, nor did it any longer feel bound to observe the classical gold-standard restraints against inflation.

While Britain's appetite was large, its major dilemma was its weakness of resources. The wracking inflation and the withdrawal from the gold standard had left the United States, not Great Britain, as the only "hard," gold-standard country. If Great Britain were to dominate the postwar monetary picture, it would somehow have to take the United States into camp as its willing junior partner. From the classic prewar pound-dollar par of $4.86 to the pound, the pound had fallen on the international money markets to $3.50, a substantial 30-percent drop, a drop that reflected the greater degree of inflation in Great Britain than in the U.S. The British then decided to constitute a new form of international monetary system, the "gold-exchange standard," which it finally completed in 1925. In the classical, prewar gold standard, each country kept its reserves in gold, and redeemed its paper and bank currencies in gold coin upon demand. The new gold-exchange standard was a clever device to permit Britain and the other European countries to remain inflated and to continue inflating, while enlisting the United States as the ultimate support for all currencies. Specifically, Great Britain would keep its reserves, not in gold but in dollars, while the smaller countries of Europe would keep *their* reserves, not in gold but in pounds sterling. In this way, Great Britain could pyramid inflated currency and credit on top of dollars, while Britain's client states could pyramid *their* currencies, in turn, on top of pounds. Clearly, this also meant that *only* the United States would remain on a gold-coin standard, the other countries "redeeming" only in foreign exchange. The instability of this system, with pseudo gold-standard countries pyramiding on top of an increasingly shaky dollar-gold base, was to become evident in the Great Depression.

But the British task was not simply to induce the United States to be the willing guarantor of all the shaky and inflated currencies of war-torn Europe. For Great Britain might well have been able to return to the original form of gold standard at a new, realistic, depreciated parity of $3.50 to the pound. But it was not willing to do so. For the British dream was to restore, even more glowingly than before, British financial preeminence, and if it depreciated the pound by 30 percent, it would thereby acknowledge that the dollar, not the pound, was the world financial center. This it was fiercely unwilling to do; for restoration of dominance, for the saving of financial face, it would return at the good old $4.86 or bust in the attempt. And bust it almost did. For to insist on returning to gold at $4.86, even on the new, vitiated, gold-exchange basis, was to mean that the pound would be absurdly expensive in relation to the dollar and other currencies, and would therefore mean that at current inflated price levels, Britain's exports—its economic lifeline—would be severely crippled, and a general depression would ensue. And indeed, Britain suffered a severe depression in her export industries—particularly coal and textiles—throughout the 1920s. If she insisted on returning at the overvalued $4.86, there was only one hope for keeping her exports competitive in price: a massive domestic deflation to lower price and wage levels. While a severe deflation is difficult at best, Britain now found it impossible, for the new system of national unemployment insurance and the new-found strength of trade unions made wage-cutting politically unthinkable.

But if Britain would not or could not make her exports competitive by returning to gold at a depreciated par or by deflating at home, there was a third alternative which it could pursue, and which indeed marked the key to the British international economic policy of the 1920s: it could induce or force *other* countries to inflate, or themselves to return to gold at overvalued pars; in short, if it could not clean up its own economic mess, it could contrive to impose messes upon everyone else. If it did not do so, it would see inflating Britain lose gold to the United States, France, and other "hard-money" countries, as indeed happened during the 1920s; only by contriving for other countries, especially the U.S., to inflate also, could it check the loss of gold and therefore halt the collapse of the whole jerry-built international monetary structure.

In the short run, the British scheme was brilliantly conceived, and it worked for a time; but the major problem went unheeded: if the United States, the base of the pyramid and the sole link of all these countries to gold and hard money, were to inflate unduly, the *dollar too* would become shaky, it would lose gold at home and abroad, and the dollar would itself eventually collapse, dragging the entire structure down with it. And this is essentially what happened in the Great Depression.

In Europe, England was able to use its domination of the powerful Financial Committee of the League of Nations to cajole or bludgeon country after country to (1) establish central banks that would collaborate closely with the Bank of England; (2) return to gold *not* in the classical gold-coin standard but in the new gold-exchange standard which would permit continued inflation by all the countries; and (3) return to this new standard at overvalued pars so that European exports would be hobbled vis-à-vis the exports of Great Britain. The Financial Committee of the League of Nations was largely dominated and run by Britain's major financial figure, Montagu Norman, head of the Bank of England, working through such close Norman associates on the committee as Sir Otto Niemeyer and Sir Henry Strakosch, leaders in the concept of close central bank collaboration to "stabilize" (in practice, to raise) price levels throughout the world. The distinguished British economist Sir Ralph Hawtrey, director of Financial Studies at the British Treasury, was one of the first to advocate this system, as well as to call for the general European adoption of a gold-exchange standard. In the spring of 1922, Norman induced the league to call the Genoa Conference, which urged similar measures.[2]

But the British scarcely confined their pressure upon European countries to resolutions and conferences. Using the carrot of loans from England and the United States and the stick of political pressure, Britain induced country after country to order its monetary affairs to suit the British—that is, to return only to a gold-exchange standard at overvalued pars that would hamper their own exports and stimulate imports from Great Britain. Furthermore, the British also used their inflated, cheap credit to lend widely to Europe in order to stimulate their own flagging export market. A trenchant critique of British policy was recorded in the diary of Émile Moreau, governor of the Bank of France, a country that clung to the gold standard and to a hard-money policy, and was thereby instrumental in bringing down the pound and British financial domination in 1931. Moreau wrote:

[2]See Murray N. Rothbard, *America's Great Depression*, 3rd ed. (Kansas City, Mo.: Sheed and Ward, 1975), pp. 159ff.

> England having been the first European country to reestablish a stable and secure money [*sic*] has used that advantage to establish a basis for putting Europe under a veritable financial domination. The Financial Committee [of the League of Nations] at Geneva has been the instrument of that policy. The method consists of forcing every country in monetary difficulty to subject itself to the Committee at Geneva, which the British control. The remedies prescribed always involve the installation in the central bank of a foreign supervisor who is British or designated by the Bank of England, and the deposit of a part of the reserve of the central bank at the Bank of England, which serves both to support the pound and to fortify British influence. To guarantee against possible failure they are careful to secure the cooperation of the Federal Reserve Bank of New York. Moreover, they pass on to America the task of making some of the foreign loans if they seem too heavy, always retaining the political advantage of these operations.
>
> England is thus completely or partially entrenched in Austria, Hungary, Belgium, Norway, and Italy. She is in the process of entrenching herself in Greece and Portugal. She seeks to get a foothold in Yugoslavia and fights us cunningly in Rumania. . . . The currencies will be divided into two classes. Those of the first class, the dollar and the pound sterling, based on gold and those of the second class based on the pound and the dollar—with a part of their gold reserves being held by the Bank of England and the Federal Reserve Bank of New York. The latter moneys will have lost their independence.[3]

[3]Émile Moreau diary entry of February 6, 1928. Lester V. Chandler, *Benjamin Strong, Central Banker* (Washington, D.C.: Brookings Institution, 1958) pp. 379–80. On the gold-exchange standard and European countries being induced to overvalue their currencies, see H. Parker Willis, "The Breakdown of the Gold Exchange Standard and its Financial Imperialism," *The Annalist* (October 16, 1931): 626 ff.; and William Adams Brown, Jr., *The International Gold Standard Reinterpreted, 1914–1934* (New York: National Bureau of Economic Research, 1940), 2, pp. 732–49.

Inducing the United States to support and bolster the pound and the gold-exchange system was vital to Britain's success, and this cooperation was ensured by the close ties that developed between Montagu Norman and Benjamin Strong, governor of the Federal Reserve Bank of New York, who had seized effective and nearly absolute control of Federal Reserve operations from his appointment at the inception of the Fed in 1914 until his death in 1928. This control over the Fed was achieved over the opposition of the Federal Reserve Board in Washington, which generally opposed or grumbled at Strong's Anglophile policies. Strong and Norman made annual trips to visit each other, all of which were kept secret not only from the public but from the Federal Reserve Board itself.

Strong and the Federal Reserve Bank of New York propped up England and the gold-exchange standard in numerous ways. One was direct lines of credit, which the New York bank extended, in 1925 and after, to Britain, Belgium, Poland, and Italy, to subsidize their going to a gold-exchange standard at overvalued pars. More directly significant was a massive monetary inflation and credit expansion which Strong generated in the United States in 1924 and again in 1927, for the purpose of propping up the pound. The idea was that gold flows from Britain to the United States would be checked and reversed by American credit expansion, which would prop up or raise prices of American goods, thereby stimulating imports from Great Britain, and also lower interest rates in the U.S. as compared to Britain. The fall in interest rates would further stimulate flows of gold from the U.S. to Britain and thereby check the results of British inflation and overvaluation of the pound. Both times, the inflationary injection worked, and prevented Britain from reaping the results of its own inflationary policies, but at the high price of inflation in the United States, a dangerous stock market and real estate boom, and an eventual depression. At the secret central bank conference of July 1927 in New York, called at the behest of Norman, Strong agreed to this inflationary credit expansion over the objections of Germany and

France, and Strong gaily told the French representative that he was going to give "a little *coup de whiskey* to the stock market." It was a *coup* for which America and the world would pay dearly.[4]

The Chicago business and financial community, not having Strong's ties with England, protested vigorously against the 1927 expansion, and the Federal Reserve Bank of Chicago held out as long as it could against the expansion of cheap money and the lowering of interest rates. The *Chicago Tribune* went so far as to call for Strong's resignation, and perceptively charged that discount rates were being lowered in the interests of Great Britain. Strong, however, sold the policy to the middle West with the rationale that its purpose was to help the American farmer by means of cheap credit. In contrast, the English financial community hailed the work of Norman in securing Strong's support, and *The Banker* of London lauded Strong as "one of the best friends England ever had." *The Banker* praised the "energy and skillfullness he [Strong] has given to the service of England" and exulted that "his name should be associated with that of Mr. [Walter Hines] Page as a friend of England in her greatest need."[5]

[4]On the *coup de whiskey*, see Charles Rist, "Notice Biographique," *Revue d'Economie Politique* (November–December, 1955): 1005; translation mine. On the Strong-Norman collaboration, see also Lawrence E. Clark, *Central Banking Under the Federal Reserve System* (New York: Macmillan, 1935), pp. 307–21; and Benjamin M. Anderson, *Economics and the Public Welfare: Financial and Economic History of the United States, 1914–1946* (New York: D. Van Nostrand, 1949).

[5]*The Banker*, June 1, 1926, and November 1928. In Clark, *Central Banking Under the Federal Reserve*, pp. 315–16. See also Anderson, pp. 182–83; Benjamin H. Beckhart, "Federal Reserve Policy and the Money Market, 1923–1931," in *The New York Money Market* (New York; Columbia University Press, 1931), 4, pp. 67ff. In the autumn of 1926, a leading American banker admitted that bad consequences would follow Strong's cheap-money policy, but added, "that cannot be helped. It is the price we must pay for helping Europe." H. Parker Willis, "The Failure of the Federal Reserve," *North American Review* (1929): 553.

A blatant example of Strong's intervention to help Norman and his policy occurred in the spring of 1926, when one of Norman's influential colleagues proposed a full gold-coin standard in India. At Norman's request, Strong and a team of American economists rushed to England to ward off the plan, testifying that a gold drain to India would check inflation in other countries, and instead they successfully backed the Norman policy of a gold-exchange standard and domestic "economizing" of gold to permit domestic expansion of credit.[6]

The intimate Norman-Strong collaboration for joint inflation and the gold-exchange standard was not at all an accident of personality; it was firmly grounded on the close ties that both of them had with the House of Morgan and the Morgan interests. Strong himself was a product of the Morgan nexus; he had been the head of the Morgan-oriented Bankers Trust Company before becoming governor of the New York Fed, and his closest ties were with Morgan partners Henry P. Davison and Dwight Morrow, who induced him to assume his post at the Federal Reserve. J.P. Morgan and Company, in turn, was an agent of the British government and of the Bank of England, and its close financial ties with England, its loans to England and tie-ins with the American export trade, had been highly influential in inducing the United States to enter World War I on England's side.[7] As for Montagu Norman, his grandfather had been a partner in the London banking firm of Brown, Shipley, and Company, and of the affiliated New York firm of Brown Brothers and Company, a powerful investment banking firm long associated with the House of Morgan. Norman himself had been a partner of Brown, Shipley and had

[6]See Rothbard, *America's Great Depression,* p. 138; and Chandler, *Benjamin Strong,* pp. 356ff.

[7]Charles Callan Tansill, *America Goes to War* (Boston: Little, Brown, 1938), pp. 70–134. On the aid given by Benjamin Strong to the House of Morgan and the loans to England and France, see ibid., pp. 87–88, 96–101, 106–08, 118–32.

worked for several years in the offices of Brown Brothers in the United States.

Moreover, J.P. Morgan and Company played a direct collaborative role with the New York Fed, lending $100 million of its own to Great Britain in 1925 to facilitate its return to gold, and also collaborating in futile loans to prop up the shaky European banking system during the financial crisis of 1931. It is no wonder that in his study of the Federal Reserve System during the pre–New Deal era, Dr. Clark concluded that "the New York Reserve Bank in collaboration with a private international banking house [J.P. Morgan and Company] determined the policy to be followed by the Federal Reserve System."[8]

The major theoretical rationale employed by Strong and Norman was the idea of governmental collaboration to "stabilize" the price level. The laissez-faire policy of the classical, prewar gold standard meant that prices would be allowed to find their own level in accordance with supply and demand, and without interference by central bank manipulation. In practice, this meant a secularly falling price level, as the supply of goods rose over time in accordance with the long-run rise in productivity. And *in practice*, price stabilization really meant price *raising*: either keeping prices up when they were falling, or "reflating" prices by raising them through inflationary action by the central banks. Price stabilization therefore meant the replacement of the classical, laissez-faire gold standard by "managed money," by inflationary credit expansion stimulated by the central banks.

In England, it was, as we have seen, no accident that the lead in advocating price stabilization was taken by Sir Ralph Hawtrey and various associates of Montagu Norman, including Sir Josiah Stamp, chairman of Midland Railways and a director of the Bank of England, and two other prominent directors—Sir Basil Blackett and Sir Charles Addis.

[8]Clark, *Central Banking Under the Federal Reserve System*, p. 343.

It long has been a myth of American historiography that bankers and big businessmen are invariably believers in "hard money" as against cheap credit or inflation. This was certainly not the experience of the New Deal or the pre–New Deal era.[9] While the most articulate leaders of the price stabilizationists were academic economists led by Professor Irving Fisher of Yale, Fisher was able to enlist in his Stable Money League (founded 1921) and its successor, the Stable Money Association, a host of men of wealth, bankers and businessmen, as well as labor and farm leaders. Among those serving as officers of the league and association were: Henry Agard Wallace, editor of *Wallace's Farmer* and secretary of agriculture in the New Deal; the wealthy John G. Winant, later governor of New Hampshire; George Eastman of the Eastman-Kodak family; Frederick H. Goff, head of the Cleveland Trust Company; John E. Rovensky, executive vice president of the Bank of America; Frederic Delano, uncle of Franklin D. Roosevelt; Samuel Gompers, John P. Frey, and William Green of the American Federation of Labor; Paul M. Warburg, partner of Kuhn, Loeb and Company; Otto H. Kahn, prominent investment banker; James H. Rand, Jr., head of Remington Rand Company; and Owen D. Young of General Electric. Furthermore, the heads of the following organizations agreed to serve as ex officio honorary vice presidents: the American Association for Labor Legislation; the American Bar Association; the American Farm Bureau Federation; the Brotherhood of Railroad Trainmen; the National Association of Credit Men; the National Association of Owners of Railroad and Public Utility Securities; the National Retail Dry Goods Association; the

[9]For examples of businessmen and bankers in favor of cheap money and inflation in American history, and particularly on the inflationary role of Paul M. Warburg of Kuhn, Loeb and Company during the 1920s, see Murray N. Rothbard, "Money, the State, and Modern Mercantilism," in *Central Planning and Neo-Mercantilism*, Helmut Schoeck and James W. Wiggins, eds. (Princeton, N.J.: D. Van Nostrand, 1964), pp. 146–54.

United States Building and Loan League; the American Cotton Growers Exchange; the Chicago Association of Commerce; the Merchants' Association of New York; and the heads of the bankers associations of 43 states and the District of Columbia.[10]

Irving Fisher was unsurprisingly exultant over the supposed achievement of Governor Strong in stabilizing the wholesale price level during the late 1920s, and he led American economists in trumpeting the "new era" of permanent prosperity which the new policy of managed money was assuring to America and the world. Fisher was particularly critical of the minority of skeptical economists who warned of overexpansion in the stock and real estate markets due to cheap money, and even after the stock market crash, Fisher continued to insist that prosperity, particularly in the stock market, was just around the corner. Fisher's partiality toward stock market inflation was perhaps not unrelated to his own personal role as a millionaire investor in the stock market, a role in which he was financially dependent on a cheap-money policy.[11]

In the general enthusiasm for Strong and the new era of monetary and stock market inflation, the minority of skeptics was led by the Chase National Bank, affiliated with the Rockefeller interests, particularly A. Barton Hepburn, economic historian and chairman of the board of the bank, and Chase National's chief economist, Dr. Benjamin M. Anderson, Jr. Another highly influential and indefatigable critic was Dr. H. Parker Willis, editor of the *Journal of Commerce*, formerly aide to Senator Carter Glass (D-Va.) and professor of banking at Columbia University, along with Willis's numerous students, who included Dr. Ralph W. Robey, later to become economist at the National Association of

[10]Irving Fisher, *Stabilised Money* (London: George Allen and Unwin, 1935), pp. 104–13, 375–89, 411–12.

[11]Fisher was also a partner of James H. Rand, Jr., in a card-index manufacturing firm. Fisher, pp. 387–88; Irving Norton Fisher, *My Father Irving Fisher* (New York: Comet Press, 1956), pp. 220ff.

Manufacturers. Another critic was Dr. Rufus S. Tucker, economist at General Motors. On the Federal Reserve Board the major critic was Dr. Adolph C. Miller, a close friend of Herbert Hoover, who joined in the criticisms of the Strong policy. On the other hand, Treasury Secretary Andrew W. Mellon, of the powerful Mellon interests, enthusiastically backed the inflationist policy. This split in the nation's leading banking and business circles was to foreshadow the split over Franklin Roosevelt's monetary departures in 1933.

The First New Deal: Dollar Nationalism

The international monetary framework of the 1920s collapsed in the storm of the Great Depression; or rather, it collapsed of its own inner contradictions in a depression which it had helped to bring about. For one of the most calamitous features of the depression was the international wave of banking failures; and the banks failed from the inflation and overexpansion which were the fruits of the managed international gold-exchange standard. Once the jerry-built pyramiding of bank credit had collapsed, it brought down the banking system of nation after nation; as inflation led to a piling up of currency claims abroad, the cashing in of the claims led to a well-founded suspicion of the solvency of other banks, and so the failures spread and intensified. The failures in the weak currency countries led to the accumulation of strains in other weak currency nations, and, ultimately, on the bases of the shaky pyramid: Britain and the United States.

The major banking crisis began with the near bankruptcy in 1929 of the Boden-Kredit-Anstalt of Vienna, the major bank in Austria, which had never recovered from its dismemberment at Versailles. Desperate attempts by J.P. Morgan, the House of Rothschild, and later the New York Fed, to shore up the bank only succeeded in a temporary rescue which committed more financial resources to an unsound bank and thereby made its ultimate failure in May 1931 all the more catastrophic. Rather than permit the outright liquidation of their banking systems,

Austria, followed by Germany and other European countries, went off the gold standard during 1931.[12]

But the key to the international monetary situation was Great Britain, the nub and the base for the world's gold-exchange standard. British inflation and cheap money, and the standard that had made Britain the base of the world's money, put enormous pressure on the pound sterling, as foreign holders of sterling balances became increasingly panicky and called on the British to redeem their sterling in either gold or dollars. The heavy loans by British banks to Germany during the 1920s made the pressure after the German monetary collapse still more severe. But Britain *could* have saved the day by using the classical gold-standard medicine in such crises: by raising bank interest rates sharply, thereby attracting funds to Britain from other countries. In such monetary crises, furthermore, such temporary tight money and checks to inflation give foreigners confidence that the pound will be sustained, and they then continue to hold sterling without calling on the country for redemption. In earlier crises, for example, Britain had raised its bank rate as high as 10 percent early in the proceedings, and temporarily contracted the money supply to put a stringent check to inflation. But by 1931 deflation and hard money had become unthinkable in the British political climate. And so Britain stunned the financial world by keeping its bank rate very low, never raising it above 4.5 percent, and in fact continuing to inflate sterling still further to offset gold losses abroad. As the run on sterling inevitably intensified, Great Britain cynically repudiated its own gold-exchange standard, the very monetary standard that it had forced and cajoled Europe to adopt, by coolly going off the gold standard in September 1931. Its own international monetary system was sacrificed on the altar of continued domestic inflation.[13]

[12]See Anderson, *Economics and the Public Welfare*, pp. 232ff.

[13]See Lionel Robbins, *The Great Depression* (New York: Macmillan, 1934), pp. 89–99. See also Anderson, *Economics and the Public Welfare*,

The European monetary system was thereby broken up into separate and even warring currency blocs, replete with fluctuating exchange rates, exchange control, and trade restrictions. The major countries followed Britain off the gold standard, with the exception of Belgium, Holland, France, Italy, Switzerland, and the United States. Currency blocs formed with the British Empire forming a sterling bloc, with parities mutually fixed in relation to the pound. It is particularly ironic that one of the earliest effects of Britain's going off gold was that the overvalued pound, now free to fluctuate, fell to its genuine economic value, at or below $3.40 to the pound. And so Britain's grand experiment in returning to a form of gold at an overvalued par had ended in disaster, for herself as well as for the rest of the world.

In the last weeks of the Hoover administration, a desperate attempt was made by the U.S. to restore an international monetary system; this time the offer was made to Britain to return to the gold standard at the current, eminently more sensible par, in exchange for substantial reduction of the British war debt. No longer would Britain be forced by overvaluation to be in a chronic state of depression of its export industries. But Britain now had the nationalist bit in its teeth; and it insisted on outright "reflation" of prices back up to the pre-depression, 1929 levels. It had become increasingly clear that the powerful "price stabilizationists" were interested not so much in stabilization as in high prices, and now they would only be satisfied with an inflationary return to boom prices. Britain's rejection of the American offer proved to be fatal for any hopes of international monetary stability.[14]

The world's monetary fate finally rested with the United States, the major gold-standard country still remaining. Federal Reserve attempts to inflate the money supply and to lower

---

pp. 244 ff.; and Frederic C. Benham, *British Monetary Policy* (London: P.S. King and Son, 1932), pp. 1–45.

[14]Robbins, *The Great Depression*, pp. 100–21.

interest rates during the depression further weakened confidence in the dollar, and gold outflows combined with runs and failures of the banks to put increasing pressure on the American banking system. Finally, during the interregnum between the Hoover and Roosevelt administrations, the nation's banks began to collapse in earnest. The general bank collapse meant that the banking system, always unsound and incapable of paying more than a fraction of its liabilities on demand, could only go in either of two opposite directions. A truly laissez-faire policy would have allowed the failing banks to collapse, and thereby to engage in a swift, sharp surgical operation that would have transformed the nation's monetary system from an unsound, inflationary one to a truly "hard" and stable currency. The other pole was for the government to declare massive "bank holidays," that is, to relieve the banks of the obligation to pay their debts, and then move on to the repudiation of the gold standard and its replacement by inflated fiat paper issued by the government. It is important to realize that neither the Hoover nor the Roosevelt administrations had any intention of taking the first route. While there was a considerable split on whether or not to stay on the gold standard, no one endorsed the rigorous laissez-faire route.[15]

The new Roosevelt administration was now faced with the choice of retaining or going off the gold standard. While almost everyone supported the temporary "bank holidays," there was a severe split on the longer-run question of the monetary standard.

While the bulk of the nation's academic economists stood staunchly behind the gold standard, the indefatigable Irving Fisher redoubled his agitation for inflation, spurred onward by his personal desire to reinflate stock prices. Since the Stable

[15]See Rothbard, *America's Great Depression*, pp. 284–99; H. Parker Willis, "A Crisis in American Banking," in *The Banking Situation*, H.P. Willis and J.M. Chapman, eds. (New York: Columbia University Press, 1934), pp. 3–120.

Money Association had been supposedly dedicated to price stabilization, and what Fisher and the inflationists wanted was a drastic raising of prices, the association liquidated its assets into the new and frankly inflationist Committee for the Nation to Rebuild Prices and Purchasing Power. The Committee for the Nation, founded in January 1933, stood squarely for the "reflation" of prices back to their pre-1929 levels; stabilization of the price level was to proceed only *after* that point had been achieved. The Committee for the Nation, which was to prove crucially influential on Roosevelt's decision, was composed largely of prominent businessmen. The committee was originated by Vincent Bendix, president of Bendix Aviation, and General Robert E. Wood, head of Sears, Roebuck and Company. They were soon joined, in the fall of 1932, by Frank A. Vanderlip, long close to Fisher and former president of the National City Bank of New York, by James H. Rand, Jr., of Remington Rand, and by Magnus W. Alexander, head of the National Industrial Conference Board.

Other members of the Committee for the Nation included: Fred H. Sexauer, president of the Dairymen's League Cooperative Association; Frederic H. Frazier, chairman of the board of the General Baking Company; automobile magnate E.L. Cord; Lessing J. Rosenwald, chairman, Sears, Roebuck; Samuel S. Fels of Fels and Company; Philip K. Wrigley, president of William Wrigley Company; John Henry Hammond, chairman of the board of Bangor and Aroostook Railroad; Edward A. O'Neal, head of the American Farm Bureau Federation; L.J. Taber, head of the National Grange; F.R. Wurlitzer, vice president of Rudolph Wurlitzer Manufacturing Company; William J. McAveeny, president of Hudson Motor Company; Frank E. Gannett of the Gannett Newspapers; and Indiana banker William A. Wirt. Interestingly enough, this same group of highly conservative industrialists was later to become the Committee for Constitutional Government, the major anti–New Deal propaganda group of the late 1930s and 1940s. Yet the committee was the major proponent of the inflationist policy of the early New Deal in reflating and abandoning the gold standard.

Also associated with the Committee for the Nation was another great influence on Franklin Roosevelt's decision: agricultural economist George F. Warren of Cornell, who, along with his colleague Frank A. Pearson, was the inspiration for the reflationist Roosevelt program of continually raising the buying price of gold.

The Committee for the Nation at first included several hundred industrial and agricultural leaders, and within a year its membership reached over two thousand. Its recommendations, beginning with going off gold and embargoing gold exports, and continuing through devaluing the dollar and raising the price of gold, were fairly closely followed by the Roosevelt administration.[16] For his part, Irving Fisher, in response to a request for advice by President-elect Roosevelt, had strongly urged at the end of February a frankly inflationist policy of reflation, devaluation, and leaving the gold standard without delay.[17] By April 19, when Roosevelt had cast the die for this policy, Fisher exulted, "Now I *am* sure—as far as we ever can be sure of anything—that we are going to snap out of this depression fast. I am now one of the happiest men in the world." In the same letter to his wife, an heiress of the substantial Hazard family fortune, Fisher added,

> My next big job is to raise money for ourselves. Probably we'll have to go to Sister [his wife's sister Caroline] again. . . . I have defaulted payments the last few weeks, because I did not think it was fair to ask Sister for money when there was a real chance that I could never pay it back. I mean that if F.D.R. had followed Glass we would have been pretty surely ruined. So would Allied Chemical [in which much of his wife's family fortune was invested], and the U.S. Govt. . . . *Now* I can go to Sister with a clean conscience.[18]

[16]Fisher, *Stabilised Money*, pp. 108–09, 118–22, 413–14; and Jordan Schwarz, ed., *1933: Roosevelt's Decision, the United States Leaves the Gold Standard,* (New York: Chelsea House, 1969), pp. 44–60, 116–20.

[17]Schwarz, *1933: Roosevelt's Decision*, pp. 27–35.

[18]Fisher, *My Father Irving Fisher*, pp. 273–76.

If Irving Fisher's interest was personal as well as ideological, economic interests also underlay the concern of the Committee for the Nation. The farm groups wanted farm prices driven up, including farm export prices, which necessarily increase in terms of other currencies whenever a currency is devalued. As for the rest of the committee and other inflationists, Herbert Feis notes:

> By the spring of 1933 diverse organizations and groups were crying aloud for some kind of monetary inflation or devaluation, or both. Most effective, probably, was the Committee for the Nation. Among its members were prominent merchants, such as the head of Sears, Roebuck, some journalists, some Wall Street operators and some foreign exchange speculators. Their purpose was to get the United States off the gold standard and to bring about devaluation of the dollar from which they would profit either as speculators in foreign exchange or as businessmen. Another group, more conservative, who stood to gain by devaluation were those who had already exported gold or otherwise acquired liquid deposits in foreign banks. They conceived that they were merely protecting the value of their capital. . . . Then there were the exporters—especially of farm products—who had been at a disadvantage ever since Great Britain had gone off the gold standard and the value of sterling had fallen much below its previous parity with the dollar.[19]

Also advocating and endorsing the decision to inflate and leave the gold standard were such conservative bankers as James P. Warburg of Kuhn, Loeb and Company, one of Roosevelt's leading monetary advisers; Chicago banker and former Vice President Charles G. Dawes; Melvin A. Traylor, president of the First National Bank of Chicago; Frank Altschul of the international banking house of Lazard Frères; and Russell C. Leffingwell, partner of J.P. Morgan and Company. Leffingwell

[19]Herbert Feis, "1933: Characters in Crisis," in Schwarz, ed., *1933: Roosevelt's Decision*, pp. 150–51. Feis was a leading economist for the State Department.

told Roosevelt that his action "was vitally necessary and the most important of all the helpful things you have done."[20] Morgan himself hailed Roosevelt's decision to leave the gold standard:

> I welcome the reported action of the President and the Secretary of the Treasury in placing an embargo on gold exports. It has become evident that the effort to maintain the exchange value of the dollar at a premium as against depreciated foreign currencies was having a deflationary effect upon already severely deflated American prices and wages and employment. It seems to me clear that the way out of the depression is to combat and overcome the deflationary forces. Therefore I regard the action now taken as being the best possible course under the circumstances.[21]

Other prominent advocates of going off gold were publishers J. David Stern and William Randolph Hearst, financier James H.R. Cromwell, and Dean Wallace Donham of the Harvard Business School. Conservative Republican senators such as David A. Reed of Pennsylvania and Minority Leader Charles L. McNary of Oregon also approved the decision, and Senator Arthur Vandenberg (R-Mich.) happily declared that Americans could now compete in the export trade "for the first time in many, many months." Vandenberg concluded that "abandonment of the dollar externally may prove to be a complete answer to our problem, so far as the currency factor is concerned."[22]

Amidst this chorus of approval from leading financiers and industrialists, there was still determined opposition to going off gold. Aside from the bulk of the nation's economists, the lead in opposition was again taken by two economists with close ties to

[20]Arthur M. Schlesinger, Jr., *The Coming of the New Deal* (Boston: Houghton Mifflin, 1959), p. 202.

[21]*New York Times*, April 19, 1933; quoted in Joseph E. Reeve, *Monetary Reform Movements* (Washington, D.C.: American Council on Public Affairs, 1943), p. 275.

[22]Schwarz, ed., *1933: Roosevelt's Decision*, p. xx.

the banking community who had been major opponents of the Strong-Morgan policies during the 1920s: Dr. Benjamin M. Anderson of the Rockefeller-oriented Chase National Bank, and Dr. H. Parker Willis, editor of the *Journal of Commerce* and chief adviser to Senator Carter Glass (D-Va.), who had been secretary of the Treasury under Wilson. The Chamber of Commerce of the United States also vigorously attacked the abandonment of gold as well as price-level stabilization, and the Chamber of Commerce of New York State called for prompt return to gold.[23] From the financial community, leading opponents of Roosevelt's decision were Winthrop W. Aldrich, a Rockefeller kinsman and head of Chase National Bank, and Roosevelt's budget director, Lewis W. Douglas, of the Arizona mining family, who was related to the J. Henry Schröder international bankers and was eventually to become head of Mutual Life Insurance Company and ambassador to England. Douglas fought valiantly but in vain within the administration against going off gold and against the remainder of the New Deal program.[24]

By the end of April 1933, the United States was clearly off the gold standard, and the dollar quickly began to depreciate relative to gold and the gold-standard currencies. Britain, which a few weeks earlier had loftily rejected the idea of international stabilization, now became frightened: currency blocs and a depreciating pound to aid British exports were one thing; depreciation of the dollar to spur American exports and injure British exports was quite another. The British had the presumption to scold the United States for going off gold; they now rested their

[23]Fisher, *Stabilised Money*, pp. 355–56.

[24]On Douglas, see Schwarz, ed., *1933: Roosevelt's Decision*, pp. 135–36, 143–44, 154–58; and Schlesinger, *Coming of the New Deal*, pp. 196–97, and passim. Douglas resigned as budget director in 1934; his critical assessment of the New Deal can be found in his Lewis W. Douglas, *The Liberal Tradition: A Free People and Free Economy* (New York: D. Van Nostrand, 1935).

final hope for a restored international monetary system on the World Economic Conference scheduled for London in June 1933.[25]

Preparations for the conference had been under way for a year, under the guidance of the League of Nations, in a desperate attempt to aid the world economic and financial crisis by attempting the "restoring [of] the currencies on a healthy basis."[26] The Hoover administration was planning to urge the restoration of the international gold standard, but the abandonment of gold by the Roosevelt administration in March and April 1933 changed the American position radically. As the conference loomed ahead, it was clear that there were three fundamental positions: the gold bloc—the countries still on the gold standard, headed by France—which desired immediate return to a full international gold standard with fixed exchange rates between the major currencies and gold; the United States, which now placed greatest stress on domestic inflation of the price level; and the British, supported by their Dominions, who wished some form of combination of the two. What was still unclear was whether a satisfactory compromise between these divergent views could be worked out.

At the invitation of President Roosevelt, Prime Minister Ramsay MacDonald of Great Britain and leading statesmen of the other major countries journeyed to Washington for individual talks with the president. All that emerged from these conversations were vague agreements of intent; but the most interesting aspect of the talks was an American proposal, originated by William C. Bullitt and rejected by the French, to establish a coordinated worldwide inflation and devaluation of currencies.

[25]Robbins, *The Great Depression*, p. 123; and Schwarz ed., *1933: Roosevelt's Decision*, p. 144.

[26]Leo Pasvolsky, *Current Monetary Issues* (Washington, D.C.: Brookings Institution, 1933), p. 14.

> [T]here was serious discussions of a proposal, sponsored by the United States and vigorously opposed by the gold countries, that the whole world should embark upon a "cheaper money" policy, not only through a vigorous and concerted program of credit expansion and the stimulation of business enterprise by means of public works, but also through a simultaneous devaluation, by a fixed percentage, of all currencies which were still at their pre-depression parities.[27]

The American delegation to London was a mixed bag, but the conservative gold-standard forces could take heart from the fact that staff economic adviser was James P. Warburg, who had been working eagerly on a plan for international currency stabilization based on gold at new and realistic parities. Furthermore, conservative Professor Oliver M.W. Sprague and George L. Harrison, governor of the New York Fed, were sent to discuss proposals for temporary stabilization of the major currencies. In contrast, the president paid no attention to the petition of 85 congressmen, including ten senators, that he appoint as his economic advisor to the conference the radical inflationist and antigold priest, Father Charles E. Coughlin.[28]

The World Economic Conference, attended by delegates from 64 major nations, opened in London on June 12. The first crisis occurred over the French suggestion for a temporary "currency truce"—a de facto stabilization of exchange rates between the franc, dollar, and pound for the duration of the conference. Surely eminently reasonable, the plan was also a clever device for an entering wedge toward a hopefully permanent stabilization of exchange rates on a full gold basis. The British were amenable, provided that the pound remained fairly cheap in relation to the dollar, so that their export advantage gained since 1931 would not be lost. On June 16, Sprague and Harrison concluded an agreement with the British and French for temporary

[27]Ibid, p. 59.

[28]Robert H. Ferrell, *American Diplomacy in the Great Depression* (New York: W.W. Norton, 1957), pp. 263–64.

stabilization of the three currencies, setting the dollar-sterling rate at about $4.00 per pound, and pledging the United States not to engage in massive inflation of the currency for the duration of the agreement.

The American representatives urged Roosevelt to accept the agreement, with Sprague warning that "a failure now would be most disastrous," and Warburg declaring that without stabilization "it would be practically impossible to assume a leading role in attempting [to] bring about a lasting economic peace." But Roosevelt quickly rejected the agreement on June 17, giving two reasons: that the pound must be stabilized at no cheaper than $4.25, and that he could not accept any restraint on his freedom of action to inflate in order to raise domestic prices. Roosevelt ominously concluded that, "it is my personal view that far too much importance is being placed on existing and temporary fluctuations." And lest the American delegation take his reasoning as a stimulus to renegotiate the agreement, Roosevelt reminded Hull on June 20: "Remember that far too much influence is attached to exchange stability by banker-influenced cabinets." Upon receiving the presidential veto, the British and French were indignant, and George Harrison quit and returned home in disgust; but the American delegation went ahead and issued its official statement on temporary currency stabilization on June 22. It declared temporary stabilization impermissible, "because the American government feels that its efforts to raise prices are the most important contribution it can make."[29]

With temporary stabilization scuttled, the conference settled down to long-range discussions, the most important being centered in the subcommission on "immediate measures of financial reconstruction" of the Monetary and Financial Commission of the conference. The British delegation began by introducing a draft resolution, (1) emphasizing the importance of "cheap and plentiful credit" in order to raise the

[29]Pasvolsky, *Current Monetary Issues*, p. 70. See also Schlesinger, *Coming of the New Deal*, pp. 213–16; and Ferrell, *American Diplomacy*, p. 266.

world level of commodity prices, and (2) stating that "the central banks of the principal countries should undertake to cooperate with a view to securing these conditions and should announce their intention of pursuing vigorously a policy of cheap and plentiful money by open market operations."[30] The British thus laid stress on coordinated inflation, but said nothing about the sticking point: exchange-rate stabilization. The Dutch, the Czechoslovaks, the Japanese, and the Swiss criticized the British advocacy of inflation, and the Italian delegate warned that

> to put one's faith in immediate measures for augmenting the volume of money and credit might lead to a speculative boom followed by an even worse slump. . . . A hasty and unregulated flood [of credit] would lead to destructive results.

And the French delegate stressed that no genuine recovery could occur without a sense of economic and financial security:

> Who would be prepared to lend, with the fear of being repaid in depreciated currency always before his eyes? Who would find the capital for financing vast programs of economic recovery and abolition of unemployment, as long as there is a possibility that economic struggles would be transported to the monetary field? . . . In a word, without stable currency there can be no lasting confidence; while the hoarding of capital continues, there can be no solution.[31]

The American delegation then submitted its own draft proposal, which was similar to the British, ignored currency stability, and advocated close cooperation between all governments and central banks for "the carrying out of a policy of making credit abundantly and readily available to sound enterprise," especially by open market operations that expanded the money supply. Also government expenditures and deficits should be synchronized between the different nations.

[30]Pasvolsky, *Current Monetary Issues*, pp. 71–72.

[31]Ibid., pp. 72–74.

The difference of views between the nations on inflation and prices, however, precluded any agreement in this area at the conference. On the gold question, Great Britain submitted a policy declaration and the U.S. a draft resolution which looked forward to eventual restoration of the gold standard—but again, nothing was spelled out on exchange rates, or on the crucial question of whether restoration of price inflation should come first. In both the American and British proposals, however, even the eventual gold standard would be considerably more inflationary than it had been in the 1920s: for all domestic gold circulation, whether coin or bullion, would be abolished, and gold used only as a medium for settling international balances of payment; and all gold reserves ratios to currency would be lowered.[32]

As could have been predicted before the conference, there were three sets of views on gold and currency stabilization. The United States, backed only by Sweden, favored cheap money in order to raise domestic prices, with currency stabilization to be deferred until a sufficient price rise had occurred. Whatever international cooperation was envisaged would stress joint inflationary action to raise price levels in some coordinated manner. The United States, moreover, went further even than Sweden in calling for reflating wholesale prices back to 1926 levels. The gold bloc attacked currency and price inflation, pointed to the early postwar experience of severe inflation and currency depreciation, and hence insisted on stabilization of exchanges and the avoidance of depreciation. In the confused middle were the British and the sterling bloc, who wanted price reflation and cheap credit, but also wanted eventual return to the gold standard and temporary stabilization of the key currencies.

As the London conference foundered on its severe disagreements, the gold-bloc countries began to panic. For on the one hand the dollar was failing in the exchange markets, thus making American goods and currency more competitive. And what

[32]Ibid., pp. 74–76, 158–60, 163–66.

is more, the general gloom at the conference gave international speculators the idea that in the near future many of these countries would themselves be forced to go off gold. In consequence, money began to flow out of these countries during June, and Holland and Switzerland lost more than 10 percent of their gold reserves during that month alone. In consequence, the gold countries launched a final attempt to draft a compromise resolution. The proposed resolution was a surprisingly mild one. It committed the signatory countries to reestablishing the gold standard and stable exchange rates, but it deliberately emphasized that the parity and date for each country to return to gold was strictly up to each individual country. The existing gold-standard countries were pledged to remain on gold, which was not difficult since that was their fervent hope. The nongold countries were to reaffirm their ultimate objective to return to gold, to try their best to limit exchange speculation in the meanwhile, and to cooperate with other central banks in these two endeavors. The innocuousness of the proposed declaration comes from the fact that it committed the United States to very little more than its own resolution of over a week earlier to return eventually to the gold standard, coupled with a vague agreement to cooperate in limiting exchange speculation in the major currencies.

The joint declaration was agreed upon by Sprague and Warburg; by James M. Cox, head of the Monetary Commission of the conference; and by Raymond Moley, who had taken charge of the delegation as a freewheeling White House adviser. Moley was assistant secretary of state and had been a monetary nationalist. Moley, however, sent the declaration to Roosevelt on June 30, urging the president to accept it, especially since Roosevelt had been willing a few weeks earlier to stabilize at a $4.25 pound while the depreciation of the dollar during June had now brought the market rate up to $4.40. Across the Atlantic, Undersecretary of the Treasury Dean G. Acheson, influential Wall Street financier Bernard M. Baruch, and Lewis W. Douglas also strongly endorsed the London declaration.

Not hearing immediately from the president, Moley frantically wired Roosevelt the next morning that "success even continuance of the conference depends upon United States agreement."[33] Roosevelt cabled his rejection on July 1, declaring that "a sufficient interval should be allowed the United States to permit . . . a demonstration of the value of price lifting efforts which we have well in hand." Roosevelt's rejection of the innocuous agreement was in itself startling enough; but he felt that he had to add insult to injury, to slash away at the London conference so that no danger might exist of currency stabilization or of the reconstruction of an international monetary order. Hence he sent on July 3 an arrogant and contemptuous public message to the London conference, the famous "bombshell" message, so named for its impact on the conference.

Roosevelt began by lambasting the idea of temporary currency stabilization, which he termed a "specious fallacy," an "artificial and temporary . . . diversion." Instead, Roosevelt declared that the emphasis must be placed on "the sound internal economic system of a nation." In particular,

> old fetishes of so-called international bankers are being replaced by efforts to plan national currencies with the objective of giving to those currencies a continuing purchasing power which . . . a generation hence will have the same purchasing and debt-paying power as the dollar value we hope to attain in the near future. That objective means more to the good of other nations than a fixed ratio for a month or two in terms of the pound or franc.

In short, the president was now totally committed to the nationalist Fisher–Committee for the Nation program for paper money, currency inflation and very steep reflation of prices, and then stabilization of the higher internal price level. The idea of stable exchange rates and an international monetary order

[33]Schlesinger, *Coming of the New Deal*, pp. 218–21; Pasvolsky, *Current Monetary Issues*, pp. 80–82.

could fade into limbo.[34] The World Economic Conference limped along aimlessly for a few more weeks, but the Roosevelt bombshell message effectively killed the conference, and the hope for a restored international monetary order was dead for a fateful decade. From here on in the 1930s, monetary nationalism, currency blocs, and commercial and financial warfare would be the order of the day.

The French were bitter and the English stricken at the Roosevelt message. The chagrined James P. Warburg promptly resigned as financial adviser to the delegation, and this was to be the beginning of the exit of this highly placed economic adviser from the Roosevelt administration. A similar fate was in store for Oliver Sprague and Dean Acheson. As for Raymond Moley, who had been repudiated by the president's action, he tried to restore himself in Roosevelt's graces by a fawning and obviously insincere telegram, only to be ousted from office shortly after his return to the States. Playing an ambivalent role in the entire affair, Bernard Baruch, who was privately in favor of the old gold standard, praised Roosevelt fulsomely for his message. "Until each nation puts its house in order by the same Herculean efforts that you are performing," Baruch wrote the president, "there can be no common denominators by which we can endeavor to solve the problems. . . . There seems to be one common ground that all nations can take, and that is the one outlined by you."[35]

Expressions of enthusiastic support for the president's decision came, as might be expected, from Irving Fisher and George F. Warren, who urged Roosevelt to avoid any possible agreement that might limit "our freedom to change the dollar

[34]The full text of Roosevelt's message can be found in Pasvolsky, *Current Monetary Issues*, pp. 83–84, or Ferrell, *American Diplomacy*, pp. 270–72.

[35]Schlesinger, *Coming of the New Deal*, p. 224. For Baruch's private views, see Margaret Coit, *Mr. Baruch* (Boston: Houghton Mifflin, 1957), pp. 432–34.

any day." James A. Farley has recorded in his memoirs that Roosevelt was prompted to send his angry message by coming to suspect a plot to influence Moley in favor of stabilization by Thomas W. Lamont, partner of J.P. Morgan and Company, working through Moley's conference aide and White House adviser, Herbert Bayard Swope, who was close to the Morgans and also a longtime confidant of Baruch. This might well account for Roosevelt's bitter reference to the "so-called international bankers." The situation is curious, however, since Swope was firmly on the antistabilizationist side, and Roosevelt's London message was greeted enthusiastically by Russell Leffingwell of Morgans, who apparently took little notice of its attack on international bankers. Leffingwell wrote to the president: "You were very right not to enter into any temporary or permanent arrangements to peg the dollar in relation to sterling or any other currency."[36]

From the date of the torpedoing of the London Economic Conference, monetary nationalism prevailed for the remainder of the 1930s. The United States finally fixed the dollar at $35 an ounce in January 1934, amounting to a two-thirds increase in the gold price of the dollar from its original moorings less than a year before, and to a 40-percent devaluation of the dollar. The gold nations continued on gold for two more years, but the greatly devalued dollar now began to attract a flood of gold from the gold countries, and France was finally forced off gold in the fall of 1936, with the other major gold countries—Switzerland, Belgium, and Holland—following shortly thereafter. While the dollar was technically fixed in terms of gold, there was no further gold coin or bullion redemption within the U.S. Gold was used only as a method of clearing balances of payments, with only fitful redemption to foreign countries.

[36]Schlesinger, *Coming of the New Deal*, p. 224; Ferrell, *American Diplomacy in the Great Depression*, pp. 273ff.

The only significant act of international collaboration after 1934 came in the fall of 1936, at about the time France was forced to leave the gold standard. Partly to assist the French, the United States, Great Britain, and France entered into a Tripartite Agreement with France, beginning on September 25, 1936. The French agreed to throw in the exchange-rate sponge, and devalued the franc by between one-fourth and one-third. At this new par, the three governments agreed—*not* to stabilize their currencies—but to iron out day-to-day fluctuations in them, to engage in mutual stabilization of each other's currencies only within each 24-hour period. This was scarcely stabilization, but it did constitute a moderating of fluctuations, as well as politico-monetary collaboration, which began with the three Western countries and soon expanded to include the other former gold nations: Belgium, Holland, and Switzerland. This collaboration continued until the outbreak of World War II.[37]

At least one incident marred the harmony of the Tripartite Agreement. In the fall of 1938, while the United States and Britain were hammering out a trade agreement, the British began pushing the pound below $4.80. At the threat of this cheapening of the pound, U.S. Treasury officials warned Secretary of the Treasury Henry Morgenthau, Jr., that if "sterling drops substantially below $4.80, our foreign and domestic business will be adversely affected." In consequence, Morgenthau successfully insisted that the trade agreement with Britain must include a clause that the agreement would terminate if Britain should allow the pound to fall below $4.80.[38]

[37]On the Tripartite Agreement, see Raymond F. Mikesell, *United States Economic Policy and International Relations* (New York: McGraw-Hill, 1952), pp. 55–59; W.H. Steiner and E. Shapiro, *Money and Banking* (New York: Henry Holt, 1941), pp. 85–87, 91–93; and Anderson, *Economics and the Public Welfare*, pp. 414–20.

[38]Lloyd C. Gardner, *Economic Aspects of New Deal Diplomacy* (Madison: University of Wisconsin Press, 1964), p. 107.

Here we may only touch on a fascinating historical problem which has been discussed by revisionist historians of the 1930s: To what extent was the American drive for war against Germany the result of anger and conflict over the fact that, in the 1930s' world of economic and monetary nationalism, the Germans, under the guidance of Dr. Hjalmar Schacht, went their way successfully on their own, totally outside of Anglo-American control or of the confinements of what remained of the cherished American Open Door?[39] A brief treatment of this question will serve as a prelude to examining the aim of the war-borne "second New Deal" of reconstructing a new international monetary order, an order that in many ways resembled the lost world of the 1920s.

German economic nationalism in the 1930s was, first of all, conditioned by the horrifying experience that Germany had had with runaway inflation and currency depreciation during the early 1920s, culminating in the monetary collapse of 1923. Though caught with an overvalued par as each European country went off the gold standard, no German government could have politically succeeded in engaging once again in the dreaded act of devaluation. No longer on gold, and unable to devalue the mark, Germany was obliged to engage in strict exchange control. In this economic climate, Dr. Schacht was particularly successful in making bilateral trade agreements with individual countries, agreements which amounted to

[39]For revisionist emphasis on this economic basis for the American drive toward war with Germany, see ibid., pp. 98–108; Lloyd C. Gardner, "The New Deal, New Frontiers, and the Cold War: A Re-examination of American Expansion, 1933–1945," in *Corporations and the Cold War,* David Horowitz, ed. (New York: Monthly Review Press, 1969), pp. 105–41; William Appleman Williams, *The Tragedy of American Diplomacy* (Cleveland, Ohio: World Publishing, 1959), pp. 127–47; Robert Freeman Smith, "American Foreign Relations, 1920–1942," in *Towards a New Past,* Barton J. Bernstein, ed. (New York: Pantheon Books, 1968), pp. 245–62; and Charles Callan Tansill, *Back Door to War* (Chicago: Henry Regnery, 1952), pp. 441–42.

direct "barter" arrangements that angered the United States and other Western countries in totally bypassing gold and other international banking or financial arrangements.

In the anti-German propaganda of the 1930s, the German barter deals were agreements in which Germany somehow invariably emerged as coercive victor and exploiter of the other country involved, even though they were mutually agreed upon and therefore presumably mutually beneficial exchanges.[40] Actually, there was nothing either diabolic or unilaterally exploitive about the barter deals. Part of the essence of the barter arrangements has been neglected by historians—the deliberate overvaluation of the exchange rates of *both* currencies involved in the deals. The German mark, as we have seen, was deliberately overvalued as the alternative to the spectre of currency depreciation; the situation of the other currencies was a bit more complex. Thus, in the barter agreements between Germany and the various Balkan countries (especially Rumania, Hungary, Bulgaria, and Yugoslavia), in which the Balkans exchanged agricultural products for German-manufactured goods, the Balkan currencies were also fixed at an artificially overvalued rate vis-à-vis gold and the currencies of Britain and the other Western countries. This meant that Germany agreed to pay higher than world market rates for Balkan agricultural products while the latter paid higher rates for German-manufactured products.

For the Balkan countries, the point of all this was to force Balkan consumers of manufactured goods to subsidize their own peasants and agriculturists. The external consequence was that Germany was able to freeze out Britain and other Western countries from buying Balkan food and raw materials; and since the British could not compete in paying for Balkan

[40]Thus, see Douglas Miller, *You Can't Do Business With Hitler* (Boston, 1941), esp. pp. 73–77; and Michael A. Heilperin, *The Trade of Nations* (New York: Alfred Knopf, 1947), pp. 114–17. Miller was commercial attaché at the U.S. Embassy in Berlin throughout the 1930s.

produce, the Balkan countries, in the bilateral world of the 1930s, did not have sufficient pounds or dollars to buy manufactured goods from the West. Thus, Britain and the West were deprived of raw materials and markets for their manufactures by the astute policies of Hjalmar Schacht and the mutually agreeable barter agreements between Germany and the Balkan and other, including Latin American, countries.[41] May not Western anger at successful German competition through bilateral agreements and Western desire to liquidate such competition have been important factors in the Western drive for war against Germany?

Lloyd Gardner has demonstrated the early hostility of the United States toward German economic controls and barter arrangements, its attempts to pressure Germany to shift to a multilateral, "Open-Door" system for American products, and the repeated American rebuffs to German proposals for bilateral exchanges between the two countries. As early as June 26, 1933, the influential American consul-general at Berlin, George Messersmith, was warning that such continued policies would make "Germany a danger to world peace for years to come."[42] In pursuing this aggressive policy, President Roosevelt overrode Agricultural Adjustment Administration chief George Peek, who favored accepting bilateral deals with Germany and, perhaps not coincidentally, was to be an ardent "isolationist" in the late 1930s. Instead, Roosevelt followed the policy of the leading interventionist and spokesman for an "Open Door" to American products, Secretary of State Cordell Hull, as well as his assistant secretary, Francis B. Sayre, son-in-law of Woodrow Wilson. By 1935, American officials were calling

[41]For an explanation of the workings of the German barter agreements, see Ludwig von Mises, *Human Action* (New Haven, Conn.: Yale University Press, 1949), pp. 796–99. Also on the agreements, see Hjalmar Schacht, *Confessions of "The Old Wizard"* (Boston: Houghton Mifflin, 1956), pp. 302–05.

[42]Lloyd Gardner, *New Deal Diplomacy*, p. 98.

Germany an "aggressor" because of its successful bilateral trade competition, and Japan was similarly castigated for much the same reasons. By late 1938, J. Pierrepont Moffat, head of the Western European Division of the State Department, was complaining that German control of Central and Eastern Europe would mean "a still further extension of the area under a closed economy." And, more specifically, in May 1940, Assistant Secretary of State Breckenridge Long warned that a German-dominated Europe would mean that "every commercial order will be routed to Berlin and filled under its orders somewhere in Europe rather than in the United States."[43] And shortly before American entry into the war, John J. McCloy, later to be U.S. high commissioner of occupied Germany, was to write in a draft for a speech by Secretary of War Henry Stimson:

> With German control of the buyers of Europe and her practice of governmental control of all trade, it would be well within her power as well as the pattern she has thus far displayed, to shut off our trade with Europe, with South America and with the Far East.[44]

Not only were Hull and the United States ardent in pressing an anti-German policy against its bilateral trade system, but sometimes Secretary Hull had to whip even Britain into line. Thus, in early 1936, Cordell Hull warned the British ambassador that the "clearing arrangements reached by Britain with Argentina, Germany, Italy and other countries were handicapping the efforts of this Government to carry forward its broad program with the favored-nation policy underlying it." The tendency of these British arrangements was to "drive straight toward bilateral trading," and they were therefore milestones on the road to war.[45]

[43]Smith, "American Foreign Relations, 1920–1942," p. 247; Lloyd Gardner, *New Deal Diplomacy*, p. 99.

[44]Lloyd Gardner, "New Deal, New Frontiers," p. 118.

[45]Tansill, *Back Door to War*, p. 441.

One of the United States government's biggest economic worries was the growing competition of Germany and its bilateral trade in Latin America. As early as 1935, Cordell Hull had concluded that Germany was "straining every tendon to undermine United States trading relations with Latin America."[46] A great deal of political pressure was used to combat German competition. Thus, in the mid-1930s, the American Chamber of Commerce in Brazil repeatedly pressed the State Department to scuttle the Germany-Brazil barter deal, which the chamber termed the "greatest single obstacle to free trade in South America." Brazil was finally induced to cancel its agreement with Germany in exchange for a $60 million loan from the U.S. America's exporters, grouped in the National Foreign Trade Council, issued resolutions against German trade methods, and pressured the government for stronger action. And in late 1938 President Roosevelt asked Professor James Harvey Rogers, an economist and disciple of Irving Fisher, to make a currency study of all of South America in order to minimize "German and Italian influence on this side of the Atlantic."

It is no wonder that German diplomats in Brazil, Chile, and Uruguay reported home that the United States was "exerting very strong pressure against Germany commercially," which included economic, commercial, and political opposition designed to drive Germany out of the Brazilian and other South American markets.[47]

In the spring of 1935, the German ambassador to Washington, desperately anxious to bring an end to American political and economic warfare, asked the United States what Germany could do to end American hostilities. The American answer, which amounted to a demand for unconditional economic surrender, was that Germany abandon its economic policy in

[46]Smith, "American Foreign Relations, 1920–1942," p. 247.

[47]Lloyd Gardner, *New Deal Diplomacy*, pp. 59–60.

favor of America. The American reply "really meant," noted Pierrepont Moffat, "a fundamental acceptance by Germany of our trade philosophy, and a thoroughgoing partnership with us along the road of equality of treatment and the reduction of trade barriers." The United States further indicated that it was interested that Germany accept, not so much the *principle* of the most-favored national clause in all international trade, but specifically for *American* exports.[48]

When war broke out in September 1939, Bernard Baruch's reaction was to tell President Roosevelt that "if we keep our prices down there is no reason why we shouldn't get the customers of the belligerent nations that they have had to drop because of the war. And in that event," Baruch exulted, "Germany's barter system will be destroyed."[49] But particularly significant is the retrospective comment made by Secretary Hull:

> [W]ar did not break out between the United States and any country with which we had been able to negotiate a trade agreement. It is also a fact that, with very few exceptions, the countries with which we signed trade agreements joined together in resisting the Axis. The political lineup follows the economic lineup.[50]

[48]Ibid., p. 103. It might be noted that in the spring of 1936, Secretary Hull refused to settle for a bilateral deal to sell Germany a large store of American cotton; Hull denounced the idea as "blackmail." The predictable result was that in the next couple of years the sources of raw cotton imported into Germany shifted sharply from the United States to Brazil and Egypt, which had been willing to make barter sales of cotton. Ibid., p. 104; Arthur Schweitzer, *Big Business in the Third Reich* (Bloomington: Indiana University Press, 1964), p. 316.

[49]Francis Neilson, *The Tragedy of Europe* (Appleton, Wis.: C.C. Nelson, 1946), 5, p. 289. For a brief but illuminating study of German-American trade and currency hostility in the 1930s leading to World War II, see Thomas H. Etzold, *Why America Fought Germany in World War II* (St. Louis: Forums in History, Forum Press, 1973).

[50]Cordell Hull, *Memoirs of Cordell Hull* (New York, 1948), 1, p. 81.

Considering that Secretary Hull was a leading maker of American foreign policy throughout the 1930s and through World War II, it is certainly a possibility that his remarks should be taken, not as a quaint testimony to Hull's *idée fixe* on reciprocal trade, but as a positive causal statement of the thrust of American foreign policy. Read in that light, Hull's remark becomes a significant admission rather than a flight of speculative fancy. Reinforcing this interpretation would be a similar reading of the testimony before the House of Representatives in 1945 of top Treasury aide Harry Dexter White, defending the Bretton Woods agreements. White declared:

> I think it [a Bretton Woods system] would very definitely have made a considerable contribution to checking the war and possibly might have prevented it. A great many of the devices which Germany and Japan utilized would have been illegal in the international sphere, had these countries been participating members.[51]

Is White saying that the Allies deliberately made war upon the Axis because of these bilateral, exchange control and other competitive devices, which a Bretton Woods—or for that matter a 1920s—system would have precluded?

We may take as our final testimony to the possible economic causes of World War II the assertion by the influential *Times* of London, well after the start of the war:

> One of the fundamental causes of this war has been the unrelaxing efforts of Germany since 1918 to secure wide enough foreign markets to straighten her finances at the very time when all her competitors were forced by their own debts to adopt exactly the same course. Continuous friction was inevitable.[52]

[51]Richard N. Gardner, *Sterling-Dollar Diplomacy* (Oxford: Clarendon Press, 1956), p. 141.

[52]*The Times* (London), October 11, 1940; quoted in Neilson, *Tragedy of Europe*, 5, p. 286.

THE SECOND NEW DEAL: THE DOLLAR TRIUMPHANT

Whether and to what extent German economic nationalism was a cause for the American drive toward war, one point is certain: that, even before official American entry into the war, one of America's principal war aims was to reconstruct an international monetary order. A corollary aim was to replace economic nationalism and bilateralism by the Hullian kind of multilateral trading and "Open Door" for American goods. But the most insistent drive, and the particularly successful one, was to reconstruct an international monetary system. The system in view was to resemble the gold-exchange system of the 1920s quite closely. Once again, all the major world's currencies were to abandon fluctuating and nationally determined exchange rates on behalf of fixed parities with other currencies and of all of them with gold. Once again, there was to be no full-fledged or internal gold standard for any of these nations, while in theory all currencies were to be fixed in terms of one key currency, which would form a gold-exchange standard on which other nations could pyramid their own supply of domestic money. But there were two crucial differences from the 1920s. One was that while the key currency was to be the only currency redeemable in gold, there was to be no further embarrassing possibility of internal redemption in gold; gold was only to be a method of international payment between central banks, and never again an actual money held by the public. In this way, the key currency—and the rest of the world in response—could expand and inflate much further than in the 1920s, freed as they were from the check of domestic redemption. But the second difference was more politically far-reaching: for instead of two joint-partner key currencies, the pound and the dollar, with the dollar as workhorse junior subaltern, the *only* key currency now was to be the dollar, which was to be fixed at $35 to the gold ounce. The pound had had it; and just as the United States was to use World War II to replace British imperialism with its own far-flung empire, so in the monetary sphere, the United States was now to move in and take over, with the pound no less subordinate than all the other major currencies. It was truly a triumphant "dollar imperialism" to parallel the imperial American thrust in the political sphere. As Secretary of the Treasury Henry Morgenthau, Jr., was later to express it, the critical and eminently successful objective was "to move the financial center of the world" from London to the United States Treasury.[53] And all this eminently was in keeping with the prophetic vision of Cordell Hull, the man who, in the words of Gabriel Kolko, had "the basic responsibility for American political and economic planning for the peace." For Hull had urged upon Congress as far back as 1932 that America "gird itself, yield to the law of manifest destiny, and go forward as the supreme world factor economically and morally."[54]

World War II was the occasion for a new coalition to form behind the New Deal, a coalition which reintegrated many conservative "internationalist" financial interests who had been thrown into opposition by the domestic statism or economic nationalism of the earlier New Deal. This reintegration of the entire conservative financial community was particularly true in the field of international economic and monetary policy. Here, Dr. Leo Pasvolsky, a conservative economist who had broken with the New Deal upon the scuttling of the London Economic Conference, returned to a crucial role as Secretary Hull's special adviser on postwar planning. Dean Acheson, also disaffected by the radical monetary measures of 1933–34, was now back as assistant secretary of state for economic affairs. And when the ailing Cordell Hull retired in late 1944, he was replaced by Edward Stettinius, the son of a Morgan partner and himself former president of Morgan-oriented U.S. Steel. Stettinius chose as his assistant secretary for economic affairs the

[53]Richard Gardner, *Sterling-Dollar Diplomacy*, p. 76.

[54]Smith, "American Foreign Relations, 1920–1942," p. 252; Gabriel Kolko, *The Politics of War: The World and United States Foreign Policy, 1943–1945* (New York: Random House, 1968), pp. 243–44.

man who quickly became the key official for postwar international economic planning, William L. Clayton, a former leader of the anti–New Deal Liberty League, and chairman and major partner of Anderson, Clayton and Company, the world's largest cotton export firm. Clayton's major focus in postwar planning was to promote and encourage American exports—with cotton, not unnaturally, never out of the forefront of his concerns.[55]

Even before American entry into the war, U.S. economic war aims were well-defined and rather brutally simple: they hinged on a determined assault upon the 1930s system of economic and monetary nationalism, so as to promote American exports, investments, and financial dealings overseas—in short, the "Open Door" for American commerce. In the sphere of commercial policy, this took the form of pressure for reduction of tariffs on American products, and the elimination of quantitative import restrictions on those products. In the allied sphere of monetary policy, it meant the breakup of powerful nationalistic currency blocs, and the restoration of an international monetary order based on the dollar in which currencies would be convertible into each other at predictable and fixed parities and there would be a minimum of national exchange controls over the purchase and use of foreign currencies.

And even as the United States prepared to enter the war to save its ally, Great Britain, it was preparing to bludgeon the British at a time of great peril to abandon their sterling bloc, which they had organized effectively after the Ottawa Agreements of 1932. World War II would presumably deal effectively with the German bilateral trade and currency menace; but what about the problem of Great Britain?

John Maynard Lord Keynes long had led those British economists who had urged a policy of all-out economic and monetary

[55]Kolko, *The Politics of War*, pp. 264, 485 ff.; Lloyd C. Gardner, *Architects of Illusion: Men and Ideas in American Foreign Policy, 1941–1949* (Chicago: Quadrangle Books, 1970), pp. 113–38.

nationalism on behalf of inflation and full employment. He had gone so far as to hail Roosevelt's torpedoing of the London Economic Conference because the path was then cleared for economic nationalism. Keynes's visit to Washington on behalf of the British government in the summer of 1941 now spread gloom about the British determination to continue their bilateral economic policies after the war. High State Department official J. Pierrepont Moffat despaired that "the future is clouding up rapidly and that despite the war the Hitlerian commercial policy will probably be adopted by Great Britain."[56]

The United States responded by putting the pressure on Great Britain at the Atlantic Conference in August 1941. Undersecretary of State Sumner Welles insisted that the British agree to remove discrimination against American exports, and abolish their policies of autarchy, exchange controls, and Imperial Preference blocs.[57] Prime Minister Churchill tartly refused, but the United States was scarcely prepared to abandon its crucial aim of breaking down the sterling bloc. As President Roosevelt privately told his son Elliott at the Atlantic Conference:

> It's something that's not generally known, but British bankers and German bankers have had world trade pretty well sewn up in their pockets for a long time. . . . Well, now, that's not so good for American trade, is it? . . . If in the past German and British economic interests have operated to exclude us from world trade, kept our merchant shipping closed down, closed us out of this or that market, and now Germany and Britain are at war, what should we do?[58]

The signing of Lend-Lease agreements was the ideal time for wringing concessions from the British, but Britain consented to

[56]Lloyd Gardner, "New Deal, New Frontiers," p. 120.

[57]Richard Gardner, *Sterling-Dollar Diplomacy*, pp. 42ff.; Lloyd Gardner, *New Deal Diplomacy*, pp. 275-80.

[58]Smith, "American Foreign Relations, 1920–1942," p. 252; Kolko, *The Politics of War*, pp. 248-49.

sign the agreement's Article VII—which merely involved a vague commitment to the elimination of discriminatory treatment in international trade—only after intense pressure by the United States. The agreement was signed at the end of February 1942, and in return the State Department pledged to the British that the U.S. would pursue a policy of economic expansion and full employment after the war. Even under these conditions, however, Britain soon maintained that the Lend-Lease Agreement committed it to virtually nothing. To Cordell Hull, however, the agreement on Article VII was decisive and constituted "a long step toward the fulfillment, after the war, of the economic principles for which I had been fighting for half a century." The United States also insisted that other nations receiving Lend-Lease sign a virtually identical commitment to multilateralism after the war. In his first major public address in nearly a year, Hull, in July 1942, could now look forward confidently that

> leadership toward a new system of international relationships in trade and other economic affairs will devolve very largely upon the United States because of our great economic strength. We should assume this leadership, and the responsibility that goes with it, primarily for reasons of pure national self-interest.[59]

In the postwar planning for economic affairs, the State Department was in charge of commercial and trade policies, while the Treasury conducted the planning in the areas of money and finance. In charge of postwar international financial planning for the Treasury was the economist Harry Dexter White. In early 1942, White presented his first plan, which was to be one of the two major foundations of the postwar monetary system. White's proposal was of course within the framework of American postwar economic objectives. The countries of the world were to join a Stabilization Fund, totaling $5 billion, which would lend funds at short term to deficit countries to

[59]Ibid., pp. 249–51.

iron out temporary balance-of-payments difficulties. But in return for this provision of greater liquidity and short-term aid to deficit countries, exchange rates of currencies were to be fixed, in relation to the dollar and hence to gold, with the gold price to be set at $35 an ounce, and exchange controls were to be abandoned by the various nations.

While the White Plan envisioned a substantial amount of inflation to provide greater currency liquidity, the British responded with a Keynes Plan that was far more inflationary. By this time, Lord Keynes had abandoned economic and monetary nationalism for Britain under severe American pressure, and his aim was to salvage as much domestic inflation and cheap money for Britain as he could possibly induce America to accept. The Keynes Plan envisioned an International Clearing Union (ICU), which, in return for agreeing to stable exchange rates between currencies and the abandonment of exchange control, provided a huge loan fund to its members of $26 billion. The Keynes Plan, moreover, provided for a new international monetary unit, the "bancor," which could be issued by the ICU in such large amounts as to provide almost unchecked room for inflation, even in a country with a large deficit in its balance of payments. The nations would consult with each other about correcting balance-of-payments disequilibria, through altering their exchange rates. The Keynes Plan, furthermore, provided automatic access to the fund of liquidity, with none of the embarrassing requirements, as included in the White Plan, for deficit countries to cease creating deficits by inflating their currency. Whereas the White Plan authorized the Stabilization Fund to require deficit countries to cease inflating in return for fund loans, the Keynes Plan envisioned that inflation would proceed unchecked, with all the burden of necessary adjustments to be placed on the hard-money, creditor countries, who would be expected to inflate faster themselves, in order not to gain currency from the deficit nations.

The White Plan was stringently attacked by the conservative nationalists and inflationists in Britain, particularly G.R. Boothby,

Lord Beaverbrook, the *Times* of London, and the *Economist*. The Keynes Plan was attacked by conservatives in the United States, as was even the White Plan for interfering with market forces, and for automatic extension of credit to deficit countries. Critical of the White Plan were the Guaranty Survey of the Guaranty Trust Company and the American Bankers Association; furthermore, the *New York Times* and *New York Herald Tribune* called for return to the classical gold standard, and attacked the large measure of governmental financial planning envisioned by both the Keynes and White proposals.[60]

After negotiating during 1943 and into the spring of 1944, the United States and Britain hammered out a compromise of the White and Keynes plans in April 1944. The compromise was adopted by a world economic conference in July at Bretton Woods, New Hampshire; it was Bretton Woods that was to provide the monetary framework for the postwar world.[61]

The compromise established an International Monetary Fund (IMF) as the stabilization mechanism; its total funds were fixed at $8.8 billion, far closer to the White than to the Keynes prescriptions. Its balance of IMF international control as against domestic autonomy lay between the White and Keynes plans, leaving the whole problem highly fuzzy. On the one hand, national access to the fund was *not* to be automatic; but on the other, the fund could no longer require corrective domestic economic policies of its members. On the question of exchange rates, the Americans yielded to the British insistence on allowing room for domestic inflation even at the expense of stable exchange rates. The compromise provided that each country could be free to make a 10-percent change in its exchange rate,

[60]Richard Gardner, *Sterling-Dollar Diplomacy*, pp. 71ff., 95–99.

[61]We do not deal here with the other institution established at Bretton Woods—the International Bank for Reconstruction and Development—which, in contrast to the International Monetary Fund, comes under commercial and financial, rather than monetary, policy.

and that larger changes could be made to correct "fundamental disequilibria"; in short, that a chronically deficit country could devalue its currency rather than check its own inflation. Furthermore, the U.S. yielded again in allowing creditor countries to suffer by permitting deficit countries to impose exchange controls on "scarce currencies." This meant in effect that the major European countries, whose currencies would be fixed at existing highly overvalued rates in relation to the dollar, would thus be permitted to enter the IMF with chronically overvalued currencies and then impose exchange controls on "scarce," undervalued dollars. But despite these extensive concessions, there was no "bancor"; the dollar, fixed at $35 per gold ounce was now to be firmly established as the key currency base of a new world monetary order. Besides, for the dollar to be undervalued and other major currencies to be overvalued greatly spurs American exports, which was one of the basic aims of the entire operation. U.S. Ambassador to Britain John G. Winant recorded the perceptive hostility to the Bretton Woods Agreement by the majority of the directors of the Bank of England; for these men saw "that if the plan is adopted financial control will leave London and sterling exchange will be replaced by dollar exchange."[62]

The proposed International Monetary Fund ran into a storm of conservative opposition in the United States, from the opposite pole of the hostility of the British nationalists. The American attack on the IMF was essentially launched by two major groups: conservative Eastern bankers and Midwestern isolationists. Among the bankers, the American Bankers Association (ABA) attacked the unsound and inflationary policy of allowing debtor countries to control access to international funds; and W. Randolph Burgess, president of the ABA, denounced the provision for debtor rationing of "scarce currencies" as an "abomination." The *New York Times* urged rejection of the IMF,

[62]John G. Winant to Hull, April 12, 1944; in Richard Gardner, *Sterling-Dollar Diplomacy*, p. 123. See also ibid., pp. 110–21.

and proposed making loans to Britain in exchange for the abolition of exchange controls and quantitative restrictions on imports. Another bankers' group came up with a "key currency" proposal as a substitute for Bretton Woods. This key currency plan was proposed by economist John H. Williams, vice president of the Federal Reserve Bank of New York, and was endorsed by Leon Fraser, president of the First National Bank of New York, and by Winthrop W. Aldrich, head of the Chase National Bank. It envisioned a bilateral pound-dollar stabilization, fueled by a large transitional American loan, or even grant, to Great Britain. Thus, the key-currency people were ready to abandon temporarily not only the classical gold standard but even an international monetary order, and to stay temporarily in a modified version of the world of the 1930s.[63]

The Midwestern isolationist critics of the IMF were led by Senator Robert A. Taft (R-Ohio), who charged that, while the bulk of the valuable hard money placed in the fund would be American dollars, the dollars would be subject to international control by the fund authorities, and therefore by the debtor countries. The debtor countries could then still continue exchange controls and sterling bloc practices. Here Taft failed to realize that formal and informal structures in the Bretton Woods design would ensure effective United States control of both the IMF and the International Bank.[64]

[63]An elaboration of the banker-oriented criticisms of the International Monetary Fund may be found in Anderson, *Economics and the Public Welfare*, pp. 578–89.

[64]Henry W. Berger, "Senator Robert A. Taft Dissents from Military Escalation," in *Cold War Critics: Alternatives to American Foreign Policy in the Truman Years*, Thomas G. Paterson, ed. (Chicago: Quadrangle Books, 1971), pp. 174–75, 198. Taft also strongly opposed the government's guaranteeing of private foreign investments, such as were involved in the International Bank program. Ibid. See also Kolko, *Politics of War*, pp. 256–57; Lloyd Gardner, *New Deal Diplomacy*, p. 287; and Mikesell, *United States Economic Policy*, pp. 199f.

The administration countered the critics of Bretton Woods with a massive propaganda campaign, which was able to drive the agreement through Congress by mid-July 1945. It emphasized that the U.S. government would have effective control, at least of its own representatives in the fund. It played up—in what proved to be gross exaggeration—the favorable aspects of the various ambiguous provisions: insisting that debtor access to the fund would not be automatic, that exchange controls would be removed, and that exchange rates would be stabilized. It pushed heavily the vague idea that the fund was crucial to postwar international cooperation to keep the peace. Particularly interesting was the argument of Will Clayton and others that Bretton Woods would facilitate the general commercial policy of eliminating trade discrimination and barriers against American exports. This argument was put particularly baldly by Treasury Secretary Morgenthau in a speech to Detroit industrialists. Morgenthau promised that the Bretton Woods agreement would lead to a world trade freed from exchange controls and depreciated currencies, and that this would greatly increase the exports of American automobiles. Since the fund would begin operations the following year by accepting the existing grossly overvalued currency parities that most of the nations insisted upon, this meant that Morgenthau might have known whereof he spoke. For if other currencies are overvalued and the dollar undervalued, American exports are indeed encouraged and subsidized.[65]

It is perhaps understandable, then, that not only the major farm, labor, and New Deal liberal organizations pushed for Bretton Woods, but that the large majority of industrial and financial interests also approved the agreement and urged its passage in Congress. American approval in mid-1945 was followed, after lengthy soul-searching, by the approval of Great Britain at the end of the year. By the end of its existence, therefore, the second

[65]Richard Gardner, *Sterling-Dollar Diplomacy*, pp. 136–37; Mikesell, *United States Economic Policy*, pp. 134ff.

New Deal had established the triumphant dollar as the base of a new international monetary order.[66] The dollar had displaced the pound, and within a general political framework in which the American empire had replaced the British. Looking forward perceptively to the postwar world in January 1945, Lamar Fleming, Jr., president of Anderson, Clayton and Company, wrote to his longtime colleague Will Clayton that the "British empire and British international influence is a myth already." The United States would soon become the British protector against the emerging Russian land mass, prophesied Fleming, and this would mean "the absorption into [the] American empire of the parts of the British Empire which we will be willing to accept."[67] As the New Deal came to a close, the triumphant United States stood ready to reap its fruits on a worldwide scale.

EPILOGUE

The Bretton Woods agreement established the framework for the international monetary system down to the early 1970s. A new and more restricted international dollar-gold exchange standard had replaced the collapsed dollar-pound–gold-exchange standard of the 1920s. During the early postwar years, the system worked quite successfully within its own terms, and the American banking community completely abandoned its opposition.[68] With European currencies inflated and overvalued, and European economies exhausted, the undervalued dollar

[66]On the American debate over Bretton Woods, see Richard Gardner, *Sterling-Dollar Diplomacy*, pp. 129–43; on Bretton Woods, see also Mikesell, *United States Economic Policy*, pp. 129–35, 138ff., 142ff., 149–52, 155-58, 163–70.

[67]Kolko, *Politics of War,* p. 294.

[68]The removal of such classical pro-gold-standard economists as Henry Hazlitt from his post as editorial writer for the *New York Times* and Dr. Benjamin M. Anderson from the Chase National Bank, coincided with the accommodation of the financial community to the new system.

was the strongest and "hardest" of world currencies, a world "dollar shortage" prevailed, and the dollar could base itself upon the vast stock of gold in the United States, much of which had fled from war and devastation abroad. But in the early 1950s, the world economic balance began slowly but emphatically to change. For while the United States, influenced by Keynesian economics, proceeded blithely to inflate the dollar, seemingly relieved of the limits imposed by the classical gold standard, several European countries began to move in the opposite direction. Under the revived influence of conservative, free-market, and hard-money-oriented economists in such countries as West Germany, France, Italy, and Switzerland, these newly recovered countries began to achieve prosperity with far less inflated currencies. Hence these currencies became ever stronger and "harder" while the dollar became softer and increasingly inflated.[69]

The continuing inflation of the dollar began to have two important consequences: (1) the dollar was increasingly overvalued in relation to gold; and (2) the dollar was also increasingly overvalued in relation to the West German mark, the French and Swiss francs, the Japanese yen, and other hard-money currencies. The result was a chronic and continuing deficit in the American balance of payments, beginning in the early 1950s and persisting ever since. The consequence of the chronic deficit was a continuing outflow of gold abroad and a heavy piling up of dollar claims in the central banks of the hard-money countries. Since 1960 the foreign short-term claims to American gold have therefore become increasingly greater than the U.S. gold supply. In short, just as inflation in England and the United States during the 1920s led finally to the breakdown of the international monetary order, so has inflation in

[69]We might mention the influence of such economists as Ludwig Erhard, Alfred Müller-Armack, and Wilhelm Röpke in Germany; President Luigi Einaudi in Italy; and Jacques Rueff in France, who had played a similar hard-money role in the 1920s and early 1930s.

the postwar key country, the United States, led to increasing strains and fissures in the triumphant dollar-order of the post–World War II world. It has become increasingly evident that an ever more inflated and overvalued dollar cannot continue as the permanently secure base of the world monetary system, and therefore that this ever more strained and insecure system cannot long continue in anything like its present form.

In fact, the postwar system has already been changed considerably, in an ultimately futile attempt to preserve its basic features. In the spring of 1968, a severe monetary run on the dollar by Europeans redeeming dollar claims led to two major changes. One was the partial abandonment of the fixed $35-per-ounce gold price. Instead, a two-price, or "two-tier," gold price system was established. The dollar and gold were allowed to find their own level in the free gold markets of the world, with the United States no longer standing ready to support the dollar in the gold market at $35 an ounce. On the other hand, $35 still continued as the supposedly eternally fixed price for the world central banks, who were pledged not to sell gold in the world market. Keynesian economists were convinced that with the dollar and gold severed on the world market, the price of gold would then fall in the freely fluctuating market. The reverse, however, has occurred, since the world market continued to have more faith in the soundness and the relative hardness of gold than in the increasingly inflated dollar.

The second change was the creation in 1969 of Special Drawing Rights (SDRs), a new form of "paper gold," of newly created paper which can supplement gold as an international currency reserve behind each currency. While this indeed put more backing behind the dollar, the quantity of SDRs has been too limited to make an appreciable difference to a world economy that trusts the dollar less with each passing year.

These two minor repairs, however, failed to change the fundamental overvaluation of the ever more inflated dollar. In the spring of 1971, a new monetary crisis finally led to a massive revaluation of the hard currencies. If the United States stubbornly refused to lose face by raising the price of gold or by otherwise devaluing the dollar down to its genuine value in the world market, then the harder currencies, such as West Germany, Switzerland, and the Netherlands, found themselves reluctantly forced to raise the value of their currencies. Their alternatives—a massive calling upon the United States to redeem in gold and thereby the smashing of the façade of dollar redemption in gold—was too much of a political break with the U.S. for these nations to contemplate. For the United States, to preserve the façade of gold redemption at $35, had been using intense political pressure on its creditors to retain their dollar balances and *not* to redeem them in gold. By the late 1960s, General Charles de Gaulle, under the influence of classical gold-standard advocate Jacques Rueff, was apparently preparing to make just such a challenge—to break the dollar standard as a move toward restoring the classical gold standard in France and much of the rest of Europe. But the French domestic troubles in the spring of 1968 ended that dream at least temporarily, as France was forced to inflate the franc for a time in order to pay the overall wage increase it had agreed upon under the threat of the general strike.

Despite these hasty repairs, it is becoming increasingly evident that they are makeshift stopgaps, and that a series of more aggravated crises will shake the international monetary order until a fundamental change is made. A hard-money policy in the United States that put an end to inflation and increased the soundness of the dollar might sustain the current system, but this is so politically remote as to hardly be a likely prognosis.

There are several possible monetary systems that might replace the present deteriorating order. The new system desired by the Keynesian economists and by the American government would be a massive extension of "paper gold" to demonetize gold completely and replace it with a new monetary unit (such as the Keynesian "bancor") and a paper currency issued by a new world reserve bank. If this were achieved, then the new American-dominated world reserve bank would be able to inflate any currencies indefinitely, and allow inflating currencies to pay for any and all deficits *ad infinitum*. While such a scheme, embodied in the Triffin Plan, the Bernstein Plan, and others, is now the American dream, it has met determined opposition by the hard-money countries, and it remains doubtful that the United States will be able to force these countries to go along with the plan.

The other logical alternative is the Rueff Plan, of returning to the classical gold standard after a massive increase in the world price of gold. But this too is unlikely, especially over powerful American opposition. Barring acceptance of a new world currency, the Americans would be content to keep inflating and simply force the hard-money countries to keep appreciating their exchange rates, but again it is doubtful that German, French, Swiss, and other exporters will be content to keep crippling themselves in order to subsidize dollar inflation. Perhaps the most likely prognosis is the formation of a new hard-money European currency bloc, which might eventually be strong enough to challenge the dollar, politically as well as economically. In that case, the dollar standard will probably fall apart, and we may see a return to the currency blocs of the 1930s, with the European bloc this time on a harder and quasi-gold basis. It is at least possible that the future will see gold and the hard European currencies at last dethrone the triumphant but increasingly uneasy dollar.

Index

(Prepared by Richard Perry)